Middle East Studies after September 11

Studies in Critical Social Sciences Book Series

Haymarket Books is proud to be working with Brill Academic Publishers (www.brill.nl) to republish the *Studies in Critical Social Sciences* book series in paperback editions. This peer-reviewed book series offers insights into our current reality by exploring the content and consequences of power relationships under capitalism, and by considering the spaces of opposition and resistance to these changes that have been defining our new age. Our full catalog of *SCSS* volumes can be viewed at https://www.haymarketbooks.org/series_collections/4-studies-in-critical-social-sciences.

Middle East Studies after September 11

Neo-Orientalism, American Hegemony and Academia

Edited by

Tugrul Keskin

Haymarket Books
Chicago, IL

First published in 2018 by Brill Academic Publishers, The Netherlands.

Published in paperback in 2019 by
Haymarket Books
P.O. Box 180165
Chicago, IL 60618
773-583-7884
www.haymarketbooks.org

ISBN: 978-1-64259-009-8

Distributed to the trade in the US through Consortium Book Sales and Distribution (www.cbsd.com) and internationally through Ingram Publisher Services International (www.ingramcontent.com).

This book was published with the generous support of Lannan Foundation and Wallace Action Fund.

Special discounts are available for bulk purchases by organizations and institutions. Please call 773-583-7884 or email info@haymarketbooks.org for more information.

Cover design by Jamie Kerry and Ragina Johnson.

Printed in United States.

10 9 8 7 6 5 4 3 2 1

Library of Congress Cataloging-in-Publication Data is available.

*I dedicate this book to Edward Said (1935–2003),
Samih Farsoun (1937–2005), and to the children of Syria....*

∵

Contents

Acknowledgements

Life is a short journey. We are born, grow up, live and die. It is as simple as an ant's life; however, a human being makes his or her life more complicated than the rest of the creatures on this earth. In this journey, we face difficulties, challenges, and obstacles that are created by other human beings, due to his or her selfish interests, for example careerism, ideologies, nationalism, patriotism, and so on. This is like the story of Martin Heidegger, spying on his former colleagues at the University of Freiburg to give the Nazis information about his Jewish colleagues. Although he was one of the greatest minds of the 20th century, he degraded the value of his scholarly work for the ideology and interests of Nazi Germany. To me, Orientalism is like what he did to his Jewish colleagues. Instead of promoting our selfish interests, we should try to understand others, learn from them, and listen to their part of the story. Before I met my wife, I held some negative views regarding Jews, originating from my own environment as is common in Muslim-populated societies. However, this is not like the anti-Semitism that existed in Europe, that racism was a hard fact. The more Jews I encountered, the more I came to understand about a people who have been discriminated against for centuries. In Muslim-populated societies, we hold conspiracy theories about the existence of a Jewish-controlled world; what a wonderful imagination we have! This is also Orientalism. What we are facing in the Middle East today is not directly related to the Jews, but is caused by our own mistakes and blindness. To me, there is no difference between a Palestinian child killed by an Israeli soldier, or a Jewish child who was killed in a terrorist attack in Israel. We should try to live together in peace and respect each other, because we have a short journey and it is a journey that we share.

For this book, I would like to thank many scholars and friends, whom I cannot list here, but appreciate their friendship, collegiality, and help on this project. I thank all the contributors for their dedication and efforts, as their thoughts comprise the core of this work. I would also like to thank my wife Sharon, for her patience. She is a wonderful wife and mother to our child, and has always greatly helped and supported my work. I also cannot thank enough my copyeditor, Sabrina Rood. She should be credited as much as me, for without her this book would have been far less polished than it now is. Also, I would like to thank David Fasenfest for his mentorship and guidance.

Last, but not least, I hope and wish that the world will become a better place, driven less by prejudice. All studies on Orientalism remind me of Nazim Hikmet's poem, *The Strangest Creature on Earth*:

You're like a scorpion, my brother,
you live in cowardly darkness
like a scorpion.
You're like a sparrow, my brother,
always in a sparrow's flutter.
You're like a clam, my brother,
closed like a clam, content,
And you're frightening, my brother,
like the mouth of an extinct volcano.
Not one,
not five-
unfortunately, you number millions.
You're like a sheep, my brother:
when the cloaked drover raises his stick,
you quickly join the flock
and run, almost proudly, to the slaughterhouse.
I mean you're strangest creature on earth-
even stranger than the fish
that couldn't see the ocean for the water.
And the oppression in this world
is thanks to you.
And if we're hungry, tired, covered with blood,
and still being crushed like grapes for our wine,
the fault is yours-
I can hardly bring myself to say it,
but most of the fault, my dear brother, is yours.

Nazim Hikmet—1947

List of Illustrations

Figures

Table

Notes on Contributors

Beyazit H. Akman
is an Assistant Professor of English Literature at Social Sciences University of Ankara. He got his B.A. degree from the Middle East Technical University in 2003. He got his M.A.in English literature at Illinois State University, USA, as a Fulbright Scholar from Turkey in 2006, and completed his Ph.D. degree at the same university in 2012. He was awarded the Smithsonian Baird Society Fellowship in 2010. He worked at State University of New York, Geneseo as a visiting professor between 2012–2014. Akman specializes on the (mis)representations of Turks and Islam in the Western discourse and is also a published novelist with four bestselling novels in Turkish. He was awarded the Grand Prize for Historical Fiction by the Writers' Association of Turkey in 2015.

Mahmoud Arghavan
obtained his PhD in American Studies at Free University of Berlin in 2013 with a dissertation entitled 'Iranian American Literature: from Collective Memory to Cultural Identity.' From 2014 to 2016 he worked as adjunct lecturer at the American Studies department of the University of Tübingen. His research interests include Iranian American Literature, Diaspora Studies, Postcolonial Studies, Critical Race Theory, and Border Studies. He is the co-editor of the book *Who Can Speak and Who Is Heard / Hurt? Facing Problems of 'Race,' Racism and Ethnic Diversity in the Humanities in Germany* (transcript, forthcoming).

Dunya D. Cakir
is Lecturer in Political Science at the National University of Singapore and holds a Ph.D. in Political Science from the University of Massachusetts, Amherst. Her research focuses on Middle Eastern politics, Islamist civil society and intellectual discourses in Turkey, and comparative political thought. On Turkish Islamists, she has contributed to the journals *Muslim World* and *International Journal of Middle East Studies*.

Emanuela C. Del Re
is a specialist in conflicts, migrations, sociology of religion. She is tenured Professor (Univ. Cusano and La Sapienza of Rome—Italy) and Jean Monnet Professor (2007–2010). She has undertaken extensive research on field (prestigious grants) in: Balkans, Caucasus, Middle East (Iraq, Syria et al.). Italian Coordinator of AIS-Sociology of Religion. Chair of *EPOS Intl. Negotiating Agency.* Leader of projects for the Syrian Civil Society funded by Italian Foreign Affairs Min.

and European Commission). Board member of leading scientific associations. Author of several publications: *Pursuing Stability and a Shared Development in Euro-Mediterranean Migrations* (Rome: Aracne, 2017) (with R. Larémont); *Border, Violence and Gender* (London: Tauris, 2017) (with S. Shekhawat, A. Mahapathra); and documentaries: *We, the last Christians of Iraq (2015); The Denied Yazidi Festival (2013).*

Babak Elahi

teaches in the School of Communication at Rochester Institute of Technology. He holds a Ph.D. in American literature from the University of Rochester. His work has been published in *Iranian Studies; Alif; Middle Eastern Literatures; Comparative Studies in South Asia, Africa, and the Middle East; International Journal of Fashion Studies*; and *Cultural Studies*. He has also reviewed books for *The American Journal of Islamic Social Sciences* and *The International Journal of Middle East Studies*. He also plays and sings folk, blues, and rock in Rochester, New York.

Manuela E.B. Giolfo

was Lecturer in Arabic at Exeter University (2008–2013). In 2013, she moved to the University of Genoa, where she is researcher in Arabic language and literature, and lecturer in Arabic language and philology. From 2014, she is also chercheuse associée in Arabic linguistics and sociolinguistics at IREMAM—CNRS—Aix-Marseille Université. She holds an MA in philosophy from Milan University, and a PhD in Arabic linguistics from Aix- Marseille Université. She edited *Arab and Arabic Linguistics* (Leiden: Brill, JSS, 34, 2014) and, with others, *Approaches to the History and Dialectology of Arabic* (Leiden: Brill, SSLL 88, 2016). She was the organizer of the international conference Foundations of Arabic Linguistics IV, Genoa University, 2016. Her current research focuses on Arabic variation and variation-driven models for proficiency enhancement in TAFL.

Shah Mahmoud Hanifi

is Professor of Middle Eastern and South Asian History at James Madison University. Hanifi earned a Ph.D. from the University of Michigan, and received a Gutenberg-e Prize from the American Historical Association that resulted in his first book, *Connecting Histories in Afghanistan* (Stanford: SUP, 2008, 2011). In addition to the AHA, Hanifi has received research grants from the Social Science Research Council, the Council of American Overseas Research Centers, the Asian Development Bank, and the Carnegie Corporation of New York. Hanifi's research and publications address colonial political economy, the history of printing, the Pashto language, photography, cartography, animal and environmental studies in Afghanistan.

Merve Kavakci
is the Director of Postcolonial Studies Research Center (PAMER) at Uskudar University. Prior to that, she was a Lecturer of International Relations at George Washington University and Howard University in Washington DC. Kavakci served as a consultant for US Congress on the Muslim world. She is among Georgetown University's the World's Most Influential 500 Muslims. Kavakci holds a Ph. D in Political Science from Howard University, an MPA from Harvard University and a BS in Computer Engineering from University of Texas at Dallas. Her books include *Headscarf Politics in Turkey: A Postcolonial Reading* (London: Palgrave Macmillan, 2010), *The Unnamed Coup at Scarfless Democracy* (published in Turkish as *Başörtüsüz Demokrasi' de Adi Konmamis Darbe* (Istanbul: Timaş Yayınları, 2004); also published in Arabic, Persian), *International Relations in the Global Village: Changing Interdependencies* (ed.) (San Diego: Cognella, 2014). A book on her political life, *The Day Turkey Stood Still* (Reading: Ithaca Press), by American writer Richard Peres, was released in 2012.

Tugrul Keskin
is an Associate Professor and a member of the Center for Turkish Studies and the Center for Global Studies at Shanghai University. Keskin was the graduate director at the Department of Political Science and International Relations at Maltepe University in Turkey. He taught previously at the Department of International and Global Studies and as an affiliated faculty of Black Studies, Sociology and the Center for Turkish Studies at Portland State University. He served as the Middle East Studies Coordinator at PSU for six years. His research and teaching interests include International and Global Studies, Social and Political Theory, African Society and Politics, Sociology of Human Rights, Islamic Movements, and Sociology of Middle East. Previously, Dr. Keskin taught as an instructor of Sociology and Africana Studies at Virginia Tech University and taught as a Visiting Assistant Professor of Sociology at James Madison and Radford Universities. He received his PhD in Sociology from Virginia Tech, with graduate certificate degrees in Africana Studies, Social and Political Thought, and International Research and Development. He is the founder and moderator of the Sociology of Islam mailing list, and the founder and editor of the *Sociology of Islam Journal* - published by Brill and is the North Africa and Middle East region editor of *Critical Sociology* - published by SAGE. His current research involves Modern Uyghur Nationalism, China and the Middle East, and US Foreign Policy in the Post-Cold War Era.

Seyed Mohammd Marandi
is Professor of postcolonial literature and North American Studies, University of Tehran. He is specialist on colonial and post-colonial studies, Iran-US

relation, Iran's nuclear program, and Iran's regional policies and he has authored and published numerous journal articles on these topics. Dr. Marandi has also appeared as a political commentator on international news networks.

Ameena Al-Rasheed Nayel
is a regional advisor for the United Nations economic and social commission for Western Asia, (ESCWA) specialist in gender, peace, conflict, race, identity and sociology of religion. Worked as coordinator and assistant professor at the United Nations mandated University for peace, in Costa Rica. Consultant on women peace and security and gender equality, worked as programme manager for the UNDP in Bahrain. Member of professional research and study groups in the UK. Author of: *Alternative Performativity of Muslimness, the Intersection of Gender Race, Religion and Migration* (London: Palgrave Macmillan, 2017). Expert in MENA region, taught at the department of political science university of Khartoum, Sudan, and at the Arabic and Middle Eastern Studies, University of Leeds, UK. Worked and taught in many countries around the world, Nepal, Iran, Iraq/Kurdistan, Somaliland, Rwanda, Eritrea. Published several articles and book's chapters.

Staci Gem Scheiwiller
is Assistant Professor of Modern Art History at California State University, Stanislaus. She received her Ph.D. in the History of Art from UC Santa Barbara in 2009. Her field is Modern and Contemporary Art with an emphasis in Iranian art and photography and a minor field in Islamic Art. Her most recent publications include *Liminalities of Gender and Sexuality in Nineteenth-Century Iranian Photography: Desirous Bodies* (New York: Routledge, 2017), an edited volume with Markus Ritter entitled *The Indigenous Lens: Early Photography in the Near and Middle East* (forthcoming 2017), and another edited volume, *Performing the Iranian State: Visual Culture and Representations of Iranian Identity* (London: Anthem Press, 2013).

Francesco L. Sinatora
is an Assistant Professor of Arabic at The George Washington University. He holds an MA in Afro-Asiatic Studies (University of Pavia) and a Ph.D. in Arabic (Georgetown University). He specializes in Arabic sociolinguistics and Arabic pedagogy. His current research analyzes political discourse and identity on Syrian social media through the tools of online ethnography and multimodality. He has taught Modern Standard Arabic and Syrian Arabic in Jordan, the UK and the US. He recently authored the chapter "Online Ethnography in the Arabic as Second Language Classroom in *Handbook for Arabic Language Teaching in the 21st Century Volume II* (New York: Routledge, 2017).

Zeinab Ghasemi Tari
is an assistant professor of American Studies at the Faculty of World Studies, University of Tehran. She is interested in colonial and post-colonial studies, US politics, Orientalism and Iran-US relations. She has published many articles related to the representation of Iran in the United States, on Iran-US relations, and on Iranian studies in the United States.

CHAPTER 1

An Introduction: The Sociology of Orientalism and Neo-Orientalism (Theories and Praxis)

Tugrul Keskin

> Knowledge means rising above immediacy, beyond self, into the foreign and distant. The object of such knowledge is inherently vulnerable to scrutiny; the object is a 'fact' which, if it develops, changes, or otherwise transforms itself in the way that civilizations frequently do, nevertheless is fundamentally, even ontologically stable. To have such knowledge of such a thing is to dominate it, to have authority over it.
>
> EDWARD SAID, *Orientalism*

•••

> Until the lions have their own historians, the history of the hunt will always glorify the hunter.
>
> CHINUA ACHEBE

•••

> Western education remains a fetish of the colonial past.
>
> THORSTEN J. PATTBERG

∴

Introduction

This book is intended as a contemporary exploration of Edward Said's thesis, first laid out in his seminal work, *Orientalism*,[1] which posits that the field of Middle Eastern studies produces policy-oriented and not value-free knowledge and, moreover, is tied to the culture of colonialism. In the post-September 11th

1 Edward W. Said, *Orientalism* (New York, NY: Pantheon Books, 1978).

era, we have witnessed an increasing tendency to establish closer, more explicit, and multifaceted relationships between universities and state institutions, and in the case of Middle East studies this may be considered one form of neo-Orientalism. There are many examples within U.S. academic study of the Middle East and Islam of work that is intimately connected to think tanks, governmental and non-governmental organizations, and driven by government interests and funding.

Said opened the door to a global discussion of Orientalism, based mainly on a theoretical approach to the concept. Many scholars have criticized the theory of Orientalism, perhaps because Said's work touched and in a sense threatened the heart of some threads of Western academic discourse. He has been criticized strongly in some Western quarters, but at the same time, has been glorified in the global south from the Middle East, Asia, and Latin America to Africa. By most accounts, *Orientalism* produced a sea change and provided the theoretical foundations for critical studies of colonialism, imperialism, and other subaltern studies. However, it did not shed any light on the practical applications of the theory of Orientalism. After the end of the Cold War and the collapse of the Soviet Union in the late 1980s into the early 1990s, we witnessed the emergence of a different trend within Middle East, Islamic, Turkish, Ottoman, Iranian, Arabic, and Kurdish studies. American hegemony, and the complex and multifaceted relationship between governments and academia, led in part to an increased emphasis on the production of policy-oriented knowledge in the United States. After September 11th, academics began to work more openly with government agencies, think tanks, and non-governmental organizations (NGOs) and institutions in order to fund and popularize their research.

In this book, we will develop a better understanding of Middle East and area studies subjects such as Iranian, Turkish, Arabic, and Islamic studies through the lenses of 'Orientals' and offer a perspective that is distinct from the interests of the U.S. academic power elite. Therefore, this book demonstrates that regional studies is a central element of American foreign policy in the post-Cold War era and involves a complex process of state interference in the social sciences. The complex relationship we currently see between state actors and American academia and Middle Eastern studies is explored from a critical perspective, in an effort to implicate and update Said's work on Orientalism. This book will bridge the gap between classical Orientalism and the neo-Orientalism that characterizes the post-September 11th era as it applies to Middle Eastern and Islamic studies in American academia. Its relevance also includes shedding light on the practical applications of Orientalism, including Title VI and flagship academic programs, the re-invigoration of Middle East studies after

2001, and the emergence of think tank politics and its influence on the field of Middle East studies.

Said's work, as a postcolonial Palestinian scholar, is less well received by some liberal Western scholars as well as conservative scholars, such as Daniel Pipes and Martin Kramer.[2] These scholars include Zachary Lockman, Robert Irwin, Edmund Burke III, and Daniel Varisco, who attempt to de-emphasize the importance of Said's argument, because it is fundamentally threatening to the very foundation of area studies, particularly the role of Middle East studies within American and European academia. Also, Orientalism is not just about Middle East studies, but also applies more generally to all area and ethnic studies, such as Chinese, African, Black, Asian, and Native American studies.

There are four important descriptive books that criticize Edward Said's work. One of the most important is Zachary Lockman's *Contending Visions of the Middle East: The History and Politics of Orientalism.*[3] This book is a good representation of the liberal critique of Orientalism, within the empire of neo-Orientalist characteristics. According to him, Lockman's main argument is to portray that there are some scholars who

> reject the entire notion of a politics of knowledge and insist that their own scholarly impartiality, critical faculties and good judgment, along with the use of tried-and-true scholarly methods, allow them to produce knowledge that is not informed by any implicit or explicit theory, model or vision of the world but is simply and objectively true.
>
> LOCKMAN, 2004, p. 4

However, in his book, he does not really criticize Orientalist knowledge production on how it is produced through Middle East studies centers; instead Lockman attacks Daniel Pipes, Martin Kramer, and neoconservative Middle East studies scholars (Lockman, pp. 201, 254, 257, 262, 265). Most importantly, the chapters of Lockman's book, In the Beginning (Chapter 1) and Islam, the West and the Rest (Chapter 2) should be considered as an Orientalist framework of what Edward Said criticized. Whatever Said criticized in Orientalism, Lockman tried to deal with Said's ghost in his argument and attempted to show that there are good old people in the Middle East studies, unlike neoconservatives. This was not Said's argument.

---

2 Martin Kramer, "Enough Said" [review of Robert Irwin, *Dangerous Knowledge*]. *Commentary*, March 2007. http://www.campus-watch.org/article/id/3082.

3 Zachary Lockman, *Contending Visions of the Middle East: The History and Politics of Orientalism* (Cambridge, England: Cambridge University Press, 2004).

By contrast, Varisco's approach is slightly closer to classical Orientalism; therefore, he defends Orientalism by attacking Said's argument as polemical. In his book, *Reading Orientalism: Said and the Unsaid,*[4] Varisco attempted to discredit Said's theory of Orientalism. According to A.J. Caschetta:

> Edward Said's reputation as a serious scholar has taken heavy blows in recent years, and those with a vested interest in Saidism have been busy attempting to repair the damage. Varisco's *Reading Orientalism: Said and the Unsaid* is one such attempt.[5]

Therefore, many Orientalist institutions appreciated Varisco's critique of Orientalism; such as the Middle East Institute, which provided a forum for Varisco to publish a collection of essays for disproving Said's work.[6]

On the other hand, some Orientalists took further steps toward criticizing Said as using non-scholarly critique. British historian Robert Irwin is one of those who tried to attack Said directly from an Orientalist viewpoint. In his book, *Dangerous Knowledge: Orientalism and Its Discontents,*[7] "Irwin claims that *Orientalism,* which indicts the entire field of Eastern studies as racist and imperialist; he characterizes in the introduction as 'a work of malignant charlatanry.'"[8] According to Irwin, *Orientalism* is a political book, rather than a scholarly argument.

Edmund Burke III and David Prochaska's edited book on *Genealogies of Orientalism: History, Theory, Politics*[9] is a mere representation of previous scholars; therefore, it received less attention from the scholarly community. Almost the entire book was written in a way critical of Said's *Orientalism* book. None of the Orientalists will accept Said's scholarly contribution to the social sciences.

---

4 Daniel Martin Varisco, *Reading Orientalism: Said and the Unsaid* (Seattle: University of Washington Press, 2017).

5 A.J. Caschetta, Review of *Reading Orientalism: Said and the Unsaid* by Daniel Martin Varisco. *Middle East Quarterly,* Winter 2010, pp. 78–80.

6 *Orientalism's Wake: The Ongoing Politics of a Polemic* (Washington, DC: The Middle East Institute, No. 12, September 2009). http://www.mei.edu/sites/default/files/publications/2009.09.Orientalism%27s%20Wake.pdf.

7 Robert Irwin, *Dangerous Knowledge: Orientalism and Its Discontents* (New York: Penguin Books, 2006).

8 William Grimes, "The West Studies the East, and Trouble Follows." *The New York Times,* Nov. 1, 2006, para. 2. http://www.nytimes.com/2006/11/01/books/01grim.html.

9 Edmund Burke III and David Prochaska (Eds.), *Genealogies of Orientalism: History, Theory, Politics* (Lincoln: Nebraska University Press, 2008).

Imperialism and Orientalism

Since the Second World War, Western academic institutions have dominated the landscape of global knowledge production due to the hegemonic economic power of the West. This was one outcome of the industrialization and technological advancement of Europe and the United States, and of the urbanization and economic advances that led to the development of the modern educational system in the early 20th century. These transformations exponentially increased the demand for resources for the society and state in the Western hemisphere. Hence, state collaboration with the educational system was advanced in order to pursue its objectives. Particularly the countries of old colonial Europe including Germany, France, and the United Kingdom established close ties with universities and scholars as they began to fund academic work on colonized geographical areas and their societies. European imperial states in the 19th century sent their 'researchers' to Africa, Latin America, the Middle East, and Asia as archaeologists, anthropologists, and historians to travel to and study colonized lands. Their main goal in funding academic research was to understand local cultures and societies in order to simplify the process of colonization, as Said argues. On the other hand, sociology, a new field in the 20th century, had not really involved the study of other cultures and societies until neoliberal globalization started to challenge global knowledge production in the 1980s. At that moment, a new subfield of sociology had begun to emerge in the late 1990s, similar to international and global studies, called transnational and global sociology. Since then, the sociology field has been dominated by grant and career-making forms of scholarship that have only slight differences from the interests of states and state-funded organizations. However, this new form of scholarship, or 'neo-Orientalism' as I refer to it, is not substantively different than the earlier Orientalist production of knowledge and is probably more damaging.

The Colonial State and Education

As early as the 19th century, European colonial states established a direct link between the state and educational system in order to use the social sciences for their own benefit and further exploit and colonialize Africa, Asia, Latin America, and the Middle East. As a result of the economic needs driven by European industrialization, colonial states began to support and finance social science fields such as history and anthropology in order to study colonized regions and design a comprehensive foreign policy vis a vis ethnicities, religions, cultures, traditions, and social structures.

We can trace the complicated relationship between Western colonialism and imperialism and the Western educational system to the 18th century. Edward Said describes this colonialist knowledge production and criticizes the motivations driving Middle East and Islamic studies in Western academia, especially in the postcolonial period. He understood the real impetus behind Orientalism as non-academic, but instead policy-oriented with the objective of further colonialism and imperialism. For example, anthropology was established as an academic field not because some people in Europe were really interested in other cultures, but due to an interest in studying other cultures and societies for the purpose of further exploitation. As a result, most of the early anthropologists were supported and financed by the French and British state in the late 19th and early 20th centuries.

Christian missionaries began to establish schools in Muslim-populated societies in the late 17th and early 18th centuries. These schools flourished in the 18th and 19th centuries, not just in the Middle East, but across colonized regions such as the Congo, Nigeria, Angola, Algeria, Egypt, Turkey, India, China, Japan, Latin America, and Australia. There were two objectives for establishing these schools: one was to 'civilize the uncivilized other' and the second was to break down the resistance to European colonialism. The main mission was not to proselytize them to Christianity, but to assist in the colonization process.

However, the collapse of the European empires in the 20th century and the emergence of new nation-states in the Middle East led to a new set of circumstances in world politics and the global economy. Former colonizers gave up their colonial lands, but left behind the cultural legacies and colonial elite who had graduated from missionary schools. The newly independent states in the Middle East did not have established modernized economy, bureaucracy, and educational systems; they were reactionary, secular, and nationalist with colonial education systems. Many colonial missionary schools later became colleges or universities in the modern nation-state era, the second half of the 20th century. These newly independent states were dominated by state-run economies.

With the emergence of the United States as global power at the end of WWII, the role of the United States was essentially a continuation of the British Empire. The United States tried to replace Britain, France, and Germany in the Middle East and Muslim-populated societies and therefore established solid relations with Turkey, Egypt, Iran, Indonesia, Pakistan, Saudi Arabia, Algeria, and others. Without its own colonial and imperialist past in the region, and with the Soviet threat, the United States had an easy time establishing good relationships with each of these countries. The military relationship was established in the early 1950s and many Turkish, Pakistani, Egyptian, Iranian, and Egyptian military, intelligence officials, and diplomats were trained in the United States. In addition, the United States helped to finance and support these newly independent states, not for their interests but in the interests of American national security strategy against the Soviet Union.

As a result of this transformation from British colonialism to American imperialism, the region became the center of the global economic battlefield because of its oil resources. Unlike Britain, Germany, and France, the United States did not have academic knowledge of the region in the form of Middle East studies, Islamic studies, and so on. It was a new player and trying to learn the social, political, and economic dynamics of the region. Consequently, three Middle East studies centers were established at American universities in the 1950s at Harvard University (1955), Princeton University (1955), and Portland State University (1959). However, very few scholars were focused on Middle East and Islam within American academia. One well-known early scholar and historian was Bernard Lewis. As far as I know, there were no sociologists focused on the region, unlike today.

The late 1950s and early 1960s became a cornerstone of the American educational system,[10] when the Fulbright scholarships and Peace Corps were established. Young college graduates, PhD students, and professors were sent to many different countries to study, research, and 'help.' This was the very early stage of what I will refer to as 'humanitarian imperialism' and its collaboration with American academia. This was also a transformational stage for U.S. foreign policy.[11] For example, the first Peace Corps volunteers were sent to four different Muslim-populated countries where the United States had already established military cooperation: Turkey, Iran, Afghanistan, and Indonesia.

Middle East Studies Associations in the United States

In U.S. academia, there are two main Middle East Studies associations;[12] the first and oldest one is the Middle East Studies Association (MESA), established in 1996. A number of scholars came together to establish the Middle East Studies Association (MESA), which is the most neo-Orientalist institution in

10 J.R. Vaughan, *The Failure of American and British Propaganda in the Arab Middle East, 1945–1957: Unconquerable Minds* (London: Macmillan, 2005), pp. 178–191.

11 M. Latham, *Modernization as Ideology: American Social Science and "National Building" in the Kennedy Era* (Chapel Hill: University of North Carolina Press, 2000).

12 Middle East Studies Association (MESA) based in University of Arizona, http://mesana.org/.

existence today. Fifty scholars met in Washington DC and established the organization; however, according to Samih Farsoun, a Palestinian sociologist who died in 2005, most of these scholars were Orientalists with close connections to governmental organizations. Today, MESA is the largest Middle East Studies association and is based at the University of Arizona. Significantly, almost half of the MESA presidents have been consultants for the U.S. government. However, as it turns out, all of these national security investments in the Middle East region did not pay back well, as evidenced by events such as the 1979 Iranian Revolution, which came as a shock to the American government as well as to American academia.

MESA is a combination of Orientalism and neo-Orientalism, as it is best characterized by a Rudyard Kipling style of white liberal scholarship. MESA has a quarterly publication called the *International Journal of Middle East Studies*.[13] In the early history of MESA, we see more classical Orientalist work by scholars such as such as Gustave E. von Grunebaum, Morroe Berger, George Hourani, R. Bayly Winder, William M. Brinner, John S. Badeau (a former U.S. Ambassador), Charles Issawi, Leonard Binder, Roderic H. Davison, L. Carl Brown, and others. Almost all of these scholars advised U.S. government agencies on Middle East issues. This is very similar today; however, they were less ideologically oriented and more scholarly than today. Edward Said's *Orientalism,* however, shocked Middle East studies scholars in the United States after 1978 and many of them were offended by the work. A year after Said's book was published, the Islamic Revolution of Iran in 1979 took place as a seminal catastrophe for Middle East studies and politics. These two important cornerstone events changed Middle East studies and led to its transformation toward neo-Orientalism with free market characteristics under the Reagan administration. Loose U.S. government control over MESA and Middle East studies was replaced with more Department of Education, Department of State, and Department of Defense involvement in the organization and additional financial support for language training programs. After the 1980s, more 'native informants' migrated to the United States and started to play more important roles in MESA and Middle East studies in the United States, which has created more diverse scholarship. On the other hand, the Israeli-Palestinian conflict began to emerge as a political division within MESA and among the academic power elite.[14] As a result, MESA has become more anti-Israeli than before, but this conflict existed the

13 *The International Journal of Middle East Studies*, https://www.cambridge.org/core/journals/international-journal-of-middle-east-studies.

14 Norvell B. De Atkine and Daniel Pipes, "Middle Eastern Studies: What Went Wrong?" *Academic Questions* Winter 1995–1996.

most clearly in the Ivory Towers, between white liberalism and conservatism, which has nothing to do with anti-imperialist attitudes. After September 11, 2001, we began to see this conflict more clearly, and created power struggle over financial resources coming from the U.S. government. Middle East studies centers, funded from the Department of Education with Title VI grant, produced a conflict between classical Orientalists and neo-Orientalists. Both sought to gain more and access to financial resources and better relations with the government in Washington DC. This was the beginning stages of misinformation to the U.S. Middle East policies.

An important book, *Ivory Towers on Sand: The Failure of Middle Eastern Studies in America,*[15] written by Martin Kramer in 2001 and published by the Washington Institute for Near East Policy, a pro-Israeli think tank, created another upheaval within Middle East studies. In his book, Kramer claims that Middle East studies should be restructured, because it is ideologically oriented and not serving U.S. national security interests. According to him, Said's *Orientalism* created guilt and turned Middle East studies into an apologetic field, while MESA had become the center of anti-Israeli propaganda. However, Kramer's motives in writing this critical analysis were based on MESA's Israeli policies; and in fact, he was not criticizing imperialist scholarship and U.S. objectives toward the Middle East. Rather, his criticism was coming from inside the beltway. In agreement with Kramer's view regarding MESA's anti-Israeli and partly anti-Semitic policies, we should not forget that this is a conflict within the 'bourgeoisie' of Washington.

In the early 1990s, some pro-Israeli academics and policy-oriented think tank scholars witnessed changes in the U.S. governmental structure of Middle East studies, and they formed another group called the Middle East Forum (MEF), founded in 1990 in Philadelphia. MEF was established initially as a think tank and its status changed to a non-profit organization in 1994. MEF began to publish an academic journal called the *Middle East Quarterly* in 1994. However, the journal did not become a peer-reviewed journal until 2009. The well-known pro-Israeli policy-oriented scholar Daniel Pipes was a leader in this organization. Patrick Clawson, Michael Rubin, and Efraim Karsh were active participants and editors for MEF and the journal. MEF's political views focus on Islamism and the Israeli political conflict, and its perspectives tend to coincide closely with that of the U.S. defense establishment. Unlike MESA, MEF is more open and transparent than MESA on the subject of U.S. interests, the Middle East, and Israel; however, they are more conservative and imperialist

15 Martin Kramer, *Ivory Towers on Sand: The Failure of Middle Eastern Studies in America* (Washington, DC: The Washington Institute for Near East Policy, 2001).

than MESA, but also promote and publish liberal viewpoints on the Middle East, women's issues, democratization, and human rights, all core aspects of liberal humanitarian imperialism. However, MEF became more controversial when David Horowitz published his book, *The Professors: The 101 Most Dangerous Academics in America*[16] in 2006. Horowitz's work was not initiated from a Middle East studies conflict but from the University of Colorado-Boulder Professor Ward Churchill's September 11 attacks essay controversy. Horowitz and Pipes have a very similar and transparent viewpoint, unlike MESA and the neo-Orientalists.

On the other hand, two important Middle East studies scholars, Bernard Lewis (Princeton University) and Fouad Ajami (Hoover Institution) founded the Association for the Study of the Middle East and Africa (ASMEA) in 2007, and both also have close relations with Daniel Pipes and MEF. ASMEA was founded in order to generate more diverse viewpoints than those available within the hegemonic and exclusionary MESA structure and academic power elite. The context of the conflict between MESA and ASMEA/MEF is an internal struggle between liberal humanitarian and neoconservative classical imperialism inside the beltway. However, some Turkish, Arab, and Iranian scholars have been caught in the middle of this conflict and some of these scholars have extensive relations with U.S. government agencies, such as Fouad Ajami, Sabri Sayari, Walid Phares, Birol Yesilada, Nadav Safran,[17] and many more. These 'native informants' played a very important role in establishing local academic connections. This is similar to the government connections held by many of the MESA presidents and officers.

Cold War to the Post-Cold War Period

Cold War politics did not allow the U.S. educational system to invest heavily in the Middle East and Islamic studies, because Russian and Soviet studies dominated the educational national security investment. Particularly at Harvard University, Indiana University, and Stanford University, Russian and Soviet studies were used by the CIA and Pentagon. In this era, Middle East and Islamic studies was controlled by the CIA.

16 David Horowitz, *The Professors: The 101 Most Dangerous Academics in America* (Washington, DC: Regnery Publishing, 2006).

17 Kristin A. Goss, "Safran to Leave Top Center Post After Inquiry Into CIA Funding," *Harvard Crimson*, January 6, 1986. http://www.thecrimson.com/article/1986/1/6/safran-to-leave-top-center-post/.

With the Reagan presidency and influence from Margaret Thatcher, American policy had changed significantly, as William Robinson also claims in his book, *Promoting Polyarchy.*[18] After Reagan came to power, his neoliberal economic policies served to shape and restructure the American educational system. Government-supported Soviet and Russian studies was at the time a decreasing trend, because the Cold War was nearing its end; however, the emergence of neoliberalism would soon change the American educational and university system forever. The cooptation of American academia began in the early 1980s during the Reagan administration, a period that marked the beginning stages of neoliberalism, which coincided with the commodification of knowledge in the name of national security interests.

According to Hayek, neoliberalism coincides with freedom, liberty, democracy, and human rights. As a demonstration of neoliberal economic policy, Reagan, similar to Kennedy, expanded the Peace Corps, Fulbright, NSF, and NEH grant structures and established the NED, NDI, IRI, USIP, and the Woodrow Wilson Center. This revolutionary change in American foreign and educational policies created a different type of scholarship, based on a modern understanding of Rudyard Kipling, or what I refer to as 'white liberalism.' However, the conditions of imperialism had also changed in this era. Reagan described this era as the 'free world,' based on his understanding of human rights, democracy, freedom, and liberty. A Western understanding of these economic, social, and political views stemming from Reagan and Hayek have been imposed on the rest of the world, especially in the Middle East and Muslim-populated countries since the mid-1980s.

The collapse of the Soviet Union in the late 1980s left Sovietologist and Russian studies scholars jobless and grantless. As a result, many Russian studies scholars became Central Asian studies scholars and we witnessed the emergence of new area studies within American universities. The Central Eurasian Studies Society was established and new centers were founded at Harvard University, the University of Wisconsin, and Georgetown University. These scholars and new scholars who were interested in Central Asia began to study and research subjects such as gender equality, democratization, human rights, minority rights, and freedom. As a result of this market-driven demand, the International Research and Exchanges Board (IREX) was established, and the United States Agency for International Development (USAID), the Peace Corps, the Fulbright scholarship, and area studies were

18 William I. Robinson, *Promoting Polyarchy: Globalization, US Intervention, and Hegemony* (Cambridge, England: Cambridge University Press, 1997).

expanded to encompass Central Asia. In the 1990s, we saw the rapid emergence of neo-Orientalist scholarship within American universities.

After Presidents Kennedy and Reagan, Bill Clinton was one of the most important neoliberal American presidents to reshape the U.S. educational system and area studies in line with imperialist objectives. Clinton fully supported USAID, the Peace Corps, and the Fulbright scholarship, as well as neoliberal ideas and concepts such as human rights, democratization, and freedom. However, the United States did not forget the Iranian Revolution and the dark effects of covering women under its Islamic regime. In this era of human rights, freedom, and democracy, the Taliban came to power in Afghanistan. Clinton, a liberal and supporter of women's rights, invited the Taliban foreign minister to the United States for a short visit and, in so doing, unofficially recognized the Taliban government in 1997.

In the aftermath of September 11th, the United States discovered certain sensitive issues in Muslim-populated countries, such as women's rights, minorities' rights, LGBT rights, human rights, dictatorship, democracy, and ethnic conflicts. As a result, the United States restructured its grant and funding opportunities for scholars, graduate and undergraduate students, and grant-giving institutions such as the National Science Foundation (NSF), National Endowment for the Humanities (NEH), Ford Foundation, Carnegie, SSRC, Boren Fellowship, Title VI, Department of State, Department of Education, and NSEP (National Security Education Program) changed their priorities to address the market-oriented concepts of human rights. This was a market-oriented education system that operated in collaboration with national security interests. In 2010, the CIA recommended that government institutions and agencies increase their research on women and gender issues in Muslim-populated societies. In this context, there were many new incentives and rules to encourage PhD students and assistant professors to study these concepts for their research, because it had become very easy to receive funding or recognition.

Sociology of Orientalism

The most important thinker and founder of this theoretical approach is Edward Said, whose book was published in 1978; however, very few scholars have studied and researched the praxis of Orientalism, which should be understood as also embedded within African studies, Middle East studies, Chinese studies, and Latin American studies in the United States and Europe after WWII. It was this context where the modern understanding of area studies was formed under the direct influence of the state apparatuses. Many of the earlier scholars were more independent than scholars after the post-Cold War era and beyond.

According to Said, Europeans used to refer to the Eastern world as the 'Orient,' a concept with vague meaning by European invention. The term is a mystic and exotic, imagined place. In fact, the geographical place referred to as 'the orient' is real, and as Said writes,

> The orient is not adjacent to Europe; it is also the place of Europe's greatest and richest and oldest colonies, source of its civilization, and languages, its cultural contestant, and one of its deepest and most recurring images of the other.[19]

The Orient has provided Europe with a convenient way to define itself, and this identity is based upon a counter-definition of the Orient.

Edward Said defined Orientalism as the process of colonialism of the Middle East and argues that the idea of Orientalism creates an artificial separation between East and West, and in so doing it generates animosity between different religions, cultures, and lifestyles. Orientalists attempt to change policy and to control the knowledge of the Orient.

The best illustration of Orientalism is found in Bernard Lewis's work. Bernard Lewis is an Islamic and Middle East historian who has worked and written on these subjects for more than 40 years. His recent work, *What Went Wrong,*[20] argues that after September 11, Islamic and Middle Eastern studies have been criticized for inadequately serving U.S. national interests, and Bernard Lewis and Martin Kramer suggest that area or Middle East studies should be restructured based on U.S. national security interests in the region. Therefore, according to this understanding, U.S. foreign policy in the Middle East should be facilitated through Israeli security interests in the region. This is a neoconservative and Orientalist representation of U.S. foreign policy within academia. On the other hand, the liberal and neo-Orientalist approach is different in that while they appear to use a more 'humanitarian' (imperialist) approach, they disregard Israeli security interests, which in their case originates from anti-Semitic tendencies within U.S. white liberal academia.

Neo-Liberalism and the State

The Ronald Reagan presidency in the U.S. marked the beginning stages of transformation in Orientalism and area studies into a new form of academia

---

19 Edward Said, *Orientalism*, p. 3.

20 Bernard Lewis, *What Went Wrong?: Western Impact and Middle Eastern Response* (Oxford, England: Oxford University Press, 2002).

driven by neoliberal interests. From 1945 to the time of the Reagan presidency, area studies had been dominated by anti-communist and anti-Russian scholarship and funding, but with collapse of the Soviet Union, a new neoliberal economic funding and research agenda began to diversify strategic interests in African, Middle Eastern, and Chinese studies in the United States.

At the end of WWII, the United States had become a global political power, but had been competing with the Soviet Union in the developing world over political influence and social spaces. As a result of Cold War politics, the United States borrowed the old imperial policies of Europe, based on classical Orientalism. Therefore, in the 1950s, the U.S. national security strategy led the design of area studies within American universities funded by the Department of Education, Department of Defense, and the Department of State. However, this policy was based not just in the universities, but also at government-funded agencies and non-governmental organizations. Therefore, the Fulbright program and Peace Corps were established, and the first Middle East studies centers were established at Harvard, Princeton, and Portland State University. This was the beginning stage of academic involvement in Turkish studies in the United States.[21] However, over the years, Turkey's strategic geopolitical importance attracted much attention from Washington's policy makers. Between 1959 and 1972, there were 27 American military bases and thirty thousand U.S. troops deployed in Turkey, in addition to many Fulbright scholars and Peace Corps volunteers. In the 1980s neoliberal era, the Orientalist approach had transformed into a more policy-oriented form of neo-Orientalism, and as a result, we have seen the growth of Turkish studies academic programs in the American education system funded by the Turkish government, the U.S. Department of State, the Department of Defense, and the Department of Education. This NATO-based academic orientation facilitated the imperial domination of Turkey by the United States. After September 11, 2001, this has continued and Turkish politics and language have become a part of the national security strategy of the United States.

In the last three decades, we have witnessed a more market-oriented neoliberal trend within American academia than ever before. We see less state support, increased tuition expense, crowded classrooms, more adjunct and fixed term instructors being hired, and most importantly, more state involvement in the American educational system. State involvement in the American educational system is not a new phenomenon; however, academia has been co-opted through the work of Middle East studies, African studies, Asian and

21 Andreas Tietze, "Orientalism and Turkish Studies," *Bogazici Universitisi Dergisi.* Vol. 8–9. 1980–81.

Central Asian studies centers, the Fulbright and Boren fellowships, the FLAS (Foreign Language Area Studies) fellowship, Peace Corps, and so on. While the state is not directly financing national security-based programs or departments, it has created funding, grant, scholarship, and fellowship opportunities through third party state-sponsored institutions such as NED, NDI, IRI, the Woodrow Wilson Center, Carnegie Endowment, U.S. Institute of Peace, Amnesty International, Freedom House, NSF, NEH, and others. This is an example of the commodification of knowledge within Middle East studies and Turkish studies and takes place through popularized concepts such as human rights, democracy, gender equality, ethnic and religious rights, the study of Christian minorities in Muslim-populated societies and Turkey, work and labor rights in the Middle East, and other current topics.

Emergence of a Euro-U.S.-Centric Liberal Discourse

In the 1980s, new economic conditions have generated and redefined some key concepts, such as human rights, democracy, women's rights, freedom of expression, press freedom, and ethnic and religious rights. Area studies began to use these redefined concepts as they applied to Western criteria and apply them to developing countries. These concepts began to be used as a platform to criticize Muslim-populated countries and African states.

A Modern Rudyard Kipling and the Western Human Rights Industry

In his famous poem, "White Man's Burden," Rudyard Kipling tried to explain the social, political, and economic responsibility that a colonial man holds toward a savage man in a colonized land. The savage man and land is thought to be modernized and civilized through his interaction with the colonial man. In this way, the emergence of the human rights industry and neo-Orientalism have produced a scholarship that serves the national interests of developed and industrialized countries.

Sociology of Neo-Orientalism

Orientalism should be considered a more theoretical approach to area studies in the West. However, as mentioned before, praxis is as important as the theory of Orientalism, which is not mere subject, and it is in a constant transformation based on market and state needs. On the other hand, the relations between educational institutions and states have become more complex than they were before 1978. We now live in a more connected and globalized world, and states and societies compete with one another over resources and the market.

Chapters of the Book

After the Islamic Revolution of Iran in 1979, the field of Iranian studies has undergone significant changes. This unexpected event in Middle Eastern history transformed what was once a peripheral subject to one that became a strategic center for U.S. national security interests and studies. Many Middle East studies centers were established as well as the Boren Fellowship and Language Flagship Programs. Another result of the Revolution was the immigration of many Iranian middle and upper class educated Iranians to the United States, where they began to play important roles in U.S. policy-making circles and academia. In his work *At the Threshold of Iranian Studies*, Babak Elahi explores recent reassessments of Iranian studies. On the one hand, critics read Iranian studies within a broader neo-Orientalist framework driven by foreign policy motivations rather than by value-free scholarly interests and pursuits. On the other hand, however, some scholars celebrate the broadening and expanding scope of Iranian or Persian studies. From yet a third perspective, some challenge the center-margin divide in Iranian studies that valorizes certain forms of study as authentically within the field, and other approaches that are viewed as falling outside the field. To reconcile these different views, this chapter examines Iranian studies through written representations of the field, as well as interviews with scholars and those moving towards it from other disciplinary and sub-disciplinary points of view, especially those focused on the Iranian diaspora. What these analyses and conversations point to is a re-conceptualization of Iranian studies neither as neo-Orientalist nor as a hard division between center and margin, but, rather, as a threshold. The concept of *threshold* can be defined in a number of ways. One is simply the notion of a doorway, a passage from one space to another. Another conceptualization of threshold focuses on the transformation of state; such as in phases of sublimation between gas, liquid, and solid. These concepts come together in anthropological notions of the threshold as a moment that is transformational for the individual or, in this case, an institution. Babak Elahi's study suggests that Iranian studies has reached a transformative moment and begins by briefly describing the current state of Iranian studies, summarizing recently published reassessments of the field, as well as vision statements from an array of Iranian studies program websites. This chapter examines how the field sees and represents itself. The second part of the chapter adds additional nuance to this 'official picture' by summarizing interviews conducted with two scholars in leadership roles in ISIS, Mohamad Tavakoli Targhi and Mehrzad Boroujerdi. Thirdly, the study examines the work of scholars working at the aforementioned 'threshold' of the field. These readings, interviews, and observations demonstrate that the current state of Iranian studies as in a dynamic point of transformation, with the theoretical concept of the threshold helping us to frame the history, state, and future of the field.

Since September 11, 2001, Afghanistan studies has become a center of policy-oriented work that has fueled increased politicization in the social sciences. In his chapter, *A Genealogy of Orientalism in Afghanistan: The Colonial Image Lineage*, Shah Mahmoud Hanifi provides a history of Orientalism in Afghanistan by focusing on images. Following brief introductions to the concept of Orientalism, he calls attention to the distorting power of images of Afghanistan in the contemporary era as illustrated by the deployment of *National Geographic* magazine's *Afghan Girl* to legitimize U.S. imperial intervention and forced cultural change in Afghanistan. He ties this to the images of Afghans and Afghanistan that were intensively marketed in Britain, British India, and British colonies across the globe in the two Anglo-Afghan wars (1839–1842 and 1878–1880). Particular foci include the map produced by the first British Indian diplomatic embassy to the Kingdom of Kabul that was led by Mountstuart Elphinstone, the lithographic images of Afghans and Afghanistan contained in the *London Illustrated News*, and photographs of the country and its people produced by John Burke and Lillias Hamilton.

Middle East language education in the United States and European universities is an important center of Orientalist knowledge production. Therefore, Arabic language education programs have become a source of the imperial policies in the post-Cold War era within Western academia. In their chapter, *Orientalism and Neo-Orientalism: Arabic Representations and the Study of Arabic,* Manuela E.B. Giolfo and Francesco L. Sinatora investigate why there has been an expansion of exchange programs and collaborations between Arab and Western universities over the past 10 years. Such collaborations have gone together with the production and dissemination of textbooks and curricula based predominantly on Modern Standard Arabic. These educational products stem from a concept of proficiency as mastering of a standardized, allegedly unified language, which effaces the dualistic perspective of the Arabic native speaker, which lies at the core of the Arabs' identity. The point conceptually is about who decides the reality of contemporary Arabic? Western powers are rather motivated to conceive of the Arab world as a unified, thus simple and manageable entity.

The European Orientalist academic framework is more complex and historical, particularly in the United Kingdom, than the Orientalist academic framework we find in American Middle East studies. In her chapter, *Middle Eastern Studies in the United Kingdom Post-September 11: A Battlefield of Orientalism*, Ameena Al-Rasheed Nayel critically analyzes Middle Eastern studies in the United Kingdom through a political and sociological lens and writes that a neocolonial discourse produces not only policy-oriented knowledge, but also propagates a neo-Oriental perspective within academia. In this way, Middle Eastern studies are truncated implicitly or explicitly to work with the state's schemes that reflect the principles of liberalism. Terrorism is constructed as a password to utilize more measures of scrutiny, the veil (*hijab*) is reproduced with alternative connotations, and the liberal policies of the state are used to spur actions that undermine the academic role of Middle Eastern studies.

Over the last two decades, the Middle East has been at the forefront of the new academic sub-field called 'democracy studies,' which was created in the 1990s. Most Middle East and Islamic studies scholars have focused on democratization, human rights, political participation, and gender inequality while ignoring the necessary foundations of democratization, which are independence and economic development. In her chapter, *The Onto-Politics of Moderation: Studying Islamist Politics and Democracy in the Middle East*, Dunya D. Cakir provides a textual analysis of academic and think tank research, and describes how ideals associated with the liberal democratic age, such as political moderation and deliberation, are assumed within scholarly works on the contemporary Middle East. The first section explores reports published by the Rand Corporation in the aftermath of 9/11 and strategies to moderate Islamist actors as an additional pillar of the U.S. War on Terror. The second section looks at moderation literature in comparative politics of the Middle East and how understanding Islamist politics through the moderation (modernity and democracy-friendly movements) paradigm leads us to think of liberalism and democracy as hand in hand. In the final section, she calls attention to the importance of scholarly accounts that seek to uncouple democracy from liberal values. She asks us to question the assumption of a direct association between democracy and liberalism. Her work therefore serves to critique scholarly approaches that frame their inquiry within primarily Western theoretical debates and knowledge and therefore miss an opportunity to move the field beyond its endemic Eurocentrism.

Gender issues have become one of the most important cornerstone topics within Middle East and Islamic studies in the United States. Since the occupation of Afghanistan, gender- and women-related panels have dominated Middle East Studies Association panels. Neo-Orientalist scholarship began to focus on gender issues with the occupation of Afghanistan, as well as a proliferation of newspaper and journal articles, panels in academic associations annual meetings, workshops focusing on what Saadia Toor calls imperialist feminism.[22] In his chapter, *The Dilemma of Postcolonial and/or Orientalist Feminism in Iranian Diasporic Advocacy of Women's Rights in the Homeland*, Mahmoud Arghavan argues that since 9/11, the Bush administration and Western mainstream media commenced a refashioned Orientalist propaganda to justify the U.S. War on Terror in the Middle East. Among others, neo-Orientalist perspectives on 'liberating Muslim women from Muslim men' was one of the driving forces of the War on Terror and led to a variety of responses from postcolonial feminists and critics of U.S. imperialism. Their efforts to combat U.S. imperialism in this way, however, have sometimes amounted to an unfortunate endorsement of the women's rights situation under some repressive regimes such as the Islamic Republic of Iran. Projecting a romanticized image of the 'Orient' as an alternative to a Western dystopia, some critics have instead overlooked human rights violations against the local population. What we see, here, is another instance of postcolonial Orientalism, as initially conceptualized by Lisa Lowe[23] in *The Desires of Postcolonial Orientalism: Chinese Utopias of Kristeva, Barthes, and Tel quell* (1991) to explain the fascination of the French leftist intellectuals with Maoist China after 1968. This chapter looks at the rhetoric of Middle Eastern academics in their denunciations of U.S. imperialist politics toward the Middle East and argues that some diaspora intellectuals have shown a tendency to conceal the local sociopolitical injustices in their homelands in order to avoid a challenge in their moral campaign for delegitimizing the Orientalist politics of the imperial powers.

Western Middle East studies scholars have been so politicized and are largely ideologically oriented and driven. For example, since 2009, we have not seen any positive news about Turkish politics written by neo-Orientalist scholarship in the popular Western media. In her chapter, *Let the Oriental Perform: A Critical Approach to Neo-Orientalism at Work in Turkish Politics*, Merve Kavakci writes that academic discourse on world politics that is produced in the West, particularly vis a vis Muslim countries, is inextricable from the realpolitik on the ground in the respective regions. The theoretical frameworks constructed by a community of knowers, and the resulting knowledge, are legitimized by

22 Saadia Toor, Imperialist Feminism Redux. *Dialectical Anthropology*. December 2012, Volume 36, Issue 3–4, pp. 147–160.

23 Lisa Lowe, *Critical Terrains: French and British Orientalisms*. (Ithaca: Cornell UP, 1991).

support from the (apparently) empirical evidence. There are two important aspects of this process. First, the relationship between the theoretical and empirical knowledge is a circular one. Theory-dependent information, which is contingent upon the day-to-day realities, in turn contributes to the alterations of realities on the ground and how these realities are perceived and re-formed anew. In other words, the philosophical discussions do not reverberate with the exact realities of the Muslim world, but rather they create their own realities to be used as leverage for the creation of other knowledge. Secondly, a cherry-picking process takes place, which allows a community of 'knowers' who have the power to create, shape, and disseminate information to do so in their own perspective, construing realities in particular ways to serve their own goal(s), divulging what is deemed important, undermining what is rendered trivial, unimportant, or worthy of dismissal. At the end, this serves to create a pseudo-reality different than what is 'factual' or real. In this chapter, Merve Kavakci explores the role of neo-Orientalism in producing knowledge in American academia in the aftermath of September 11, 2001, specifically in the Middle East studies field, and how that process impacted the politics of the region and the American response to it. Using Turkey as a case study, Mamdani's 'good' Muslim versus 'bad' Muslim categorization is considered, and the relationship between moderate Islam and neo-Orientalism.

In her chapter, *(Neo)Orientalism: Alive and Well in Contemporary Art—A Case Study of Contemporary Iranian Art,* Staci Gem Scheiwiller argues that contemporary Iranian art, as well as contemporary Middle Eastern art and contemporary Islamic art, has been subsumed within the discourses of 'contemporary art' or into the newest nomenclature of 'global art,' and away from the more traditional identification as part of the historical subfield of 'Islamic art.' Although these rubrics took shape in the 1990s, their presence in the discipline of art history and in the art marketplace expanded dramatically after the events of 9/11, and with the later wars in Afghanistan and Iraq as interest in the cultures of the Middle East expanded. This result may seem to be a bittersweet outcome of these violent conflicts, but the integration of contemporary Iranian art into the discourses of contemporary and global art has in fact been awkward, because of the prevailing (neo)Orientalist views still entrenched in the art market, art history, and academia, particularly in North America and Europe. This unsettling marriage of contemporary Iranian art to the framework of contemporary art has produced weak scholarship, because many scholars who have never been to Iran and do not have the language skillset now write on contemporary Iranian art. Compounding the situation, the art market continues to focus on contemporary Iranian (and Middle Eastern) art that strongly represents an ethnic or cultural identity; hence, if an Iranian artist seeks international fame and plays into the already established tropes of the global art scene, his or her compatriots accuse the artist of 'self-Orientalizing,' while 'white' artists from Europe and North America do not face the same critique when exhibiting their artwork. The author also questions the idea of a 'neo-Orientalism' and writes that Orientalism itself has never died out. Scholars writing on contemporary Iranian and Middle Eastern art continually invoke the terms 'East' and 'West' when describing artwork and artists, do not provide nuanced understandings of the artwork at hand, and 'East' and 'West' are euphemisms for 'Orient' and 'Occident,' which still divide the world ideologically.

During the presidency of George W. Bush, the neo-conservative movement dominated the U.S. political system and foreign policy toward the Middle East. However, this political network used a similar social and political paradigm toward Middle East and Muslim-populated countries and societies to the neoliberals. Although the neoconservative movement used a more direct approach than neoliberals, its objectives are the same as demonstrated within foreign policy. Therefore, if we compare MESA and ASMEA in terms of common themes and panels at their annual meetings, we see this clearly. In his chapter, *Neo-Orientalism, Neo-Conservatism, and Terror in Salman Rushdie's Post-9/11 Novel*, Beyazit Akman examines the Orientalist discourse in Salman Rushdie's *Shalimar the Clown* (2005), one of the author's most problematic works and his first novel after 9/11. Akman argues that rather than questioning the assumptions about the '*Islamic* terrorist' and its place in the Western collective consciousness, Rushdie reinforces and licenses the intellectual neo-Orientalist discourse of 'the axis of evil' perpetuated by the Bush administration by applying the stereotypes and clichés about the East, without engaging in a dialogue to understand or historicize the subject matter. Rushdie's so-called 'insider' status due to his Indian origin and having lived among Muslims made him more credible in the eyes of his readership, particularly among the literary intelligentsia of the West. Unlike many intellectuals, Rushdie positions himself among the neo-conservatives of the United States. His work is examined in the context of other post-9/11 novels to situate these works in a contextual framework. Akman also briefly looks at John Updike's *The Terrorist* (as an American example) and Ian McEwan's *Saturday* (a British example).

Another important aspect of neo-Orientalism is hidden in the colorful revolutions that have been perpetuated through Western online media, Twitter, Facebook, and NGOs by using the argument of democracy, human rights, ethnic and religious rights, women's rights, freedom of press, and academic freedom. In her chapter, *The Jasmine in the Fist: International Democratization Strategies in the Arab Spring and Beyond*, Emanuela C. Del Re discusses the April 6 movement; the initiator of the protest in Egypt that brought down

Mubarak, and its roots of inspiration in Otpor, the Serbian group that overthrew Milošević. This indicates that there exists an international network for democracy, financed and inspired by the United States. An interesting movement of thought has developed from those events in two directions, with a wide spectrum of interpretations arising from them; from rational to strongly ideological. On the one hand, the idea that societies can be manipulated by big powers who make use of small elitist groups of people who are able to apply a nonviolent and anti-regime methodology to any context at any moment, whatever the consequences and long-lasting results could be; on the other, the idea that the application of global patterns of democratization processes in different contexts—the color revolutions—have in fact promoted a paradigm shift by which democracy is no longer seen as a privilege of the West, but as a natural aspiration by any population. Problems arise in the post-revolution phase, when the foreign pattern that succeeded in achieving significant and striking results in the key moment must face the test-bed of consolidation of the embryo of democracy. The Arab Spring and Egypt, in particular, are significant cases. This chapter analyses this interesting movement of thought and the concrete actions that the global democratization networks inspires, also exploring the role of social media and the internet, and in light of these challenges, identifies prospects for the future.

For neo-Orientalists, knowledge production[24] is a vital element of dominating the field of Middle East studies. Therefore, they attempt to control Middle East and Islamic studies and related associations and are the gatekeepers for academic or journalistic publishing and academic hiring in the United States and Europe. On the other hand, Iranian studies is different than Turkish and Arabic studies, because the field of Iranian studies is dominated by Iranian scholars. In their chapter, *Iranian Studies in the United States and the Politics of Knowledge Production on Post-Revolutionary Iran*, Seyed Mohammd Marandi and Zeinab Ghasemi Tari argue that Iranian/Persian studies began in the early 20th century as part of the classical academic model of Orientalism in the United States. The program first began as a philological endeavor and had an archaeological approach with more emphasis on ancient Iranian civilization and language. Later, after WWII, the focus moved more to the study of Iran from a more modern and international academic perspective, as a part of area studies programs in the United States. However, the 1979 Iranian Islamic Revolution altered Iranian studies programs in the United States drastically and gave them a political significance. The authors provide an overview of the

24 Sari Hanafi, "Global Knowledge Production in the Social Sciences: A Critical Assessment." *Journal of the Brazilian Sociological Society*. SID, Porto Alegre, v. 2, n. 1, pp. 16–30, Jan.–Jun. 2016.

developments and evolutions of Iranian studies programs in the United States and the changes that took place in knowledge production toward Iran since the early years of its establishment until the present time. Marandi and Tari focus on one of the leading journals about Iran, the *Iranian Studies Journal,* as a case study to understand some of the properties of the mainstream academic discourse on post-revolutionary Iran. The chapter examines particular passages from several articles published by female writers from 1980, a few months after the Islamic Revolution, to August 2012. Two broad criticisms are addressed: limitations regarding access to the journal, and framing of the issues related to post-revolutionary Iran, as well as concerns regarding the sources that are used by writers to describe post-revolutionary Iran.

In short, I hope you will enjoy reading diverse views on neo-Orientalism from critical perspectives. My motive is to understand the complexity of practical applications of Orientalism in the post-Cold War era in the United States, which has led to the production of neo-Orientalist forms of scholarship. As a result of this new academic discourse, I strongly believe that the U.S. policy-making structure has been misinformed in many ways and the result has been devastating for the Middle East and Muslim societies more generally. The occupations of Iraq, the Civil War in Syria, Yemen, Somalia, Libya, Lebanon, the emergence of ISIS, and many more social, political, and economic problems are directly or indirectly linked with the rise of neo-Orientalism and its complicated relations with the governmental organizations and state structure in the United States and Europe. However, this is a vicious cycle of academic funding that has trapped the U.S. government, from which it cannot extricate itself. As an academician, my goal is to lay out this network of deception that is hidden in the academic careerism and interest of the academic power elite, as C. Wright Mills rightly pointed out half a century ago.

CHAPTER 2

At the Threshold of Iranian Studies

Babak Elahi

Part 1: Critical Contexts

Approaching Iranian Studies

This chapter explores the disciplinary pathways opening out of and into Iranian studies today, both from related disciplines, but also, perhaps more importantly, from activist communities outside academe. This last opening is more important than ever today as I write in the first weeks of the Trump administration in the United States. While much of this chapter was written during Obama's second term (when his administration tried to walk a line between continued sanctions and a nuclear deal to ease those sanctions), it will be going to press during Donald Trump's presidency, and we are already seeing a renewed need to put knowledge into action. Of course, much of the power structure that has made Trump possible was already present under Obama's presidency, particularly the latter's foreign policy. Moreover, Congress's hawkishness on Iran, which has now reached a moment of crisis, has been there for decades. Today, we find an even greater need to link knowledge to action. This chapter, then, is at least in part an encouragement of my colleagues to step through any thresholds (or borders or barriers) that separate their epistemological communities and disciplines both from each other and from performative practices in the world.

The field of Iranian studies seems to be at a threshold in three ways. It is at a transformative moment as scholars rethink new 'agendas' for Iranian studies and as the name and nature of the field are being reconsidered. Secondly, those who find themselves on the margins of Iranian studies—either approaching the field from outside or teaching and writing in other areas despite their training with Iranian or Near Eastern studies—are working to create rituals of liminality, such as 'thematic conversations' at national and international conferences that allow for the exploration of the threshold between intellectual identities. Thirdly, and most importantly, Iranian studies is pragmatically interdisciplinary, and as such, those in leadership within the field, as well as those on its margins, are proactively attempting to keep disciplinary doorways open between Iranian studies, its various subfields, other related academic and scholarly endeavors, and the broader public discourse. In what follows I argue for this pragmatist understanding of Iranian studies as an interdisciplinary passageway not only between disciplines, but also an engagement with the world.

Although its origins lie in Orientalist scholarship—primarily philological study—and while it might be argued that some areas of Iranian studies have fallen prey to instrumentalist and political motivations since September 2001, the central dynamic of the field is one of opening to new possibilities staked out by social science as well as critical theoretical approaches from the humanities. Scholars with graduate training in Iranian studies now often find themselves contributing to a broad range of areas in their professional lives including English or American literature programs, comparative literature departments, centers for postcolonial studies, feminism, and schools within the social sciences. By the same token, some scholars some scholars, like myself, not trained during graduate school in Iranian studies, begin to contribute to the field not only because they might have been born in Iran, but also because their field—film studies in particular—can no longer ignore Iranian culture and society. These disciplinary, anthropological, and pragmatist dynamics mark a field at a threshold, a term I will define more extensively below.

The current opening of disciplinary pathways occurs, interestingly, not in a time of stability and stasis but, rather, at a time when, it might be argued, the discipline of (or set of disciplines that constitute) Iranian studies is buffeted by the actual politics of Iran's place in wider geopolitical concerns. This destabilization has become even more pronounced as I write in the first months of 2017, with threats of war between the United States and Iran given Michael Flynn's recent provocative and unfounded statements about Iran's destabilizing presence in the region. More specific to the field of Iranian studies, the preeminent Iranian studies organization in the world has had to change its name from the International Association for Iranian Studies to the Association for Iranian Studies to avoid the unfortunate acronym. Given the current climate, the field is under particular stress and strain.

This is not to say that disciplines and institutions are ever free of such geopolitical influences, but that the past decade, and recent months in particular, has seen an increase in pressure from such events and changes. In these times, how do scholars outside the field find their way in, and what kind of reception are they given? More importantly perhaps, how do we, including those of us who are latecomers to the field, engage with the broader discourse on Iran. I hope to suggest some answers to these questions by considering the concept of threshold. Iranian studies, I would argue, finds itself today at a threshold moment, and scholars find themselves in a threshold space. Based on my own experience, and through interviews with other scholars, I hope to show how this threshold is experienced and what it might mean for the road ahead.

Scholarly Location and Relocation

Because I am concerned with institutional and disciplinary boundaries as well as intellectual identities, it will be important to identify my own location within these boundaries and not to pretend that I can situate my scholarly point of view in some objective space. Hence, I begin with an autobiographical account. In 1993, when I entered a Ph.D. program in American Literature at the University of Rochester, I had the opportunity to take courses in that university's program in Visual and Cultural Studies. One of the first seminars I took was about video art and politics, which included consideration of Hamid Naficy's (1993) *The Making of Exile Cultures*. For me, as for many Iranian Americans in and out of academe, the work was a signal event. Although scholars such as Georges Sabagh and Mehdi Bozorgmehr had been writing about Iranian émigrés and exiles as early as 1987, Naficy's work underscored the interdisciplinary approach to his subject that was now possible. Sabagh and Bozorgmehr had, clearly, brought behavioral science research into the realm of Iranian studies which was still mainly guided by the archival and textual studies—literary history, philology, art history, and so on. However, it was Naficy who brought literary and cultural studies scholarship into relation with data-driven social sciences. His research method—like the subject he analyzed—was hybrid. This seemed like a great model to follow.

Though I was inspired by and drawn to this scholarship, I had personal and professional reasons (though I sometimes question the latter) for postponing or potentially abandoning the possibility of research on Iranian diasporic culture at the University of Rochester at that time. The requirements of travel and language re-acquisition, the absence of an Iranian studies program or even any Iran scholars at my university, and because of family obligations, I felt it was inadvisable to make the move from American literature, a much more manageable textual and archival kind of work, to Iranian cultural studies. At the time, the more familiar and stable discipline seemed like the more prudent choice over what was for me an as yet inchoate area of study. I ended up studying American literature, with a focus on discourses of immigration. I wrote a dissertation that dealt primarily with Russian Jewish immigrant writers of the late 19th and early 20th centuries, but concluded the document with a reading of the contemporary cultural politics of immigration—which had reached a boiling point in the mid-1990s, and where we find ourselves again at the outset of the Trump administration.

However, after completing my dissertation in 2000, the opportunity to respond critically to Iranian American cultural production presented itself. Indeed, by the mid-2000s, and in the political aftermath of September 11, 2001, there was a personal and professional urgency to go back to Naficy's (1993) observations and conclusions and apply them to the explosion of Iranian diasporic memoirs being published at the time. Debates around the politics of Azar Nafisi's *Reading Lolita in Tehran* in 2004 gave this motivation added urgency. As I began to work on this material, I found fellow scholars who were similarly positioned and who were drawn to the same set of questions and topics. Fellow writers and scholars including Persis Karim and Nasrin Rahimeih gave me courage to continue contributing to these discussions.

One important question that emerged from the study of this material was: Where—at which points of disciplinary contact—should critical debates over a work like Nafisi's be conducted? As an immigrant American writer, Azar Nafisi's work could be approached from an American studies perspective. But clearly there were postcolonialist implications, as well as questions concerning feminism, cultural studies, and, indeed, Iranian studies. I found myself entering Iranian studies through these debates over the politics of exilic Iranian self-fashioning. As an Americanist, I was interested once again in the ways in which immigrants construct their identities in the complex relations of politics in both home and host cultures. Between 1993 and 2004, Naficy and Nafisi, each in his or her own way, drew me to Iranian studies through my academic grounding in American cultural studies, my interest in combing humanist with social science approaches, and my personal stake in what it means to identify as Iranian in the United States.

Since earning tenure at Rochester Institute of Technology, where there are no programs in Middle East or Iranian studies, no tracks in Middle East studies within the International and Global Studies program, and no literature or English degree program, I have mainly contributed to general education course offerings. In a sense, this has been liberating in that my scholarly work need not fit within a narrow disciplinary frame. This has allowed me to divide my scholarly efforts between American literary and cultural studies on the one hand, and Iranian diasporic cultural studies on the other. My work has ranged from a study of American literary realism to a qualitative study of an Iranian website and its engagement with a diasporic audience. In fact, I believe that this combination of a deep understanding of American cultural history and Iranian diasporic culture (within a broader Iranian literary and cultural context) is an important combination, one that gives me a way of understanding how these two nations and their people engage with, misunderstand, and conflict with one another.

Thus, for those of us on the outside of Iranian studies looking in, we feel that important debates about Iran are afoot and that we have something to say, even if we must beg, borrow, steal, and invent the critical language required to say what needs to be said.

Faustian Bargain?

As some have observed, after September 2001 Iranian studies was caught in a double bind in which their work risked being recruited into hawkish attitudes towards Iran. For the most part, I would argue that scholars have resisted this pressure. It is part of a wider pressure identified in which certain research outcomes take on a politicized or ideological tinge. Meta-anthropologist Lesley Gill at Vanderbilt University, for example, has demonstrated, based on over one hundred interviews, "that academics who criticize the Israeli state, especially its treatment of Palestinians, and denounce US militarism contend with threats to their careers and risk of harassment" (2016, p. 555). This may be evidence of a wider sense, to quote Gills's title, of being on "the edge" rather than at the threshold of a scholarly field. To what extent is Iranian studies pushed towards a similar edge?

One way to answer this question in relation to post 9/11 pressures is to see where sponsored research opportunities appeared—in other words to see what kinds of research are *encouraged* rather than *discourages*. Because tenure and promotion are increasingly tied not only to publishing but also bringing in sponsored research dollars, scholars may find their career development tied to opportunities that serve Orientalist research agendas. The perceived imperative of more clearly understanding Islamic societies and Southwest Asia history and politics—albeit mainly for strategic rather than cultural or even diplomatic motivations—led to increased opportunities for sponsored research and even for the development of new programs. However, at the same time, the expected outcomes and some of the research itself were increasingly instrumentalist. Some would argue that increased interest in academic study of Iran over the past decade has been influenced (though not wholly determined) by fairly narrowly conceived American foreign policy interests. As early as 2002, an article in *The Atlanta Journal-Constitution* was recognizing the potential for growth around Iranian studies specifically (Patel, 2002). The article described briefly, for a general non-academic audience, how Georgia State University was benefiting from an award from Nader Rastegar, allowing the university to expand its Iranian Studies program. The article did not reflect on what this gift might mean in terms of possible research pursued, but it is an early indication of the occasionally reactive way in which Iranian studies might grow. Since then, some programs have expanded; others have newly emerged. Certainly, after 2001 and 2003, there was greater academic interest in Iranians, Arabs, and Muslims living in North America and Europe. But there was also political (and partisan) interest in them as well. This further complicated the situation and situated-ness of those of us at the threshold of Iranian studies.

In his "Brief History of Area Studies and International Studies," Hossein Khosrowjah (2011) makes a compelling and convincing case that Iranian studies (and Middle Eastern and Islamic studies) are all-too-often guided in the post-9/11 context by this Faustian bargain with narrowly conceived U.S. foreign policy interests. Khosrowjah offers a history of area studies in the United States, showing clearly the links between the academic field and the American strategic motivations. He argues convincingly that the Iran Democracy Project and Abbas Milani's work comprise a key case of how Iranian studies is coopted into U.S. national security concerns. The specific programs and projects he examines do, indeed, seem to reflect a reactive and reactionary concern for regime change in Iran, and they reflect a limited understanding and appreciation for the histories of colonialism and empire that have led to the relationship between 'the West' and 'the Middle East' in late capitalist society. I find Khosrowjah's arguments convincing and feel that we should remain aware of the potential he identifies.

However, I think there is also another story to tell, and one that I hope complements his story. First, the argument is very familiar, in that it re-applies Edward Said's (1979) critique of Orientalism to what Khosrowjah (2011) identifies as a renewed version of that discourse. Again, I would agree that Said's signal work identified a phenomenon that continues to hold sway on many scholars. However, we should also acknowledge that Said's work has had an important influence, has engendered debates, and may, indeed, have redirected disciplinary discourses and practices. A look at what might be termed disciplinary self-fashioning in Iranian studies might help us understand a more complex and nuanced situation, one that I hope will complement Khosrowjah's timely and important observations.

I offer my own observations in this paper not as a corrective to his position but, rather, as the potential for intellectual and scholarly agency that Iranian studies institutions have attempted to open up. This opening-up has happened at the margins, boundaries, and edges of the field, but increasingly, even those at the heart of the Iranian studies organizations are meeting scholars from a wide range of disciplines at the threshold of the field. Thus, while in the post-9-11 world we need to remain cognizant of how institutional and structural development of certain academic fields can be events driven, I would distinguish between the kind of instrumentalist programs that Khosrowjah (2011) identifies and the more disciplinarily open and dynamic sorts of programs that are opening up Iranian studies to diverse ways of understanding Iranian culture.

Agendas for Iranian Studies

Reflections on the state of the field suggest that Iranian studies has been moving outward (but not away) from distinctly philological and historicist approaches in order to include ones that are broadly inter- or at least multidisciplinary. For instance, in her overview of Iranian studies at the University of Toronto, Rivanne Sandler (2009) concludes by noting that

> in the decades since its beginning in the 1960s, Iranian studies has developed from a language-based discipline of an earlier generation of scholars into a multifaceted program, drawing on a diverse and yet cohesive cadre of academic talent, who address a wide variety of academic and community interests. (p. 620)

Noting Mohamad Tavakoli Targhi's stewardship of the program at Toronto, Sandler documents the broadening of methodological approaches and diversification of subjects that students, faculty, and visiting scholars address. According to Sandler's assessment, the field is expanding its scope.

Similarly, Garry W. Trompf, from the University of Sydney, writes in a 2008 article about what he calls "a new agenda for Persian studies," although he qualifies this in his title with a question mark. Writing some 15 years after an earlier article titled "An Agenda for Persian Studies," Trompf narrows his discussion in two ways: by looking at the development of the *Encyclopedia Iranica* and by focusing on the subfield of early Persian language and studies of Zoroastrianism. It is important to note that Trompf's interests come out of long-standing philological approaches that sustained a much older Orientalist approach. In his remarks on the occasion of the 1994 Mehregan Festival Conference proceedings in Australia, Trompf prefaced his agenda for Persian studies with a brief history of philological study of Iran going back to Friedrich Max Müller. He represents the longer history of Persian studies in Europe and, in some instances, as part of European philological histories. I point this out because Trompf's earlier argument reflects his philological credentials and ethos. Thus, these observations, coming from such a scholar, are even more striking: Even a scholar with a fairly traditional academic pedigree sees an expanding field. Though limiting his case study, Trompf's claims have broader implications about the field. Trompf (2008) writes:

> Since the 1994 Seminar, indeed, the possibilities of relevant research seem to me so much more greatly expanded, and as far as singling out matters distinctly Persian, the potential Agenda would have to be much vaster. I find myself asking endless questions that I never imagined arising before; and of course that means asking about "a new agenda for Persian Studies." (p. 386)

Singling out the role *Encyclopedia Iranica* has played in this process, Trompf (2008) goes on to say that it "has been part of the role of *Iranica*, it seems, to raise as many new questions as its entries set out to answer!" (p. 386). I would add that one of these entries in *Iranica* is precisely what has drawn many outsiders to the field. The entry on *diaspora* covers a broad historical sweep and widening linguistic and transnational concerns. If, as Trompf observes, the subfield of Persian studies is diversifying, then Iranian studies tout court has been widening its focus even more. However, by widening its focus, does the field risk blurring its vision?

Part 2: Threshold Theories

First Threshold: Transformation

The term *threshold* means different things in different epistemologies. In psychology, it means the first point at which a stimulus results in response. In chemistry, it is a point of transformation. In anthropology, it is the point of transition from one stage of life or one social structure into another. In common parlance, it is the entrance or doorway, made symbolically important in the traditional cliché of the groom carrying the bride into the home. I use the term in three ways. It is (borrowing from chemistry) a point of transformation; it is (borrowing from anthropology) a liminal and often ritualized state of experience and situated-ness vis a vis a culture or society; and it is (borrowing from pragmatist philosophy) a point of ingress and egress from a field of knowledge or discipline. Before going on to discuss the thresholds of Iranian studies, I want to offer this theoretical framing of the term itself.

The first way to think of a threshold is as a point of transformation—similar, by analogy, to the point at which solid sublimates to liquid or liquid to gas. The question becomes: Is Iranian studies at such a transitional point? Is it becoming something other than what it has been? Do the current changes in the agendas of Iranian studies, as discussed by Sandler (2009) and Trompf (2008), amount to a moment of qualitative rather than incremental change?

How might such a transformation be measured? Any extensive survey of articles published, symposia organized, or conference panels convened at both the Middle East Studies Association (MESA) and the Association for Iranian Studies (AIS), formerly the International Society for Iranian Studies is beyond the scope of this paper. However, a few key indicators of a transformative moment might be noted here. For a discipline to be qualitatively (rather than merely incrementally) different from an earlier state (and, hence, transformed), then it is not simply that more of a certain kind of activity is going on, but that the conditions for these kinds of activity are changed. One such new kind of activity is already almost 15 years in the making—the Iranian Alliance Across Borders (IAAB) organization,[1] whose mission is not primarily scholarly, but which has come to include an important annual conference that brings together a more open scholarly enterprise including legal and political activists, artists and writers, and digital archivists, along with more traditional scholars. Moreover, the organization sees as its object of analysis diasporic community. Brubaker goes on to say that his intention is not "to deflate diaspora, but rather to de-substantialize it, by treating it as a category of practice, project, claim and stance, rather than as a bounded group" (p. 13). IAAB, in my view, is based on practice—on taking a stance and making a claim. The claim is encapsulated in its prepositional name: alliances across borders. As noted in its mission statement,[2] IAAB embraces a dynamic vision of the diasporic community, one shaped and reshaped by its actions and alliances across borders rather than a pre-existing ethnicity or identity that only consequently takes actions (IAAB, 2017). In so doing, the organization helps to contribute to a transformative moment in Iranian studies by not a national or even linguistic category, but the diaspora itself. If, as Rogers Brubaker (2005) has argued, the condition of diaspora is not so much a community as it is a stance, then IAAB takes this stance. According to Brubaker, a diaspora is not a pre-existing community that takes a stand or makes a claim, but rather it is through the act of taking a stance and making a claim that forms a not just expanding, but transforming the scope of scholarly study of what we mean by 'Iranian' culture, society, and identity.

As IAAB contributes to a transformative moment from outside the discipline, it remains more attuned, perhaps, to the need for activism than it does to the need for epistemological community building. Two brief examples over the past 5 years might show how IAAB sees itself as a dynamic organization taking stances and making claims in response to the needs of a 'community' that does not stand still, that is always changing, and that is not limited to a scholarly discourse community, but linked to activist imperatives. First, during the increased sanctions against Iran during the Obama administration, IAAB directed visitors to its website to an "Iran Sanctions Economic Toolkit"[3] and an informational page on Iranian international students affected by the

1 http://iranianalliances.org.

2 http://iranianalliances.org.

3 http://iranianalliances.org.

sanctions.[4] These efforts suggest that this organization is focused not so much on building knowledge, as it is in what Brubaker calls a 'category of practice' described above. This stance taking is expressed once again today as I write in the shadow of Donald Trump's executive order to ban entry of refugees, students, immigrants, and travelers of all kinds from Iran, Iraq, Syria, Somalia, Sudan, Yemen, and Libya. In response to this troubling development, now halted by the American courts, IAAB (and other Iranian studies organizations) have made clear statements and, more importantly, opened up opportunities to build coalition and take collective action. The dominant Iranian studies organization, AIS, has also made a statement on this issue, appearing above current President Touraj Daryaee's signature.[5] The statement is clear in condemning Trump's Executive Order, and expresses concern about the ability to hold the next biennial (2018) in Irvine, California. Clearly, such organizations have to make such statements at a moment such as we have entered.

What distinguishes IAAB's efforts on this occasion of the travel ban order is that they open up a more interactive response; they invite scholars and citizens across their threshold. By establishing #BannedLives,[6] IAAB solicits the life stories of its members and affiliates and friends. The page on IAAB's website asks for visitors to fill out a form and include their story of migration, immigration, and border crossing. With the permission of those who submit their stories, IAAB uses the immediacy of oral history/narrative and the dissemination of the internet to post these stories on its Twitter page at #RejectHate.[7] For IAAB, any epistemological work on the development of a discipline must be linked to performative work in rhetorical, cultural, and political action. I do not want to suggest, by any means, that IAAB is the *only* organization in this field that sees and responds to the imperative of active political engagement. However, given its less formally institutionalized profile, I would argue that it can be nimbler than most scholarly organizations in the field in responding to immediate needs that affect its constituents, who are themselves broadly imagined as a wide alliance.

In addition to these activist dialectics between the field of Iranian studies and the broader cultural and political landscape, the field itself has, at least since 2013, been considering ways of re-imagining itself. For example, a 2013 call for papers sent out to the AIS/ISIS listserv from the Iranian Studies Initiative at Yale signals the ways in which even fairly established and traditional programs

4 http://iranianalliances.org.

5 https://associationforiranianstudies.org/president-trump-executive-order.

6 http://iranianalliances.org.

7 https://twitter.com/iaabsays.

of Iranian Studies or Near East Studies are actively seeking to transform—or respond to the transformation of—the field and collection of disciplinary approaches that now constitutes Iranian studies as a richly cross-pollinated intellectual endeavor. The call for papers was for a workshop scheduled for May 2014 which explores the possibility of establishing 'Persianate studies' as a scholarly framework. The desire to rename a field, or to add a new category to an existing field, is a sign of that field's transformation, and the question surrounding the potential of the term 'Persianate' indicates a rethinking of Iranian studies to move "beyond language and literature" to include other forms of scholarship, on objects of analysis that might be imagined to fall outside traditional parameters. As the call for papers puts it:

> The workshop asks whether the term "Persianate" works as a conceptual framework beyond language and literature to such areas as habitat, economy and trade routes, and political and material cultures. Are there tangible historical ties in the pre-modern and early modern eras among such diverse regions as Anatolia, the Iranian plateau and the greater Khorasan region, the Caucasus, the southern rim of Central Asia, Western Xingjian, and the Indian subcontinent? Can these ties create a viable field of study beyond Middle Eastern, Central Asian, South Asian and East Asian studies to underscore subtle interregional connections and longue durée commonalities? What circumstances, on the other hand, reoriented these regions and helped break up the Persianate oecumene in modern times?[8]

Clearly, the field itself is responding to a sense within its own scholarly ranks, and through the ingress of interest from related and associated disciplinary areas that a re-imagining of, in this case, the notion of 'Persian' is in order. Even though this conversation dates back to 3 years before the completion of this chapter, it points to an ongoing desire to rename, and even re-orient the field in response to the dynamism of its diasporic histories and constituencies.

If a transformation can be understood as a moment of qualitative change when new kinds of questions are asked about new or divergent objects as yet inadequately or not at all considered by a disciplinary community, then these two developments (the establishment and now longevity of IAAB, and expressed interest in re-naming a field of study) indicate a transformative moment. However, this is not the only way to think of the 'threshold' of Iranian studies. In addition to being a point of transformation, the notion of threshold can be thought of as a ritualized moment of transition.

---

8 http://cmes.macmillan.yale.edu/top-stories.

Second Threshold: Rituals of Intellectual Identity

It is important to consider the anthropological definition of threshold because it can potentially be applied to the individual scholar's transition (process of becoming) as she moves from one field into another, and the kinds of, in this case, informal rituals (if we can consider the various events involved in conferences, for example, to be such rituals) that move the individual scholar through this transition. Naficy (1993), in discussing the liminality of Iranian exilic culture, relies on Victor Turner's definition of the liminal as it relates to rites of passage. While I find this useful in my use of the term *threshold*, I want to make it clear that I am not adopting this theory whole cloth from anthropology and adopting it here. There are important aspects of this theory that can inform my consideration of the threshold of Iranian studies, but there are also some important limitations. The movement of scholars from, say, American literature to Iranian studies is *not* the same as ritual rites of passage. But anthropological notions of threshold states can help us understand how individual scholars move from particular institutional structures to others.

Rites of passage, according to Turner (1970), "are not restricted, sociologically speaking, to movements between ascribed statuses. They also concern entry into a new achieved status, whether this be a political office or membership of an exclusive club or secret society" (p. 95). The difference between inhabiting an ascribed status and entering an achieved one in the case of this field is that those moving toward a "new achieved status" as Iranian studies scholars are increasingly becoming partners in establishing the terms of the rituals that admit them. This is not a matter of a mature society admitting initiates, but rather, of an organization and its potential members negotiating the terms of entry. In this sense, then, Naficy's (1993) adaptation of Turner's application of Van Gennep's concepts of inbetweenness might be further adopted and adapted to consider how scholars negotiate their own identities at the threshold between disciplines, between scholarly organizations, and between intellectual projects.

Attending to these thresholds between disciplines can also help us understand how those disciplines are shifting as well. Here I would cite the thematic conversation on the Iranian diaspora—"Whither the Iranian Diaspora"—organized by Amy Motlagh for the 2010 meeting of MESA (now archived on the Public Affairs Alliance of Iranian Americans website who advertised the event to the broader public in Los Angeles at the time)[9] as an example of this kind of threshold position. As a thematic conversation rather than a panel, the

9 http://www.paaia.org/CMS/mesa-whither-the-iranian-diaspora-methodological-questions-for-activists-and-scholars.aspx.

conversations might be seen as a ritualized practice that allows those outside the organization (including activists as well as scholars) to join the conversation. The fact that the PAAIA promoted a panel of an academic conference is already telling, suggesting a point of contact (or an opening) between this "private, non-profit, non-political learned society" (as MESA calls itself),[10] and "a nonprofit, nonpartisan, nonreligious 501(c)(4) organization that serves the interests of Iranian Americans and represents the community before U.S. policymakers and the American public at large."[11] By embracing these points of contact and these openings, we can remain vigilant against a re-Orientalization of the discipline into an epistemological community (or "learned society") based on knowledge accumulation, and be open to engaging with a wider range of interlocutors towards transformational ends.

Indeed, during that conference the terms of who could attend these conversations had to be negotiated and renegotiated in the process of setting them up. Would these conversations include members of MESA only, representatives from organizations like National Iranian American Council (NIAC) or Public Affairs Alliance of Iranian Americans (PAAIA) as guests of the conference, and the local communities where the conference is being held? This in itself points to the kinds of haggling that goes on at the threshold of disciplinary, institutional, and organizational structures. The thematic conversations aimed at something different from the standard panel at which three to five scholars read completely written papers formally, a discussant responds to these papers which he or she has, ideally, read beforehand, and the panel chair takes questions in the time remaining, which is usually very brief because most panelists go at least a few minutes over their allotted time. The standard approach to conference presentations is not open, and this is not limited to MESA but is the case with most national and international conferences, whether it be the Modern Language Association or similar organizations in the social sciences. This is not to say that even in these fairly rigid forms, conference panels do not offer a kind of liminal space for the scholar, especially for the young, inexperienced scholar to move from the space of protégé to that of mentor as he or she offers his or her work in this formalized space of the national academic conference.

However, what I believe Motlagh's formation of the thematic conversation around diaspora allowed was a doorway, an opening, a threshold between that ritualized academic space and the broader social, practical, and cultural concerns of a community that included the academic along with the professional, artistic, activist, and so on. It is, perhaps, at the threshold of the political and

10 http://mesana.org/about/index.html.

11 http://www.paaia.org/CMS/about-us.aspx.

the scholarly, however, that we need to take the most care, and I understand and appreciate any organization's desire to remain neutral in relation to potentially contentious political questions. However, I also believe that allowing spaces—alongside those traditional sites of the formal panel made up of a series of formally written and delivered 'papers'—where the unrehearsed discussion takes precedence over the prepared essay will open up thresholds not only between disciplines, but also between the academy and the wider community. Keeping the anthropological conception of threshold as the liminal space between achieved statuses *and* between social formations is a useful way to think of Iranian studies.

Third Threshold: The Pragmatism of Disciplinary Doorways

Another way of thinking about thresholds—an analogy, really—might help us consider how one might approach Iranian studies from other disciplinary locations. The analogy comes from William James, the American philosopher and psychologist, and brother to Henry James, the expatriate American novelist. In his lecture on the subject "What Pragmatism Means," delivered as part of a series of lectures James gave in Boston between 1906 and 1907, he uses the analogy of the corridor of a hotel to define pragmatism. He writes that pragmatism

> has no dogmas, and no doctrines save its method. As the young Italian pragmatist Papini has well said, it lies in the midst of our theories, like a corridor in a hotel. Innumerable chambers open out of it. In one you may find a man writing an atheistic volume; in the next someone on his knees praying for faith and strength; in a third a chemist investigating a body's properties. In a fourth a system of idealistic metaphysics is being excogitated; in a fifth the impossibility of metaphysics is being shown. But they all own the corridor, and all must pass through it if they want a practicable way of getting into or out of their respective rooms.
>
> JAMES, 2000, pp. 28–29

I think AIS and a number of other Iranian studies centers and organizations embody this pragmatic approach to Iranian studies, just as James (2000) encouraged a pragmatic philosophy more broadly. The upshot of James's analogy is this: "No particular results then, so far, but only an attitude of orientation, is what the pragmatic method means. *The attitude of looking away from first things, principles, 'categories,' supposed necessities; and of looking towards last things, fruits, consequences, facts*" (p. 29). I believe this view of Iranian studies can be helpful to those of us approaching it from what I would encourage us to think only contingently as the outside. Without diminishing the integrity of the field, or blurring its boundaries to the point of not recognizing the field's distinctiveness, we might argue that the thresholds of Iranian studies are multiple, allowing entry (and exit) from many sides.

Part 3: Disciplinary Doorways

The Storefront: Doorways into Iranian Studies

As a college administrator, I am keenly aware of the importance of an institutions web presence. Though clearly not a deep representation of what we do, the digital doorway into our institutions marks one kind of doorway. Many think of this as a storefront. It is the initial identifier of an organization, an institution, even a discipline. Earlier I asked whether broadening the focus of Iranian studies risks blurring the field. One way to answer this question is to examine Iranian studies vision statements. As a genre, vision statements attempt to encapsulate a way of knowing into a short condensed form that, nevertheless, appeals to a wide audience and is not loaded down with specialized jargon. In this sense, it might be considered a pragmatic threshold, rather than transformative or ritualistic. It speaks to a range of disciplinary and interdisciplinary readers, and to both specialists within academe and interested parties (including donors, community partners, activists, and both governmental and non-governmental agencies). In this sense, it is a succinct yet significant expression of the field's entry point.

In this section, I will examine the vision statements presented on the websites of a number of programs in Iranian studies: Columbia University's Center for Iranian Studies, the Iranian Studies Group at MIT, Stanford's Hamid and Christina Moghadam Program, the London Academy of Iranian Studies, the Foundation for Iranian Studies (which publishes *Iran Nameh*), the Scandinavian Society for Iranian Studies (established only in 2010), the Toronto Initiative for Iranian Studies, UC Irvine's Samuel Jordan Center for Persian Studies and Culture, UT Austin's Department of Persian and Tajiki Studies, and, of course, AIS. This exercise, I believe, can give us a sense of how the field views itself institutionally. Though not scientific, this survey of web pages can, I believe, provide the beginnings of something like an institutional anthropological study. These vision statements amount to statements of self-definition for audiences both within and outside the field. Though reading and analyzing these statements might seem like a fairly shallow understanding of the field (and I agree that it is), such a reading does offer a look at the threshold—the entryway into the field's view of itself, the field's field of vision, if you will. Combined with what I trust are deeper explorations above (in reading Trompf and

Sandler's agendas for Iranian studies, as well as referring to Khosrowjah's 2011 critique) and below (in exploring the center and margins of the field through interviews with scholars), and a theoretical framework that acknowledges the importance of both surfaces and interiors, this understanding can be very useful in exploring the social and cultural meanings and the political implications of disciplinary and interdisciplinary work. If the discipline is expanding, a look at these statements of identity can give us some insight into how this transformation is given meaning and whether this meaning can be pinned down.

If, as Trompf (2008) suggests, *Encyclopedia Iranica* is the prime example of the new expanding agenda for Iranian studies, then its home at Columbia University's Center for Iranian Studies (2016a) may well be the flagship of the transformation of Iranian studies in recent years. The vision statement for Columbia focuses on three key points: the stewardship of the Center by Ehsan Yarshater since 1968, its sponsorship of cultural and scholarly events for both the public and students at Columbia, and, most importantly, "the main focus of its activities ... an extensive program of scholarly publications and several related projects" (Center for Iranian Studies, 2016a, para. 1). Clearly, this self-description emphasizes an ethos of scholarly reliability founded on the longevity of the Center and of its specifically named director, the well-known, highly respected, and increasingly public figure of Yarshatar. It also distinguishes the Center either from a department or from a think tank by naming the wider community and students in general rather than other specialists, governments, or the media. Finally, it points attention to the Center's projects, which are specified elsewhere on the site. The site's Welcome page tells the visitor that the Center's major project is a "multi-disciplinary reference work and research tool concerned with Iranian history and civilization and its contacts with other cultures and peoples" (Center for Iranian Studies, 2016b, para. 1). Along with this specifically "multi-disciplinary" project that looks at Iran in terms of its encounters, the site also lists a History of Persian Literature and a critical edition of *The Shahnameh* as two more of its major projects. The Columbia Center's emphasis on literary projects suggests that it is true to an older Orientalist approach to understanding Iran. However, as Trompf suggests in his assessment of the ongoing work of the *Encyclopedia Iranica*, the Center continues to help guide Iranian studies toward a multidisciplinary and post-national view of Iranian studies. These elements of interdisciplinarity and post-national scholarship suggest, for me, that Iranian studies remains open to new approaches, at least as Columbia University's Center conceives of the field.

Several Iranian studies organization websites emphasize interdisciplinarity, privilege a historical perspective, and continue to espouse humanist approaches to scholarship. Looking a bit more closely at some of these, we can begin to see some distinctions in their implied or more openly expressed political leanings. MIT's Iranian Studies Group (ISG), for example, seems to present a clearly liberal, even neo-liberal, endorsement of knowledge/power dynamics. ISG's statement on its Our Vision page employs key words like *uniqueness*, *personal*, and *individual* in order to frame other key ideas like *civil society*, all of which is couched in its analytical approach, emphasizing "independence" and a "democratic spirit."[12] MIT's Group seems to endorse an image of the scholar as free and independent entrepreneur. Interestingly, the Group also gives a broad definition of Iranian identity, itself, claiming that ISG "promotes a unique analytical approach to long-term issues that are important to *Iranians worldwide*." By addressing Iranians worldwide, the group affirms the idea that the boundaries of the nation, and perhaps the object of its unique analysis transcend rigid national boundaries. Iranianness, itself, seems uncontainable within the nation but is, rather, something transnational. In this sense it echoes what I see as Columbia University's post-national conception of Iranian culture and civilization.

Some institutional statements of self-definition seem to counterbalance what Khosrojah identifies as an instrumentalist, policy-driven approach in some Iranian studies centers. The London Academy of Iranian Studies' vision statement, for instance, engages the very question of Iran's contemporary political situation, not shying away from the question. Indeed, the London Academy does so in a way that seems, at least at first, to challenge rather than adopts a U.S. foreign policy agenda. The About Us statement on the London Academy's (2010) website lists, in brief bullet points, the Academy's aims:

> Academic research on contemporary social, political, and cultural affairs of Iran; Dialogue between Iranian and western elites; Making clear Iran point of view on world social, political and cultural affairs; Organizing conferences and seminars on Iran, Middle East, CIS, Muslim's world and Iran & West. (para. 1)

This is quoted verbatim, including some of the somewhat awkward wording. The insistence on clarifying the Iranian "point of view on world social, political, and cultural affairs" does seem to challenge a Eurocentric and North American orientation (London Academy of Iranian Studies, 2010, para. 1). In this sense, the Academy identifies itself as a corrective to U.S. foreign policy-oriented approaches. However, it does continue to rely—at least on this superficial level

12 http://isgmit.org/about/index.php?page=Our%20Vision.

of its web presence—a reductive dichotomy between 'Iranian' and 'Western,' focusing, furthermore on dialogue between 'elites' rather than peoples.

Other vision statements tend to emphasize concepts such as heritage, reflecting perhaps the motivations of contributors whose exilic privileging of a cultural and civilizational past is as important as any contemporary questions. However, by and large, these centers, groups, and initiatives tend to emphasize the kind of openness and breadth of study espoused by Trompf and Sandler that I note above. Three of these centers are particularly thoughtful in expressing this openness in their vision statements: Toronto's Initiative, the Scandinavian Society, and AIS.

There is not enough space here to cover all of these, but I will highlight the Scandinavian Society for Iranian Studies in particular because of its more recent development (since 2010), because of its openness to various kinds of research, and because of its central image and metaphor of the Simorgh as an emblem for its scholarly worldview. It offers a finite and clear definition of Iranian studies, defining interdisciplinarity in a particularly humanist context of philology, history, and religious studies. Its logo, and its commentary on the logo are interesting: SSIS emphasizes the aspect of the Simorgh as a mythological figure that fosters the birth of Iranian civilization. However, what is perhaps unstated here is the notion that the Simorgh embodies the search for knowledge as having two complementary components: the search for the self in community and for the community in the self. The end of the 30 birds' quest brings that community before a mirror. This might be as good a definition as any for the kind of Iranian studies that would be open to the outsider. As membership of the community changes, both its sense of identity and its mission change. This vision statement turns the scholarly gaze back onto the socialized self—the community of scholars.

Shifting Center and Moving Margin

The forgoing discussion has been based on readings of a fairly static, abstract, and reductive genre: the institutional vision statement. It would be unfair to reduce Iranian studies' self-definition to these electronic storefronts. Thus, to round out my definition of how the field sees itself, I conducted two interviews with scholars currently at the heart of the discipline: Mohamad Tavakoli-Targhi, and Mehrzad Boroujerdi (both, past presidents of AIS/ISIS). Tavakoli-Targhi has been instrumental in developing Toronto's Initiative in Iranian Studies. And Boroujerdi has played a key role in creating a Middle Eastern Studies program at Syracuse University. Tavakoli-Targhi confirmed for me the sense that, very much like the SSIS, Toronto's program aims to move Iranian studies forward by linking it across disciplinary boundaries, and bringing new objects of study into the discipline's scholarly purview (M. Tavakoli-Targhi, personal communication, July 13, 2012). Students in the program are conducting research on a range of interesting new areas, including dance, for example. Tavakoli-Targhi pointed out that even in terms of regional historical studies, scholars not only of Russian or British history, but even scholars of German history move into Iranian studies based on emerging knowledge and research agendas about Iran, reflecting innovative approaches to understanding these histories (M. Tavakoli-Targhi, personal communication, July 13, 2012). Most importantly, the door opens both ways—with Iranian studies scholars moving out to teach and contribute research in related disciplines. Even though the field is diversifying, and new programs are emerging, it is still difficult to find a tenure-track position in Persian or Iranian studies. Thus, some scholars bring their work to programs in Middle Eastern studies, literature, history, and other fields.

This pragmatic reason is also why the program at Syracuse embraces the broader rubric of Middle Eastern studies. According to Boroujerdi's informal history of the field, which he offered to me in a phone interview, Iranian studies has shifted toward a broader interdisciplinarity, and this methodological movement has been accompanied by a shift in institutional structures and funding models, driven in part by the shifting demographics of Iranians in diasporic communities, and by global events such as 9/11 (M. Boroujerdi, personal communication, July 11, 2012). Before the Iranian Revolution and looking back historically at the decades preceding it, the field was dominated by the study of language, literature, and history, and much of this was descriptive rather than critical—it introduced the reader to Iranian culture. Much of this included translation of works from Iranian cultural history. The Shah's patronage of Iranology was a contributing factor in these less critical approaches. Polarization in the government, and the work of expats to secure and privilege concepts of heritage were also contributing factors in a particular approach that upheld the history of Persian civilization above contemporary research agendas concerned with sociological and political questions.

After 1979 the field's literary approaches became more varied than in the past and included some comparative rather than merely descriptive work. As more scholars left Iran after the Revolution, more interesting work on Iran began to emerge among the expat community than within Iran itself. Also, the methodological approach seemed to shift not so much away from philological and historical approaches, but to expand to include sociological, cultural, and anthropological approaches. Moreover, more attention is now given to previously neglected groups such as women, the working class, and ethnic minorities. The field remains largely literary and historicist, but these new approaches shift the study of literature and history toward neglected traditions and groups.

However, notwithstanding Boroujerdi's claim that more attention is being given to previously neglected groups, one might argue that this attention should be conducted with a more pointed and critical interdisciplinarity than the field currently reflects (M. Boroujerdi, personal communication, July 11, 2012). Although multidisciplinary approaches may have emerged, and despite the inclusion of certain social science approaches to Iranian studies, the range of feminist, postcolonial, queer studies, and post-national viewpoints remains narrow. It is from other areas, and particularly from those trained in fields such as English, cultural studies, and certain areas of anthropology that this critical interdisciplinarity can enter the conversation.

Boroujerdi describes his own early work as coming from a political science perspective, and continuing in the historicist vein (M. Boroujerdi, personal communication, July 11, 2012). His history of intellectuals in Iran uses a familiar methodological approach—that is, one that is primarily archival. However, his more recent work draws on much more quantitative and empirically driven study of contemporary society. Boroujerdi also noted, more modestly and simply, the wisdom of the clichéd notion that "if you build it, they will come." He explained that naming something, housing it in a building, and giving it institutional recognition already moves it toward establishment.

However, although this is an interesting, and probably correct, observation, this instrumentalist view of a discipline can also undermine the potential for counter narratives. Institutionalization is an important and necessary step, but it should occur in the context of critical reflection. I do not dispute that Boroujerdi and others are doing this—building the institution while remaining critically aware of its pitfalls and limitations. However, I still want to emphasize the point here that once institutionalized, other fields have shown the potential to limit their perspectives. For instance, cultural studies and American studies begin have had to reinvent themselves at the level of research once they have become institutionalized at the level of curriculum.

According to Boroujerdi, some of the challenges have been the same as establishing any other program: the challenges of fund-raising, and the politics of both curricular and financial challenges (M. Boroujerdi, personal communication, July 11, 2012). He also observed, however, that as opposed to Arabic or Turkish programs, Iranian expats seem less inclined to support these kinds of programs. In terms of scholarly approaches and new voices entering the discussion, Boroujerdi told me that, from his point of view, the data-driven sociological approach remains under-represented in the field but has been gaining momentum, and this is partly due to a perception that there is a growing need to understand the demographic lay of the land in Iran (M. Boroujerdi, personal communication, July 11, 2012). Moreover, the deteriorating political climate in

Iran has led many professionals in non-academic fields such as engineering and medicine to turn to scholarship in political science and sociology because they feel compelled to understand and explain for others the critical political terrain of Iran. Though anecdotal, Boroujerdi's evidence for this is compelling, as he reports having received numerous requests for help on empirical research from independent scholars whose day jobs—or former work—are in medicine and engineering.

The Question of Authenticity

By contrast to Hossein Khosrowjah's (2011) critique of how some Iran policy think tanks are implicated in U.S. foreign relations concerns, other scholars see the field of Iranian studies as limited not by its links to the legacies of imperialist ideology, but, rather, as delimited by certain forms of scholarship seen to be 'authentic.' Although area studies, as Nima Naghibi puts it, is "marked by a history of being dominated by cultural 'outsiders' not always attuned (or particularly sympaethetic) to the specificities of the culture or nation under study," Iranian studies is sometimes marked by a cultural or national protectiveness that champions the history, civilization, literature, and language of Iran through particular kinds of historical and linguistic scholarship (N. Naghibi, personal communication, May 11, 2011). For Naghibi, whose training is in English studies and whose methodological approach is informed by feminist and postcolonial analytical models, the field found certain rhetorical analytical approaches to be suspect. Some forms of critical analysis based on rhetorics and politics of discourse were often seen as inauthentic, and because they were overly theorized, their results were seen as speculative rather than empirical. Furthermore, the objects of analysis we 'outsiders' turn to have been documents and artifacts produced within the contemporary diaspora, and often in English. Whether based mostly on our own anxieties or on actual responses to our work, it seemed that these theoretical approaches and nontraditional objects of study were viewed as inauthentic and were on the margin, if not completely outside of Iranian studies, and more suited to areas such as feminist studies or American ethnic studies.

Persis Karim, whose work as an editor has not only helped shape the field of Iranian diasporic studies but also provided some of the primary texts we analyze, discusses a similar sense of working on the margin of Iranian studies. My own involvement in the field is due, in large part, to encouragement and dialogue with scholars like Karim and others. Karim noted the significance of Hamid Naficy's (1993) *The Making of Exiled Cultures* as providing a kind of impetus to this new kind of approach (P. Karim, personal communication, May 11, 2011, July 10, 2012). I would add some of the work of Mehdi Bozorgmehr and others writing from a distinctly social science perspective that also helped open methodological as well as subject-matter possibilities. Karim's case is instructive in that she has moved back and forth across disciplinary thresholds, but has also donned different intellectual identities. Karim's master's degree is in Middle Eastern Studies from the University of Texas, Austin, well known for its Iranian Studies program, including in the area of literary translation. Karim then went on to study comparative literature. Her work in soliciting, sustaining, and disseminating literary production by writers in the Iranian diaspora and immigrant communities speaks to the ways in which she brings together her personal stake in activism and community building, with her disciplinary identities in Middle Eastern Studies and Comparative Literature.

In the interest of full disclosure, but also to further illustrate the point that scholars in this field move across intellectual thresholds, Karim and I recently edited a section of a recent issue of *Comparative Studies in South Asia, Africa and the Middle East* dedicated to the Iranian diaspora from political, sociological, cultural, and literary perspectives. Karim has gone on to edit a similar volume for the journal *Iranian Studies*. Interestingly, this work in more traditionally conceived scholarly approaches to Iranian studies comes on the heels of (and, in fact, in tandem with) Karim's work on Iranian diaspora literary collections—*A World Between* (Karim & Khorrami, 1999), *Let Me Tell You Where I've Been* (Karim & Young 2006), and, most recently, *Tremors* (Amirrezvani & Karim 2013). Karim's journey across these thresholds between creative and scholarly work suggests that we need to understand Iranian studies not in the traditional sense of an object of study and the tools used to study it, but, rather, as a dynamic intellectual enterprise in which the distinction between the critical and the creative are often blurred. In the context of the diaspora, at least, this kind of threshold space between different intellectual approaches is necessary given that the 'object' of analysis is itself dynamic, performative, and changing.

Though well-established today, behavioral scientific analysis of contemporary questions inside Iran and across the diaspora seemed radical and new in the early 1990s. As Mehrzad Boroujerdi pointed out to me in conversation from 2012, the tradition of Iranian studies had been mainly historicist, philological, literary, and art historical rather than critical, at least up to the revolution (M. Boroujerdi, personal communication, July 11, 2012).

The anthropological and sociological approaches have matured only relatively recently. But, again, postcolonial, cultural studies, and feminist approaches have come to the table recently. Ultimately, I would argue that some of the new approaches are more interdisciplinary than earlier claims about interdisciplinarity would suggest. The field of Iranian studies has always been multidisciplinary, but only recently have truly interdisciplinary approaches emerged.

However, while both Karim and Naghibi noted the tension between center and margin in the field, both also told me that they have witnessed a shift in the past several years, going back perhaps to the MESA conference of 2005 held in Montreal, Canada, where many of us met for the first time (P. Karim, personal communication, May 11, 2011, July 10, 2012; N. Naghibi, personal communication, May 11, 2011, July 16, 2012). Since then, and particularly since the AIS/ISIS biennial of 2010, both Karim and Naghibi have seen the field respond to different methodological approaches and to recognize Iranian diasporic studies as an important and legitimate concern. The thematic discussion of the Iranian diaspora that Amy Motlagh organized for MESA between 2010 and 2012 is a key example of this shift. This is why I would argue that rather than merely finding ourselves at the margin, we might find ourselves at a threshold. In fact, those of us approaching Iranian studies from different disciplinary positions can approach through multiple doorways. Given the various agendas and changing terrain of the field and its related and cognate disciplines, this multiply open approach seems to me both pragmatic and productive.

Conclusion: The Threshold of Historical Novelty

To conclude, I would like to point to a very specific debate that has emerged precisely because Iranian studies and those disciplines that approach it and that it approaches have remained open to each other. This specific topic is the discussion of Michel Foucault's relationship to the Iranian Revolution as it has emerged from the confluence of philosophy, historicism, gender studies, and Iranian studies. In 2005, Janet Afary and Kevin Anderson published *Foucault and the Iranian Revolution: Gender and the Seductions of Islamism.* Afary and Anderson came to the Iranian Revolution equally through Foucault's encounter and from Iran's history itself. Moreover, this approach to the subject was informed at least in part by gender studies, where Foucault's thought has had a significant influence. Furthermore, his work has also had an important impact on the development of the critique of Orientalism beginning with Edward Said's use of Foucault's concept of discourse. In this mix of disciplinary and theoretical traditions, Afary and Anderson offered an explanation of continental philosophy's encounter with the Iranian Revolution that can be summed up in one Iranian feminist's criticism of how the left had been seduced by the Islamist disruption of modernity. This activist accused Foucault and his contemporaries of endorsing the cleric's prescription of a "cure" that was worse than the "disease" (Afary & Anderson, 2005, p. 210). Coming after 9/11 and after the U.S. invasion of Iraq, Afary and Anderson's book reconsidered important questions about how the left in Europe and North

America can engage movements of liberation in regions with legacies of colonialism.

Partly in response to Afary and Anderson, just this past year (2016) Behrooz Ghamari-Tabrizi published *Foucault in Iran: Islamic Revolution after Enlightenment*, in which he offers a stronger defense of both Foucault and the revolutionary movement in Iran, arguing that Afary and Anderson's reading falls into a pattern of neo-liberal and left handwringing that demonizes Islam as monolithically Islamist. By contrast, entering into debates revolving around the Enlightenment and its legacies in neo-liberal politics and postcolonial contexts, Ghamari-Tabrizi argues that Afary and Anderson's critique of Foucault is based on a concept of 'History' in which the events of the past and future follow a predictable schema. This predictable version of History gives rise to terms like the 'Arab Spring,' suggesting a dark Winter of the past and a bright future lit by the brightness of modernity as a Western historical development, historical schema grounded in Western notions of temporality and the subject in history. What Foucault identified and identified *with* in the Iranian Revolution was a complete break from such schemas of history.

I have rehearsed this recent and ongoing debate about philosophy, historicism, and Iran because Ghamari-Tabrizi (2016) uses the term 'threshold' about 'history' in a way similar to the way I have tried to apply it to disciplines. Ghamari-Tabrizi re-conceptualizes Foucault's response to the Iranian Revolution by arguing that the French philosopher saw these events in terms of a 'threshold' moment:

> In Iran, Foucault tried to see the revolution as a phenomenon of history and, at the same time, as a phenomenon that defies it. He perceived those who marched on the streets of Tehran as subjects of history who had risen to make history the subject of their revolutionary acts. He encouraged his readers to see Iranians at the threshold of a novelty rather than subjects of the discursive authority of a world that is perpetuated in tired conceptions of "History." (p. 2)

He repeats this later, painting an even clearer picture of how 'threshold' marks a limit and opening in a temporal and ideological mapping of history:

> What made [Foucault's] essays on the Iranian Revolution exceptional was his willingness to observe the revolution without the temporal map of a universal history. He observed the revolution as a moment at the threshold of a novelty, as something radically new outside the tired conceptions of linear revolutionary politics.
>
> GHAMARI-TABRIZI, 2016, p. 7

Ultimately, we might say the same thing about what is most compelling about a discipline and its interdisciplinary revolutions: interdisciplinary transformations happen at threshold spaces that fall outside the boundaries and question the standard conceptions of any single discipline, particularly one, like Orientalism itself, that is a geographical entity. Ghamari-Tabrizi's work—and Afary and Anderson's, for that matter—explores and steps through these disciplinary thresholds. At this post-9/11 moment, in the era of Trump, questioning disciplinary and disciplined constructions of Iran is crucial, not just in politics, but also in academe.

References

Afary, J., & Anderson, K.B. (2005). *Foucault and Iranian Revolution: Gender and the seductions of Islamism.* Chicago, IL: The University of Chicago Press.

Amirrezvani, A., & Karim, P. (Eds.). (2013). *Tremors: New fiction by Iranian American writers.* Fayetteville, AR: University of Arkansas Press.

Brubaker, R. (2005). The "diaspora" of diaspora. *Ethnic and Racial Studies, 28,* 1–19. doi: 10.1080/0141987042000289997.

Center for Iranian Studies, Columbia University in the City of New York. (2016a). *About us.* Retrieved July 7, 2017 from http://cfis.columbia.edu/about-us.

Center for Iranian Studies, Columbia University in the City of New York. (2016b). *Welcome.* Retrieved July 7, 2017 from http://cfis.columbia.edu.

Ghamari-Tabrizi, B. (2016). *Foucault in Iran: Islamic Revolution after the Enlightenment.* Minneapolis, MN: University of Minnesota Press.

Gill, L. (2016). Ethnography at its edges: Compulsory Zionism, free speech, and anthropology. *American Ethnologist, 43,* 555–559. doi:10.1111/amet.12346.

Iranian Alliances Across Borders. (2017). *Our mission.* Retrieved July 7, 2017 from http://iranianalliances.org.

James, W. (2000). *Pragmatism and other writings.* New York, NY: Penguin Books.

Karim, P.M., & Khorrami, M.M. (Eds.). (1999). *A world between: Poems, short stories, and essays by Iranian-Americans.* New York, NY: George Braziller.

Karim, P.M., & Young, A. (Eds.). (2006). *Let me tell you where I've been: New writing by women of the Iranian diaspora.* Fayetteville, AR: University of Arkansas Press.

Khosrowjah, H. (2011). A brief history of area studies and international studies. *Arab Studies Quarterly, 33,* 131–142. Retrieved July 7, 2017 from http://www.jstor.org/stable/41858661.

London Academy of Iranian Studies. (2010). *About us.* Retrieved July 7, 2017 from http://iranianstudies.org/about.

Naficy, H. (1993). *The making of exile cultures: Iranian television in Los Angeles.* Minneapolis, MN: University of Minnesota Press.

Nafisi, A. (2004). *Reading Lolita in Tehran: A memoir in books.* New York, NY: Random House.

Patel, U. (2002, July 10). Iranians in Atlanta help GSU's Persian Studies program take off: Two metro Atlanta universities reach out into community to build global stature. *The Atlanta Journal-Constitution,* F1.

Said, E. (1979). *Orientalism.* New York, NY: Vintage.

Sandler, R. (2009). Iranian Studies at the University of Toronto. *Iranian Studies, 42,* 611–620. doi:10.1080/00210860903106329.

Trompf, G. (1994). An agenda for Persian Studies. *Mehregan-Persian Studies 1994 Conference Proceedings,* 1–6.

Trompf, G. (2008). Encyclopaedia Iraenica—35: A new agenda for Persian studies? *Iran & the Caucasus, 12,* 385–396. doi:10.1163/157338408x406137.

Turner, V. (1970). *The forest of symbols: Aspects of Ndembu ritual.* Ithaca, NY: Cornell University Press.

CHAPTER 3

A Genealogy of Orientalism in Afghanistan: The Colonial Image Lineage

Shah Mahmoud Hanifi

Definitions and Context

There is no country on earth more subject to misrepresentations based upon Orientalism than Afghanistan. To support this surely contested but certainly strong claim, working understandings of the two terms in question, *Orientalism* and *Afghanistan*, are required.

Orientalism

A discussion of Orientalism can usefully begin with the Professor of English and Comparative Literature and Palestinian activist Edward Said (1935–2003). Said (1978/2003) attached three very broad meanings to the term *Orientalism* in his pathbreaking book of that title that appeared on the cusp of the Islamic Revolution in Iran, an historical coincidence that greatly magnified the book's impact. Orientalism in general and each of the three fields of action comprising the phenomena have subsequently received considerable elaboration from Said (1978/2003, 1985, 1989) and others (Abu El-Haj, 2005; Breckenridge & Van der Veer, 1993; Lockman, 2004; Ludden, 1993; Macfie, 2000), as well as a wide variety of sometimes quite extended critiques (Irwin, 2007, 2008; Varisco, 2004, 2007).

The first component of the term Orientalism identified by Said (1978/2003, 1985, 1989) was primarily the work of academics who study and teach about the Orient. Said's attention to this group of scholars, historians, and linguists and the knowledge they produce was grounded in Antonio Gramsci's (1972) consideration of intellectuals; in this regard, Said's cultural consciousness and political activism fueled his sustained attention to the role of intellectuals in the U.S. public arena.

The second general component of Orientalism addressed much wider fields of sometimes imaginary activity and cultural production, including the work of writers, artists, and state officials who share an ontological and epistemological perspective predicated on an impermeable binary opposition between the East and the West or the Orient and the Occident. This strand of Orientalism has come to be associated with the concept of 'othering,' and as such has pried open what may be called a can of worms involving complex and highly charged debates about cultural identity across a wide range of disciplines.

Said also identified a "Western style for dominating, restructuring, and having authority over Orient" as the third aspect of Orientalism (1978/2003, p. 3). This feature of Orientalism can be associated with the concept of power generically, empires generally, Western imperialism especially, and U.S. imperialism most specifically. At all levels, the power of Orientalism takes shape through established ways of talking, writing, thinking, and acting that comprise a given discourse, with discourse being a conceptual tool that Said adopted from Michel Foucault (1970/1994, 1972, 1979).

For present purposes, Orientalism can be understood to be a complex set of relationships between knowledge, power, and representation (Said, 1978/2003). These generic conceptual relationships informing Orientalism have concrete historical articulations. In other words, particular groups of people practice their own culture and represent other cultures in tangible ways in specific institutional, national, and imperial contexts. Orientalism has a history that is composed of many separate histories of Orientalism.

"Orientalized" Afghanistan

The Orientalism of Afghanistan involves large numbers of different types of scholars, artists, scientists, and policy makers operating within multiple national and imperial institutional frameworks across many centuries. Afghanistan must not be separated from Afghans, and both terms carry considerable cultural and historical complexity and ambiguity. There is no fixed meaning to either term, and usage of both words appears to originate outside of the territory and population in question.

In general terms, Afghans as an oxonymic social referent emerge as minor actors in Persian language texts roughly one thousand years ago, but Afghans do not begin to appear regularly in chronicle histories until the Mughal era (c. 1526–1857). As used by both indigenous populations and cultural outsiders, the term *Afghan* has been made more opaque by its frequent interchangeability with the words *Pashtun* and *Pathan*. Again, as a term applied by outsiders, *Afghanistan* as a regional referent appears faintly in indigenous Persian and Turkish language sources roughly 500 years ago, but it never gained traction in Mughal texts. The founder of the Afghan kingdom in the mid-18th century did not use the term Afghanistan. Although still somewhat imprecise and not ordinarily used by inhabitants of the territory, the term Afghanistan became routinely used in the late 19th century when maps were entering an increasingly Anglicized textual world, cartography was emerging as a bona fide science, and borders were being inscribed in increasingly violent ways upon national and imperial landscapes. Momentarily understood ahistorically to include the 'full run' of time, not just the modern period, Afghanistan has the characteristic of being ill-defined even when conceptualized as bounded space. These territorial ambiguities arise from the unusually permeable nature of its ancient and modern borders and borderlands, especially the modern eastern and southern frontier border zones around the so-called Durand Line that is so unusually configured when compared to other state territories and border systems.

There are ways to productively address and surmount these semantic challenges. One route in that direction is to re-emphasize a basic point. It is absolutely essential to understand that the people living in the area we now call Afghanistan have diverse and changing cultural profiles inflected by immigrant 'newcomers,' traditional migrant 'outgoers,' and culturally repackaged 'returnees,' all of which combine over millennia to lend a significant degree of extra-territoriality and mobility to the evolving cultural complexion of Afghans inside and outside Afghanistan. However, this is precisely the problem of Orientalism. In general terms, the Orientalism of Afghanistan has worked toward two interrelated goals: to erase the historical realities of mobility of Afghans and fluidity of cultural relations among them by imposing a totalizing imaginary epistemology of geographically immobilized, racially distinguished, culturally homogeneous Afghan people in a timeless place called Afghanistan.

Orientalism's primary illusionary fantasy of misrepresentation involves the self-aggrandizing and unsustainable idea that Afghan women need Western, particularly American, assistance to be 'liberated' from various forms of oppression, be it Soviet, Islamic, or ethnic. This highly politicized and artificially gendered view of Afghanistan is best represented by what is arguably the world's most famous photograph, the June 1985 *National Geographic* cover image of the *Afghan Girl* that has been usefully decoded by Schwartz (2005, 2006; Schwartz-Dupre, 2007). With a generation-long wave of an American cultural and imperial hand, in 2018 this photo takes concrete expression in the form of local and international institutions, policies, resources, and wars geared toward 'freeing Afghan women' from what is in many ways an imaginary prison of Orientalism. As per the dialectic between representation and reality, the delusional Orientalist illusion of 'saving Afghan women' has transformed Afghanistan into a literal prison where all Afghans are constantly under surveillance and always exposed to a 'tip of the spear' by a growing fleet of planes, blimps, drones, and other forms of high-tech imaging, monitoring, and killing machines. Cutting-edge killing technology costing billions of dollars is deployed to insure compliance with the imperial and epistemological violence of forced cultural change in Afghanistan, which is predicated upon an absurd genocidal equation that to save urban Persian-speaking Afghan women, rural Pashto-speaking men must be killed. By tragic extension this means that at its core, U.S. policy is designed to save Kabul by exterminating its hinterland.

American Orientalism and the *National Geographic* Magazine *Afghan Girl* Cover Image

How has a single picture of a solitary, then anonymous Afghan refugee woman acquired its own agency among those forces responsible for the catastrophic harm suffered by the people of Afghanistan over the last generation? To answer, we must understand Orientalism as an ongoing historical process whereby colonial powers generate specific bits of cultural information from cultures targeted for colonization, then repackage and reframe these tidbits from the Other culture for circulation and consumption within the institutional matrix of the imperial culture. This imperial recirculation serves commercial, political, and strategic goals that are contradictorily separated but dependent upon representations of the Other culture. Seen with the aid of this unspecified and therefore dim light, generic Orientalism works through representations in imperial contexts that amplify, magnify, and thereby distort elements of cultural Others in tangible ways for tangible reasons that serve to further the goals of the colonizing imperial culture at the expense of the authenticity and reality of the colonized culture. The Other culture's response to their colonial misrepresentation typically includes nationalism that is problematically often saturated with colonial orientations.

To understand the Orientalism effect of the *Afghan Girl* image, we must situate Orientalism in American cultural and political life, and the photograph itself in the institutional context of *National Geographic* magazine (NGM). For the cultural and political context, Osamah Khalil (2016) demonstrated the influence of Orientalism on U.S. foreign policy from the Inter-War period through the Cold War by detailing its prevalence in U.S. intelligence agencies, think tanks, academic institutions, and the field of Middle East studies generally. Douglas Little (2002) found approximately a dozen articles published in the NGM in the 1920s and 1930s that highlight a widening political and cultural gap between the Orient and the Occident. Following cultural studies theorists of the Frankfurt School who focus on the consciousness-molding effects of the media, Lutz and Collins (1993) argued that NGM represents 'mass culture' or materials created and disseminated by powerful interests for the consumption of the working classes. Lutz and Collins concluded that the magazine's highly stylized mass-produced images speak to a limited number of themes and serve to further government and corporate interests at the interstice of which we can locate the magazine's umbrella organization, the National Geographic Society. By the 1980s, the Orientalism of Islam, Muslims, Arabs, and the Middle East was well established in American popular culture and institutionally entrenched in the U.S. academy and government, and the NGM was an important and highly visible realm of expression for the American version of Orientalism.

A multi-generational, institutionally diverse American Orientalism within which the NGM figures prominently sets the general context for the 1985 *Afghan Girl* cover image. The specific historical context of the photograph was conditioned by the Cold War development duel in Afghanistan between the United States and Soviet Union. The combined U.S. and U.S.S.R. aid provided to Afghanistan from the 1950s through the 1970s made the country the largest per capita recipient of development assistance in the world (Calluther, 2002; Van Vleck, 2009).

Transportation infrastructure was a primary arena of Cold War competition, and President Harry S. Truman's 1949 Point Four Program made technical assistance to developing countries a cornerstone of global cold warring by coordinating the resources and institutional relationships necessary to advance U.S. Cold War interests around the world. For Afghanistan in the 1950s, the Point Four Program created the context for Pan American Airways to organize the Afghan national carrier, Ariana Afghan Airlines, and for the Morrison-Knudsen Corporation to build the Qandahar International Airport in the image of Washington Dulles International Airport. During the 1960s both superpowers also invested heavily in irrigation and damming projects in Afghanistan. These projects included the USAID program, outsourced yet again to Morrison-Knudsen for the ultimately failed Helmand (and later Arghandab) Valley Development Project that was modeled on the Tennessee Valley Authority.

The dynamics of the Cold War development duel between the two superpowers were substantially transformed by the April 1978 coup d'etat or Saur Revolution in Afghanistan. The 1978 revolution ended the monarchy and brought progressive forces to power; this development triggered an immediate covert response from the United States that in turn precipitated the Soviet military invasion of the country in December 1979. The Soviet invasion was a key issue in the 1980 U.S. presidential election. When elected, President Ronald Reagan promptly authorized a growing stream of covert funding, military supplies, and logistical support to a variety of groups that came to be collectively known as the Afghan Holy Warrior Freedom Fighters or *mujahideen* (Coll, 2004; Cooley, 2000; Weiner, 1990).

Reagan made many very public statements about the distant cause of the mujahideen that were loudly amplified and widely disseminated U.S. national interests so that remote Afghanistan could receive the requisite attention for consent to national policies toward the country to be extracted from the American public. Reagan dedicated the launch of the Space Shuttle Columbia on March 22, 1982 to the people of Afghanistan, and he hosted leaders of the Afghan mujahideen at the White House in February 1983, where he declared his guests to be the "moral equivalents of our Founding Fathers" (Reagan, 1982, 1983; Ronald Reagan Presidential Library and Museum, 1983). During the early 1980s the U.S. president publicly drew attention to the extensive, growing, and supposedly covert U.S. support of the anti-Soviet Afghan guerrilla forces by, for example, declaring March 21, 1983 Afghanistan Day and by repeatedly referencing Afghanistan in State of the Union speeches, formal addresses to Congress, and less formal remarks to the mass media (Reagan, 1983). By 1985 when the NGM cover appeared, Orientalism had been instrumental in making the American public well aware of what were marketed as unjustly threatened American interests in Afghanistan.

The combined message for the American public was that the *Afghan Girl* must be saved from the clutches of the Evil Soviet Empire, and that the Afghan insurgent mujahideen fighting against a Soviet-supported regime required immediate and extensive cultural and political support. As a result, on the political front, in 1986 the little known but highly influential Texan Congressman Charlie Wilson secured top of the line high technology anti-aircraft Stinger missiles for the mujahideen. In terms of cultural production, in 1988 TriStar Pictures in Hollywood released the motion picture *Rambo III*, wherein the American hero is successfully embedded with the heroic mujahideen to do both godly and patriotic work against evil-doing Soviets (Crile, 2003; Feitshans, Kassar, Munafo, Vajna, & MacDonald, 1988).

During the 1970s and 1980s, the American Louis Dupree was by far the most influential figure at the apex of a vast web of networks of U.S. university, corporate, and government interests including the Central Intelligence Agency and the Fulbright and Peace Corps programs that extend deeply into multiple national bureaucracies in Afghanistan and the United States (S.M. Hanifi, 2009). Dupree was a World War II veteran, Harvard-trained archaeologist, and author of the encyclopedic tome *Afghanistan* (Dupree, 1973/1980). Under the formal direction, informal tutelage, and personal networking capacity of Louis Dupree and his second wife Nancy Hatch Dupree, a large number of U.S. academic authorities, particularly in the field of anthropology, lent their patriotic and intellectual support to the Afghan mujahideen (see, for example, many of the chapters in Shahrani & Canfield, 1984). With broad-based academic consent and support, national policy directives regarding the Afghan mujahideen kicked into high gear, and mass media in the form of popular films and widely circulated print journalism explicitly and publicly adopted an allegedly covert Afghan *cum* American national cause. The 1985 NGM *Afghan Girl* cover image appeared in an already very active discursive and imperial field of action that united the United States and Afghanistan through a known set of institutions, personalities, and resources; the photograph rapidly gained weight in American popular and policy mindsets, both of which were then saturated with illogic and misrepresentation founded on Orientalism.

By the mid-1980s, American Orientalism of Afghanistan carried its own political capital; as an industry, it became able to institutionally reproduce and mass-market itself. Since the 1985 NGM cover appeared, there has been an enormous amount of American cultural production based upon images of Afghans, both men and women. This general trend was exponentially amplified by the events of September 11, 2001. The Taliban were implicated in 9/11, and an understanding of the Taliban cannot be had without grounding in the U.S. extension of extensive overt and covert funding to Afghan and international mujahideen in the 1980s, including Osama Bin Laden. Images of Afghan women in particular gained exponentially added value in American public and political arenas after 9/11. Since that date, there has been very little academic or public time or space devoted to the substantive American cultural distortions of Afghanistan that have assumed a reality of their own, very much to the detriment of U.S. foreign policy and tens of millions of ordinary innocent inhabitants of the country.

American Orientalism regarding Afghanistan has become increasingly entrenched since 2001. Despite this general trend, and beyond Schwartz's important contributions (Schwartz, 2005, 2006; Schwartz-Dupre, 2007), it is important to note at least a handful of significant critiques of American caricatures of Afghan and Muslim women predicated on Orientalism that have appeared in academic journals, within which the work of Jennifer Fluri figures prominently (Abu-Lughod, 2001; Fluri, 2008a, 2008b, 2009a, 2009b; Hirschkind & Mahmood, 2002; Khalid, 2011; Russo, 2006; Toor, 2012). This important but limited critical academic production stands in marked contrast to the mass production and high visibility of periodicals such as NGM and more recently *Time* magazine with its nose-less Aisha cover image (M.J. Hanifi, 2010; Stengel, 2012) that remain steadfastly faithful to the lucrative market for representations of Afghans and other Muslim cultural Others that perpetuate Orientalism.

Printing, Mapping, and Photography: The Colonial Technologies Deployed to Imag(in)e Afghanistan

The full spectrum of Orientalism as it operates in and on Afghanistan involves multiple centuries of imperial interests, multiple centers of imperial power, multiple mutually reinforcing although sometimes contradictory expressions of imperial Orientalisms, and multiple forms of local Afghan elite appropriations of technologies and cultural tastes that reproduce global international Orientalism locally in the national context. Regarding the ancient period, it is may be possible to see the residue of Greek artistic forms in the territory that later became Afghanistan as a form of Orientalism, understood broadly to mean artistic and architectural styles and technologies imposed by the West upon the East in the context of imperial wars. However, due to limitations of historical evidence, there is not enough cultural data about this period to see Orientalism at work in the Greek or Hellenic period. It is important to consider the possibilities for other 'proto-Orientalisms' to have been embedded within the processes of Persianization, Islamization, and in a more limited and complicated way, Buddhization, in a long-term historical view of Afghanistan.

Printing 1: Language

Orientalism as a modern scholarly tradition is grounded in the study of languages. Arguably the most famous British Orientalist, Sir William Jones (1746–1794), expressed a keen interest in the Pashto language (Trautmann, 1995, 1998). Jones's attention to Pashto was contextualized by his larger interest in connecting the histories of ancient and modern peoples including Greeks, Indians, Persians, and English speakers to other past and present Eurasian cultures through linguistic analysis. Jones' work helped to establish historical linguistics and comparative philology as the foundational sciences of intellectual Orientalism that soon gave way to political Orientalism. The institutional context for Jones's study of Oriental languages was the Asiatic Society of Bengal that was founded in 1784. In 1788 the Society began to publish a journal, first known as *Asiatic Researches* and later as the *Journal of the Asiatic Society of Bengal*, wherein a great deal of science of Afghanistan ranging from linguistics to geology and geography to history was collected for the use of British colonial authorities in India and British scholars in Europe. In 1790 Jones published an article in *Asiatic Researches* entitled "On the Descent of the Afghans from the Jews" in which he presented a "Specimen of the Pushtoo Language." Jones argued that the Pashto language was related to Chaldaic, a position that fed into his theorization about the historical relationships among speakers of what later came to be known as Indo-European languages.

Due to the large number of contemporaneously pirated copies and subsequent re-printings of *Asiatic Researches* in Asia and Europe, it is unclear whether Jones's first printing of Pashto occurred through lithography or through moveable type printing. Moveable type printing was definitively first applied to the Pashto language through the American William Carey's Baptist Missionary

Serampore Press, which produced a typeset printed version of the New Testament in Pashto in 1821 (Center for Study of the Life and Work of William Carey, n.d.). As indicated by the career of the British East India Company's most accomplished student of Pashto, Henry George Raverty (S.M. Hanifi, 2011b), moveable type printing of the Pashto language was institutionally organized by the military exam system for colonial officers. The colonial exam system engaged local languages in a myriad of ways that compromised such key elements as the number of characters used to represent the spectrum of sounds in Pashto. In this regard, for example, Raverty used 40 characters for his version of Pashto, while the military exam system adopted a 20-character system, thus erasing at least half of the language's morphological and phonological spectrum for students and instructors alike. In the early phase of this particular cultural encounter between East and West, British Orientalism discovered, transformed, and redeployed the Pashto language for its own purposes, and in these processes printing technology was a primary agent of change.

Mapping

Orientalism compels its powerful Western practitioners to use their fragmentary knowledge in pursuit of imperial objectives at the expense of the authenticity and integrity of Eastern cultures. British India was the key arena for the establishment of Orientalism as intellectual and political enterprise, and Afghanistan occupied a strategically important imperial frontier of the British colonial project in South Asia. During the 19th century the British acted diplomatically, coercively, and scientifically at various times and in varying degrees on the young Afghan kingdom that co-emerged with colonial rule in India. The first accredited British Indian diplomatic ambassador to be received by an Afghan king was Mountstuart Elphinstone (1779–1859), who was hosted by the soon-to-be-exiled ruler Shah Shuja (r. 1803–1809 and 1839–1842) in Peshawar in 1809. By the time Elphinstone arrived in Peshawar, Shuja had already lost control of Kabul, a city Elphinstone recognized as being so central and definitional to the Afghan kingdom that he titled the memoirs of his journey *An Account of the Kingdom of Caubul* (Elphinstone, 1815/1992; Hopkins, 2008). Elphinstone never made it beyond Peshawar, and Shuja spent roughly the next thirty years as an exile in British Indian territory before being forcibly repatriated by the colonial Army of the Indus that occupied Kabul in summer of 1839 at the beginning of the first Anglo-Afghan war (S.M. Hanifi, 2012). The Army of the Indus experienced utter annihilation in the course of a desperate retreat from the city in January 1842, and the vengeful terror inflicted by the Army of Retribution on the inhabitants of eastern Afghanistan in the fall of 1842 marks the end of the first Anglo-Afghan war. Three editions of Elphinstone's *Account* appeared—in 1815, 1819, and 1839—indicating an increasing market for knowledge about this exotic corner of the British Imperial Oriental bazaar leading up to the first Anglo-Afghan war.

The most important image contained in Elphinstone's book is a map of the *Kingdom of Caubul* upon which the word *Afghaunistaun* appears faintly. One of the most tangible and consequential projections within British colonialism was to bring Afghanistan itself to cartographic life, episodically and, arguably, largely ineffectually through a series of boundary-making endeavors in the late 19th century (S.M. Hanifi, 2008, 2011a; Hopkins, 2007). The asymmetrically co-authored British imperial/Afghan national bordering scheme left the eastern boundary or Durand Line with what is now Pakistan particularly contested and periodically subject to closures and the possibility of revision or erasure. The historic height of these eastern border troubles was from the late 1940s to the late 1960s. In that period, a series of diplomatic jousts and public demonstrations occurred in Kabul and Peshawar, primarily, regarding a separate third polity termed Pashtunistan, which straddled the eastern border between the recognized but increasingly 'failed' nation-states of Afghanistan and Pakistan (S.M. Hanifi, Forthcoming B). The noteworthy issue at present is the high degree of importance that Elphinstone attached to the map that accompanies his book.

Beyond its extensive use of local manual and intellectual labor, Elphinstone's embassy contained a number of European specialists, including Lieutenant John Macartney, who was responsible for the vital and prized map the Elphinstone mission was commanded and contracted to produce. By identifying and scientifically locating environmental, cultural, and political features of the landscape, a map stands as both a key symbol and a primary technical instrument for the articulation of imperial power over subjected peoples and territories, thus raising the rhetorical question as to whether such maps as Macartney's enable or result from imperial conquest. In the first edition of his book, Elphinstone included a separate five-page "Notice Regarding the Map," indicating that the embassy was conducting a particular kind of route survey (Elphinstone, 1815/1992, vol. 1, pp. xii–xvii).

To produce route surveys, directions, distances, and times were determined by imprecise technical measurements obtained from new scientific instruments and including compasses, perambulators (or surveyor's wheels), and clocks (Edney, 1997). From the British perspective, all forms of their modern route survey scientific data were destabilized by the labor and information necessarily collected from native informants and employees. Route survey data was routinely cross-checked but always suspect, due in large measure to local terminological variation regarding settlements and natural features of the environment that constantly challenged the linguistic competencies and scientific authority of colonial cartographers. Fully inflected by human imprecision during the collection phase, all of this route survey data was further scientifically collated and manipulated in the form of complex printed maps that became first points of reference for colonial authorities and strategists. Colonial maps such as Macartney's distilled multiple forms of science and knowledge and as such represent a textual pinnacle of Imperial authority to represent Other cultures.

Elphinstone's notice about Macartney's map pays tribute to James Rennell, the Surveyor-General of the East India Company from 1764–1777, whose maps of Bengal and Hindustan retained discursive authority in 1808 (Elphinstone, 1815/1992). It is clear that Elphinstone viewed Macartney's cartographic efforts that he oversaw as a scientific advance following and extending Rennell's famous route surveys and maps. Macartney's memoir detailing the Kabul map's production through a process of triangulation reveals how inexact, imprecise, and at times speculative the whole mapmaking enterprise was in this era, as Edney illustrates on a larger scale through his analysis of the Great Trigonometrical Survey of India (Edney, 1997; Elphinstone, 1815/1992).

It should be emphasized that the Elphinstone embassy did not know precisely where Kabul was, and that an important part of their mission was to bring that city, as well as Qandahar, Herat, Balkh, and intervening locations into the colonial cartographic orbit by 'fixing' or 'settling' their position in relation to other scientifically charted areas of India. The Elphinstone embassy never proceeded beyond Peshawar, so Macartney's scientific route survey ceased there, leaving native information as the basis of the map beyond that point. Despite these cartographic limitations and setbacks, Elphinstone was satisfied that Macartney's work advanced the "surveyed line hundreds of miles beyond Rennell's map" (Elphinstone, 1815/1992, vol. I, p. xiv). In the brief one-page Preface to the second edition of an *Account*, Elphinstone mentioned the map as having escaped the printing errors the text itself suffered during the book's first printing. The third edition of the book appeared in 1838 during the far from secretive but not fully public buildup to the first Anglo-Afghan War. Elphinstone dedicated the entirety of the longer five-page Preface of this edition to corrections that came to his attention over the previous two decades or so and, rather ominously, to the cartographic work that remained to be in and around Kabul. Elphinstone and Macartney's extensive commentary about mapping Kabul and Afghanistan reveal what Edney calls *cartographic anxiety*, which is produced when unpredictable, inconsistent, and contradictory human agencies inflect and destabilize Western cartographic science harnessed for imperial service in Eastern contexts. The technical printing history of Elphinstone's map and the scientific advances made by the ill-fated first colonial occupation army in furthering the imperial mapping project for Afghanistan await future archival research.

Similar to the division of labor behind the printing of Macartney's first map, the second British imperial map of Afghanistan was also a collective production. Alexander Burnes' *Travels into Bokhara* (1834/1992) was a widely acclaimed and circulated account of his undercover travels through Peshawar and Kabul to Bukhara. The book was enormously popular, and Burnes was ceremoniously received and féted in London at various public and private events. He received the gold medal of the Geographical Society of England, the silver medal of the Geographical Society of Paris, and the Athenæum Club admitted him as a member without ballot (Prior, 2004/2008). He was most conspicuously knighted by Queen Victoria in 1839, shortly after which he joined the Army of the Indus in Kabul. Burnes's execution by mob there on November 2, 1841 is commonly said to mark the beginning of the revolt that led to the Army of the Indus's suicidal retreat two months later.

Burnes's Persian-speaking Kashmiri guide, interpreter, and secretary, Mohan Lal, also gained fame in England. Lal made a much-celebrated return of Burnes's personal papers to the celebrity's grieving father in Scotland, and he participated in high profile public debates about the tragic course of the Afghan war in London, where Burnes's actions came under close parliamentary scrutiny (Fisher, 2004; Lal, 1846/2009). It is important to note that Lal sought and received formal training as a surveyor very shortly after concluding his journey with Burnes to Kabul and Bokhara. That prompt pursuit of institutional certification, combined with his linguistic service and the close personal, political, professional, and economic relationship between the two, prompts one to deduce a large but unrecognized role for the Lal when Burnes states that he (Burnes)

> gave *my* original manuscript surveys, protractions, and the whole of the observations which I had made during a period of nine years (to M. John Arrowsmith who) … embodied these in a large and comprehensive map (containing) the latest and best information on the various countries within the limits of the map … (that was to be) … sold separately by all booksellers. (my emphasis, Burnes, 1834/1992, vol. 1, un-paginated *Advertisement Regarding The Map of Central Asia and the Indus*)

To produce the second publicly circulated British map of Afghanistan, the famed printer and cartographer John Arrowsmith (Baigent, n.d.) collated the data provided by Burnes, whose access to local information was mediated primarily by Lal. The profit to be made from maps and other information about Afghanistan should not escape readers' notice.

To highlight how Orientalism works across cultural, scientific, and political fields, I have traced a brief history of the application of moveable type printing technology on the Pashto language by European intellectuals and American missionaries. Carey's Pashto translation of the New Testament and Jones's brief sample of the language are texts that demonstrate the power of Western technology and ideas as applied to Eastern languages and cultures. The powerful impact of printing technology has a related but distinct effect when applied to images. As a particular genre of images, maps are emblematic of Orientalism's power to represent and produce scientific and political legitimacy, but maps also inherently distort local geographic and cultural realities involving languages and territory, at least. Readers have been provided with accounts of the first two British Imperial mapping exercises in and around Kabul and Afghanistan commonly associated with Elphinstone and Burnes, each of whom delegated and outsourced through contract much of the labor and scientific knowledge and technology necessary to construct the maps identified with each colonial actor.

Printing II: Images (Drawings, Paintings, and Lithographs)

The lithographic printing of manually produced drawings and illustrations was a well-known and available technology during the early 19th century when Elphinstone journeyed to Peshawar and Burnes traveled to Kabul and Bokhara. Elphinstone's *Account* contains 14 additional plates, 13 of which are portraits of locals (Elphinstone, 1815/1992; Hanifi, Forthcoming A). Elphinstone does not indicate who originally prepared and modified the non-map plates, but in an age of standardized handwriting, Elphinstone's penmanship stands out as conspicuously poor, so it is doubtful he had a hand in preparing them. However, after Elphinstone many of the British adventurers and officials who traveled to and through Kabul and its hinterland personally produced an increasingly large set of images. Burnes's *Travels* contains nine plates: "Portrait of Runjeet Sing, Costume of Bokhara, Colossal Idols at Bameean, Bactrian and other Coins (two plates), View of Hydrabad on the Indus, Natives of Cutch, Natives of Sinde, View of Sindree" (Burnes, 1834/1992, vol. 1, un-paginated List of Plates). Without the necessary archival research, it cannot be determined who produced the plates accompanying Burnes's *Travels* or precisely when or how they were generated for publication.

The phenomenon of including illustrations with travel narratives is explained by a number of factors, including a growing imperial and market interest in Kabul, the increasing availability of lithographic printing, and the apparently insatiable metropolitan cultural appetite for adventure stories and exotic images from the colonies and imperial frontiers. The narratives of these texts allowed readers to follow the footsteps of these swashbuckling British heroes and travelers, and the accompanying illustrations provided opportunities to view and imaginatively interact with the Indians, Persians, and Afghans hailing from these imperial heartlands and peripheries. The texts and illustrations, together with the sciences and technologies behind them, combined through Orientalism to mark Victorian moral and racial boundaries between the modern civilized colonizing Western British and the colonized traditional Eastern Others.

Between roughly 1827 and 1838, Charles Masson, also known as James Lewis, located, collected, sketched, and analyzed what were then termed 'antiquities,' meaning in modern parlance pre-historic archaeological materials, ranging from coins to pottery to Buddhist structures called *topes* or *stupas* (Errington, 2004; S.M. Hanifi, 2011a; Masson, 1842/1997; Whitteridge, 1986). As with the Afghan war-driven market demand for a third edition of Elphinstone's seminal *Caubul* text, Horace Hayman Wilson (Wilson & Masson, 1841/1998) compiled and published two of Masson's essays, as well as a large number of Masson's drawings and sketches of coins, caves, topes, temples, vases, seals, caskets, cups, and figurines. In his philological efforts, Masson also collected samples of what he hypothesized to be an ancient 'Arianian' alphabet from the artifacts he unearthed in and around Kabul, Begram, and Hadda, primarily. These writing samples were subsequently determined to contain multiple languages and scripts, such as Bactrian and Kharosthi, from different historical eras.

Errington (2004) indicates that a great deal more of Masson's artwork and illustrations are archived at the British Museum, and there is also considerable archival material from Masson at the British Library. Among the archived holdings at the British Library are two maps comparing what Masson argues to be the route taken by Alexander the Great through the area and his own route (Richardson, 2013). Masson's maneuver was to superimpose an emerging cartographic unity upon an established philological unity between ancient Greece and modern England established by Sir William Jones. Orientalism's effects on the cartographic sciences generally, and the ongoing colonial and more recent neo-colonial engagement of Afghanistan through cartography specifically, require separate treatment. As such, I will suspend further discussion of maps and mapping and turn my attention to the early history of mass-produced images of the inhabitants of the country.

The annihilation of the Army of the Indus generated an active market for Afghanistan-related texts and images, and a rapidly expanding British reading public craved information about the infamous imperial war. Among the hordes of people who entered the market built upon the war in Afghanistan was Godfrey Thomas Vigne (1842/ 1982), who published an account of his 1836 journey to and residence in Kabul at the war's end. Vigne's book is distinguished by black and white lithographic reproductions of his sketches of various structures, landscapes, and people at the heading of each of the 12 chapters. Vigne was an avid amateur artist who produced at least 70 prints, drawings, and paintings of people and places in the Ottoman Empire, Arab world, Persia, and Afghanistan, for which there are 19 black and white sketches and color paintings. These images are archived at the Victoria and Albert Museum and their acquisition details reveal an active market for images produced in the "Orientalist Style" (Victoria and Albert Museum Collection, n.d.).

Vigne's (1842/1982) book does not highlight or emphasize images; rather, its strengths and market orientation were textual. However, a vast industry of imperial image production primarily for the British market arose in the general context, particularly the aftermath of the first Anglo-Afghan war. Approximately 100 lithographic images of Afghanistan were published by a handful of participants in the first British Indian occupation of Kabul, Qandahar, and other locations in eastern Afghanistan (Atkinson, 1842; Eyre, 1843; Hart, 1843; Jackson, 1840; Rattray, 1847). These industrially mass-produced images portray historical sites, political elites, and local populations in isolation from each other, and the narratives accompanying these images reinforce the cultural distance between local Afghans and an imperial army whose total destruction was immortalized in British national consciousness through the British popular press.

In the British public imaginary, the place of the colonies comprising the empire was inscribed primarily by the rise of popular middle-class journalism, and British newspapers increasingly relied on visual stimuli to convey highly politicized, militarized, and exoticized narratives of the societies subjected to imperial action. *The Illustrated London News* (ILN) was the first industrially produced mass-circulation weekly newspaper to emphasize the use of images, and Afghanistan figured prominently in its very first words and pages. The inaugural issue on May 14, 1842 opens by noting a decade-long

> revolution in illustrative arts ... (wherein) ... art has become the bride of literature ... (and) ... penetrated all departments of our social system ... (and in the ILN) ... intelligence reaching our shores will be sifted with industry and illustrated with skill ... so whether the cowardice of China or the treachery of Affghanistan be the theme of your abhorrence or resentment, you shall at least have as much historical detail of both as, while it

> gratifies general curiosity, shall minister to the natural anxieties at home of those who have friends and relations amid the scenes delineated and events described.
>
> *The Illustrated London News*, 1842, p. 1

The second page of ILN's first issue contains one image of Kabul and another image of Ghazni. These images accompany a narrative that emphasizes the plight of British captives still held by Afghans, whose duplicity and treachery were then being narratively and visually actively inscribed in the imperial public mindset (ILN, 1842). The ILN devoted considerable attention to Afghanistan in the first half year of its existence, and Afghanistan content contributed in no small way to the early success of the new publication. These were the months when the British Army of Retribution was organized to rescue the British hostages whose captivity was later and somewhat problematically illustrated by Eyre (1843) as having been quite comfortable. Afghanistan continued to appear regularly in the pages of ILN as the revolutionary newspaper grew well over ten-fold in the first two decades of its existence, from the 26,000 copies of the first issue printed in 1842 to copy runs exceeding 300,000 by the early 1860s (Leary, n.d.).

The most celebrated of the many very well-known images of the first Anglo-Afghan war is an 1879 painting titled *Remnants of an Army* by the Imperial war artistic memorialist Elizabeth Thompson Butler (Butler, 1922; Usherwood, n.d.; Wynne, 2011). The picture depicts Dr. William Brydon, who is often but incorrectly identified as the sole survivor of the British troops massacred on an ill-conceived retreat out of Kabul in the dead of winter in January 1842, clinging to life on a horse that is also barely alive and straggling to salvation at the British garrison at Jalalabad. The painting is designed to elicit the British nation's patriotic duty to avenge the first Afghan war disaster with support for the contemporary second Afghan war (1878–1880) that was progressing less than satisfactorily.

Elizabeth Thompson (later Butler) gained fame with her 1874 *Roll Call* painting that drew attention to the heroic sacrifices of ordinary British foot soldiers during the Crimean War (Butler, 1922). The artistic view of heroism through suffering was innovative, but she was also unique for being the first noteworthy female painter of military scenes. With its combined forms of originality, *Roll Call* quickly gained notoriety of such an extent that it was purchased by Queen Victoria, who allowed engravings of it to be made for mass printing and wide public circulation. This crown patronage made Thompson arguably the most famous painter in England when *Remnants of an Army* appeared in spring 1879 in the early phases of the second Anglo-Afghan war.

In 1877 Elizabeth Thompson married the British Army Officer William Francis Butler. Butler gained fame across the empire first as a soldier and to a lesser extent as a writer about his travels and imperial exploits, including increasingly standardized commentary about the first Afghan war and the "timeless, wild, fanatical, revengeful" Afghans (Butler, 1880, p. 159) in a book titled *Far Out* (Butler, 1880; Wynne, 2011). When *Remnants of an Army* and *Far Out* appeared, the independently and jointly famous Butlers were painting and writing for empire at a time when a powerful new technology, photography, was taking center stage as the primary visual tool for the modern imperial documentation of Eastern cultural exotica, traditionalism, and inferiority.

Photography

Remnants of an Army was nearing completion in March of 1879, the month of a frightening and much publicized drowning of 45 cavalry officers and untold numbers of local attendants in the Kabul River near the eastern Afghan city of Jalalabad. This event was later memorialized in the imperial ink of Rudyard Kipling in his poem *Ford O' Kabul River* (Kipling, 1922). For a reading and viewing public thirsty for ever more readily available information about the empire and wars that defined it, the Kabul River disaster signaled how eerily tenuous the second invasion and occupation had yet again become for British forces and strategic interests in Afghanistan. Of concern at present are the new technologies used in the second Afghan war when compared to the first conflict. One cannot over-appreciate that between the end of the first war in 1842 and the beginning of the second war in 1878, railroads, steamships, telegraphy, and industrial killing had become not just common, but normative and necessary for Britain to articulate its dialectical relationship with a growing and increasingly interconnected global empire. How photography was deployed to represent cultures subjected to imperial power will be examined through the photographs of John Burke and Lillias Hamilton.

Within the British forces that invaded Afghanistan, John Burke was attached to the Bengal Sappers and Miners, but precisely how remains obscure. It is not known exactly how many photographs Burke took, nor do we currently have details about the Europeans, Indians, and Afghans who assisted him and how they did so, technically and regarding social and political access to his local photographic subjects. We do know that Burke made available for purchase approximately 400 photographs of the occupation forces as they progressed from Peshawar through the Khaibar Pass and Jalalabad to Kabul (John Burke Archive, n.d.; Khan, 2002). Prior to his time in Afghanistan, Burke spent a brief amount of time in the British Army, and his photographic skills became known to the British Indian public and through it the wider British imperial public in the 1850s. In 1859 Burke established a long-term working partnership with William Baker, who had previously established himself as a prominent photographer in Peshawar.

Burke and Baker were influential enough to photograph the Afghan Amir Sher Ali (r. 1863–1866 and 1868–1879) at least twice: first in 1869, as he attended a colonial durbar or public court in Ambala, and then again in 1871 in Peshawar in the context of Lord Mayo's tour of India as Viceroy. Perhaps as a result of his independent work with the Archaeological Survey of India, Burke branched out on his own in 1873.

Sher Ali fled Kabul shortly before the British captured Jalalabad in December 1878 and died in flight near Mazar-e Sharif in February 1879. Upon Sher Ali's death, his son Yaqub Khan assumed control of Kabul. The British advanced toward Kabul from Jalalabad but secured the terms they were looking for via the May 1879 treaty signed with Yaqub at the symbolically highly potent site of Gandamak, where the last remnants of the Army of the Indus, less William Brydon, were annihilated in January 1842. After a difficult start with substantial losses of life at Paiwar Kotal and Khurd Kabul, the Gandamak treaty marked a highly successful avenge-the-past ending to the first stage of the second war. This treaty relinquished control over Afghanistan's foreign affairs to the British in return for a hefty subsidy, which was a political low point for those invested in an independent state-centered view of Afghanistan. Yaqub attended the Gandamak meeting in a white European uniform most unlike the clothing of his father that was far less attuned to Western sensibilities.

The most celebrated of the photographs Burke took of Yaqub at Gandamak was reproduced in illustrated form along with another sketch of Burke at work in processing the photographic negative. These famous images appeared in the very widely circulated newspaper *The Graphic* on July 12, 1879 under the title and subtitle "The End of the Afghan War: Photographing the Ameer." *The Graphic* was established in 1869 to compete with the ILN. *The Graphic* was explicit in its intention to increase the quantity and quality of images included in it pages compared to the ILN, thus improving the pay of working artists and undermining the latter's local and global market shares. In a feast of wording consummating Orientalism's construction and consumption of the cultural Other, *The Graphic* narrated the technology of photography as a means of imperial dominance through Yaqub's dress, which became a symbol of colonized consent while also serving as an allusion to a natural resemblance between the Afghan Amir and British Royalty:

> After Mr. Burke had taken (the photograph) of him in his gorgeous uniform of white and gold, the Ameer showed great anxiety to see the

> results, and Mr. Cavagnari explained to him the process of photography ... and with regard to the brilliant uniform in which the Ameer arrayed himself for the occasion ... the costume was perfectly European in all its details ... probably German ... or Russian ... with a steel helmet ... that when removed presented a curious likeness to the Duke of Edinburgh.
>
> *The Graphic*, 1879

The announcement of the war's end was exceedingly premature, nevertheless, as the second Afghan war wore on, over 40 of Burke's photos would appear via illustrated reproduction in *The Graphic* (1879). Burke accompanied the invasion force to Kabul and his photographs of the city's populace are all necessarily staged given the technology involved. The very ability to stage such photos and the mass rendering of Kabul's inhabitants into anonymized Western categories inherently reflects the coercive and representational power of Orientalism. The following are samplings of the titles Burke gave to photographs in his Kabul portfolio that indicate a combination of local and external economic and social categories, with priority given to non-local terminology: *High Priests and Mulahs of Kabul, Central Asian Dealers, Kizzelbash Chiefs of Kabul, Wealthy Hindus of Kabul, Surgeons and Physicians of Kabul, Beggars, Kafiristan Slaves, Kohistani Hazara Combatants, Kabul Nautch Girls, Nautch Girls with Musicians, Landowners and Labors, Kabulee Police, Representatives of Science and Art of Kabul, The Family of the Dost* (Mohammad). Burke privately marketed his Afghan war photos, and he encountered two main competitors in the wider Indian photographic market. The first of Burke's competitors was Sir Benjamin Simpson and the second was the most famous photographic team British India during the second half of the 19th century, Samuel Bourne and Charles Shepherd.

Burke's photography business thrived in this active market, and he maintained access to official circles after the encounter with Yaqub at Gandamak. His success and connections allowed him to photograph Yaqub's replacement as the colonially appointed Amir of Kabul, Abd al-Rahman (r. 1880–1901). The British appointed Abd al-Rahman to the Kabul Amirate in July 1880 in an attempt to provide local political cover for their military evacuation. In return for significantly increased material support, Abd al-Rahman accepted all terms of the diplomatically neutering Gandamak Treaty, with the sole colonial 'concession' being the British resident newswriters in Afghanistan were to be Indian Muslims, not European Christians or Hindus. The British success in achieving Afghanistan's political isolation from the perceived threat of Russian aggression in Central Asia required an elaborate colonial bordering project for the polity assigned to him. As such, colonial patronage of Abd al-Rahman was subsumed within a larger set of British imperial border policies for Afghanistan that structurally impoverished and systemically peripheralized this historically vibrant regional political economy. Afghanistan assumed its current cartographic disposition during Abd al-Rahman's reign, and there is a clear historical correlation between the bordering of the country and its economic and political regression that have combined to fracture state-society relations.

When Abd al-Rahman assumed the Amirate of Kabul and British patronage, only the Perso-Afghan boundary in Sistan had been previously demarcated in 1873 by the F.G. Goldsmid Mission, for which Sher Ali received a payment of 1.5 million Rupees (Balland, 1990; Hopkins, 2007). Abd al-Rahman's subsidy increased progressively in return for colonial border agreements culminating in the largest and arguably most problematic 1893 Durand Line divide between eastern Afghanistan and the North-West Frontier Province of British India, thus increasing what colonial officials termed the Kabul Subsidy 50% from 1.2 to 1.8 million Rupees (S.M. Hanifi, 2011a). What is often referred to as the 'Panjdeh incident' began in late March 1885 and it marks the height of the many 'boundary crises' in the northern and northwestern regions of the Afghan frontier with Russia. These crises often involved territorial claims relating to the Oxus/Amu Darya River and its tributaries.

The Panjdeh crisis began with a military skirmish between the British and Russian Boundary Commissions wherein a body of Afghan troops attached to the British Commission was overrun by Russian forces. The British imperial and British Indian components of the British Boundary Commission produced maps, route surveys, and travel narratives about northern Afghanistan for Government officials and the public-at-large (Holdich, 1885a, 1885b, 1885c; A.C. Yate, 1887; C.E. Yate, 1888) in printed fashions made familiar by the previous generation of colonial authors addressing eastern Afghanistan. The Panjdeh incident provoked a flurry of local, regional, and international diplomatic activity that took place just as Abd al-Rahman was making his way from Kabul to a British durbar in Rawalpindi. At the durbar Abd al-Rahman received the ceremonial title "Knight Grand Commander of the Most Exalted Order of the Star of India" (Khan, 2002, p. 156), publicly thanked Queen Victoria for all her favors, and expressed solidarity with the British in resisting external adversaries. The Rawalpindi durbar consummated Abd al-Rahman's material and symbolic subordination to British capital and colonialism, and we are fortunate that Burke was there to photograph some of the proceedings (Khan, 2002).

The Rawalpindi durbar marked a critical stage of play in what only later became known as the Great Game, a phrase popularized largely through the effect of Rudyard Kipling's *Kim* that appeared originally as a serial publication in 1900. Said highlights Kipling's race-based Orientalism as typified by the "White

Man's Burden" poem to highlight how a pathology of cultural, physical, and epistemological violence is found behind the "White Masks" of imperial representatives such as Kipling and T.E. Lawrence (Said, 1978/2003, pp. 226–229, *passim*).

Burke and other photographers took a large number of pictures of Abd al-Rahman and his entourage in Rawalpindi. Burke's images of the Rawalpindi durbar include some of the most well-recognized and widely circulated photographs of Abd al-Rahman, his confidantes, and bodyguards. Arguably the most famous of these is a view of the Afghan Amir on the veranda of a bungalow surrounded by British officials. In this photograph, Abd al-Rahman appears to be leaning rather heavily on his walking stick, due to what durbar observers understood to be gout (Khan, 2002). Kipling took note of Abd al-Rahman's infirmity in the context of his journalist reporting on the Amir's high-profile travel from Peshawar to Rawalpindi for the *Lahore Civil and Military Gazette* newspaper (Moran, 2005). Kipling characterized Abd al-Rahman's much anticipated formal entrance to the durbar proceedings as immediately revealing him to be "very lame" (Moran, 2005). The Afghan Amir has subsequently been shown to have had a number of severe and debilitating illnesses that rendered him psychologically unsettled and physically unable to conduct state business for multiple months at time for most of his reign (Lee, 1991).

Abd al-Rahman's unremitting illnesses and his personal connections to British Indian officials combined to bring the Australian-Scottish nurse Lillias Hamilton to Kabul. Hamilton arrived at Abd al-Rahman's court in the spring of 1894 and departed in 1896 under very unclear, arguably mysterious circumstances (Cohen, 2004). Hamilton wrote a novel about an Afghan girl titled *A Vazier's Daughter* (1900/2002) that serves up narratives of Afghans and their homeland for a market insatiably hungry for Eastern exotica skewered by Orientalism. Hamilton's book is predicated on personal experience based upon her time in Kabul. However, she deploys a fictional narrative designed to appeal to the sensibilities the reading public had come to understand of Afghanistan at a distance. Similar to the effect of Khaled Hosseini's (2003) book *The Kite Runner* on U.S. public opinion and policy in the wake of September 11, 2001, this intermediate historical fiction genre reaffirmed an Orientalism-inspired truth for a rapidly growing market of readers:

> If my readers complain that there is no brightness, no happiness in my book, that it is a story without one ray of hope, I can but reply, "Then I have succeeded but too well in my task of drawing a fair picture of life as it is in Afghanistan." There is no such thing as joy there. There is no such thing as peace, or comfort, or rest, or ease. There is never a moment when any one

> is sure he is not the subject of some plot or intrigue. There is no amusement, no relaxation; the people don't know how to enjoy themselves.
>
> HAMILTON, 1900/2002, p. 6

We are fortunate to be able to position Hamilton's writings in relation to a large number of photographs she took during her time in and around Kabul, roughly 100 of which are now archived at the Wellcome Institute Library in London (Wellcome Images, n.d.). Many of these photographs are of Abd al-Rahman's court, confidantes, and harem. These formal pictures of Abd al-Rahman's world in Kabul are unique and important and they reflect the kind of staging Burke used and therefore reveal Hamilton's access and presence in Kabul to be fully dependent upon imperial state patronage. As such, these court-centered photographs are products of the power structures undergirding Hamilton's presence in Kabul and thus carry the structural potential to convey the cultural exotica of Orientalism, which they do articulate, but only in part.

The limits on Hamilton's images servicing Orientalism are found in a separate subset of her archived material that includes non-court photographs taken outside of the royal palace complex context. These photographs were subject to some degree of state disciplining and oversight, but much less rigid and strict than at court. The content and context of these non-court photos fall to the margin of the imperial forces undergirding Orientalism. Despite appearing more hurried and blurry than stage-managed, they are more clearly focused on larger groups of ordinary Afghan people informally gathered, for example, at bread, fruit, and sweet shops in the Kabul market or washing clothes on the banks of the Kabul River. The most important point of emphasis is that many of these ordinary Afghans are smiling and would therefore appear to Western sensibilities as happy. The contradiction to note is that Hamilton exposes Afghan realities in photography that she elides in print.

Unlike her book, Hamiliton's photos were never publicly circulated, at least in part because they contradict her own fictional narrative focusing on a universal and therefore singular plight of oppressed women in Afghanistan. Hamilton's photos of the ordinary popular classes of Afghan people include multiple photographs of very different kinds of women in Kabul and its immediate hinterland. For example, on the outskirts of Kabul city, nomad women who look worlds apart from the women of Abd al-Rahman's court are visually captured. There is an especially striking photograph of two anonymous smiling women in 'Turkoman dress.'

It was primarily the fiction of Afghan women that Hamilton marketed to the British public through a widely circulated and much anticipated book, not the distinct, diverse, and complex realities of very different life circumstance for urban and rural and elite and lower-class women in Afghanistan that she revealed in her photographs.

The Exchange and Agency of Technology Within Orientalism

In reviewing the history of 19th-century British colonial images of Afghanistan, we have seen the cumulative nature of Orientalism at work through a variety of technologies. Printing provided a new form of expression that distorted the Pashto language, and the mapping of Kabul and boundary making around Afghanistan were accomplished scientifically, but imprecisely, through a form of bribery known as subsidization that characterizes asymmetrical colonial and imperial relationships. The colonial subsidies to the Afghan state ended due to the Third Anglo-Afghan war of 1919 that resulted in Afghanistan's political independence, which in turn opened up a variety of new corridors for technological exchange beyond those routed through the British and their restrictive policies toward this Indian buffer state.

The Afghan ruler Amanullah's (r. 1919–1929) declaration of independence from the British on May 6, 1919 prompted the short-lived third colonial war that officially ended with an August 8 armistice. However, the war ended in practice at the end of May as a result of the application of a recently developed technology, namely aerial bombardment. The British bombed Jalalabad on May 19 and 20, and the addition of Kabul to the target list on May 24 prompted Amanullah to sue for peace. During and after the war, Amanullah and other state officials dedicated a substantial amount of diplomatic time and structurally now much more limited state resources to the acquisition of airplanes. In a nationalist intensification of the colonial legacy of Orientalism, Amanullah's application of air power mimicked the British use of this coercive and frightening technology against "rebellious" Pashtun tribal populations (Adamec, 1996, pp. 48–49).

Airplane technology is unique because of its extensive division of labor and requisite training. The larger comparative lesson to come from aviation history is that as new technologies became available to Afghan state officials, new classes of Afghan technocrats were exposed to the ideologies contextualizing these material and scientific exchanges. And it is here in the cultural and social interstices of technological exchange that the local adoption and adaptation of Orientalism by Afghan elites can be located. Technology has been a pathway for Orientalism's hegemonic effects to be absorbed by Afghan elites and transferred to Afghan civil society through new institutions, industries, and projects designed in support of a national air carrier such as Ariana Afghan Airlines, for example.

Van Vleck (2009) identifies Ariana Airlines as a site for the local and global co-production of hegemony during the Cold War. However, the state quest for airplanes and other material expressions of modernity in Afghanistan was institutionalized in the 1920s and 1930s, when large groups of students including females were sent to India and France, at least (Andersson, n.d.; Williams Afghan Media Project, n.d.). These privileged students and their state patrons became vehicles for the installation of ideologies such as nationalism and modernity among a small but influential class of urban elites in Kabul. Western technology was a primary attraction for these urban elites and traditional intellectuals who also became the repositories for Orientalism in Afghanistan, regarding Pashtun tribes in particular. The ideological hegemony of Orientalism in Afghanistan was expressed by local agents and agencies that were mobilized and motivated by technology fetishes, as we have briefly addressed through airplane technology in the 20th century and as we can perhaps extend to drone technology in the 21st century.

The brief 20th-century airplane excursus helps us appreciate the pathways through which the ideology of Orientalism was previously indigenized in Afghanistan during the colonial period through the transfer and deployment of earlier technologies such as those associated with mechanical printing, cartography, lithography, and photography. These technologies were acquired from and associated with modern Western power, states, and imperialism. As primary vehicles for representing Afghanistan through images, those technologies also carried the ideological potential to distort, misrepresent, and decontextualize cultural realities among Afghans themselves.

The Afghan national reproduction of Orientalism is epitomized by a book titled *Afghanistan Observed, 1830–1920* (The British Library, 2010). This volume merely repackages British and French hand-sketched, lithographic, and photographic images and descriptions of Afghanistan, including multiple images produced by individuals referenced above such as Masson, Rattray, Atkinson, and Burke. The Foreword to the volume by the Afghan Minister of Culture and Information praises European travelers for "their insights that should be of interest to Afghans" (n.p.). There is no critical commentary addressing the colonial context of these images, only uncritical Afghan state acceptance of British imperial activity. *Afghanistan Observed*, although impressed with the official seal of the Islamic Republic of Afghanistan, is in fact an outsourced production of the Agha Khan Trust and the British Library. The images, textual context, and production of this volume are drenched in Orientalism as understood through its activity, ideology, and artifacts. There is now a desperate need to surmount the Orientalism of Afghanistan. In that regard, until Afghan state officials can take control of, reinterpret, and redeploy their own national image heritage—from colonial images to the *National Geographic* and *Time* Magazine *Afghan Girls* to the imaging technologies deployed on the imperial fleets of airplanes, blimps, and drones hovering in Afghan airspace—Afghanistan will continue to be the world's primary victim of the epistemological and coercive violence of Orientalism.

References

Abu El-Haj, N. (2005). Edward Said and the political present. *American Ethnologist, 32,* 538–555. doi:10.1525/ae.2005.32.4.538.

Abu-Lughod, L. (2001). "Orientalism" and Middle East feminist studies. *Feminist Studies, 27,* 101–113. doi:10.2307/3178451.

Adamec, L.W. (1996). *Dictionary of Afghan wars, revolutions, and insurgencies.* Lanham, MD: The Scarecrow Press.

Andersson, L. (n.d.). *The first thirty years of aviation in Afghanistan, Part I.* Andersson Aviation History Site. Retrieved July 27, 2017 from http://www.artiklar.z-bok.se/Afghanistan-1.html.

Atkinson, J. (1842). *Sketches in Afghaunistan.* London, England: H. Graves.

Baigent, E. (n.d.). Arrowsmith, John (1790–1873). In L. Goldman (Ed.), *Oxford dictionary of national biography.* Oxford, England: Oxford University Press. doi:10.1093/ref:odnb/701.

Balland, D. (1990). Afghanistan: Boundaries. In *Encyclopædia Iranica* IV/4, 406–415. Retrieved July 27, 2017 from http://www.iranicaonline.org/articles/boundaries-iii.

Breckenridge, C.A., & Van Der Veer, P. (Eds.). (1993). *Orientalism and the postcolonial predicament: Perspectives on South Asia.* Philadelphia, PA: University of Pennsylvania Press.

The British Library. (2010). *Afghanistan observed, 1830–1920.* London, England: British Library.

The British Library, Oriental and African Studies Reading Room. (n.d.). *Mountstuart Elphinstone Papers.* Mss Eur F88/474 "Bills and Accounts 1808–1820" and Mss Eur F88/107 "Caubul Expense Report." London, England: British Library.

Burnes, A. (1834/1992). *Travels into Bokhara; Being the account of a journey from India to Cabool, Tartary, and Persia; Also a narrative of a voyage on the Indus* (3 vols.). New Delhi, India: J. Jetley for Asian Educational Services.

Butler, E. (1922). *An autobiography.* London, England: Constable.

Butler, W. (1880). *Far out: Rovings retold.* London, England: W. Isbister.

Calluther, N. (2002). Damming Afghanistan: Modernization in a buffer state. *The Journal of American History, 89,* 512–537. doi:10.2307/3092171.

Center for Study of the Life and Work of William Carey, D.D. (1761–1834). (2012). *Baptist Missionary Society*. Retrieved July 27, 2017 from http://www.wmcarey.edu/carey/bms/bms.htm.

Cohen, S.L. (2004). Hamilton, Lillias Anna (1858–1925). In H.C.G. Matthew & B. Harrison (Eds.), *Oxford dictionary of national biography*. Oxford, England: Oxford University Press.

Coll, S. (2004). *Ghost wars: The secret history of the CIA, Afghanistan, and Bin Laden, from the Soviet invasion to September 10, 2001*. New York, NY: Penguin Press.

Cooley, J.K. (2000). *Unholy wars: Afghanistan, America, and international terrorism*. London, England: Pluto Press.

Crile, G. (2003). *Charlie Wilson's war: The extraordinary story of how the wildest man in Congress and a rogue CIA agent changed the history of our times*. New York, NY: Grove Press.

Dupree, L. (1973/1980). *Afghanistan*. Princeton, NJ: Princeton University Press.

Edney, M.H. (1997). *Mapping an empire: The geographical construction of India, 1765–1843*. Chicago, IL: University of Chicago Press.

Elphinstone, M. (1815/1992). *An account of the Kingdom of Caubul, and its dependencies in Persia, Tartary, and India*, 2 Vols. Karachi, India: Indus.

Errington, E. (2004). Charles Masson. In *Encyclopædia Iranica*. Retrieved July 27, 2017 from http://www.iranicaonline.org/articles/masson-charles.

Eyre, V. (1843). *Prison sketches: Comprising portraits of the Cabul prisoners and other subjects*. London, England: Dickinson and Son.

Feitshans, B., Kassar, M., Munafo, T., & Vajna, A.G. (Producers), & MacDonald, P. (Director). (1988). *Rambo III* [Motion picture]. United States: TriStar Pictures.

Fisher, M.H. (2004). *Counterflows to Colonialism: Indian travellers and settlers in Britain, 1600–1857*. Delhi, India: Permanent Black.

Fluri, J.L. (2008a). Feminist nation building in Afghanistan: An examination of Revolutionary Association of the Women of Afghanistan (RAWA). *Feminist Review, 89*, 34–54. doi:10.1057/fr.2008.6.

Fluri, J.L. (2008b). Rallying public opinion and other misuses of feminism: How U.S. militarism in Afghanistan is gendered through congressional discourse. In C.t. Mohanty, R.L. Riley, & M.B. Pratt (Eds.), in *Feminism and war: Confronting U.S. imperialism* (pp. 143–157). London, England: Zed Books.

Fluri, J.L. (2009a). "Foreign Passports Only": Geographies of (post) conflict work in Kabul, Afghanistan. *Annals of the Association of American Geographers, 99*(5), 986–994. doi:10.1080/00045600903253353.

Fluri, J.L. (2009b). The beautiful "other"—A critical examination of "Western" representations of Afghan feminine corporeal modernity. *Gender, Place & Culture, 16*, 241–257. doi:10.1080/09663690902836292.

Foucault, M. (1970/1994). *The order of things: An archaeology of the human sciences*. New York, NY: Vintage Books.

Foucault, M. (1972). *The archaeology of knowledge and the discourse on language*. New York, NY: Pantheon Books.

Foucault, M. (1979). *Discipline and punish: The birth of the prison*. New York, NY: Vintage Books.

Gramsci, A. (1972). *Selections from the prison notebooks of Antonio Gramsci*. New York, NY: International.

The Graphic. (1879). "Mr. Burke Posing the Ameer" and "Fixing the Negative," 12 July 1879.

Hamilton, L. (1900/2002). *A vizier's daughter: A tale of the Hazara War*. Bubendorf, Switzerland: Foundation Bibliotheca Afghanica.

Hanifi, M.J. (2010). Is Time Magazine's "cover girl" really a victim of mutilation by the Taleban? *Zero Anthropology*. Retrieved July 27, 2017 from http://zeroanthropology.net/2010/08/05/is-time's-afghan-"cover-girl"-really-a-victim-of-mutilation-by-the-taleban/.

Hanifi, S.M. (2008). *Connecting histories in Afghanistan: Market relations and state formation on a colonial frontier*. New York, NY: Columbia University Press. Retrieved July 27, 2017 from http://www.gutenberg-e.org/hanifi/index.html.

Hanifi, S.M. (2009, May). *Comparing regimes of colonial knowledge in Afghanistan, 1809–2009*. Paper presented at the Eurasian Studies Working Group Spring Seminar, Stanford University, Stanford, California.

Hanifi, S.M. (2011a). *Connecting histories in Afghanistan: Market relations and state formation on a colonial frontier*. Stanford, CA: Stanford University Press.

Hanifi, S.M. (2011b). Henry George Raverty and the colonial marketing of Pashto. In C. Talbot (Ed.), *Knowing India: Colonial and modern constructions of the past* (pp. 84–107). New Delhi, India: Yoda Press.

Hanifi, S.M. (2012). Shah Shuja's "hidden history" and its implications for the historiography of Afghanistan. *South Asia Multidisciplinary Academic Journal*. Retrieved July 27, 2017 from http://samaj.revues.org/3384.

Hanifi, S.M. (Forthcoming A). A book history of *An Account of the Kingdom of Caubul*. In S.M. Hanifi (Ed.), *Mountstuart Elphinstone in South Asia: Pioneer of British Colonial rule*. New York, NY: Oxford University Press.

Hanifi, S.M. (Forthcoming B). Producing Pashtunistan in British India, Kabul and the United States: Colonial knowledge, industrial technologies and modern ideologies in tribal territory. In S.M. Hanifi (Ed.), *Power hierarchies and hegemony in Afghanistan: State building, ethnic minorities and identity in Central Asia*. London, England: I.B. Tauris.

Hart, L.W. (1843). *Character and costume of Afghaunistan*. London, England: Henry Graves.

Hirschkind, C., & Mahmood, S. (2002). Feminism, the Taliban, and politics of counter-insurgency. *Anthropological Quarterly, 75*(2), 339–354. doi:10.1353/anq.2002.0031.

Holdich, T.H. (1885a). Afghan Boundary Commission: Geographical notes I. *Proceedings of the Royal Geographical Society, 7*(1), 39–44.

Holdich, T.H. (1885b). Afghan Boundary Commission: Geographical notes II. *Proceedings of the Royal Geographical Society, 7*(3), 160–166.

Holdich, T.H. (1885c). Afghan Boundary Commission: Geographical notes III. *Proceedings of the Royal Geographical Society, 7*(5), 273–292.

Hopkins, B.D. (2007). The bounds of identity: The Goldsmid mission and the delineation of the Perso-Afghan border in the nineteenth century. *Journal of Global History, 2,* 233–254. doi:10.1017/s1740022807002276.

Hopkins, B.D. (2008). *The making of modern Afghanistan.* New York, NY: Palgrave Macmillan.

Hosseini, K. (2003). *The kite runner.* New York, NY: Riverhead Books.

The Illustrated London News. (1842, May 14). Article. 1–2. Retrieved July 27, 2017 from http://gale.cengage.co.uk/product-highlights/history/illustrated-london-news.aspx.

Irwin, R. (2007). *For lust of knowing: The Orientalists and their enemies.* London, England: Penguin.

Irwin, R. (2008). *Dangerous knowledge: Orientalism and its discontents.* Woodstock, NY: Overlook Press.

Jackson, K. (1840). *Views of Affghaunistaun—The campaign of the Army of the Indus, c. 1839.* London, England: W.H. Allen.

John Burke Archive. (n.d.). *Burke + Norfolk: Photographs from the War in Afghanistan by John Burke and Simon Norfolk.* Retrieved July 27, 2017 from http://www.simonnorfolk.com/burkenorfolk/intro.html.

Khalid, M. (2011). Gender, Orientalism and representations of the "Other" in the War on Terror. *Global Change, Peace & Security, 23,* 15–29. doi:10.1080/14781158.2011.540092.

Khalil, O.F. (2016). *America's dream palace: Middle East expertise and the rise of the national security state.* Cambridge, MA and London, England: Harvard University Press.

Khan, O. (2002). *From Kashmir to Kabul: The photographs of John Burke and William Baker, 1860–1900.* Munich, Germany: Prestel.

Kipling, R. (1922). *Rudyard Kipling's verse: Inclusive edition, 1885–1918.* New York, NY: Doubleday, Page & Company.

Lal, M. (1846/2009). *Travels in the Panjab, Afghanistan, and Turkistan: To Balkh, Bokhara, and Herat.* London, England: W.H. Allen.

Leary, P. (n.d.). *The Illustrated London News Historical Archive, 1842–2003.* Andover, England: Gale Cengage Learning.

Lee, J. (1991). Abd al-Rahman Khan and the "*maraz ul-muluk.*" *Journal of the Royal Asiatic Society, 1,* 209–242. doi:10.1017/s1356186300000584.

Little, D. (2002). *American Orientalism: The United States and the Middle East since 1945*. Chapel Hill, NC: University of North Carolina Press.

Lockman, Z. (2004). *Contending visions of the Middle East: The history and politics of Orientalism*. Cambridge, England: Cambridge University Press.

Ludden, D. (1993). Orientalist empiricism: Transformations of colonial knowledge. In C.A. Breckenridge & P. Van der Veer (Eds.), *Orientalism and the postcolonial predicament: Perspectives on South Asia* (pp. 250–278). Philadelphia, PA: University of Pennsylvania Press.

Lutz, C., & Collins, J.L. (1993). *Reading National Geographic*. Chicago, IL: University of Chicago Press.

Macfie, A.L. (Ed.). (2000). *Orientalism: A reader*. New York, NY: New York University Press.

Masson, C. (1842/1997). *Narrative of various journeys in Balochistan, Afghanistan and the Panjab, including a residence in those countries from 1826 to 1838* (3 vols.). New Delhi, India: Munshiram Manoharlal.

Moran, N.K. (2005). *Kipling and Afghanistan: A study of the young author as a journalist writing on the Afghan border crisis of 1884–1885*. Jefferson, NC: MacFarland & Company.

Prior, K. (2004/2008). Burnes, Sir Alexander (1805–1841). In H.C.G. Matthew & B. Harrison (Eds.), *Oxford dictionary of national biography*. Oxford, England: Oxford University Press.

Rattray, J. (1847). *Scenery, inhabitants, & costumes of Afghaunistan*. London, England: Hering & Remington.

Reagan, President R. (1982). *Dedication of Space Shuttle Columbia launch 21 March*. Retrieved from http://www.youtube.com/watch?v=ipszh14WPFY.

Reagan, President R. (1983). *Proclamation of Afghanistan Day 21 March 1983*. Retrieved July 27, 2017 from http://www.thefullwiki.org/Afghanistan_Day_Proclamation.

Richardson, E. (2013). Mr. Masson and the lost cities: A Victorian journey to the edges of remembrance. *Classical Receptions Journal, 5*, 84–105. doi:10.1093/crj/clsoo8.

Ronald Reagan Presidential Library and Museum. (1983). *Meeting with Afghan Freedom Fighters to discuss Soviet atrocities in Afghanistan on 2 February 1983. C12820–32*. Retrieved July 27, 2017 from http://www.reagan.utexas.edu/archives/photographs/atwork.html.

Russo, A. (2006). The Feminist Majority Foundation's Campaign to Stop Gender Apartheid—The intersections of feminism and imperialism in the United States. *International Feminist Journal of Politics, 8*(4), 557–580. doi:10.1080/14616740600945149.

Said, E.W. (1978/2003). *Orientalism*. New York, NY: Vintage Books.

Said, E.W. (1985). Orientalism reconsidered. *Cultural Critique, 1*, 89–107. doi:10.2307/1354282.

Said, E.W. (1989). Representing the colonized: Anthropology's interlocutors. *Critical Inquiry, 15,* 205–225. doi:10.1086/448481.

Schwartz, R.L. (2005). Graphing the National: The rhetoric of National Geographic's Afghan Girl. In P. Riley & C. Willis-Chun (Eds.), *Engaging argument: Selected papers from the 2005 NCA/AFA Summer Conference on Argumentation* (pp. 121–127). Washington, DC: National Communication Association.

Schwartz, R.L.A. (2006). *Rhetorically refiguring public policy: Rhetoric, post-colonialism, and the strategic redeployment of National Geographic's Afghan Girl* (Doctoral dissertation, Ph.D. Thesis, University of Iowa).

Schwartz-DuPre, R.L. (2007). Rhetorically representing public policy: National Geographic's 2002 Afghan Girl and the Bush Administration's biometric identification policies. *Feminist Media Studies, 7*(4), 433–453. doi:10.1080/14680770701631620.

Shahrani, M.N., & Canfield, R.L. (1984). *Revolutions and rebellions in Afghanistan: Anthropological perspectives.* Berkeley, CA: Institute of International Studies, University of California, Berkeley.

Stengel, R. (2012, July 29). The plight of Afghan women: A disturbing picture. *Time Magazine.* Retrieved from http://www.time.com/time/magazine/article/0,9171,2007415,00.html.

Toor, S. (2012). Imperialist feminist redux. *Dialectical Anthropology, 36,* 147–160. doi:10.1007/s10624-012-9279-5.

Trautmann, T.R. (1995). Indian time, European time. In D.O. Hughes & T.R. Trautmann (Eds.), *Time: Histories and ethnologies* (pp. 167–197). Ann Arbor, MI: University of Michigan Press.

Trautmann, T.R. (1998). The lives of Sir William Jones. In W. Jones & A. Murray (Eds.), *Sir William Jones, 1746–1794: A commemoration* (pp. 91–121). Oxford, England: Oxford University Press.

Usherwood, P. (n.d.). Butler, Elizabeth Southerden, Lady Butler (1846–1933). In L. Goldman (Ed.), *Oxford dictionary of national biography.* Oxford, England: Oxford University Press. Retrieved July 27, 2017 from http://www.oxforddnb.com/view/article/32209.

Van Vleck, J. (2009). An airline at the crossroads of the world: Ariana Afghan Airlines, modernization and the global Cold War. *History and Technology, 25,* 3–24. doi:10.1080/07341510802618158.

Varisco, D.M. (2004). Reading against culture in Edward Said's "Culture and Imperialism." *Culture, Theory and Critique, 45,* 93–112. doi:10.1080/1473578042000283817.

Varisco, D.M. (2007). *Reading Orientalism: Said and the unsaid.* Seattle, WA: University of Washington Press.

Victoria and Albert Museum Collection. (n.d.). *Godfrey T. Vigne, Afghanistan.* Retrieved July 27, 2017 from http://collections.vam.ac.uk/search/?listing_type=imagetext&offset=0&limit=15&narrow=1&extrasearch=&q=vigne%2C+

afghanistan&commit=Search&quality=0&objectnamesearch=&placesearch=&after=&after-adbc=AD&before=&before-adbc=AD&namesearch=&materialsearch=&mnsearch=&locationsearch=.

Vigne, G.T. (1842/1982). *A personal narrative of a visit to Ghuzni, Kabul, and Afghanistan, and of a residence at the Court of Dost Mohamed: With notices of Ranjit Sing, Khiva, and the Russian expedition*. Lahore, Pakistan: Sang-e-Meel Publications.

Weiner, T. (1990). *Blank check: The Pentagon's black budget*. New York, NY: Warner Books.

Wellcome Images. (n.d.). *Lillias Hamilton*. Retrieved July 27, 2017 from http://wellcomeimages.org/.

Whitteridge, G. (1986). *Charles Masson of Afghanistan: Explorer, archaeologist, numismatist, and intelligence agent*. Warmister, England: Aris and Phillips.

Williams Afghan Media Project. (n.d.). *Khalil Enayat Seraj collection. Items A–224–855 A–226–857, A–228–859, A–229–860, and A–275–906*. Retrieved July 27, 2017 from http://contentdm.williams.edu/wamp/web/kesSearch.htm.

Wilson, H.H., & Masson, C. (1998). *Ariana Antiqua: A descriptive account of the antiquities and coins of Afghanistan*. New Delhi, India: Asian Educational Services.

Wynne, C. (2011). From Waterloo to Jellalabad: The Irish and Scots at war in Elizabeth Thomas Butler and W.F. Butler. *Journal of European Studies, 41*, 143–160. doi:10.1177/0047244111399719.

Yate, A.C. (1887). *Travels with the Afghan Boundary Commission: England and Russia face to face in Asia*. London, England: William Blackwood and Sons.

Yate, C.E. (1888). *Afghanistan—Letters from the Afghan Boundary Commission*. London, England: William Blackwood and Sons.

CHAPTER 4

Orientalism and Neo-Orientalism: Arabic Representations and the Study of Arabic

Manuela E.B. Giolfo and Francesco L. Sinatora

Introduction

The concepts of Orientalism and neo-Orientalism have been approached through and have shaped the academic discourse in the humanities and the social sciences. Whereas Said's (1978) notion referred to a stereotyped representation of the Orient by the West for political and colonialist purposes, the more recent notion of neo-Orientalism is generally understood in literature across the humanities and the social sciences as an exacerbation of Orientalism and in reaction to post-9/11 Western Islamophobic representations of Islam.

In this chapter, we argue that language is a central element in the interpretation of the concepts of Orientalism and neo-Orientalism. In particular, this work approaches these two notions through an analysis of the Arabic representations and the study of Arabic. It starts by outlining the Western interest in Arabic throughout history and how it clashed with the Arab dominant representation of Arabic. It identifies Modern Arabic as the linguistic component of Arab renaissance and Modern Standard Arabic as a neo-Orientalist linguistic policy. Unlike traditional understandings of the notions of Orientalism and neo-Orientalism, which are framed within a West-East dichotomy, our operative definition of neo-Orientalism is informed by that of Indian scholar Avadhesh Kumar Singh. Quoting Singh, Nair-Venugopal (2012) defines neo-Orientalism as the new avatar of Orientalism:

> Neo-Orientalism stands for the "discourse about (sic) Orient by the people of the Orient located in the West, or shuttling between the two" ... or

* Although the ideas expressed in this chapter come from a joint research project by both authors, Manuela E.B. Giolfo is the author of the Introduction, and the sections Arabic and Orientalism, Modern Standard Arabic and Neo-Orientalism, and MSA and Neo-Orientalism in Western Academia; Francesco L. Sinatora wrote the sections The Western Interest in Arabic, Arab-Dominant Representation of Arabic: Arabic as One and Unique, Arab Renaissance and Modern Arabic, and the Concluding Remarks.

> the "discursive practices about the Orient by the people from the Orient ... located in the non-Orient for the people of the non-Orient" (p. 13). In its latest manifestation as neo-neo-Orientalism [sic], it is a "discourse about the Orient, constructed by the Occident (West = America) and Orient in collaboration." (p. 236)

Such a collaboration can be found in the development of the concept of Modern Standard Arabic as a monoglossic representation in contemporary postcolonial Arab countries as well as its implementation in the Western curricula of Arabic as a foreign language. The chapter concludes with some positive examples in the Arab world and in Western academia which go towards a holistic and translingual understanding of Arabic in a globalized world.

The Western Interest in Arabic

Western interest in Arabic was initially motivated by a polemical intent. The appropriation of the Arabic language was functional to the refutation of the Islamic message. Arabic became at a later stage necessary for the understanding of Western philosophical thought. As a matter of fact, until the 15th century Aristotle's work was available only in Arabic, through the work of translation conducted by Arab scholars. The study of Arabic was therefore functional to the investigation of the roots of Western civilization. However, as soon as the original Greek sources became accessible, the interest in Arabic saw a dramatic downturn. This decline was also motivated by the Western scholars' conviction that the Arabic translations were permeated by Islamic thought, in a context in which Islam was still perceived as a threat to Christian Europe. Hence, the study of Arabic survived solely as an ancillary to the study of medicine, mathematics, and astronomy, as well as to the study of biblical Hebrew.

Three centuries later, Humanism and Enlightenment sparked an interest in exotic languages and cultures. Arabic became a subject of 'Oriental languages and literatures.' These included languages that were not Semitic, such as Persian, and languages that were detached from the Islamic culture, like Chinese. Such a characterization of Arabic as an exotic language went hand in hand with a vision of the Arab world as backward and underdeveloped, as opposed to a putatively enlightened and superior Western civilization. In the 19th century, within the new paradigm of Semitic comparative linguistics, Arabic became one of the languages of the Semitic family, along with languages that represented the roots of Judeo-Christian civilization. Its study became motivated by a merely classificatory intent.

To recapitulate, the dynamics emerging from this historical bird's-eye view can be interpreted as an orientalist cycle of appropriation in which Arabic was firstly feared as the language of the threatening Other, later exorcized as the language of the exotic and inferior Other, and finally appropriated within the Semitic paradigm, thus emptied of its cultural and religious peculiarity. Furthermore, the study of Arabic within the new comparative paradigm strengthened Western interest in the Arabic vernaculars. The valorization of the vernaculars clashed with the Arabs' representation of them as corrupted forms of the language of the Qur'ān and of literary production.

The Western vision of the linguistic situation in the Arabic-speaking world developed along the lines of an important dichotomy. If up to the 18th century the Western interest in Arabic was exclusively in its literary and codified form, only at a later stage emerged an exclusively Western interest in Arabic dialectology. While some Western scholars continued focusing solely on literary Arabic, thus neglecting dialects, early Western dialectologists devoted themselves entirely to the study of Arabic vernaculars. However, it was only in the 20th century that the linguistic complexity intrinsic to the peculiarity of Arabic was taken into consideration. That indeed makes room for a holistic vision of Arabic as a complex linguistic reality, what Larcher (1998, p. 417) called "*la convergence des sociolinguistes arabisants sur l'idée d'un arabe hétérogène, 'pluriel,' pour employer un mot a la mode.*"

The contemporary interest in the study of Arabic appears to be framed within the major political, economic, social, and cultural issues that dominate Western discourses and Western international agendas. The economic and sociopolitical dynamics between the Arab world and the West in the second half of the 20th century had a deep impact on the development of Arabic language materials and curricula in a way that Ryding (2006, p. 16) described through the concept of "reverse privileging." Unlike the teaching of European languages, in which a focus on "primary discourses of familiarity among family and friends" prevailed over "secondary discourses of public life in a vast range of settings" (Byrnes, 2002, p. 38), in the context of Arabic, as observed by Ryding, the situation was reversed. This was at odds with the communicative model which gained ground in the teaching of European languages and propagated by the Common European Framework of Reference for Languages (CEFR) and the American Council on the Teaching of Foreign Languages (ACTFL). In Arabic, such a communicative competence focused on one single linguistic form based on literary Arabic, namely Modern Standard Arabic (MSA).[1] In this sense, MSA

1 The meaning attributed to MSA by such approaches is different from that of more recent holistic and porous pedagogic strands. In the latter, its study does not exclude the teaching of the vernaculars.

appears as a compromise between Western communicative intents and the Arabs' representation of Arabic. Such a compromise, based on Nair-Venugopal's (2012) definition, may be understood as a neo-Orientalist approach.

In what follows, our main argument about the neo-Orientalist character of MSA is contextualized in the light of the Arab dominant representation of Arabic and the Arab reaction to 19th-century Western Orientalist representations.

Arab-Dominant Representation of Arabic: Arabic as One and Unique

A relevant Arab representation of Arabic appeared in the first centuries of the Arab–Islamic civilization. During this time frame, a process of standard language codification occurred, which was arbitrarily based on two sources of literary Arabic, namely the Qur'ān and pre-Islamic poetry. Such a partial corpus (Anghelescu, 1993) constitutes at the same time the cornerstones of the Arab–Islamic civilization and of Arab–Islamic identity, respectively its religious and its ethnic components. The codification was motivated by the needs of a rising empire: facilitating communication in the newly conquered territories, maintaining control, and regulating the expansion of lexicon. The early grammarians' codification effort had the purpose to lead the peoples of the empire "towards" (*naḥw*) the language of the Arabs.[2] What was codified as the language of the Arabs actually consisted of a form of literary Arabic that would ideally represent the Arab–Islamic civilization.

During this phase, the purpose that guided scholars was to describe this language with the intent to export it to the newly conquered territories. This representation of the Arabic language had the goal of making the Arabs themselves aware of the rising of an Arab–Islamic civilization as a politically independent and a culturally self-referential reality. On the other hand, it was functional to the political and sociocultural project of the Neo Empire. In light of these considerations, this standardization process appears to be a form of linguistic policy informed by the creation of a conquering Arab and Islamic unity.

Grammarians claimed that they were basing their observations on Bedouin informants, together with the above mentioned literary sources. Until now scholars disagree on whether the language codified by grammarians was a uniformed language, i.e., the language of the Qur'ān, that of pre-Islamic poetry and that of the Bedouin tribes, or rather a religious-poetical *koine* used as a

2 Ibn al-Sarrāğ (quoted by Versteegh, 2006) notes that the Arabic word for grammar (*al-naḥwu*) derives from *naḥwa* ("towards").

shared elevated code transcending the Bedouin tribes' vernaculars. What is important to emphasize is that the codified language needed to comprise an ethnic and a religious component. This would guarantee linguistic and cultural continuity with the pre-Islamic past despite the Islamic metanoia.

The ethnic component was reinforced during the classical age through a mythification of the 'authentic native speaker,' i.e., the Bedouin. However, as emphasized by Owens (2006) and Versteegh (2006), classical grammarians were prone to elicit from their Bedouin informants their pre-conceived ideas. Interestingly, Versteegh (2006) noted that the target of these grammars were not only the newly conquered populations, but also Arabic native speakers. Such a linguistic corpus justifies the partiality of the corpus on the one hand and the mythification of the Bedouin as authentic native Arabic speaker on the other.

It is important to note that neither early grammarians nor other Arab scholars treated linguistic variation as detrimental to the Arabic language. "In the grammarians' writings we find many references to linguistic differences between the tribes, the so-called *luġāt*, but these differences did not destroy the essential unity of the language" (Versteegh, 1997, p. 154). Within the grammarians' representations there was no space for a diachronic vision of language change. As will be explained below, Western emphasis on Arabic vernaculars as a separate empirical entity was at odds with the Arabs' dominant representation of Arabic that can be understood in the light of Eisele's (2002) *topoi* of unity, purity, continuity, and competition. These *topoi* are recurrent motifs in the most dominant tradition about which Arab representations of Arabic cluster. Within such a representation, variation was contemplated, synchronically, as intrinsic to Arabic as *one* and *unique*.

Arabic and *Orientalism*

Arab and non-Arab scholars, as remarked by Anghelescu (1993), have long struggled to come up with a widely accepted definition of Arab identity other than one which does not have language as a central component. This applies to an understanding of Arab identity both in the pre-Islamic and Islamic eras. The very meaning of the adjective 'Arab' is explained in purely linguistic terms. The answer to the question *Who are the Arabs?* is generally *the owners of the Arabic language*. Whereas the clans of pre-Islamic nomadic tribes were connected internally through solidarity, a more or less definite sense of unity existed among clans and tribes which inhabited the Arab peninsula. This sense of unity was grounded in the belief of the existence of a common ancestor and was strengthened by a common language, which transcended dialectal differences.

A true consciousness of the existence of an Arab identity emerged in concomitance with the arrival of Islam. As noted by Anghelescu (1993), this appears as a paradox, considered that Islam proposed to efface ethnic differences among all ethnicities. The Qur'ān was revealed in Arabic. Therefore, the supremacy of the Arabic language, of which Arabs deem themselves to be the owners, became an element of the Islamic dogma. As a consequence, Islam led to the re-construction of Arab ethnicity based no longer on purely linguistic criteria, but rather linguistic and religious ones.

Because Arab identity was constructed primarily on linguistic grounds, Arabs also perceived themselves as superior. It is important to note here that the language which constitutes such Arab identity and which underlies the Arabs' perception of superiority is that pure and one poetical-Quranic language which transcends dialectal differences. By virtue of the linguistic bond between Arabic and Islam, Arabs developed a representation of themselves at the center of the Islamic civilization. This perception of superiority remained essentially unaltered even during their subordination to the Ottoman empire.

> Claims that Arabic was superior to Turkish were promoted to endow the Arabs with a string sense of self-esteem. This was not difficult to accomplish owing to the status of Arabic as the primary language of Islam, doctrinally and intellectually, and to its status as a donor language to Turkish.
> SULEIMAN, 2004, p. 18

It was not until the 19th century, when the Arabs were confronted with Western modernity and with the rising colonial aspirations of France and England in the Arab world, that this perception of superiority was challenged. This challenge consisted of the perception of a Western-imposed linguistic separation which undermined the topos of unity (Eisele, 2002).

Because the linguistic component is at the core of the Arab conception of superiority, the undermining of this very linguistic component through dichotomous separation constitutes in our view the most important factor that led to a later conception of Western scholarship as Orientalist. In other words, by creating an image of the Arabs that did not correspond to how the Arabs viewed themselves, Western scholars and their academic interests were considered to be at service of Western hegemonic powers and their strategy of *divide et impera*. The Arabs' depreciation of the vernaculars actually arose only as a reaction to such a dichotomous representation. Such a depreciation consists in our view of an Arab-Islamic reaction to Orientalism which paved the way for neo-Orientalist orientations.

Nineteenth-century Western linguistic representation of Arabic imposed a separation of what was not perceived by the Arabs as separate. Interestingly, this separation was even defined 'schismatic' by some contemporary Arab scholars.[3] This adjective implies a projection of the religious-political dimension on the linguistic one, in that it portrays such separation as internal disagreement among factions of a same religious confession.

As a matter of fact, Western powers treated the language and the religion of their colonies as backward and as an obstacle to their *mission civilisatrice*. The idea prevailed that the European language and culture should be introduced in the colonies. When for the first time the West realized that they needed to communicate with the Arabs (and not only read their literary production) on a larger scale, Arabic appeared to them as a complex, multifarious reality. The interest in the vernaculars, which started in the previous centuries with the Christian missionary work, grew simultaneously with the emergence of a new discipline, that of anthropology, whose aim was to study the roots of humankind in all its forms, including the study of primitive human language, represented by the vernaculars of remote and exotic tribes. This Western dichotomous representation clashed with Eisele's (2002) *topoi* of unity, purity, continuity, and competition.

If on the one hand the Arabs' perceived association between the Western growing interest in the dialects and their colonial aspirations led the Arabs to think that their cultural identity could actually be threatened by Western representation of their language as a multifarious linguistic reality, on the other, as observed by Versteegh (2006), as a matter of fact the European colonial powers destroyed the existing educational system. Because such an educational system was characterized by and aimed at safeguarding the literary language, the destruction of such a system was a fierce attack to the core of Arab cultural identity.

From this time on, it seems to us that the Arabs began reflecting on their own language and civilization from a defensive perspective, as their image of Arabic began to be influenced by their experience as being subordinate to a new hegemonic system. The sense of linguistic backwardness and fragmentation that had been emphasized by the West could be overcome through a process at the same time of linguistic modernization and standardization.

Arab Renaissance and Modern Arabic

The 'encounter' with the West and its modernity triggered an Arab reaction known as "Arab renaissance" (*nahḍa*). The *nahḍa* initially emerged as a cultural notion and laid the foundations for the Arab political nationalist thought that developed in the second half of the 19th century. While several scholars

3 Cf. AlBzour & AlBzour (2015, p. 12).

(Antonius, 1938; Haddad, 1970; Hourani, 1962; Kallas, 2008) argued that the debate over modernization had its roots in the work of Christian missionaries from the beginning of the 18th century, other authors (Khoury, 2003 [1983]; Tibawi, 1971) argued that the *nahḍa* is a drift that comes from within the Arab world. Quoting Swedenburg (1980), Khoury explained that

> the *nahḍa* then was not so much a missionary-inspired resuscitation of a "dead" language, as the reworking, modification, and streamlining of the Arabic language by native Syrians (with missionary ties) to make it serviceable for the introduction of Western ideas, particularly positivist science, into the area. (2003 [1983], p. 110, footnote 14)

This Arab "awakening" or "rebirth" arose from the desire to integrate Western positivist ideas in the Arab society and to adjust to the concept of Western modernity. This desire, which seems to have emerged from an unprecedented sense of inferiority and backwardness vis-à-vis the Western culture and which consolidated during the colonial period along with a strong sense of vulnerability, triggered a debate within the Arab world in which it was clear to all that societal modernization could not happen without linguistic modernization.

In an article published posthumously in the online weekly *Al-Ahram*, Edward Said (2004) observed that:

> The modern classical is the result mainly of a fascinating modernisation of the language that begins during the last decades of the 19th century—the period of the *Nahḍa*, or renaissance—carried out mainly by a group of men in Syria, Lebanon, Palestine and Egypt (a striking number of them Christian) who set themselves the collective task of bringing Arabic as a language into the modern world by modifying and somewhat simplifying its syntax, through the process of Arabising (*istiʿrāb*) the 7th century original, that is introducing such words as "train" and "company" and "democracy" and "socialism" that couldn't have existed during the classical period, and by excavating the language's immense resources through the technical grammatical process of *al-qiyās*, or analogy (a subject brilliantly discussed by Ste[t]kevych who demonstrates in minute detail how Arabic's grammatical laws of derivation were mobilised by the *Nahḍa* reformers to absorb new words and concepts into the system without in any way upsetting it); thereby, in a sense, these men forced on classical Arabic a whole new vocabulary, which is roughly 60 per cent of today's classical standard language.

Twentieth-century Western Arabists defined modern Arabic as a modern form of Classical Arabic. Scholars assigned different names to this variety. These included *arabe moderne* (Monteil, 1960), "living Arabic" (Pellat, 1952), "neo-Arabic" or "neo-Classical" Arabic (Lecerf, 1933), and "New High Arabic" (Wehr, 1934). Arabs, on the other hand, call it *al-ʿarabiyya* "the Arabic language" or *al-fuṣḥā* "the purest [language]." Rarely do they use more specific terms such as *al-ʿarabiyya al-ḥadīta* "new Arabic," *al-ʿarabiyya al-ʿaṣriyya* "Modern Arabic," or *al-ʿarabiyya al-muʿāṣira* "contemporary Arabic."

As observed by Lecerf (1933), Modern Arabic, before becoming a literary language, was primarily the language of a group of nationalist movements and their press. In 1960, Monteil observed that some remarks concerning the unification of modern Chinese on the basis of what Lo Tchang-Pei defines as the masses' need for a "common national, unified, and normalized language" (p. 26) could apply to the situation of modern Arabic, described as:

> the "common" language of communication, of the institutions and the academia, of the press and the radio, a language that allows an educated Lebanese or an educated Iraqi to communicate with a Moroccan, thus an inter-Arabic and pan-Arabic language, which needs to be at the same time according to the expression of Sāṭiʿal-Ḥuṣrī (1958: 42) "unifying" (*muwaḥḥida*) and "unified" (*muwaḥḥada*).
>
> MONTEIL, 1960, p. 26

In 1956, Lo Tchang-Pei, however, emphasized that

> the influence of this common language is limited. Plays in this language do not attract massive audiences, some movies have dialect subtitles, the radio broadcasts programs in dialect as well as other in the "common" language, and also in numerous schools teaching occurs in the dialect.
>
> MONTEIL, 1960, p. 26

With reference to Arabic, Said (2004) similarly confirmed that:

> TV serials, were made principally in Egypt, and thus their spoken idioms became familiar to and were learned by Arabs everywhere else.... During the 1970's and 1980's, as part of the oil boom of those years, TV dramas were made in other places as well, and they went in for spoken classical Arabic drama, which rarely caught on.... For the inveterate surfer of today, even the most hastily put together Egyptian *mousalsal* (or serial) is

> infinitely more fun to watch than the best of the best-regulated classical-language dramas.... Only Egyptian dialect has this kind of currency.

As a matter of fact, Monteil (1960) at first characterizes Modern Arabic only as a written language, not distinguishable from "Classical Arabic" in terms of grammar system, with the exception of some syntactic simplifications and innovations. The only important trait of Modern Arabic seems to be that its phraseology and stylistics "contain elements of European origin, in contrast with the spirit of the *ʿArabiyya*" (Monteil, 1960, p. 26). This trait arises from "the practical need to translate new notions" (p. 26). Interestingly, however, 20th-century Western scholars conclude that modern Arabic has also become a *spoken* language. Not only Monteil (1960), but also Lecerf (1933) had noted that "the daily use of neo-classical Arabic in teaching, administration and politics, makes of it what it was not anymore, i.e. a not only written, but also a spoken language" (p. 186), and in 1934 Wehr had predicted, somewhat enthusiastically, that "in the future the classical language will be more and more the daily language of educated people" (p. 10). This prediction did not come true.

In fact, as observed by Said (2004),

> [A]n educated person has two quite distinct linguistic personae in the mother-tongue.... [T]he spoken dialect is invariably the language of intimacy.... Somehow there is an implicit pact that governs which Arabic is to be used, on which occasions, for how long, and so forth .... [E]ducated Arabs actually use both the demotic and the classical, and that this totally common practice neither prohibits naturalness and beauty of expression nor in and of itself does it automatically encourage a stilted and didactic tone.... The two languages are porous and the user flows in and out of one into another as an essential aspect of what living in Arabic means.... In private, popular leaders like Arafat and Nasser, with some of whom I had contact, used the colloquial to much greater effect than the Marxists (who were also better educated than either the Palestinian or the Egyptian leader) I thought at the time; Nasser in particular did, in effect, address his masses of followers in the Egyptian dialect mixed with resounding phrases from the *fuṣḥā*. And, since eloquence in Arabic has a great deal to do with dramatic delivery, Arafat usually emerges in his rare public addresses as a below-average orator, his mispronunciations, hesitations and awkward circumlocutions seeming to an educated ear to be the equivalent of an elephant tramping aimlessly through a flower-patch.

Despite the defensive pan-Arab nationalist myths, the daily language of 'educated people' is well expressed by Said's autobiographical linguistic experience, which vividly and beautifully renders the quotidian occurrence of Arabic variation:

> I think of ... [my mother's] wonderfully expressive Arabic, vacillating charmingly between the demotic of her native Nazareth and Beirut, and that of her long later residence in Cairo.... And then, more recently, my wife Mariam's Arabic, a language learned naturally in national school without the disturbance of English and French at first, although both were acquired a little later. Hence her ease in moving back and forth between classical and colloquial, which I could never do as she does or feel as completely at home in as she does.

In these autobiographic reflections, Said captured the centrality of language in the issue of Arabs' identity, and consequently, its relevance to the debate on Orientalism. Whereas the notion of Modern Arabic, as it is understood by Said, does not imply a standardization that effaces the presence of several linguistic varieties, such a type of standardization was implied by the concept of Modern Standard Arabic.

Modern Standard Arabic and Neo-Orientalism

The collapse of the Ottoman empire and the rise of France and Britain as colonizing powers left as the only solution that of nationalism: creating the conscience of an Arab unity, independently from the professed religion. Although some intellectuals initially sustained regional nationalisms, the idea that prevailed was that of Arab nation. The idea of nation-state, defined on the basis of territory, language, culture, and law is external to Islam. It arrived in the Middle East as an import from 19th-century Europe. It was in fact in Europe that, after the French revolution, nationalism, and the colonial enterprise, a new political identity arose.

The foundation of the nation-state was grounded in a sentiment of identity and solidarity which arose from within. This was counterposed to the religious community, which proceeds through the revolt against colonialism and establishes a continuity with a golden age. For the Egyptians, it was the Pharaohs. For the Lebanese, it was the Phoenicians. Until the 19th century, the term *waṭan* is used to design the birthplace and is often confused with patriotism. Throughout the 20th century, following the territorial dissolution of the Ottoman empire and following the colonialist attack and the subsequent territorial re-organization, based on artificially set boundaries, the term *waṭan* took on the ambiguous meaning of "nation." When *waṭan* is taken to mean "nation" it becomes fraught with ideological motivations that clash with the Islamic values, such as ethnic pluralism and multi-loyalism, which characterize the Arab-Islamic Weltanschauung. To indicate the concept of nation, Islam had adopted the term *Umma*. Only in the 20th century did this term start to be used to denote the Arab nation (Giolfo, 1998, 2000).

As shown in the previous paragraphs, language played a central role throughout the centuries in the construction of Arabs' identity and representations. The 20th century was characterized by a shift from multilingual to monolingual policies. Paraphrasing Baggioni (1997), Miller (2003, p. 2) emphasized that "empires tend to be multilingual while contemporary Nation-States tend to become monolingual (19th century European nationalism)." The terms *waṭan* ("homeland") and *qawm* ("progeny") are unified by the fathers of the Arab linguistic nationalist movement (Saṭiʿ al-Ḥuṣrī, al-Arsuzi and Aflaq) through the concept of "common language." "Speaking Arabic was to be an Arab" (Tibi, 1981, p. 122, quoted in Suleiman, 1994, p. 11).

Given the political fragmentation and arbitrariness of the territorial boundaries of the new Nation-States and the multireligious affiliations of their citizens, the need arose to create an abstract language which could serve as the language of the nation and the language of the new Arab citizens. As argued by Miller (2003), within this vision the dialects were considered tantamount to minority languages, namely as a menace to the creation of a project of nation based on linguistic homologation. Education and national mass media were instrumental to the creation of this common language and this new national identity. These institutions guaranteed the secular character of this language.

The *ḫāṣṣa* ("special, elitarian language")—which was the language of archaic pre-Islamic poetry, the Qur'ān, and Classical literary production, as well as the language of that form of Arabic which arose from the 'encounter' with the West, namely Modern Arabic—in the light of this linguistic project, had to replace each *ʿāmma* (i.e., "the vernaculars of the commoners") and become itself the *ʿāmma* (i.e., "the new common language of the commoners"). Whereas colonial powers had destroyed the education system and applied a linguistic policy at the expenses of Classical Arabic, the monolingual policy of the Arab nation(s) aimed at the suppression of the vernaculars and minority languages. This was instrumental to the consolidation of a language for the *Umma* ("The Arab Nation") as the only unifying factor. One single language (*al-ʿarabiyya*, "The Arabic language"), for one single *waṭan* ("The Arab Homeland") and one single *qawm* ("Bedouin progeny"). Whereas for Islamists language was only a means to reconnect with the divine message within a theocratic society, the community (*Umma*) of all believers who surrender to the divine law, for Arab nationalism and pan-Arabism, language is not a means but an end, not a given manifestation of the divine, but an ongoing political and ideological project.

It is in the light of this sociopolitical context that Modern Standard Arabic should be envisioned. This is the language that in the words of one of the fathers of Arab nationalism, Sāṭi'al-Ḥuṣrī (1958, p. 42), should be "unified" (*muwaḥḥada*) and "unifying" (*muwaḥḥida*). Said's (2004) emphasis on the porous, and therefore inclusive character of Arabic, in line with the dominant Arab linguistic ideology, in which *al-fuṣḥā* ("the purest language") was linked to the topos of purity (cf. Eisele, 2002), with Modern Standard Arabic the concept of purity becomes a purging and excluding element. Its 'common' aspect is to be intended as illusionary, as it served as an instrument of subjugation in the hands of postcolonialist Arab leaders.

Based on these considerations about postcolonialist Arab monoglossic policies, we suggest that neo-Orientalism can be seen as a reaction to Orientalism that actually surrenders to Orientalism. In fact, Arab postcolonial monoglossic reactions led to the loss of the inclusive and holistic features of the Arab dominant representation of Arabic. The illusion of a monoglossic linguistic system is an underrepresentation of what living in Arabic means, a self-deprivation of the inclusive and holistic features of Arabic as a hegemonic language. That is to say an *ad usum occidentis* representation of Arabic for a Western Orientalist stage.

In what follows, we show how the teaching of Arabic in the West highlighted the collaborative component of neo-Orientalism, as it was envisaged in Nair-Vanugopal's (2012) definition. Furthermore, as explained in the introduction, the collaborative component of neo-Orientalism, as it is pointed out by Nair-Venugopal, manifested itself, in our view, in the teaching of Arabic in the West.

MSA and Neo-Orientalism in Western Academia

In the second half of the 20th century, collaborations between Arab and Western scholars in the preparation of teaching materials of Arabic as a foreign language have affirmed their dominance in Western academia. Such collaborations have gone hand in hand with the production and wide diffusion of textbooks as well as the implementation of curricula based predominantly or exclusively on Modern Standard Arabic. In Western textbooks of Arabic pedagogy, MSA was introduced in the 1960s with the implementation of audio-lingual methods applied to the teaching of Arabic, which conceptualized proficiency as the learners' achievement of overall communicative competence in the four linguistic skills, namely reading, writing, listening and speaking. A series of widely used textbooks based on the acquisition of MSA was published by the University of Michigan and included *Elementary Modern Standard Arabic* (Abboud, 1968) and *Intermediate Modern Standard Arabic* (Abboud, 1971).

As noted by Ibrahim (2009) and Ryding (2005), a full agreement on the definition of MSA has not yet been reached. In her comparative typological study, Mejdell (2008, p. 49) argues that "[MSA] is not a typical standard in its relative lack of polyfunctionality, that is, it does not cover most spoken styles and registers." Whereas MSA was defined as a primarily written language (El-Hassan, 1977; Mahmoud, 1982; Meiseles, 1980), in the textbooks of Arabic as a foreign language, MSA was imparted for both written and spoken purposes. This corresponds, in our view, to a standardizing intent.

The use of MSA for speaking purposes was explained in Schulz et al., (2000) as follows:

> This book is based on the well-tried *Lehrbuch des modernen Arabisch* by Guenther Krahl, Wolfgang Reuschel and Eckehard Schulz and has been conceived as a comprehensive course for beginners, in which particular attention is given to a speaking-focused training. It presents the basic grammar, vocabulary and phraseology of written and spoken Modern Standard Arabic (MSA). (p. ix)

Schulz et al. (2000) envisaged MSA primarily as Media Arabic. Blanc (1960) showed that radio broadcast contributed to the diffusion of Modern Standard Arabic as a spoken language. Linguists also noted that MSA is not as unified as it is presented in textbooks of Arabic as a foreign language. Wilmsen (2006) posited that such a presentation is

> somewhat misleading in that it fosters in novice learners the impression that they are about to acquire a form of the language that is in some sense analogous to other standard spoken language forms, for instance, RP English, which it is not. In the more sophisticated, it serves to maintain the fiction that this form is standard to all regions of the Arab world. (p. 135, note 2)

In our view, MSA, as it is defined in textbooks of Arabic as a foreign language, can be conceived of as a neo-Orientalist tool. In fact, Alosh (2000) affirmed that the implementation of Modern Standard Arabic for speaking purposes is a desirable solution inasmuch as MSA is readily understood throughout the Arab world, although it does not reflect the native speaker performance. The replication of such a performance is impeded by practical reasons, such as the limited nature of the classroom. Teaching only this language, which is the language of education in the Arab world, serves the purpose of the foreign student of being understood within the Arab world, not the purpose of understanding that world. It is unilateral. Such unilateral characteristic, though, is desirable as it conceals that rich complexity in which Orientalists are fallaciously and guiltily interested. The use of MSA is not only predominant in textbooks, but also in teaching curricula and practices. Due to the pervasive implementation of MSA-based curricula, MSA has acquired the meaning of language of communication with the Other, i.e., the language of the (neo-colonialist) foreigner.

In sum, the features that led us to an understanding of MSA as neo-Orientalist are an implicit acceptance of unilaterality (the language for the foreigners to make themselves understood in the Arab world), a desire to project a representation of Arabic as a unified and modern language, as an official European language. Such a representation is motivated by a 19th-century defensive stance which emerged in the colonial period, during which the Arabs perceived the Western scholars' emphasis on the vernaculars as Orientalist. MSA appears as Arabic for the West, in that it is Arabic expurgated of its holistic complexity. It is a form of neo-Orientalism in the sense that it corresponds to the image the Arabs in the West offer about the Arab world for the Westerners. At the same time, such a solution reflects a Western interest in Arabic dictated for the most part by political and economic agendas.

Concluding Remarks

In this chapter, we shed light on a shift in the motivations underlying the Western interest in Arabic and in the Arabs' representation of Arabic in light of the rise of the West as a hegemonic power. The introduction of secular and positivist concepts occurred primarily through Modern Arabic in order to overcome the gap with the 'modern' West. Whereas until the 18th century Arabic served as a marker of an Arab-Islamic identity, the desire to modernize the Arab world through the integration of Western secular notions led to an emphasis on the ethnic over the religious component. In the second half of the twentieth century, Western textbooks of Arabic as a foreign language extended the use of Modern Arabic to spoken purposes. While presented by some pedagogues as a practical strategy of simplification, we see the exclusive teaching of MSA for all linguistic skills as a defensive stance which rejects the Western 'orientalist' characterization of Arabic as a fragmented language.

The concept of proficiency underlying MSA-based educational materials and teaching practices appears to us to be the manifestation of a new ideology that results from an Arab–Western collaboration, i.e., a 'neo-Orientalist' approach.

In conclusion, it is important to emphasize that, following the expansion of social-media communication and the socio-political uprisings in 2011, a new positive trend emerged in Arabic linguistics and pedagogy. This suggests to look at Arabic as one and integrated (Al-Batal, 2017; Brustad et al., 2014; Wahba, Taha, & England, 2017; Younes, 2014, 2015). Such an orientation does not consider *fuṣḥā* and the vernaculars as mutually exclusive, thus surpassing at the same time the Orientalist Western dichotomy and the neo-Orientalist monoglossic representation. In other words, this direction re-unites what Orientalism and neo-Orientalism divided.

We hope to have made clear that embracing the complexity of Arabic does not mean adopting an 'Orientalist' approach. Rather, it would represent a reverse tendency with respect to the Western utilitarian approach to Arabic towards a more holistic study of the language of the Arabs and Islam. A focus on integrating complexity in the Arabic curriculum would ultimately overcome 'Orientalist' and 'neo-Orientalist' representations and contribute to a mutual and more nuanced understanding and communication.

References

Abboud, P. (1968). *Elementary modern standard Arabic*. Ann Arbor, MI: Inter-University Committee for Near Eastern Languages.

Abboud, P.F. (1971). *Modern standard Arabic: Intermediate level*. Ann Arbor, MI: Center for Near Eastern and North African Studies.

Al-Batal, M. (Ed.) (2017). *Arabic as one language: Integrating dialect in the Arabic language curriculum*. Washington, DC: Georgetown University Press.

AlBzour, N.N., & AlBzour, B.A. (2015). Arabic Uniglossia: Diglossia revisited. *Studies in Literature and Language, 10*(3), 7–12. Retrieved July 7, 2017 from http://www.cscanada.net/index.php/sll/article/view/6388. doi:http://dx.doi.org/10.3968/6388.

Alosh, M. (2000). *Ahlan wa sahlan functional modern standard Arabic for beginners*. New Haven, CT: Yale University Press.

Anghelescu, N. (1993). *Linguaggio e cultura nella civilta' araba*. Torino, Italy: Zamorani.

Antonius, G. (1938). *The Arab awakening: The story of the Arab national movement*. London, England: H. Hamilton.

Baggioni, D. (1997). *Langues et nations en Europe*. Paris, France: Payot & Rivages.

Blanc, H. (1960). Style variations in spoken Arabic: A sample of interdialectal educated conversation. In C. Ferguson (Ed.), *Contributions to Arabic linguistics* (pp. 81–158). Cambridge, MA: Harvard University Press.

Brustad, K. et al. (2014). *Al-Kitaab fii ta'allum al-'Arabiyya: A textbook for beginning Arabic* (3rd ed.). Washington, DC: Georgetown University Press.

Byrnes, H. (2002) Toward academic-level foreign language abilities: Reconsidering foundational assumptions, expanding pedagogical options. In B.L. Leaver & B. Shekhtman (Eds.), *Developing professional-level language proficiency* (pp. 34–58). Cambridge, England: Cambridge University Press.

Eisele, J. (2002). Approaching diglossia: Authorities, values, and representations. In A. Rouchdy (Ed.), *Language contact and language conflict in Arabic: Variations on a sociolinguistic theme* (pp. 3–23). London, England: Curzon.

Giolfo, M. (1998). Ummah: identità etnica o identità religiosa? In M. Petriccioli & A. Tonini (Eds.), *Identità e appartenenza in Medio Oriente* (pp. 105–114). Firenze, Italy: Università degli Studi di Firenze, Dipartimento di Studi sullo Stato.

Giolfo, M.E.B. (2000). Egizianità, arabicità, islamicità: quale appartenenza identitaria? In P. Branca (Ed.), *Tradizione e modernizzazione in Egitto 1798–1998* (pp. 182–200). Milano, Italy: Franco Angeli.

Haddad, R.M. (1970). *Syrian Christians in Muslim society: An interpretation*. Princeton, NJ: Princeton University Press.

el-Hassan, S. (1977). Educated spoken Arabic in Egypt and the Levant: A critical review of diglossia and related concepts. *Archivium Linguisticum, 8*(2), 112.

Hourani, A.H. (1962). *Arabic thought in the liberal age, 1798–1939. Issued under the auspices of the Royal Institute of International Affairs*. London, England: Oxford University Press.

Ibrāhīm, Z. (2009). *Beyond lexical variation in modern standard Arabic: Egypt, Lebanon and Morocco*. Newcastle upon Tyne, UK: Cambridge Scholars.

Kallas, E. (2008). Nationalism and language. In *EALL, 3*, 343–353.

Khoury, P.S. (2003 [1983]). *Urban notables and Arab nationalism: The politics of Damascus 1860–1920*. Cambridge, England: Cambridge University Press.

Larcher, P. (1998). La linguistique arabe d'hier à demain: Tendances nouvelles de la recherche, *Arabica, 45*, 409–429.

Lecerf, J. (1933). L'arabe contemporain comme langue de civilisation. *Revue africaine, 356*, 269–296.

Mahmoud, Y. (1982). Arabic after Diglossia. In J. Fishman (Ed.), *The Fergusonian impact* (p. 239). Berlin, Germany: Mouton de Guyter.

Meiseles, G. (1980), Educated spoken Arabic and the Arabic language continuum. *Archivum Linguisticum, 11*(2), 118–148.

Mejdell, G. (2008). Is Modern Fusha a "standard" language? In Z. Ibrahim & S. Makhlouf (Eds.), *Linguistics in an age of globalization* (pp. 41–52). Cairo, Egypt: The American University in Cairo Press.

Miller, C. (2003). Linguistic Policies and the issue of ethno-linguistic minorities in the Middle East. In A. Usuki & H. Kato (Eds.), *Islam in the Middle Eastern studies: Muslims and minorities* (pp. 149–174). Osaka, Japan: JCAS Symposium Series 7.

Monteil, V. (1960). *L'Arabe moderne.* Paris, France: Klincksieck.

Nair-Venugopal, S. (2012). *The gaze of the West and framings of the East.* New York, NY: Palgrave Macmillan.

Pellat, C. (1952). L'Arabe vivante. In V. Monteil (1960), *L'Arabe moderne* (pp. 217–224). Paris, France: Klincksieck.

Ryding, K. (2005). *A reference grammar of Modern Standard Arabic.* Cambridge, England: CUP.

Ryding, K. (2006). Teaching Arabic in the United States. In K.M. Wahba, Z.A. Taha, & L. England (Eds.), *Handbook for Arabic language teaching professionals in the 21st century* (pp. 13–20). Mahwah, NJ: Lawrence Erlbaum Associates.

Said, E. (1978). *Orientalism.* New York, NY: Pantheon Books.

Said, E. (2004) Living in Arabic. *Al-Ahram. Weekly On-line.* Retrieved July 1, 2017 from http://weekly.ahram.org.eg/archive/2004/677/cu15.htm.

Schulz, E., Krahl, G., Reuschel, W., & Dickins, J. (2000). *Standard Arabic: An elementary-intermediate course.* Cambridge, England: Cambridge University Press.

Suleiman, Y. (1994) Nationalism and the Arabic language: An historical overview. In Y. Suleiman (Ed.), *Arabic sociolinguistics* (pp. 3–24). Richmond, Surrey: Curzon.

Suleiman, Y. (2004). *A war of words: Language and conflict in the Middle East.* New York, NY: Cambridge University Press.

Swedenburg, T.R. (1980). *The development of capitalism in greater Syria, 1830–1914: An historic-geographical approach* (Unpublished master's thesis). University of Texas, Austin, Texas.

Tibawi, A.L. (1971). Some misconceptions about the Nahda. *Middle East Forum, 47* (Autumn & Winter), 15–22.

Tibi, B. (1981). *Arab nationalism. A critical enquiry* [M. Farouk-Sluglett, Ed. & Transl.]. London, England: Macmillan.

Versteegh, K. (2006). History of Arabic language teaching. In K.M. Wahba, Z.A. Taha, & L. England (Eds.), *Handbook for Arabic language teaching professionals in the 21st century* (pp. 3–12). Mahwah, NJ: Lawrence Erlbaum Associates.

Versteegh, K. (1997). *Landmarks in linguistic thought III: The Arabic linguistic tradition.* London, England: Routledge.

Wahba, K.M., Taha, Z.A., & England, L. (Eds.). (2017). *Handbook for Arabic language teaching in the 21st century, Volume II*. London, England: Routledge.

Wehr, H. (1934). Die Besonderheiten des heutigen Hocharabischen. *MSOS, XXXVII*, II, 1–64.

Wilmsen, D. (2006). What is communicative Arabic? In K.M. Wahba, Z.A. Taha, & L. England (Eds.), *Handbook for Arabic language teaching professionals in the 21st century* (pp. 125–138). Mahwah, NJ: Lawrence Erlbaum Associates.

Younes, M. (2014). *'Arabiyyat al-Naas*. London, England: Routledge.

Younes, M. (2015). *The integrated approach to Arabic instruction*. London, England: Routledge.

CHAPTER 5

Middle Eastern Studies in the United Kingdom Post-September 11: A Battlefield of Orientalism

Ameena Al-Rasheed Nayel

> Colonial discourse does not refer to a body of texts with similar subject matter, but rather refers to set of practices and rules which produced those texts and the methodological organization of the thinking underlying them.
>
> MILLS, 1997, p. 96

∵

Introduction: On Balancing Authority and Objectivity

Drawing from the experience of working with a Middle Eastern Studies department, this chapter will interrogate Orientalism and the cross-cutting edges of Muslimness, ethnicities, social class, and performativity in Middle Eastern studies in the United Kingdom. The authority and capacity on speaking about the subject is intrinsically related to our religious performativity, ethnicity, social class, and gender. Mainstreaming a particular performativity of Muslimness creates a hierarchical power dynamic that makes Muslims' appearances[1] and performativities the yardstick for inclusion and exclusion.

---

1 In contrast to the Wahabi sect that dominates the United Kingdom, the origin of the Sufi thought encompasses narratives of the Sufi men and women. Some examples show the contrast as wine and alcoholic imagery, for example, in the Sufi understanding is a metaphor for the spiritual ecstasy experienced in moments of profound union with the divine. A prominent Sufi woman was Rabi'ah al Adawiyyah (c.717–801). She was one of the most famous saint women of Islam and Sufi tradition. Rabi'ah gave ecstatic voice to the theme of Divine love. Like Rabi'ah Al-Hallaj (858–922) (Huasyn ibn Mansour Al-halaj), whose ecstatic utterances and his condemnation for heresy and subsequent execution made him the most controversial of the classical Sufis. Hallaj's passionate love for the Beloved and union with the Beloved were the principles of his poetry. The attributes of the Beloved are also known as the Divine

This chapter investigates the discursive features of the body of knowledge that is produced currently in the United Kingdom, reflecting how the Orient as a repository of Western knowledge and as a society and culture functioning on its own terms, is represented in the field of Middle Eastern studies in academia. Sociological interrogation of Middle Eastern studies in the United Kingdom demonstrates that a neocolonial discourse that produces not only policy-oriented knowledge, but rather a neo-Oriental discourse in academia, is well constructed and made functional. The field of Middle Eastern studies is affected by such discourses and tended implicitly or explicitly to work with the state's new schemes that reflect the principles of liberalism.

The anatomy of Middle Eastern studies in the United Kingdom in general reflects how these units of study have been oriented towards reinvestigating old colonial conquests. Issues of terrorism, Muslim women, and performativities, as well as the *hijab*, are listed as the core themes in the study of the Middle East. These topics are the auxiliary of the old colonial curiosity project in the era of colonialism, and they represent an extension of efforts made to unpack the East from within the same Western discourse at this time in the West. The project of constructing an Oriental scene in United Kingdom universities could be easily explained from the fact that; such a project is not tailored towards research and studies that investigate other performativities, colonialisms, and its effects; but rather, it reflects a denial of the neocolonial discourses and the overall colonial heritage of the British empire. Thus the neocolonial discourses were not constructed as a subject worthy of research to unpack the current hostility and contestation that covers the Middle Eastern world towards the politics of colonial powers.

The colonised 'Other' has been conceptualized as the uninformed, primitive, less and lack; such views of the Other are portrayed against the authentic Western values and the regime of truth produced to inscribe Western liberal norms. At the heart of Middle Eastern studies in the U.K. universities, issues of the female body were explored from the discourses that reproduce difference and the ones that reflect power dynamics and old scenarios.

Orientalism is the way in which the Orient has been represented in Europe through an imaginative geography that divides East and West, confirming Western superiority and enabling it (Said, 1979). Orientalism opened up the possibility for others to go further in exploring the Orientalist discourse and provide a strong rationale for historical and anthropological research. The historical recovery and existence of Middle Eastern studies had, in fact, emerged

---

names. One of these at-tribute is al-Haqq (The truth), when Halaj said "Ana Lahqq," I am the truth or I am God, he had preached incarnationism and was therefore guilty of heresy.

from this new abundance of research stimulated by the eccentric and exotic re-examination project of the Middle East, where political engagement cannot be segregated from scholarship.

The political engagement as well as the geopolitics of Middle Eastern studies illustrates how issues of the Islamic female body are highlighted and situated in the core themes of the Middle Eastern studies agenda. The construction of Middle Eastern studies resembles that same pattern and efforts constantly made to create a council of Muslims in the United Kingdom that represents all Muslim communities. Neither the case of establishing Middle Eastern studies with its aims and objectives nor establishing the council of Muslims with its assigned tasks are historically specific. From Said's (1993) critical perspective, the role of the scholar is to point to the constitutive role theories play, as opposed to contributing to the maintenance of the status quo; the role played by Middle Eastern studies in the United Kingdom was the one that preserved the status quo and presented knowledge that served the interests of the imperial power.

In the Middle Eastern studies centres based in U.K. universities, there is a British prevalence, which is reflected in the thinking patterns and modes of representation used by Middle East specialists. Such patterns could easily be illustrated in the work and research of the Middle Eastern studies that address the gender dimension of the Middle East. Localizing Middle Eastern studies is a process that takes place while viewed as a positive trend; it reflects, however, the power dimension that constructed the Middle East in accordance with the imperial power's discourse and interest. Middle Eastern studies expected to echo, display, and criticise Orientalist discourse in knowledge yet the body of research constructed inform about such discourse using the same colonial language and research.

The body of research of Middle Eastern studies is linked to the Ministry of Defence, research and training units, in particular during the war in Iraq, Syria, and Libya, that decide which projects are liable to funding. Often, an intrinsic link exists between the government's state of anxieties and the interests developed to inform Middle Eastern studies; both sides, the academics as well as the political practitioners, serve each other thereafter. The core interest developed is the use of disciplined methodologies to generate knowledge that would help prevent the horrors of war and terrorism and improve the world around them.

As maintained by Kramer (2001), "The ideal Middle East specialist is a modern-day Machiavelli who produces knowledge to inform policy making" (p. 53). Such discourse gives legitimacy to the government policies through the reproduction of tenets of official canons and conventions on the Middle East, just as it highlights the government's search for information and consultation with scholars and experts.

Civilizing women in Iraq, Afghanistan, and Libya is a core policy of intervention, shown in the Western media in relation to these countries and others in the Middle East. The European Union (EU) presence in Libya has already established the absence of gender machinery in these countries, as well as the absolute submissive and subjugated role of their women. No historical specificity has been paid to inform and to construct real images of these women. The images produced would legitimize the intervention and justify further military and army operations in these countries. In the coming section, an exploration of the geopolitics of the female body within Middle Eastern contexts will take place, and all will lead to probing the current absence and resentments towards gender studies in these units and confirm the current existence of colonial pedagogical discourse informing about Middle Eastern women.

Location, Identity, and the Female Body in Middle Eastern Studies Oriental Discourse

The issue of the female body has begun to attract attention globally as well as locally. The main trend within feminist theory has been a preoccupation with questions of identity and the body, initiating a debate that has shifted towards the acknowledgement of the complex interactions between categories of sex, class, race, and gender, e.g., minority studies in the United States (Kofman, 2000). Within this trend, there has been an increasing recognition of the importance of the role of women in global politics and the formulation of the female body and identity.

A dichotomy that is widely expressed within the scholarly work in the West maintains that gender relations and sexuality are crucial in defining cultural boundaries and binary opposition between European and North African/ Middle Eastern standards. The intersection of gender, religion, and sexuality brings to the fore religious issues at the same time as fundamentalism is posing a threat to international politics.[2] In altered traditional models, religion

2 There are many Muslim sects, Muslims are Sufi, shitte, and many other diverse sects. Sufism, or Islamic mysticism, was something of an exception in Islam, providing relatively greater religious space for Muslim women. In early Islam, one female figure in the ranks of the mystics included Rabia al-Adawiyah (d. 901), who is considered to be one of the great early formative influences in the development of Sufi doctrine. In popular Sufism, women and men have been recognized as Awliyaa ("friends" of God) who perform miracles and arbitrate and communicate with God from a closer distance. After death, the graves of the Awliyaa usually become shrines for visitation and places of prayer and fidelity. However, even within Sufism, due to the prevailing cultural attitudes towards women and the daily construction of what is

has become the key signifier of perceived incompatible differences. As Kofman (2000) stated, "Islamic groups regulated by patriarchal structure are singled out as being too distinctive in their lives and social norms to be able to cohabit with groups whose practices are derived from Christian traditions" (p. 37).

Christianity is central in shaping European culture. It is vital to understand this centrality when we conceptualize gender differences within Middle Eastern cultures. It is also significant to cite the complex relationships between Europe and the colonized 'Other,' and that the modernity we all seek is the secularized Christianity. It is defined through a Christian European perspective and is produced within the whole project of the regime of truth, imposed within specific power relations. Arabic scholar and poet Adonies (2004) stressed that Muslim scholars have failed in neutralizing and secularizing the religious discourse in the Muslim world. This might be one of the challenges facing Muslim scholars and intellectuals. It is evident as well that such a stand towards transforming old religious discourses across the Middle East is much needed to transform the structurally truncated system in Middle Eastern studies.

The very project of 'civilization' was marked by a dominant Christianity and the way it related to bodies and sexualities as uncivilized. The sense that the West presented a 'higher' form of civilization was expressed through a Christian disdain for these aspects. Thus, as the 'human' came to be defined through a radical contrast with the 'animal,' so people could only aspire to being moral/spiritual beings through "rising above their 'animal' natures," in Kant's terms. In this way Middle Eastern came to be positioned as 'less than human' because of their relationship with the bodily and the 'material.' Because Christianity was able to 'rise above' its religious sources, so it denigrated any Other tradition, from which it supposedly had nothing to learn, nothing to acknowledge or respect. At some level, this vision of 'rising above and superseding' shaped the relationship between the colonizer and the uncivilized, trapped in an earlier, more primitive stage: the colonized. Such discourse that reproduces and reinvents the exotic subject is informing the context of Middle Eastern studies in the United Kingdom. The parameters that constructed Middle Eastern studies in the United Kingdom are the same that informed the shape and the discourses of defining the subject in the colonial era.

"Western" and what is not, through a long process of stereotyping and stigma that works as well the other way round, such examples remained a minority in a society in which women were often seen as potential sources of moral and social disorder. Overall, the power and influence of Sufi orders are fading and declining against the very strong and male-centered testament discourse used by orthodox Islamists.

An ephemeral anatomy of the body of knowledge produced by Middle Eastern studies in the United Kingdom exhibits how the subjects that used to feed the Western curiosity have been introduced pedagogically in these studies. Women in Muslim societies are a marker subject in all Middle Eastern studies that attracts attention for all the wrong reasons, where those who were eager to learn about Muslim women should at first have been provided with rationale and justifications for veiling women in the Middle East. The Middle Eastern studies construct the veil as an authentic manifestation of Islam. Muslim scholars who challenged Islamic political discourses in the Middle East at large are not present in the body of knowledge presented about the Middle East.

Middle Eastern studies in the United Kingdom—and this could so easily be a categorical position for all U.K. universities and high institutes—reflecting the importance of the presence of Middle Eastern subjects as perceived by the West, read veiled female scholars, religiously and conservative oriented male scholars, images of subjugated women, cultural practices of female genital mutilation,[3] honour killings, and arranged marriages as signifiers of the Middle East. These images are often an intrinsic part of the curriculum developed in Middle Eastern studies in U.K. universities. The representation of Middle Eastern studies is to challenge old colonial discourse. However; Western liberal ideology preserved these images and attempts to reproduce them by designing the subjects that are essential in defining the Middle East and incorporating such definitions in the constructions of Middle Eastern studies.

One would question how Middle Eastern studies in the United Kingdom undertake the responsibility of Middle East representation, while they fail categorically in accurately representing the Middle East in its vibrant cultural and historical context that is intrinsically built on the ethics of challenging hegemonic discourses and dominance. Middle Eastern studies are constantly being represented by the conservative, liberal images of the West and categorically rejecting the presentation of an alternative Middle East that is able to integrate capacity and power in challenging colonial discourses.

Reproduction of a single story of the Middle East is a relentless discourse of how Middle Eastern studies are constructed. The images that produced the current Middle East encompass many features and performances. Such studies

---

3 Those are the main core interests of the Middle Eastern studies across the United Kingdom. The veil is an essential signifier of Muslimness and Middle Easternness. The veil's presence in most of the United Kingdom is a significant factor in establishing the authentic Middle Eastern studies; this space does not allow an interrogation on how the Middle Eastern studies resented and still resent the presence of unveiled Middle Eastern women, despite many claims of openness and accommodations.

are unimaginable with the absence of veiled Muslim scholars who inform the colonial image of the Middle East and confirm the old Oriental production. Investigating as well as teaching pedagogy would illustrate the same pattern on what the United Kingdom needs to explore and to investigate. The exotic subjects and eccentric performativities are present in a way that feeds into the old colonial habits and fulfills the curiosity of the West.

Suffice it to say that the powerful Western discourse of representation has featured and constantly imaged Middle Eastern women with the prominent feature of identification—the veil—standing as a signifier of the religious identity of Muslim women and a powerful representation of the Middle East. In the following section, the study will explore how Middle Eastern studies reproduced Middle Eastern women and how the geopolitics of the Middle Eastern female body is constructed.

Middle Eastern studies in the United Kingdom bear the responsibility of the Middle East's representation. The Middle East is constantly represented by the conservative, liberal images of the West. The field of Middle Eastern studies is categorically rejecting the presentation of an alternative Middle East, a Middle East that integrates capacity and power in challenging colonial discourses, a Middle East that is not present in the United Kingdom or the West. It is perceptible to envisage Middle Eastern studies in the United Kingdom in its remarkable affinity to mosques/Masjids, entering the department like entering a mosque, the discourse of religiosity and emphasis placed on Islam, performativity, and culture reflecting how Middle Eastern images have not been decolonized.

Bernasek (2008) maintained that:

> Middle Eastern Studies is generally taken to mean the study of the languages, cultures, history, politics and societies of the Arab world from Morocco in the west to Iraq and the Arabian Peninsula in the east, as well as Israel, Turkey and Iran. Afghanistan and other predominantly Muslim countries or regions in Central Asia, and in North, West or East Africa, may also be included in the definition. Despite this broad geographical scope, study of Arabic and the Arab world tends to predominate in current programmes of study and research. Scholarship in Middle Eastern Studies is carried out within a wide range of academic disciplines, including languages and literature, history, archaeology, social anthropology, religious studies, geography, economics, political science and international relations. (p. 2)

It is significant to question the languages, cultures, history, and politics of the Middle East as presented by Middle Eastern studies across the United Kingdom. In the process, it is imperative to understand how these studies are established, promoted, and financially supported. Suffice it to say that Middle Eastern studies in the United Kingdom are predominantly supported, funded, and built by either Saudi Arabia sources or other rich Gulf States sources. The support for Middle Eastern studies in the United Kingdom very much resembles the old structural adjustment program imposed over sub-Saharan Africa in the 1970s, with a catalogue of strings attached.

On the other hand, Vesper (2008) warned concerning the sharp rise in Saudi funding of the Middle Eastern studies in the United Kingdom. It is funding that reflects the nature and the ideology and pedagogy constructed to inform about the Middle East. Middle Eastern studies are unimaginable with the absence of veiled Muslim scholars who inform the colonial image of the Middle East and confirm to the old Oriental production. The Saudi stabilization projects that target Middle Eastern studies in the Middle East help in constructing and boosting the same Oriental image of the Middle East. These projects help to inform the conquest of the imperial United Kingdom.

In general, there is an absence of a robust postcolonial perspective in the work of Middle Eastern studies. Notable Middle Eastern thinkers have ceased to exist under the current construction of the discipline and the studies. Middle Eastern scholars including Ebn Rushd (1126–1198), Hussain Morowa, and Farag Foda (1946–1992) are rarely acknowledged or presented, and if presented, a catalogue of resistance is set in place to limit the scope for appropriate positioning within the academic pedagogy to such pivotal contributors in knowledge and philosophy who inform about the Middle East.

The Middle Eastern studies conventionally echo and reproduce images produced from the colonial era and then reflect it in the current pedagogy of studies that inform about the Middle East in a way that, such images present the essence of neoliberalism while silencing voices that reject the neoliberal and neocolonial representation and the present construction of Middle Eastern studies in the United Kingdom.

I will address issues of the veil and its origin and meaning in relation to the female body construction in Islamic culture and Islamic discourse. The coming section will tackle the geopolitics of the female Islamic body and its relation to the feminist perspective on the veil.

The Geopolitics of the Veil: A Blueprint of Middle Eastern Studies in the United Kingdom

Tackling the issue of the veil requires questioning how the Middle East is reproduced and how the geopolitics of the female body manifests not only a representation of a middle class culture and discourse, but rather, a liberal representation of the Middle East and an Oriental discourse that portrays the Middle East as the exotic, eccentric, and unconventional subject, where veiled women and *hareem* structure prevails.

Postcolonial political elites are created after independence, featuring the lower and middle class dominance. Women's movements are originated from this class structure. The capitalist structure of the sexualized female body objectifies women equally. In postcolonial society, capitalism never owns; capitalism cohabits with the traditional society. Traditional societies and capitalism produce and safeguard the patriarchal structure that subjugates women. The subjugation of women in Muslim culture is a product of patriarchal capitalism merging with Islamism and Arabism old discourses, preserved by the virtue and power of neoliberalism (El Sadawi, 1989; Mernissi, 1988).

In postcolonial eras, the Arab woman's body was traditionally constructed, propertized, terrorized as a sexual honor, thus resembling the construction of the female body under capitalism. A project constructed collectively is manifested in the construction of Muslim female bodies, a double construction of both capitalist and traditional.

It is noticeable that the project that subjugates women and targets their bodies within the Middle Eastern discourses is mainly originated from the upper middle class women, while they were themselves spared harsh experiences and body regulations. Feminist discourses sound foreign when they are originated in an Islamic location, full of jeopardy for women who dare to challenge old patriarchal discourses mixed with religious ones. The rhetoric of the veil illustrated various positions: the veil as empowering, in the case of the Iranian women challenging Khomeini rules; the veil tends to transform to ideology and a political stand point as well when addressed within the context of different geographic space, i.e., Muslims in Europe. The veil in Western British culture did exist; however, it is not highlighted, stigmatized, or disdained. Headscarfs are common culture in Christianity, Judaism, and other religions. How the 'Muslim women' category is constructed, singled out, and how it performs this Muslimness is a significant question that needs to be addressed.

One vigorous Middle Eastern female body representation and iconic feature of our world is the *veil*. The issue of veiling has grown more complex. While the veil (as claimed) remains a sign of Islamic affiliation and traditional piety, for many women the veil is a token of liberation, an indication of a public engagement of women, and an announcement of these women's sense of religious practice (Siddiqi, 2009). For many secular feminists from the Islamic world (Afshar, 1992; Mernissi, 1988), the Islamic norms and laws are the main impediment to women's advancement, and some stress that Islam is incompatible with feminism (Ahmed, 1993). Al Hibri (1982) and Hassan (1995), on the other hand, attempted to show the so-called egalitarian and emancipatory content of the Quran. Different views and diverse understanding are manifested from the standpoints of various Muslim entities. All emphasize and reflect the multifaceted nature of Islam.

Veiling of the female body signifies an Arabic Islamic discourse that has different layers in terms of its manifestation: female genital mutilation, foot hitting, arranged marriages, etc. There are other practices that are culture specific and made legal through manipulated religious texts and through the power and hegemony of the Arabism discourse across the Muslim world.

The ideology of the veil is manifested as the *hijab*, where the geopolitics of the Middle Eastern discourse images the body and the signs, activities, and performativities of Muslim women. Commodification of the Middle Eastern female body is a process that is embedded in the deep cultural heritage of the Middle Eastern Arabian Peninsula and some far-reaching cultural norms in such places as Iran and Afghanistan.

Clyne (2003) claimed that the religious reasons for wearing the *hijab* such as modesty, privacy, and protection are rarely understood by non-Muslims. She further defined the *hijab* within a Muslim woman's perspective as "a subtle form of non-verbal communication, which conveys a number of messages about women's religious behaviour, perhaps her social status or political beliefs and cultural background" (Clyne, 2003, p. 19). Reference has constantly been made to Algerian women wearing the *hijab* during the war against the French colonial power, also the Iranian women challenging Khomeini's regime and using the *hijab* as a symbol for challenging the Islamic regime's war against women workers.

The Middle Eastern Female Body and Its Discontents: Contesting Representations

The category of 'Muslim women' is constructed through various discursive channels including the local, national, and international media, as well as the state and academia. This category has emerged most prominently as an object of scrutiny for social scientists since the 1960s and goes back to the era of colonialism and pre-colonialism. Explorers' accounts of the *hareem* are one of the prominent products of the colonial discourse of Othering. The veil in Western culture is a clear representation of subjugation and oppression of Muslim women. Reproduction of Orientalist discourses has never ceased to exist. But on the other hand, constructing the veil/*hijab* as a signifier of Middle Eastern

Muslim women and as a subject to inform about Middle Eastern women is in itself Oriental and neocolonial. A justification of new forms of imperialism, the 'Third World women'—with 'Muslim women' often assumed to be the most oppressed members of this group—became the focus of attention for Western feminists (Badran, 1991; Kandiyoti, 1991; Mohanty et al., 1991). A second wave of interest in 'Muslim women' occurred during the mid-1980s and early 1990s in response to the national debates occurring around the issue of personal laws, suppression of women, the veil, and gender structure. Also the events of September 11, 2001 gave rise to a desire to explore the eccentric, exotic subject of women (Hasan & Menon, 2004; Hussain, 1994; Kazi, 1999; Lateef, 1989).

Within this discourse, 'Middle Eastern women,' 'Muslim women,' and 'veiled women' stand as symbols of the Middle Eastern community as a whole, both for Muslim conservative groups who echo Orientalist discourse by arguing that it is the oppression of Muslim women by Muslim men that proves the inferiority and backwardness of Muslims in general, and for the liberal groups that attempt to historicize and construct a liberal discourse to explicate women's position (Bacchetta, 1994).

Literature that portray Middle Eastern women should challenge the idea of a fixed category of Middle Eastern women by looking at the multiple identities, women who may be identified as Muslims and coming from the Middle East may also carry with them multiple intertwined identities. As such, multiple fluid categories may be produced in the space of neoliberal politics of the United Kingdom. The stories told of Middle Eastern women are stories of political power, as well as stories of representation. The pedagogy used in teaching about the Middle East is also the pedagogy of power, reflecting powerful positions of donors and beneficiaries of Middle Eastern studies. This marks an attempt to provide an alternative approach in narratives and representations.

Paying homage to the diversity and shifting historical contexts of the Middle East and reconstructing the existing Oriental images is an essential task that could lead to a better understanding of the Middle East and could challenge the circle of power the produces Middle Eastern studies in its current shape of liberalism and fundamentalism. The chronicle of Middle Eastern history would then address issues of rights, representations, and politics as well as women's resistance and struggle.

It is important to implement a narrative of multiplicity of perspectives and the plurality of experiences within Middle Eastern studies. In this sense, it is important to capture the fluidity and dynamism of the different cultural imperatives, historical forces, and localized realities conditioning the Middle East and informing about its culture, history, politics, and resistance.

A vigorous approach will discuss Middle East 'power' or 'powerlessness' concepts and argue along pre-colonial and postcolonial lines, by examining their position in these two historical contexts. It is more comprehensive also to look at these positions of power. relatively by illustrating how the intervention of the colonial period created a situation where the earlier relatively powerful positions were eroded by the introduction of the new power paradigms and opportunities. However, within the whole process of such power erosion, new avenues to power were created in the process. Collins (2010) called the unequal power relations "the matrix of domination" (p. 6), focusing on the nexus of interlocking systems of oppression where the positions of oppressor/oppressed shift. Colonialism conquered Middle Eastern subjects, and neocolonial discourse produced images of the same colonized Middle East in the United Kingdom.

The liberal perspectives on the Middle East advocated by the very pedagogy followed by Middle Eastern studies in general, recount the image of the 'ignorant' backward and 'inferior' in the castrated Middle East. Such perspectives stood as affirmation of the civilizing mission of colonialism and neocolonialism. Such positions are still advocated by many Western scholars, as well as Westernized scholars, as they persistently reproduce images of *hijab*, terrorism, and performativities, without contextualising the very specific historical contexts under which these representations are produced and hence consumed.

Western and Westernized scholars were mainly driven to such positions through the desire to acquire recognition and to generate support from systems that advocate such discourse. In a way, this is a process and a method of generating sustainable funding, while addressing such accounts of oppressed beasts subject to drudgery and degrading practices (Cornwall, 2005). Constructing research subjects in Middle Eastern studies is governed by the power and hegemony of those who help and fund the institutions.

Questions of power identity and difference are important; the establishment of Middle Eastern studies in its current position reflects dominance and hegemonic discourses of both liberalism and Islamic fundamentalism. The Middle East incorporates different cultures, ethnicities, 'races,' countries of origin, traditions, and Muslimness that is complicated by performativity. There is no one authentic Middle Eastern identity. The performative expectations, and the enquiry about whether the Middle East is noticeable in its diverse performances, demonstrate that the accomplishment of social membership is governed by culture as doing, race as being, and by performance (Dyer, 1997). The exclusion of an alternative Middle East, the one that challenged the reproduction of old colonial discourse, is almost impossible, given the hegemonic nature of the discourse produced by Saudi Arabia and the Gulf States as the sole funders of Middle Eastern projects in the United Kingdom.

In his article "New Ethnicities," Hall (1996) presented his critique of black experiences and of the cultural politics and strategies that developed around these experiences in the United Kingdom. Hall presented two principal objectives, namely access to rights of representation and contestation of marginality, as emblematic of the position of the black British community. By the current discourse of Middle Eastern studies in the United Kingdom, the Middle East remains outside of the dominant current politics, as it reproduces the same colonial subject and colonial discourse, and hence remains invisible. Hall's conceptualisation of the movement of black politics from the war of manoeuvre to the war of position, as suggested by Gramsci, might well constitute a step towards overcoming calculated marginality and misrepresentation that the Middle Eastern studies encounter in Europe, and in the United Kingdom in particular. The Middle Eastern studies need to be positioned equally in the academic sphere of the United Kingdom, where the studies represent the diverse multifaceted nature of the Middle East in its politics, economics, and social development.

While Orientalism's impact on Middle Eastern studies cannot be denied, the departments in the United Kingdom kept the field of research that informs about the Middle East accessible and tailored to policy makers. Examining women and Islam and the different performativities dictates tackling topics of veil/*hijab* and issues of harmful cultural practices as signifiers and informers of Middle Eastern women. There is almost no research or subject in Middle Eastern studies in the United Kingdom that addresses women's issues without references to what they wear (veil/*hijab*) and how they wear it. Civilizing women in the Middle East has become the vision and the undertaking of scholarly work that is welcomed in the publication houses as well as in academic settings of Middle Eastern studies.

Towards a Multiple Category of the Middle East

Middle Eastern studies in the United Kingdom are reflecting the power dynamics of the Middle East region, where the representation of Middle Eastern studies encompasses powerful manifestations and hegemony of the wealthy Arabic world states. The hegemony and dominance of the *wahabi sect* overwhelmed Middle Eastern spaces in academia in the United Kingdom. The main research study in many U.K. universities are the studies that address and study issues of the study of Islam and the Middle East, Arabic language, and Islamic culture and relations between Muslims and the wider world. The programme encourages the study and understanding of Islam by means of lectures, seminars, conferences, and publications. At different departments, the Middle Eastern studies provides academic links and exchanges between institutions and scholars of Islam in Muslim countries, Europe and the rest of the world, Leeds University, Durham University, Edinburgh University,[4] and many other universities in the United Kingdom. Mapping all the resources provided will show how the main focus of the work of Middle Eastern studies is governed by funding provided either by Prince Talal bin Abdelaziz or any other Saudi institution; hence, the main research study provided would be in conformity with the requests of the donors.

One aspect of Islamic studies that would cease to exist within the current structure of the Middle Eastern studies in the United Kingdom is the history of religion critique in the Islamic world in general and Arabic Islamic world in particular, as it is doomed as a no-entry arena, not possible to be penetrated and involved in a comprehensive articulation and criticism of its practices and concepts. The hegemony of fanaticism within Islamic religion eliminated any possible space for articulation and reproduction of new conceptions and understanding of the Islamic teachings. The history of Islam as integrated in the Middle Eastern studies curricula reflects the same Oriental themes and is sourced from colonial perspectives. The politics of resistance in the Middle East has been illuminated from the pedagogy and teaching syllabuses, while Islam is presented and perceived the way it has been produced in the Western imagination. Islam is introduced within the boundaries of glorification of the religion and its practices, rather than critically engaging recipients in a robust discussion on its origin roots and politics. The conflicting and contesting views on Islam, and the wide Middle Eastern cultural practices, were reduced into the production of one homogenous Middle East.[5]

The hegemonic discourse of representation in Middle Eastern studies in the United Kingdom has overlooked sound representations and perspectives produced in the Middle East. The Orientalist discourse adopted dismisses an outstanding contributors of knowledge production on Islam and the Middle East, for example the writings of Ebn Rushd (1169–98), Hussyain Murruwa,

---

4 Mapping the Middle Eastern studies in the United Kingdom will show a similar pattern in constructing educational programmes; however, the syllabuses, curriculums, and the approach in teaching the courses reflect one-sided views and a conservative one.

5 My perception is that Muslims through the reading /misreading of the text and of the Quran misunderstood or took literally the glorifying texts of Arabism, read (*Wa Kuntum Khir Ommatin Okrigat Lilnas*) *you were the best nations created /formed/produced to people.* Eventually the glorification and in the process undermining others who were perceived as non-Arab built deep in the Muslim's consciousness.

and the Abu Alla Almaree seem to occupy a very limited space in the teaching of the Middle East literature and politics. The current discourse seems to focus researching terrorism, and revisiting old Islamic practices. It is vital to challenge generalization and depiction of the Middle East as one homogenous category of study, and to challenge the power dynamics that produces such unified and homogenous image of Islam

The limitation of the notion of 'Middle East' itself is that different categories of the Middle East—culture, location, religion, and ethnicity—provide a direct challenge to the simplistic characterization of the Middle East. Identifying Islam as the identity marker of the Middle East does no justice, nor does it represent robust historical specificity to the religion itself.

The Middle East is rendered as voiceless and powerless, in front of the hegemonic capitalist discourse and the power of the international neoliberal politics. The stigma and stereotype overlooks the complexity of the region. The adoption of a critical approach at this time and in the global contexts is essential. The image of Middle East is increasingly used in order to justify various forms of violence and oppression, when tackling religion and Islam as authentically Middle Eastern, along with Kandiyoti's (1991) argument that "Islam cannot be viewed in isolation of other societal factors such as political systems, kinship systems, or the economy" (p. 19). Religious identity cannot be disconnected from other societal positions such as class, regional identifications, education, or age, nor can it be understood in isolation from other religious groups, as all identities are relational. The call for the veil is itself a middle class hegemonic discourse. According to Kahf (1999), "real change in Western representations of Muslim women does not occur until decolonization struggles alter the material conditions of discourse, until the Muslim world and Muslim women begin to speak back in the language of the colonizer" (p. 179).

In recent years, concerns about new nationalism in the context of Europe were echoed. Apart from the reproduction of the old colonial images of Islam and veiled Muslim women, Fortress Europe is consolidated with corroborating the EU. Ethnic wars are designed and serve to put across to international attention questions of racism and nationalism in Europe. The Dutch writer Harry Mulisch[6] (1993) opened one of his lectures by claiming that "the ghost of nationalism is roaming over Europe" (p. 20), paraphrasing Marx's famous introduction to *The Communist Manifesto*:[7] "the ghost of communism is roaming over Europe" (1848, p. 14). While the first negates the ghost, the latter celebrates its expedition (Lutz et al., 1993).

6 Mulisch, H (1993) Een Spookgeschiedenis, Bezige, Bij.

7 https://www.marxists.org/archive/marx/works/1848/communist-manifesto/.

Europe's 'imagined communities' entail exclusion from the nations and the structuring of new communities of Europeanism, welfare chauvinism, and racism. Such discourses produced the Other and were used to exclude, inferiorise, and exploit the Other. Racialised groups are not homogeneous, and class, ethnicity, gender, and sexuality are relevant. An interesting articulation of ethnicity is presented by Lutz et al., (1993), illustrating the ways in which ethnic agents are constructed to be men with fundamentalist religious beliefs in communities constructed as authentic Other.

In the case of the Middle East, it is veiled women who are considered to be the most authentic symbols of their group (Lutz et al., 1993). The construction of women as symbols for ethnicisized and racialized groups is derogatory to women, in that it allows existing gender oppression to be legitimated to some extent, suppresses intergroup differences, and thus has an essentialized effect. As Lutz et al. stated: "Women are positioned differently from each other according to whether they are construed as to be protected or to be violated" (p. 10). Lutz et al. used the crossfire metaphor from Collins (2000, 2010) to express several positions and positioning of women in Europe.

Women are caught physically and symbolically in the angry crossfire produced by ethnic, national, and racist conflicts in Europe. Such positioning makes women targets of gendered racism and nationalism. Middle Eastern women were produced as national symbols of Islam and were homogenized within the Western context, while differences continue to be central to exclusions, as Muslim/African/Black (with all categories of black) all continue to exercise yet another discourse of exclusion, that is more racialized through colour and ethnicity.

Propagating a historical specificity to the subject of Middle Eastern women, tackling reductionism, essentialism, and singularity in the study of Muslims, and challenging the depiction of these women as evolving in non-historical time is pivotal. In other words, the exploration of these Middle Eastern performativities needs to challenge the neoliberal production of a homogeneous Middle Eastern studies in the United Kingdom and a homogenous production of Middle Eastern women.

Decolonizing Middle Eastern Studies in the United Kingdom

Kramer stated (2001) that:

> The Middle East in recent years has exposed grave weaknesses in the West's military and intelligence capabilities vis-à-vis this region; it has

> also, as profoundly if less dramatically, highlighted an intellectual failure: widespread and profound weaknesses in the ability of outside experts to analyse and understand the politics of this region. Here intelligence failure by states is matched by a serious crisis of academic and journalistic comprehension and competence, a failure which has contributed—and, given the lead time involved in creating a professional expertise in area studies, will long contribute—to impoverishing public policy debate and broader public opinion alike. (p. 954)

The very intellectual failure of Middle Eastern studies in fact is a candid upshot of the above proclamation, which measures the Middle Eastern studies failure against its capacity to profoundly inform policy making that should be pursued in the Middle East by the military and intelligence of the United States and United Kingdom. Such claims would prove the much-assigned role of Middle Eastern studies, in informing policies and approaches that should be adopted in order to excel the whole process of interventions.

Since September 11, 2001, the intellectual crisis of the Middle East took different forms, as envisaged by Kramer (2001), who maintained the importance of intellectually revisiting concepts of identity, terrorism, and religion as taught in the Middle Eastern studies, and the importance of constructing the very question of identity as a question of religion and its performances.

The statements made by Kramer (2001) when he explored the two camps of those who oppose the war and those who are proponents of war—both being described as paralyzed camps, backing the wrong horse—are in fact a reflection of the very current structure of Middle Eastern studies; this is so not in failing to inform policies for the U.K. government, but rather in failing to decolonize the academic sphere of the Middle East. Middle Eastern studies in the United Kingdom is innately constructed to serve policies that attempt to contain the Middle East, policies that were well proven incompetent and deemed to failure since the early years of colonialism in the region.

Middle Eastern studies in the United Kingdom has not failed or acceded when it could not predict the Iranian Khomeini revolution, nor does it fail for not informing about a possible Arab spring. Rather, the failure of Middle Eastern studies in the United Kingdom is the failure of intellectually relating to the politics of resistance in the Middle East and to informing intellectually about the imperial conquest of the West and the United Kingdom. The structure of the Middle Eastern studies is intrinsically and originally constructed to serve the imperial conquest and cannot be blamed for its failure.

The paradoxes in the West and particularly in the United Kingdom are revealed in the sense that Middle Eastern studies has been constructed through the very neoliberal ethics that seeks to extract answers to so many questions about the Middle East that can help easing the way towards its occupation. Eventually the failure of U.K. policies in the Middle East would paradoxically be blamed on the very establishment of the Middle East as thought of by the United Kingdom. The neocolonial, neo-Orientalist discourse that constructs the very pedagogy and teaching ethics at the Middle Eastern studies should be challenged on the same ground that the Middle Eastern people have challenged the presence of colonialism itself.

The Middle Eastern studies in the United Kingdom as it appears is not historically specific and it does not reflect the complex dimensions of the Middle East, as rightly stated by Halliday (2004):

> A considerable amount of the literature on Islamic and Islamist thinking of the 1980s and 1990s was indulgent, what I have elsewhere termed "Islam Lite"; that the claim of a growing democratic, or at least civil society, space in the Arab world of the 1990s was greatly exaggerated; that the debate on "Orientalism" obscured rather than clarified methodological and substantive, area-related, issues; that much writing by academics and policy specialists on the contemporary Middle East has ignored historical context. (p. 559)

On the analysis of Middle Eastern studies in the United Kingdom from a sociological and gender perspective, it is evident that the study of the Middle East has been reduced to the study of female performativities where issues of veil,[8] female genital mutilation, and honor killings become substantive and central in how it informs about Middle Eastern women. Rather than employing a historically specific subject of the Middle East and the Middle Eastern women, the studies have indulged in a discourse that formulates sophisticated, reproduced old images of the Middle East in a neocolonial setting.

Some scholars maintained that Middle Eastern studies in the United Kingdom has not been as caught up in the rancorous debates of security and national interest as is the case in the United States, where such debates have been considered threats to academic freedom since 2001 (Lockman, 2004). Nonetheless, entering the Middle Eastern studies in the United Kingdom is strikingly

8 Women and Islam is one of the core courses provided across the Middle Eastern Studies departments in the United Kingdom, despite that fact that such studies are presented from—supposedly—postcolonial perspectives; however, the study itself is feeding the Western curiosity on the exotic and eccentric subjects.

similar to visiting a mosque or a very strict conservative space, where the veil is constructed as an authentic Islamic dress and where the curriculum developed in these departments is directed towards teaching women, and Islam from a very conservative perspective.[9]

In their attempts to generate funds for these studies, the British Society for Middle Eastern Studies has lobbied the government for more funding for various fields of training languages and religions of the region, and for a broad spectrum of humanities and social science disciplines of the Middle East. All are intrinsically related and linked to the very questions of national security and international stability as rightly stated by Ehteshami (2002). The Ministry of Defence (MOD) training stands as an important activity and body that required well established training programmes conducted at many Middle Eastern Studies departments across the United Kingdom.

The Higher Education Funding Council for England and the Scottish Funding Council, the Arts and Humanities research council (AHRC), and the economic and social research council (ESRC) have all named their funding strategy as an initiative for "Strategically Important and Vulnerable Subjects." Funding structures and issues of 'national interest' have clearly shaped the discipline over its history, and particularly at the present time, with research and teaching focused on topics of direct strategic significance, i.e., the MOD training.[10] This focus occurs despite the fact that many Middle Eastern studies scholars do work on topics with no clear strategic interest.

Middle Eastern studies in the United Kingdom remains an active and vibrant field, with researchers pursuing a wide array of topics and issues of clear relevance to contemporary society. However, the overall activities and

9 A very significant representation in the Middle Eastern studies in the United Kingdom is the presence of veiled women, scholars and students alike; there is almost no Middle Eastern studies in the United Kingdom that lacks veiled women.

10 Likewise in the United States in Summer 2003, the issue of the future of Middle East studies was taken up by the U.S. Congress, where critics voiced their conviction that Middle Eastern specialists were abusing government funds provided under Title VI of the National Defense Education Act (under which grants to area centres have been administered since 1958) and producing extreme and one-sided criticisms of American foreign policy. These criticisms build upon Kramer's book, where the author takes issue with Middle East specialists on both disciplinary grounds (for failing to explain and predict changes in the Middle East) and political grounds (for failing to serve U.S. policy needs and interests). Kramer's suggestion is that if the academy remains defiant, the government should step in and use the lever of financial support to initiate reform (Kramer, 2001).

the strategies built in Middle Eastern studies echo a substantial work and discourse of reproducing neocolonial discourses and neo-Orientalism in the United Kingdom.

One of the most lucid and conventional suggestions is that the scholars working in Middle Eastern studies in the United Kingdom build an intellectual engagement with all parts of the Middle East, taking into consideration the multifaceted nature of performativities of religions, identities, and culture, integrating all regions and academic communities working inside and outside the Middle Eastern studies. The regime of truth established by Western scholars in Middle Eastern studies needs to be challenged and the reproduction of colonial, neocolonial, and neo-Orientalist discourse in the studies needs to be equally exposed, defined, and transformed. The project of reinventing Middle Eastern studies as academia that should be related to the public policy issues in the United Kingdom is in itself bankrupting the studies, where the academic work is to be dictated by the government and should in the end help the government cause in informing about the Middle East. There is more to women in the Middle East than what they wear, and eventually there are more subjects worthy of exploring in terms of the region's resistances, politics, and transformation.

Appendix: Related Links

University departments and research centres:
Centre for the Advanced Study of the Arab World (CASAW)
www.casaw.ac.uk
Durham University, Department of Arabic
www.dur.ac.uk/mlac/arabic
Durham University, Institute for Middle Eastern and Islamic Studies
www.dur.ac.uk/sgia/imeis
School of Oriental and African Studies, Department of the Languages and Cultures of the Near and Middle East
www.soas.ac.uk/nme
University of Cambridge, Faculty of Asian and Middle Eastern Studies
www.ames.cam.ac.uk
University of Cambridge, Centre of Middle Eastern and Islamic Studies
www.cmeis.cam.ac.uk
University of Edinburgh, Department of Islamic and Middle Eastern Studies
www.imes.ed.ac.uk

References

Afshar, H. (1992). Women and work, ideology and adjustment at work in Iran. In H. Afshar & C. Dennis (Eds.), *Women and the adjustment policies in the third world* (pp. 205–229). Basingstoke, England: Macmillan.

Ahmed, L. (1993). *Women and gender in Islam, historical roots of a modern debate.* New Haven, CT: Yale University Press.

Al-Hibri, A. (1982). *Women and Islam.* New York, NY: Pergamon.

Bacchetta, P. (1994). "All our goddesses are armed": Religion, resistance and revenge in the life of a militant Hindu nationalist woman. In K. Bhasin, R. Menon, & N. Said Khan (Eds.), *Against all odds: Essays on women, religion and development from India and Pakistan* (pp. 133–156). New Delhi, India: Kali for Women.

Badran, M. (1991). Competing agenda: Feminisms, Islam and the state in nineteenth and twentieth century Egypt. In D. Kandiyoti (Ed.), *Women, Islam and the state* (pp. 201–236). Hong Kong: Macmillan. doi:10.1007/978-1-349-21178-4.

Bernasek, L. (2008). *Middle Eastern studies in the United Kingdom.* Retrieved July 27, 2017 from https://www.llas.ac.uk/resources/gpg/3192.

Clyne, I. (2003). Muslim women: Some Western fictions. In H. Jawad & T. Benn (Eds.), *Muslim women in the United Kingdom and beyond experiences and images* (pp. 19–38). Boston, MA: Brill.

Collins, P.H. (2000). *Black feminist thought: Knowledge, consciousness, and the politics of empowerment.* New York, NY: Routledge.

Collins, P.H. (2010). *Another kind of public education: Race, schools, the media, & democratic possibilities.* Boston, MA: Beacon Press.

Cornwall, A. (2005). Perspectives on gender in Africa. In A. Cornwall (Ed.), *Readings in gender in Africa.* Bloomington, IN: Indiana University Press.

Dyer, R. (1997). *White: Essays on race and culture.* London, England: Routledge.

Ehteshami, A. (2002). *The foreign policies of Middle Eastern states.* Boulder, CO: Lynne Rienner.

El Saadawi, N. (1989). *The circling song.* London, England: Zed Books.

Hall, S. (1996). New ethnicities. In D. Morely & K.H. Chen (Eds.), *Critical dialogues in cultural studies* (pp. 441–449). London, England: Routledge.

Halliday, F. (2004). 9/11 and Middle Eastern Studies past and future: Revisiting *Ivory towers on sand. International Affairs, 80,* 953–962. doi:10.1111/j.1468-2346.2004.00427.x.

Hasan, Z., & Menon, R. (2004). *Unequal citizens: A study of Muslim women in India.* New Delhi, India: Oxford University Press.

Hassan, R. (1995). *Women's rights and Islam: From the I.C.P.D. to Beijing.* Private publication. ASIN: B000RKZWT2.

Hussain, F. (1994). *Women in the Qur'an, traditions and the interpretation.* New York, NY: Oxford University Press.

Kahf, M. (1999). *Western representation of Muslim women.* Austin, TX: University of Texas Press.

Kandiyoti, D. (Ed.). (1991). *Women, Islam and the state.* Hong Kong: Macmillan.

Kazi, M. (1999). *Islam: Selected work.* Ann Arbor, MI: Nazrul Institute, University of Michigan.

Kofman, E. (2000). The invisibility of skilled female migrants and gender relations in studies of skilled migration in Europe. *International Journal of Population Geography, 6,* 45–59.

Kramer, M. (2001). *Ivory towers on sand: The failure of the Middle Eastern studies in America.* Washington, DC: The Washington Institute for Near East Policy.

Lateef, S. (1989). *Muslim women in India: Political and private realities, 1890s–1980s.* New Delhi, India: Kali for Women.

Lockman, Z. (2004). *Contending visions of the Middle East: The history and politics of Orientalism.* Cambridge, England: Cambridge University Press.

Lutz, H., Phoenix, A., & Yuval-Davis, N. (1993). *Crossfires: Nationalism, racism, and gender in Europe.* London, England: Pluto Press.

Mernissi, F. (1988). *Doing daily battle: Interviews with Moroccan women.* London, England: Women's Press.

Mills, S. (1997). *Discourse.* London, England: Routledge.

Mohanty, C., Russo, A., & Torres, L. (Eds.). (1991). *Third world women and the politics of feminism.* Bloomington, IN: Indiana University Press.

Said, E. (1979). *Orientalism.* New York, NY: Vintage Books.

Said, E.W. (1993). *Representations of the intellectual: The 1993 Reith lectures.* London, England: Vintage.

Siddiqi, D.M. (2009). Taslima Nasrin and others: The contest over gender in Bangladesh. In A. Razi (Ed.), *(Re)reading Taslima Nasrin: Contexts, contents and constructions* (pp. 15–37). Dhaka: Shrabon Publishers.

Vesper, I. (2008). Sharp rise in Saudi funding raises concerns. *Research Fortnight.*

CHAPTER 6

The Onto-Politics of Moderation: Studying Islamist Politics and Democracy in the Middle East

Dunya D. Cakir

Introduction

This chapter explores two distinct, yet related, sites of knowledge production in the area of Islamist politics and democracy in the Middle East: U.S. think tanks (specifically the Rand Corporation) and social sciences (specifically the academic discipline of political science). Although these sites are explored separately, it is in fact difficult to demarcate the discursive boundaries of the knowledge produced by policy analysts at think tanks from that produced by social scientists affiliated with universities or research units. The knowledge manufactured in think tanks percolates not only into the public domain by affecting the making of American foreign policy in the Middle East, but it also infiltrates into academic analyses in unexpected ways. The opposite is also true: scholarly categories such as civil Islam, democratization, and civil society, and scholarly theorems such as the inclusion-moderation hypothesis frequently appear in the publications of think tanks.

Through textual analysis of academic and think tank research, the chapter aims to excavate the ways in which normative ideals attached to a (liberal) democratic age such as political moderation and deliberation figure in and get appended to scholarly representations of the contemporary Middle East. The first section explores the reports published by the Rand Corporation in the aftermath of 9/11, regarding strategies to moderate/deradicalize Islamist actors as an additional pillar of the U.S. War on Terror. The second section analyzes the moderation literature in comparative politics of the Middle East and fleshes out the ways in which reading Islamist politics through the moderation paradigm solidifies prevalent political reflexes to think democracy through the normative repertoire of liberalism, while concealing its affinity with a distinctly bourgeois ethics that equates democratic agency with reasoned deliberation and cooperation in the public sphere. The final section explores an exemplary comparativist text on public spheres in the Middle East and calls attention to the analytical centrality of deliberative virtues to scholarly accounts of publics, including those that seek to uncouple democracy from liberal values.

Such work complicates the common association of democracy with liberalism (unlike much of the moderation literature), but still frames its inquiry of non-Western political practices through Western theoretical debates and categories of knowledge. In doing so, it misses an opportunity to move the field (i.e., comparative politics of the Middle East) beyond its endemic Eurocentrism.

I use the term 'onto-politics' to refer to the analysis of how certain basic units are presupposed by a given proposition, theory, or interpretation as well as the broader (albeit unintended) political effects of such presuppositions. Unpacking the onto-political components of scholarly discourse sheds light on the work that 'moderation,' used as a scholarly category of analysis, performs as a political discourse of normativity and subjectivity; thus the term onto-politics captures the (political) production of a certain category of subjectivity (moderate religious subjectivities) by the very analytic categories that seek to explain and understand Islamist politics. Specifically, the chapter highlights how framing the study of Islamist politics through the moderation paradigm consolidates a liberal/bourgeois ethic of conduct as the centerfold of democratic politics. Similarly, I argue, reading public sphere(s) in the Middle East through the lens of deliberative practices turns deliberation into the normative touchstone of democratic agency and subordinates the study of non-Western political practices (such as qat chews in Yemen) to Western theoretical frameworks and debates. In that sense, the scholarly discourses analyzed here are implicated not only in a set of political effects that suture the association of democracy with liberal norms of conduct, but also in a mode of subjectivation insofar as they presuppose and bring about a democratic subject marked by a set of ethical-dispositional characteristics (such as moderation, pluralism, tolerance, and cooperation). Collectively, such discourses consolidate an understanding of what it means to be democratic and act democratically that remain conceptually tied to Western theoretical paradigms, debates or categories of analysis.

As Connolly (1995) suggested, every political interpretation or theorization has an onto-political character in that "its fundamental presumptions fix possibilities, distribute explanatory elements, generate parameters within which an ethic is elaborated, and center (or decenter) assessments of identity, legitimacy, and responsibility."[1] In exploring the particular onto-political character of contemporary think tank and social scientific research on Islamist politics and democracy in the Middle East, I aim to demonstrate the salience of a liberal imaginary that grounds such research on distinctly bourgeois ethics, wherein

1 William Connolly, *The Ethos of Pluralization* (Minneapolis, MN: The University of Minnesota Press, 1995), 2.

an understanding of democratic 'being,' or being democratic, becomes equated with practicing deliberation amongst moderate subjectivities.

Moderating Islamists: Knowledge Production in the Rand Corporation

In this section, I explore the textual landscape of knowledge production in a prominent American think tank, the Rand Corporation, and investigate the presumptions that inform their analysis of democracy in the Middle East, the typologies and hypotheses upon which policy suggestions are predicated, the local social phenomena that are problematized as obstacles to democratization, and the corrective strategies that are devised in response. In other words, I seek to flesh out the discursive contours of what is entailed in the promotion of democracy in the Middle East as understood by researchers in the Rand Corporation, specifically focusing on the projects and reports sponsored by the Rand Corporation in the aftermath of 9/11 regarding the question of political Islam.

Established on October 1, 1945 as a private organization under the name Project RAND out of a perceived need to connect military planning with research and development decisions, the Rand Corporation has since exemplified the imbricated nature of knowledge production with apparatuses of power. Historically, the Corporation as an epistemic institution has been one of the most influential think tanks shaping American foreign policy and decision-making with the research briefs and reports of its research staff. In the last two decades, the Rand Corporation has actively encouraged the moderation of Islamists as an integral part of U.S. policy of democracy promotion and civil society development in the Middle East.

The Muslim World After 9/11 is the Corporation's earliest study on the impact of 9/11 and the ensuing sequence of events, including Operation Enduring Freedom, the global war on terrorism, and the invasion of Iraq.[2] In hindsight, it is clear that this work has set a strong precedent for subsequent research on Islam and democracy conducted by the Rand analysts. This influence is most noticeable in the prevalent use of a typology of ideological tendencies among Islamic groups in the Middle East, first laid out in *The Muslim World After 9/11*, and intended to demarcate the future allies of the United States in its campaign to promote democracy and stability. Following this initial publication,

2 Angel Rabasa, Cheryl Benard, Peter Chalk, Christine Fair, Theodore Karasik, Rollie Lal, Ian Lesser, and David Thaler, *The Muslim World After 9/11* (Santa Monica, CA: The Rand Corporation, 2004).

later research turned to the causes underlying religious extremism and to detailing major cleavages across religious, national, or sectarian lines among Islamic groups (lines which would constitute opportunities for American foreign policy).

In the face of extensive networks developed and sustained by radical Islamic groups, the Rand analysts primarily recommend foreign policy makers to consider the U.S. role as an external catalyst in "promoting moderate network creation" at the international level. This is because "the battle for Islam requires the creation of liberal groups to retrieve Islam from the hijackers of the religion."[3] Accordingly, this catalyst role is best performed through "funding for education and cultural programs run by moderate, secular Muslim organizations to counter the influence of radical groups."[4] An additional but related suggestion concerns supporting expression of "civil Islam," a category defined by Rabasa et al. as "Muslim civil society groups that advocate moderation and modernity."[5]

In substantiating their policy prescriptions, Rabasa et al. (2004) draw insights from the moderation literature in comparative politics that traces the development of Islamist groups and political parties following their inclusion in democratic processes. The authors maintain that despite the possibility that an Islamist party, once in power, may move against democratic freedoms, the inclusion of Islamist groups within existing, open democratic institutions is to be supported as this may have the effect over time of taming the threat Islamists pose to the system, i.e., the denunciation of democratic freedoms. Therefore, the authors stress that the process of engaging Islamist groups in 'normal politics' and allowing them to participate in democratic electoral processes promise to generate political moderation. To reduce the threat of eventual systemic change through democratic means, the Rand report suggests that democratic inclusion of Islamists should be conditional on the presence among the group members of an unequivocal commitment to nonviolence and democratic processes. To refer to this ideological prerequisite for democratic inclusion, the researchers use the term "the infrastructure of democratic political processes" that includes a liberal worldview (whether founded on Western or Islamic philosophical traditions) including respect for freedom of expression, association, and religion support for individual rights, building of alliances with other political actors, etc.[6]

3 Ibid., xxii.

4 Ibid., xxiii.

5 Ibid., xxiv.

6 Ibid., 6.

Among the numerous implications of the global war on terrorism (and expanded U.S. counter-terrorism operations abroad), the Rand researchers particularly stress the "sharpening of the divide between moderate and radical Muslims, producing new political risks and opportunities for governments and political actors alike."[7] In that juncture, it is argued, the appropriate strategy in the War on Terror requires deliberate attempts at strengthening moderate Muslim voices and incorporating them as allies into the project of eradicating Islamic terrorism. Through this discursive move, the work of the Rand Corporation not only ranks and classifies Islamic groups along the moderate-radical axis using the U.S. national interests as a yardstick, but also generates a discourse problematizing "the silence of the moderates" (referring to a liberal, moderate majority of Muslims who denounce the activities of transnational Islamist terrorist networks) as a field requiring political intervention. Having thus identified the site of intervention, the Rand report then articulates and projects a regulative and corrective logic in its call for "empowering moderate Muslim networks" and "educational reform in madrassas and mosques" to foster religious moderation.[8]

Within the broad universe of political Islam, the Rand identifies radical Islamists as a minority, qualitatively different from other political denominational categories such as scriptural fundamentalists, traditionalists, modernists, liberal secularists, and authoritarian secularists. Traditionalism, understood as the predominant orientation among the Muslims, incorporates many Sufi aspects and practices together with "moderate political attitudes, a focus on social and cultural aspects of Islam rather than politics, a commitment to pluralism and tolerance etc."[9] The report traces the rejection of Sufism among Sunni fundamentalists back to the writings of Ibn Taymiyya in the 13th century, echoed by modern exponents of radical Islamism. Their victimization by Wahhabis and Salafis, it is held, makes Sufis and traditionalists natural allies of the West in the struggle with radicals to define the place of Islam in the modern world. The Rand favors traditionalist groups on the grounds of their accommodationist approaches that endorse the privatization of religion associated with the modern liberal state and as part of a grand scheme propagating, what Metcalf calls, "patterns of Islamic a-politicism that foster a modus vivendi with democratic and liberal traditions."[10] The authors of the report claim that

---

7 Ibid., 51.

8 Ibid., 61–62.

9 Ibid., 373.

10 Barbara Metcalf, *Traditionalist Islamic Activism: Deoband, Tablighis, and Talibs* (Leiden, Netherlands: ISIM Papers, 2002), 16.

moderation, toleration, and opposition to political activism and violence make up the core values promoted by the Sufi traditionalist-Western alliance against Islamism.

A subsequent 2005 report on political Islam by Rabasa continues the earlier focus on identifying and capitalizing on the distinctions between radical and moderate strands of Islam.[11] Presented to the United States House of Representatives in 2005, Rabasa's testimony contests the prevalent scholarly conceptions of radical Islam based on support for terrorism or other forms of violence as too narrow. Instead, he proposes to incorporate "the larger universe of fundamentalist or Salafi groups who may not themselves practice violence, but that propagate an ideology that creates the conditions for violence and that is subversive of the values of democratic societies" into our understanding of radical Islam.[12] Extended this way, the term "radical" contains any and all discourse and practice expressing antidemocratic tendencies, thereby potentially breeding violent and jihadist orientations.

As this move illustrates, analytic categories are consequential for policy making. Envisaging a broader scope for the concept 'radical,' Rabasa (2005) prepares his audience for what he deems a more effective counter-terrorism policy. If radicalism transcends the boundaries of the public performance of violent acts to pursue political objectives, then it becomes imperative to revise policies to confront Islamic terrorism in a way that addresses the ideological aspect of radicalization. To distinguish between radical and moderate currents of Islamic thought, Rabasa develops a framework that categorizes Islamist groups on the basis of their preferred forms of government (Islamic state or secular government), their political and legal orientation (Shari'a or man-made law), and their attitudes toward the rights of women and religious minorities. Representing the spectrum of Muslim political thought in this manner, Rabasa's typology sorts Islamic groups and individuals into either the category of "moderates who advocate democracy and tolerance and reject violence as a means to attain political goals" or the category of "radicals who oppose democratic and pluralist values and embrace violence."[13] This typology is designed to assist policy makers in deciding which Islamic groups must be supported as their allies in an interpretive battle over the meaning of Islam.

Building on previous Rand research on moderate Islam (Benard, 2004; Rabasa et al., 2004), the Rand Center for Middle East Public Policy prepared a

11 Angel Rabasa, *Moderate and Radical Islam* (Santa Monica, CA: The Rand Corporation, 2005).

12 Ibid., 1.

13 Ibid., 3.

report in 2007 addressing the question of how to build moderate and liberal Muslim networks in order to disseminate the message of the moderates within the broader Muslim world.[14] The report endorses an external catalyst (American foreign policy) to realize such network formation. This suggestion is meant to complement the existing policies of the U.S. government that work towards this objective, such as programs of democracy promotion and civil society development. Democracy promotion mandates are often carried out through the Department of State and U.S. Agency for International Development (USAID), which sub-contracts non-governmental organizations, principally the National Endowment for Democracy (NED), the International Republican Institute (IRI), the National Democratic Institute (NDI), the Asia Foundation, and the Center for the Study of Islam and Democracy (CSID). All are non-governmental organizations (NGOs) funded by the U.S. government. The Middle East Partnership Initiative (MEPI), a new office in the Department of State's Bureau of Near Eastern Affairs (NEA), represents a novel attempt to bypass the government-to-government approach characterizing the pre-9/11 initiatives, instead relying on funding U.S. NGOs, which then distribute resources to local NGOs working in the field of democratic governance. In addition to initiatives launched by the U.S., there have also been multilateral projects designed to promote democracy, good governance and civil society development in the Middle East, such as the Broader Middle East and North Africa Initiative (BMENA) launched in 2004 by the United States together with the G8 countries. An outgrowth of the BMENA Initiative, the BMENA Foundation for the Future provides financial and political capital from the U.S. and the European Union to civil society associations in the region in order to initiate and sustain shifts toward Islamic moderation.

As a complement to existing regional initiatives, the report calls for "moderate Muslim network building" as a new pillar in the U.S. aid relations with local NGOs in the Middle East. Accordingly, priority should be given to "liberal and secular Muslim academics and intellectuals, young moderate religious scholars (moderate traditionalists including Sufis), community activists, women's groups engaged in gender equality campaigns and, moderate journalists and writers."[15] The report also proposes a set of assistance programs in the area of "democratic education," including projects that search Islamic texts and traditions for authoritative pronouncements that affirm democratic and pluralist values. For such a project to be sustainable and viable, the report requires

14 Angel Rabasa, Cheryl Benard, Lowell Schwartz, and Peter Sickle, *Building Moderate Muslim Networks* (Santa Monica, CA: The Rand Corporation, 2007).

15 Ibid., xxii.

active U.S. support in sponsoring a liberal, modernist hermeneutics of Islam by Muslim scholars and intellectuals. As part of the policy of "moderate Muslim network building," the Rand promotes the comparatively more moderate and pro-liberal examples of Islamism in Turkey and Indonesia, suggesting that "important texts originating from thinkers, intellectuals, activists, and leaders in the Muslim diaspora, in Turkey, in Indonesia and elsewhere should be translated into Arabic and disseminated widely."[16]

As part of the objective of inducing political moderation among Islamist actors, the question of how individuals or groups abandon extremist ideologies drives both academic and think tank research. In a 2010 report entitled "Deradicalizing Islamist Extremists," sponsored by the National Security Research Division of the Rand Corporation, the authors develop a two-tiered conception of moderation as a set of both ideational and performative changes in the actors' action-oriented worldview and discuss the effectiveness of deradicalization programs implemented by European, Middle Eastern, and Southeast Asian governments in the form of prison-based rehabilitation.[17] They propose that such programs should "work to break the militant's affective, pragmatic, and ideological commitment to the group."[18] The techniques used to reform the detainees, to indoctrinate them into the state-sanctioned interpretations of Islam, rely mainly on religious debates and dialogue. However, the authors argue that this alone does not break militants' affective and practical ties to a radical movement.

Instead, Rabasa et al. (2010) claim, successful deradicalization should induce not only change in behavior, termed 'disengagement' from militant Islamist organizations, but also in the individual's underlying beliefs. To guard against feigned moderation, the authors propose that deradicalization programs "continue to monitor former detainees and offer extensive support after their release."[19] Such aftercare can take the forms of theological counseling, placing the ex-radical in a supportive environment, facilitating his reintegration into society, even the assigning of a "credible interlocutor" to provide ongoing emotional support to the ex-radical and ensure genuine and sustained moderation. To encourage group deradicalization, they also emphasize the need for disclosure of ex-radicals' arguments and writings to incite others to renounce extremism. Such public disclosure not only extends the pedagogical

16 Ibid., xxiii.

17 Angel Rabasa, Stacie Pettyjohn, Jeremy Ghez, and Christopher Boucek, *Deradicalizing Islamist Extremists* (Santa Monica, CA: The Rand Corporation, 2010).

18 Ibid., xvi.

19 Ibid., xviii.

reach of the moderation apparatus beyond the individual psyche of the imprisoned militant but also locates moderation and its demonstration effects in the realm of public spectacle. It is for a similar demonstration effect that the Rand calls the U.S. government to support and sponsor reformist Muslim intellectuals' moderate voice, mobilizing the latter as the theosophical vanguard that anchors the multiple operational layers of the moderation apparatus.

Through a textual analysis of the Rand reports produced in the aftermath of 9/11, this section seeks to uncover the analytical components of a discursive regime of moderation that targets radical interpretations of Islam in Muslim politics for corrective policy interventions. First, in calling for policy measures designed to produce, sustain and disseminate an infrastructure of *moderation* (targeting political Islam) in the context of the War on Terror, the Rand reports reformulate moderation: their analysis mobilizes an ethical norm of self-conduct as a political practice designed to remake religious subjectivities along liberal lines. Promoted in the context of democratic development in the Middle East, moderation comes to suture our understanding of democratic agency around liberal norms of conduct. In other words, the onto-political presuppositions that underlie such research are most manifest in the harnessing of an ethical norm for a political agenda that subsumes democratic subjectivities under liberal values. Secondly, this brief review of the Rand's reports after 9/11 illustrates the imbricated nature of academic and policy communities as two intrinsically enmeshed epistemic networks. Think tanks as institutions of knowledge production are crucial nodes bridging academic and policy communities. As illustrated in the Rand research on moderating Islamism, think tanks *smuggle* scholarly categories of analysis and frames of inquiry (political vs. civil Islam, moderate vs. radical Islam, moderation-inclusion hypothesis) into the policy universe by devising specific policy recommendations on the basis of the concepts, typologies, and arguments oftentimes adopted from the academic literature.

Comparativists Study Islamist Politics: The Inclusion-Moderation Hypothesis

Much of recent comparative scholarship about democratization in the Middle East has directly or tacitly addressed prevalent political anxieties about non-democratic worldviews and political actors who may strategically use democratic openings and competitive, pluralist elections to empower themselves and abolish these very procedures. Since the end of the Cold War, and in the wake of 9/11, such anxieties have mainly centered on Islamist groups, broadly seen as calling for Islamizing all facets of human existence according to Islamic law which, it is often pointed out, contravenes some of the main principles of democratic citizenship (notably women's rights and minority rights) in its historical articulation. Against this backdrop, the prospects of democratization in the Middle East boil down to whether "Islamist opposition leaders and groups [can] be 'tamed' by inclusion within the political process."[20]

Since the early 2000s, a growing body of comparative scholarship on political Islam has examined the shifting commitments and practices of Islamist parties and actors through the inclusion-moderation hypothesis. Borrowed from studies of party politics in the West, this hypothesis asks whether political actors become more moderate as a result of their inclusion in pluralist political processes. Scholars advance different causal arguments, identify different mechanisms at work, or differently sequence the identified mechanisms in explaining the specific conditions under which electoral competition results in the moderation of Islamist groups. Some emphasize ideological over behavioral elements of moderation, while others focus on individuals rather than groups as the evidentiary basis of the sort of political learning called moderation.[21] The range of scholarly models notwithstanding, it is clear that "the idea that inclusion leads to moderation has now emerged as *the* issue at stake in debates about Islamist political participation."[22] Moreover, a shared analytical framework undergirds much of the literature on the evolution of Islamist politics: at the heart of scholarly models is a process-based typology that describes moderation as a movement along a continuum, a gradual "metamorphosis"[23] of radicals to moderates, the latter typically viewed as "supporting liberal democratic reforms" and normatively "tied to liberal notions of individual rights and democratic notions of tolerance, pluralism, and cooperation."[24]

In other words, not only the very existence and value of some phenomenon that can be usefully termed moderation has mainly gone unchallenged, but the literature has also prevalently deployed a binary typology used to denote (and evaluate) the evolution of Islamist actors subsequent to their participation in formal political processes. This is not to ignore the presence of revisionist

20 Carrie Rosefsky Wickham, "The Path to Moderation: Strategy and Learning in the Formation of Egypt's Wasat Party," *Comparative Politics*, Vol. 36, No. 2 (Jan. 2004), p. 205.

21 For a detailed review of the recent literature on the inclusion-moderation hypothesis, see Jillian Schwedler, "Can Islamists Become Moderates? Rethinking the Inclusion-Moderation Hypothesis," *World Politics*, Vol. 63, No. 2, (April 2011), pp. 347–376.

22 Jillian Schwedler, "Democratization, Inclusion and the Moderation of Islamist Parties," *Development*, 2007, 50 (1), 59.

23 Wickham, "Path to Moderation," 225.

24 Schwedler, "Can Islamists Become Moderates?" 348, 352.

voices within the field, which seek to advance alternative definitions of moderation,[25] complicate the neat causality posited in many models, reverse the sequencing of mechanisms that lead to moderation, or call for abandoning the terms moderate and radical as categories describing political actors and address shifting beliefs and practices on the basis of single issues.[26] My argument is that they are subsumed by a prevalent move that marks the vast majority of the literature: an analytics that explores Islamist politics through a developmental frame, and places a positive normative value on moderation as the end goal of democratic participation (and a virtue with a legitimate place in political judgment and action).

Despite the variety of scholarly models, much of the literature has conceptualized moderation as a process of ideological and behavioral transition from radical to moderate, wherein "moderate Islamists are often defined as those who are willing to participate in the democratic system, whereas radical Islamists are deemed as those who reject participation largely due to their rejection of secularism."[27] This conceptual binary is part of the modus operandi of the comparative politics of moderation, and is shared across previous works and the more recent revisionist voices. As one of the earliest examples in the field, Wickham's study of the Egyptian Muslim Brothers proposes a single, cross-cultural definition of moderation to assess whether and how the ideological evolution of radical Islamist groups take place. For Wickham, ideological moderation entails a move away from radical goals that are either abandoned or revised to adapt to the reciprocal environment of competitive electoral politics, and refers to "a shift toward a substantive commitment to democratic principles, including the peaceful alternation of power, ideological and political pluralism, and citizenship rights."[28] Similarly, Schwedler, comparing the political inclusion of Islamist parties in Jordan and Yemen, defines moderation as a spectrum ranging from ideological (based on a relatively closed and rigid worldview that precludes the legitimacy of alternative

25 Browers notably differs from others in defining moderation as a position of *wasatiyya:* "an intellectual trend characterized or claiming characterization as centrist or moderate, or said to occupy the middle between extremist alternatives." Michaelle Browers, *Political Ideology in the Arab World: Accommodation and Transformation* (New York: Cambridge University Press, 2009), p. ix.

26 Janine Clark and Jillian Schwedler, "Who Opened the Window? Women's Activism in Islamist Parties," *Comparative Politics* 35, No. 3 (April, 2003): 293–313.

27 Janine Clark, "The Conditions of Islamist Moderation: Unpacking Cross-Ideological Cooperation in Jordan," *International Journal of Middle East Studies*, Vol. 38, No. 4 (Nov. 2006), p. 541.

28 Wickham, "Path to Moderation," 206.

views) to post-ideological politics based on increased tolerance of alternative perspectives and pluralism.[29]

The theoretical premises of the inclusion-moderation hypothesis is that inclusion in the democratizing state and cooperation with non-Islamist parties and groups are presumed to lead to the ideological moderation of Islamist political thought as moderates convince radicals of the value of working within a democratic system and with other parties, and as moderates themselves have increasing contact with diverse ideologies and worldviews.[30] As formerly radical groups turn into vote-seeking electoral parties with centrist platforms, not only do they moderate but this process also contributes to democratic transition and consolidation.[31] The literature has broadly identified three mechanisms that produce moderation: (a) the institutional context that presents a set of opportunities or constraints for actors in devising new political strategies such as electoral participation (El-Ghobashy, 2005); (b) internal party debate involving ideological issues raised by electoral participation (Schwedler, 2006); and (c) cross-ideological cooperation between Islamist and secular opposition leaders in pursuit of common goals and in a spirit of compromise that transcends mere tactical thinking (Clark, 2006; Wickham, 2004). These three factors form the broad parameters for assessing the prospects for moderation of religious actors and parties in specific contexts.

The first variable stresses the importance of institutional dynamics and changes to the political strategies available to political actors, referring both to the party organization and/or the broader formal institutional context (Kalyvas, 2000; Schwedler, 2013). Institutions often provide incentives for previously marginalized groups to "enter the system, abandon more radical tactics, and play by the rules."[32] The broader institutional incentives for moderation have been mainly discussed in the context of the Middle East as regime-controlled partial liberalization attempts, wherein incumbents seek to incorporate opposition groups into the system without losing control of the process of opening. For some scholars, such limited institutional openings, short of democratization, can be sufficient to "generate strategic incentives for moderation and create opportunities for political learning, or experience-driven change in individual

29 Schwedler, "Moderation of Islamist Parties," 59.

30 Clark, "Islamist Moderation," 541.

31 Gunes M. Tezcur, *Muslim Reformers in Iran and Turkey: The Paradox of Moderation* (Austin, TX: University of Texas Press, 2010), 69.

32 Schwedler, "Can Islamists Become Moderates?" 35.

leaders' core values and beliefs."[33] The sequencing of moderation in this model starts with institutional incentives that alter actors' strategic choices, which first produce behavioral effects with actors moderating their behavior and rhetoric to appeal to a broader audience and then ideological effects in the sense of a shift in actors' beliefs and orientation. While behavioral moderation often denotes a change in public rhetoric and practices based on strategic calculations, ideological moderation refers to cognitive change as a result of political learning.[34]

Though many models posit a nearly mechanistic causality between institutional incentives and ideological moderation,[35] there are others who argue that these institutional dynamics such as political liberalization, a necessary first step, do not mechanistically bring about moderation.[36] For instance, Wickham notes that cross-ideological cooperation between Islamist parties and their secular rivals is the major mechanism that produces ideological moderation.[37] Clark, on the other hand, demonstrates that even when such cross-ideological cooperation takes place, certain redlines such as "issues that are fully addressed by shari'a,"[38] may block ideological moderation. For Schwedler, however, these redlines may shift over time as a result of internal party debates and discussion of ideological justifications for the newly adopted strategies (of electoral competition, and cross-ideological cooperation). It is this variable, according to Schwedler, that explains why Jordan's Islamic Action Front became relatively more moderate through participation in pluralist political processes while Yemen's Islah Party did not: "The IAF had serious and sustained internal party debates about whether participation in pluralist politics could be justified on Islamic grounds."[39] Schwedler also notes that it was not so much

33 Wickham, "Path to Moderation," 205.

34 Tezcur, for instance, defines ideological moderation as "a process through which political actors espouse ideas that do not contradict the principles of popular sovereignty, political pluralism, and limits on arbitrary state authority" while behavioral moderation "concerns the adaptation of electoral, conciliatory, and non-confrontational strategies that seek compromise and peaceful settlement of disputes at the expense of non-electoral, provocative, and confrontational strategies that are not necessarily violent but may entail contentious action." Tezcur, *Muslim Reformers*, 10–11.

35 Mona El-Ghobashy, "The Metamorphosis of the Egyptian Muslim Brothers," *International Journal of Middle East Studies* 37, No. 3 (August 2005): 373–395.

36 Jillian Schwedler, *Faith in Moderation: Islamist Parties in Jordan and Yemen* (Cambridge: Cambridge University Press, 2006); Clark, "Islamist Moderation," 539.

37 Wickham, "Path to Moderation."

38 Clark, "Islamist Moderation," 2.

39 Schwedler, "Can Islamists Become Moderates?" 359.

the actual content of such intra-party debates that mattered for the relative ideological moderation of the iaf as the fact that the debates took place.

Conceiving moderation as a multidimensional and dynamic model along behavioral and ideological change, Tepe argues that moderation of religious parties can be facilitated by extraneous (institutional) factors, while the limits of their moderation hinge on internal (ideological) factors and their interaction with electoral goals.[40] For most of the literature, as for Tepe, the electoral incorporation of religious parties serves as a necessary first step in their behavioral moderation but is not the main determinant of their ideological transformation. It is the party's ability to forge new ideologically coherent positions and engage with the demands of previously unrecognized actors that defines whether and how inclusion leads to a shift in parties' commitments.[41] Not only institutional incentives and electoral strategies do not stand in a singular causal relationship to moderation, but some Islamist parties cannot be argued to have moderated as a result of inclusion for a different reason: in Jordan and Yemen, "Islamist parties that participated in regime-controlled electoral processes were never radical in the first place and in fact were long allied with the ruling regime against leftist and secular threats."[42] Even in such cases where moderation cannot be said to follow from inclusion, Schwedler argues, the "elevation of relative moderates can have an isolating effect on radicals, thus producing an overall effect of moderation within the political sphere."

In an effort to demonstrate the different political effects of both inclusion and moderation, some of the recent work in the field call for greater caution in correlating moderation with democratization (Somer, 2014; Tezcur, 2010; Turam, 2007). Some propose that questions of moderation should be posed of all sorts of political actors, secular as well as religious (Somer, 2014). Others maintain that different patterns of transformations are subsumed under the term moderation (Tepe, 2012). Still others revisit the link between moderation and democratization, complicating its hasty conclusions in the paradoxical cases of Iran and Turkey where the rise of Muslim reformers attesting to the compatibility of Islamic values and democratic commitments did not generate a democratic transition or consolidation (Tezcur, 2010). Tezcur's revision proposes to see the moderation process as a double-edged sword: it could contribute to democratizing the authoritarian regime or end up domesticating

40 Sultan Tepe, "Moderation of Religious Parties: Electoral Constraints, Ideological Commitments, and the Democratic Capacities of Religious Parties in Israel and Turkey," *Political Research Quarterly*, Vol. 65, No. 3 (2012), 483.

41 Ibid., 481.

42 Schwedler, "Moderation of Islamist Parties," 8.

Muslim reformers, i.e., making them averse to challenging the authoritarian aspects of the regime. Thus, Tezcur concludes, prospects for democratic consolidation have more to do with the organizational resources of oppositional groups and institutional characteristics of the ruling regimes rather than the ideological commitments of the opposition.

Similarly, for Somer (2007, 2014), the more pressing question related to democratization is not moderation per se (or even, the ideological commitments of political actors regarding pluralism), but the creation and institutionalization of a democratic centre. He argues that the content of moderation and its effects on democracy will vary across countries depending on its domestic and international context—a country's centre—and political rivals' reactions. A country's mainstream context (i.e., its centre) influences actors' political calculations about how to access and maintain power. It is this intervening variable that shapes the content and consequences of moderation on democracy. Somer does not conceive moderation as a move towards pluralism and tolerance, but treats the very content of the concept as a variable to be explored cross-temporally and cross-nationally. This, he argues, helps better explicate the relationship between moderation and democratization.[43]

To sum up, recent work in the moderation literature has advanced the following propositions in an effort to challenge and revise the singular causal logic of the inclusion-moderation hypothesis: moderation is better seen as (a) interactive between religious and secular actors, (b) multidimensional, limited, and reversible; and (c) the effect of inclusion on moderation is overdetermined by the institutional contexts in which Islamist parties function. In the light of these works that articulate the limits of the inclusion-moderation hypothesis with regards to ideological moderation in given contexts, Schwedler proposes to rethink the hypothesis as "less of a single hypothesis with a single logic, but a series of propositions about the relationship between institutional constraints, the structures of a field of political contestation, and the normative commitments of individual and group actors."[44]

Defined either as a shift toward a substantive commitment to democratic principles, adoption of post-ideological politics based on increased tolerance and pluralism or as a shift toward a country's mainstream context/center, the concept of moderation is understood in terms of the acquisition of some

43 Murat Somer, "Moderation of Religious and Secular Politics, a Country's 'Centre' and Democratization," *Democratization*, 21, 2 (2014), 246.

44 Jillian Schwedler, "Islamists in Power: Inclusion, Moderation, and the Arab Uprisings," *Middle East Development Journal*, Vol. 5, No. 1 (2013), 16.

attribute or a set of attributes thought to distinguish political actors which have experienced these transformations from those which have not. Reading political change through this lens, the moderation literature (with some exceptions as Somer and Tezcur) anchors the concept of change to the individual and collective acquisition of a certain ethico-political disposition that is normatively attached to democratic political agency. Secondly, the set of referents through which the concept is defined in operational terms serve not only to describe but also order the experience of these transformations. That is, the use of moderation as an analytic category has both denotative and evaluative aspects insofar as its most common referents are not a mere empirical shorthand for the adoption of liberal democratic values but also attach a liberal teleology to the way we come to think of the political agency of Islamist actors in democracies. In that sense, to borrow from Skinner, the use of the term "performs the speech act of commending what is described."[45] For these reasons, the moderation literature makes itself vulnerable to the same set of critiques leveled against modernization theory a few decades ago: "stripped of its scientific pretensions, the concept of moder(niz)ation becomes little more than a classificatory device distinguishing processes of social change deemed 'progressive' from those which are not."[46]

In part, one could argue that the dichotomous approach developed by social evolutionists during the late 19th century continues to haunt social scientific accounts of sociopolitical change, as manifest in the consecutive analytical pairs through which human societies have been evaluated: civilization vs. barbarism, modernity vs. tradition, moderation vs. radicalism. In a similar vein, today's moderation theory continues to evaluate political change like its 19th-century forbears, by its proximity to the institutions and values of Western, and particularly Anglo-American societies. Using liberal values and dispositions as the criterion for assessing the degree of political learning and the normative end of political participation, the field continues the business of grounding the analysis of non-Western societies upon European experience. Not only categories modeled after European experience are projected upon Islamist communities to order their political present but through its inherent directionality the term moderation also provides a glimpse of the future of these societies as well: a glimpse comforting to the West by the assurance it

45 Quentin Skinner, "The Empirical Theorists of Democracy and Their Critics: A Plague on Both Their Houses," *Political Theory*, Vol. 1, No. 3 (Aug., 1973), 298–299.

46 Dean Tipps, "Modernization Theory and the Comparative Study of Societies: A Critical Perspective," *Comparative Studies in Society and History*, Vol. 15, No. 2 (Mar., 1973), 222.

gives that Islamist actors would follow along its own familiar path to moderate, pluralist politics.

Moreover, the reification of moderation as a framework for understanding Islamist politics obstructs a fuller understanding of the diversity of Islamist politics, as it continues to marginalize those Islamist worldviews that are not amenable to an egalitarian, and relativist exchange with democratic norms. Firstly, this blind spot approximates modernization theorists' analytical objectification of the category of 'traditional man' seen as devoid of agentive power to enact positive social change. The traditional/radical must give way to the modern/moderate who alone is the historical actor of progressive political change. Secondly, it elides the broader question of how to understand fundamentalist actors who defy liberal requirements of epistemological humility, relativism, pluralism and tolerance in the public sphere without assimilating them to the logic of Western-derived social scientific categories. It absolves comparative researchers from the more pressing methodological challenges that accompany attempts to understand, interpret and translate the political agency of Islamist groups in their own terms and from within the discursive framework that shapes their perspectives.

That said, the moderation literature diverges from the modernization theory in one important respect: while the latter is implicated with the Orientalist cosmology that is founded on a sense of radical difference between the East and the West, the former explicitly seeks to complicate such presumptions. In the context of the Middle East, often seen through its 'democracy gap,' the moderation literature (with its investigation of the mechanisms through which Islamist parties adapt to or adopt democratic procedures and norms) has served to demonstrate the ideological flexibility of Islamist actors. This has the practical effect of calling into question prevailing neo-orientalist views about the anti-democratic fixity of Islamist politics. However, the impulse to correct essentialist accounts of Islamist politics as inevitably antidemocratic gets implicated in a struggle driven to substitute one truth for another without exploring the shared normative foundations of the debate. Countering Orientalist representations of Islamism by falsifying its argument of incompatibility between the call for Shari'a rule and democracy does not question why the terms of the dialogue are set such that one party is required to speak in the idiom of the other. This reactive response of the moderation literature to neo-Orientalism ends up reifying the unacknowledged hierarchy of values in politics between popular sovereignty on the one hand and submission to God's law on the other. That is, it reproduces the global hegemony of a specific grammar of politics without fully engaging with the alternative lifeworld of the Islamist actors under analysis.

From Analytical Constructs to Liberal Onto-Politics: Unpacking the Moderation Discourse

By focusing on the mechanisms that domesticate the counter-hegemonic challenge posed by Islamist opposition movements to the political status quo, the scholarly analytics of moderation serve to regulate the political anxieties generated by the Islamic revivalist movements and their increasing political appeal and public visibility, thereby serving liberal ends. As a result, (a) moderation becomes a moral virtue with an unquestioned legitimacy in political action and judgment, (b) it comes to operate as a political instrument used against illiberal Others, an achievement expected from them, and a normative touchstone to evaluate the political evolution of "liberalism's remaindered subjects"[47] with their non-democratic, and illiberal doctrines. Through its implication with a political pedagogy that investigates the making of radical religious actors into democratic citizens, the moderation literature reproduces the civilizational frame of the liberal public sphere. That is, the end of political participation comes to be construed as a form of pedagogy and corrective regulation that targets illiberal actors, blanketed with the neutrality of a moral ethos, and not the renegotiation of the very parameters of the political field (the very terms of citizenship, political participation and agency) beyond liberalism. In this discursive regime, fundamentalist religious actors (who may hold anti- or nondemocratic political worldviews) come to be negatively defined through a lack (of moderation) and concomitantly, the social scientific conceptualization of their agency hinges on rendering them toothless; in much of the scholarly models of moderation, fundamentalist Islamists become political agents (capable of progressive change) insofar as they can subsume their commitments under the transforming egalitarianism of democratic inclusion. When the terms of democratic participation and competition is set, those "who are not directly amenable to conversation are given no chance to dissent to its imposition."[48] As a result, democratic politics becomes subsumed by a liberal modality of government that makes recognition of illiberal Others conditional on the domestication of their difference. As such, more than inclusion, moderation serves the liberal end to manage and depoliticize difference.

47 Wendy Brown, "What is Important in Theorizing Tolerance Today?" *Contemporary Political Theory*, 14 (2015), 162.

48 Leigh K. Jenco, "What does Heaven Ever Say? A Methods-Centered Approach to Cross-cultural Engagement," *The American Political Science Review*, Vol. 101, No. 4 (Nov., 2007), 744.

Notwithstanding scholarly intentions, the moderation discourse (used in both social scientific and think tank research on political Islam) is poised to contribute to the naturalization of an apparatus of moderation/deradicalization of Islamist groups, including internationally sponsored projects of democracy promotion and training in the Middle East. This naturalization most powerfully acts at the level of theoretical presuppositions underlying the field's causal postulates, which specifically pertain to the nature and ends of the democratic political system, and to political agency. Analysts' use of moderation as a basis for applying criteria as to what sorts of transformation of Islamist ideas is to be expected from democratic inclusion brings with it an assumed framework for understanding the nature of the democratic political system (as a pedagogical order) and the ethical-dispositional characteristics that make this order possible (moderation, pluralism, tolerance, cooperation). As a result, moderation comes to refer to a pedagogically achieved state of emancipation from radical (revolutionary) comprehensive doctrines, enabled by processes of pluralist democratic competition. Secondly, political agency in democracies as well as the normative end of democratic participation comes to be defined in terms of a post-ideological (liberal) norm of moderation. These two postulates, I argue, make up the onto-political structure of the moderation discourse. This underlying structure of the moderation paradigm has the effect of solidifying prevalent political reflexes to think democracy through the normative repertoire of liberalism, while concealing its affinity with a distinctly bourgeois ethics that equates democratic agency with reasoned deliberation and cooperation in the public sphere. The centrality of 'cross-ideological cooperation' and 'internal debates' to the moderation of Islamist actors in the literature suggests that deliberative norms operate as the normative touchstone of democratic participation and political agency.

Locating Democracy in the Middle East: Beyond Liberal Norms but within Western Frames of Inquiry?

There is another way in which social scientific representations of the Middle East come to naturalize deliberation as a normative touchstone of democratic participation and agency. In addition to the moderation literature on Islamist political parties, this discursive feat is also noticeable among scholarly accounts of the (traditional or nascent) public sphere(s) in the Middle East. To a certain extent, it is even present in work that differs from the moderation literature in actively seeking to uncouple democratic practices from liberal norms, and that opens up theoretical space to think democracy beyond the terms of liberalism in the Middle East.

In the last decades, there has been a growing scholarly tendency to use the term 'public sphere' to refer to the burgeoning religious revivalism in Muslim societies, oftentimes explored in relation to democratic development. For Eickelman and Anderson (1999), the religious components of the new public brought an element of rationalization to the public sphere by fragmenting and contesting political and religious authority. Accordingly, the open contests between state authority and the emerging Muslim public sphere(s) promise a democratic move toward greater accountability of governmental power and the creation of a civil society (Deeb, 2006; Esposito & Burgat, 2003; Hefner, 2001; Lynch, 2006; Salvatore, 2007; Salvatore & LeVine, 2005). The emerging Muslim public spheres manifest the opening up of a "public space that is discursive, performative and participative, and not confined to formal institutions recognized by state authorities."[49] Examining the manifestations of this new Muslim public, White emphasizes its roots in the intersection of class, traditional culture, and national politics, whether organized around Islamist political parties or civic activities.[50] She argues that it is neither print nor joint interests but interpersonal trust between neighbors and family members that fosters a sense of community among the constituents of this new pious public. These accounts of the new Muslim public spheres commonly weave together the concepts of communication, mutual participation, and performance as the main pillars of this emerging public, and define the public sphere as a space of freedom and reasonable communication generated through the daily exchanges and practices of ordinary people.

As understood by Habermas, the public sphere presupposes the formation of bourgeois private selves whose "coming together as a public" constitutes the public sphere.[51] In addition to the conception of a civil society of private citizens preceding the public sphere, the founding features of the Habermasian model are a secular rationality on which publicness thrives, deliberation about matters of public concern among moral and political equals on the basis of uncoerced, egalitarian, sincere, and truthful dialogue, which Habermas calls the "ideal speech situation" governed by communicative reason, and the

49 Dale Eickelman and Jon Anderson, "Redefining Muslim Publics," in Eickelman and Anderson (eds.), *New Media in the Muslim World: The Emerging Public Sphere* (Bloomington, IN: Indiana University Press, 1999), 2.

50 Jenny White, "Amplifying Trust: Community and Communication in Turkey," in Eickelman and Anderson (eds.), *New Media in the Muslim World: The Emerging Public Sphere* (Bloomington, IN: Indiana University Press, 1999), 177.

51 Jurgen Habermas, *The Structural Transformation of the Public Sphere: An Inquiry into a Category of Bourgeois Society* (T. Burger, trans.) (Cambridge, MA: Massachusetts Institute of Technology Press, 1962/1989), 27.

function of the public as a counterweight to the absolutist state and a means of rationalizing domination. Following the poststructuralist turn in social sciences, Habermas' conception of the modern public sphere has increasingly come under theoretical criticisms that set out to reveal the exclusionary nature of the bourgeois modalities of publicness, particularly across gender and class lines.[52] Others point to the analytical limitations of the Habermasian model in explaining the origins, formation, and functioning of public spheres in the non-Western world.

This section will concentrate on and discuss one such ethnographically grounded criticism of the Habermasian public sphere, the work of Lisa Wedeen on qat chew gatherings (framed as public spheres) in Yemen.[53] Through a discussion of Wedeen's study, the section will illustrate a prevalent scholarly reflex in comparative politics of the Middle East to subsume the study of non-Western practices and ideas under Western theoretical frames and debates. This move is present even in accounts, such as Wedeen's, that explicitly seek to overcome the Eurocentrism of social scientific analysis and reveal the limitations of seeing non-Western practices through the prism of Western models.

Wedeen's (2008) work is thought provoking, for it asks us to look at qat chews as sites of democratic practice in their own right. Wedeen argues that "the democratic nature of qat chews stems from the kind of political subject formation that takes place through the practice of discussion and deliberation in public."[54] This distinct form of personhood performed in these deliberative, quotidian publics revels in "peaceful disagreement" with strangers who "foreswear the use of violence to accomplish political ends."[55] These gatherings "promote citizen awareness and produce subjects who critically debate political issues, allowing participants to build an agonistically inclined political world in which disagreements are entertained in common."[56]

Wedeen is careful to distinguish the work that the daily practice of qat chewing does. It enables the "performance of an explicitly democratic subjectivity that relishes deliberation," which is not to say that it "produce[s] explicitly liberal debates or forms of personhood."[57] In Wedeen's own words:

---

52 Well-known critiques include, but are not limited to Dryzek, 2002; Fraser, 1993; Haas, 2004; Mouffe, 1992, 1996; Warner, 2005; and Young, 2001.

53 Lisa Wedeen, "The Politics of Deliberation: Qat Chews as Public Spheres," in *Peripheral Visions: Publics, Power, and Performance in Yemen* (Chicago, IL: University of Chicago Press, 2008).

54 Ibid., 140–141.

55 Ibid., 115, 139.

56 Ibid., 120.

57 Ibid., 145.

> The very activity of deliberating in public contributes to the formation of democratic persons, but does so in conditions fundamentally different from the ones Habermas identified as seminal in Western Europe.... I argue that close attention to the case of Yemen raises a crucial distinction between democratic practices and liberal values.... As I will show in this chapter, the example of Yemen demonstrates that any political analysis that fails to take into account participation and the formation of "public spheres" as activities of political expression in their own right falls short of capturing what a democratic politics might reasonably be taken to include.[58]

Akin to other studies of Muslim public spheres, Wedeen's reading of Yemeni qat chews revolves around a similar semantic orbit (of a scholarly universe that I tentatively call Habermasian). On the one hand, her study exemplifies a performative approach to (democratic) politics by attending to democratic phenomena that exist outside of electoral and other formal organizational confines. In that respect, it contests the narrow analytical focus of institutional accounts of democracy, and in doing so extends scholarly conceptions of democracy by rescuing the concept from the throes of a minimalist, liberal proceduralism. Uncoupling democratic practices from liberal values, her reading of qat chews underlines how "democratic persons are produced through quotidian practices of deliberation" even in the absence of free and fair elections.[59] On the other hand, in attending to the non-bourgeois forms of public sphere in Yemen—that is, a performance of deliberation that does not "arise out of bourgeois notions of individuality"[60]—the analysis remains nevertheless tied to the ethical framework of Habermas. In Wedeen's work, we travel to Yemen, destabilize the liberal foundation of Habermasian deliberation, but his emphasis on deliberation remains with us upon return. We dynamite the (infra)structure of Habermas' theory and simultaneously recuperate its ethics.

Wedeen argues, contra Habermas, that what makes deliberation productive of democratic subjectivities is its very form, rather than its ultimate institutional effects. However, the criteria by which a practice is deemed democratic by Wedeen remain in accord with Habermas' communicative ethics. This raises the following question: if we do not need more than Habermasian communicative ethics (its basic premise of deliberation as constitutive of a democratic public sphere) to conceptualize (paradoxically, a non-liberal) democracy, what

58 Ibid., 105.

59 Ibid., 3.

60 Ibid., 117.

is then the theoretical utility of postcolonial ethnographies (other than confirming the fundaments of our theoretical horizons rooted in Western democratic theory)?

Among comparative political scientists, the acknowledgement of the "imperialism of [Euro-American] categories"[61] has led to a call for epistemological reflexivity, spearheaded by the interpretivists who stress the local and particular self-understandings of social actors as a point of departure for research, the situated and partial character of knowledge, and the connective relations between the researcher and the researched. In defense of interpretive methods in political science, Wedeen notes:

> Ethnographic observations can raise questions about the concepts and paradigms currently informing social science projects and invite novel ways of imagining the political. They can negotiate the tensions between the particular lived experience of social actors and the analytic categories we use to generalize about them.[62]

In her work on qat chews, Wedeen (2008) manages the tension highlighted above by focusing on the observed experience of social actors, which appear to subsume her informants' voice (and their categories of practice) under the analytic privileging of the researcher's interpretive grid. However, as she aptly notes quoting Pitkin, "practices, like human actions, are ultimately dual composed of what the outside observer can see and of the actors' understanding of what they are doing."[63] I argue that it is this second dimension (the Yemeni participants' own understanding of the practices they are engaged in) that has been downplayed in her ethnographic insights on qat chews in Yemen. This is a consequential move, illustrative of a broader trend in the discipline (even among the interpretivists): in coming to terms with cultural and historical difference by rethinking the Western categories of knowledge (as illustrated in the interpretivist turn), political scientists still remain largely beholden to Western theoretical debates, thereby compromising the possibility of thinking beyond the West. As comparative political theorist Jenco notes, one irony in

61 Susanne H. Rudolph, "Presidential Address: The Imperialism of Categories: Situating Knowledge in a Globalizing World," *Perspectives on Politics*, Vol. 3, No. 1 (Mar., 2005), pp. 5–14.

62 Lisa Wedeen, "Ethnography as Interpretive Enterprise," in Edward Schatz (ed.) *Political Ethnography: What Immersion Contributes to the Study of Power* (Chicago, IL: University of Chicago Press, 2009), 90.

63 Ibid., 87.

much cross-cultural work in the contemporary academy is that non-Western voices and cases are included "by means of those very discourses whose cultural insularity is what prompts critique in the first place."[64]

Alternatively, ethnographic work in political science of the Middle East could treat local actors' insights as a distinct source of political theorizing that comes to discipline the researcher's theoretical framework. Doing so allows the analyst to go a step further in destabilizing West-centered categories of knowledge by not only problematizing (or decentering) the presumed bourgeois/liberal foundations of the public sphere in non-Western contexts, but also re-centering our theoretical frame of inquiry by way of the meanings, experiences, and self-understandings of local actors in these contexts. This way, scholarly readings of emerging publics in the Middle East could counter the Eurocentrism implicit in the act of reaffirming the centrality of Western theoretical debates and categories (e.g., Habermasian public sphere) to cross-cultural inquiry.

Scholarly work that seeks to think beyond Western categories of analysis requires attention to local, situated manifestations of publicness that may not easily map onto communicative ethics especially when the members of that public understand their activities in terms other than producing democratic persons. This would make the activities of civil society actors in non-Western societies intelligible to us without at the same time distorting or discarding their meanings, that is, forcing them *to speak to us*. Eventually, these meanings and self-understandings of non-Western actors should not matter to scholars *only* when they resonate with and can be translated into our established debates about political life (e.g., practices of public sphere that seek to rationalize domination or express the making of democratic persons).

Conclusion

The first three sections of this chapter explored the different sites in which a moderation discourse has been articulated and propagated by epistemic and policy circles in the context of the U.S. War on Terror and concomitant policy objectives to fight Islamist radicalization. Although the comparativist moderation literature in political science explicitly seeks to problematize the civilizational rhetoric of the War on Terror, this chapter argues that it nevertheless operates as an analytic component of a discursive regime of moderation, which targets radical interpretations of Islam in politics for diagnostic, regulative, and corrective policy interventions. In both think tank and social

64 Jenco, "What does Heaven Say?" 741.

science research, the analytical pairing of moderate-radical does a distinct political work: It conceals the ways in which an ethical norm comes to operate as a political practice and a liberal modality of rule that revolves around the remaking of religious subjectivities. It disavows its own implication with a liberal ethics, and this disavowed implication secures the uninterrupted operation of a liberal developmentalism that has marked much of Western social science since the 19th century. The brief review of this comparativist literature reveals the diversity of definitions, causal relations, and sequencing of the mechanisms conceived to be at work between inclusion-moderation and moderation-democratization. Taken together, however, scholarly accounts of Islamist politics clustered along the moderate-radical axis serve to constitute or consolidate/naturalize the very political identities and practices that they purport only to explain. In that respect, the field's internal diversity notwithstanding, its latent content speaks of a unity through which the exceptionality, eccentricity, and perils of fundamentalist (or non-liberal articulations of) Islam is rendered constant.

As noted by Rudolph, "social scientific categories are also modes of creating and controlling" in that "dominant peoples use ideal types and stereotypes to control the dominated by ranking and creating cultural social registers."[65] Categories may not be by themselves and directly involved with subjection and power inequalities between the societies that produce the observer and the observed respectively, but taken together they cannot be easily separated from contemporary projections of imperial power, and forms of stratification the latter relies upon, notably, by elevating liberal, moderate Islamist actors and evading non-liberal or post-liberal articulations of Islamist politics. In this literature on Islamist politics, the use of moderation as the privileged analytic framework serves to secure an ethical norm, foundational to bourgeois society, for the transformation of fundamentalist religious subjectivities into liberal ones.

The final section looked beyond the moderation literature into critical, interpretive work in political science (notably Wedeen's) that explicitly seeks to dissociate democracy from liberalism (unlike the moderation literature) and yet shares with the latter a common move to subsume the study of public spheres in the Middle East under Western theoretical debates and categories of analysis (such as Habermasian public sphere as the site of democratic deliberation).

I have used the term 'onto-politics' to refer to the (political) production of a certain category of subjectivity by the very analytic categories that seek to

65 Rudolph, "The Imperialism of Categories," 6.

explain and understand Islamist politics or democracy in the Middle East. The term points to how both of these scholarly discourses (on moderation and deliberation) analyzed here are implicated in a set of political effects that fix democracy's affinity with liberal norms of conduct, and in a mode of subjectivation that joins democratic agency to a set of ethical-dispositional characteristics (such as moderation, deliberation, pluralism, tolerance, etc.). Collectively, such discourses consolidate an understanding of what it means to be democratic, and act democratically that are expressed through Western theoretical debates and categories of analysis. Insofar as our political commitments to democracy in the Middle East remain tied to a Western theoretical framework (e.g., the practice of democratic deliberation between moderate subjectivities), our accounts remain implicated in the 'imperialism of categories' and the moral universe of bourgeois liberalism.

References

Benard, C. (2004). *Civil democratic Islam*. Santa Monica, CA: The Rand Corporation.

Browers, M. (2006). *Democracy and civil society in Arab political thought: Transcultural possibilities*. Syracuse, NY: Syracuse University Press.

Browers, M. (2009). *Political ideology in the Arab world: Accommodation and transformation*. New York, NY: Cambridge University Press.

Brown, W. (2015) What is important in theorizing tolerance today? *Contemporary Political Theory, 14*, 159–164. doi:10.1057/cpt.2014.44.

Clark, J. (2006). The conditions of Islamist moderation: Unpacking cross-ideological cooperation in Jordan. *International Journal of Middle East Studies, 38*, 539–560. doi:10.1017/s0020743806412460.

Clark, J., & Schwedler, J. (2003). Who opened the window? Women's activism in Islamist parties. *Comparative Politics, 35*, 293–313. doi:10.2307/4150178.

Connolly, W. (1995). *The ethos of pluralization*. Minneapolis, MN: The University of Minnesota Press.

Deeb, L. (2006). *An enchanted modern: Gender and public piety in Shi'i Lebanon*. Princeton, NJ: Princeton University Press.

Dryzek, J. (2002). Liberal democracy and the critical alternative. In *Deliberative democracy and beyond: Liberals, critics, contestations*. New York, NY: Oxford University Press.

Eickelman, D., & Anderson, J. (1999). Redefining Muslim publics. In D. Eickelman & J. Anderson (Eds.), *New media in the Muslim world: The emerging public sphere*. Bloomington, IN: Indiana University Press.

El-Ghobashy, M. (2005). The metamorphosis of the Egyptian Muslim Brothers. *International Journal of Middle East Studies, 37,* 373–395. doi:10.1017/s0020743805052128.

Esposito, J., & Burgat, F. (Eds.). (2003). *Modernizing Islam: Religion in the public sphere in the Middle East and Europe.* New Brunswick, NJ: Rutgers University Press.

Fraser, N. (1993). Rethinking the public sphere: A contribution to the critique of actually existing democracy. In C. Calhoun (Ed.), *Habermas and the public sphere.* Cambridge, MA: MIT Press.

Haas, T. (2004). The public sphere as a sphere of publics: Rethinking Habermas's theory of the public sphere. *Journal of Communication, 54,* 178–184. doi:10.1093/joc/54.1.178.

Habermas, J. (1962/1989). *The structural transformation of the public sphere: An inquiry into a category of bourgeois society* (T. Burger, Trans.). Cambridge, MA: MIT Press.

Hefner, R.W. (2001). Public Islam and the problem of democratization. *Sociology of Religion, 62,* 491–514. Retrieved July 27, 2017 from https://edocs.uis.edu/Departments/LIS/Course_Pages/LIS411/readings/Hefner_Public_Islam.pdf.

Jenco, L.K. (2007). What does Heaven ever say? A Methods-centered approach to cross-cultural engagement. *The American Political Science Review, 101,* 741–755. doi:10.1017/s0003055407070463.

Kalyvas, S.N. (2000). Commitment problems in emerging democracies: The case of religious parties. *Comparative Politics, 32,* 379–398. doi: 10.2307/422385.

Lynch, M. (2006). *Voices of the new Arab public: Iraq, Al-Jazeera and Middle East politics today.* New York, NY: Columbia University Press.

Metcalf, B.D. (2002). *Traditionalist Islamic activism: Deoband, tablighis, and talibs.* Leiden, Netherlands: ISIM Papers.

Mouffe, C. (1992). Democratic citizenship and the political community. In C. Mouffe (Ed.), *Dimensions of radical democracy: Pluralism, citizenship, community.* London, England: Verso.

Mouffe, C. (1996). Democracy, power, and the political. In S. Benhabib (Ed.), *Democracy and difference: Contesting the boundaries of the political.* Princeton, NJ: Princeton University Press.

Rabasa, A. (2005). *Moderate and radical Islam.* Santa Monica, CA: The Rand Corporation.

Rabasa, A., Benard, C., Chalk, P., Fair, C., Karasik, T., Lal, R., & Thaler, D. (2004). *The Muslim world after 9/11.* Santa Monica, CA: The Rand Corporation.

Rabasa, A., Benard, C., Schwartz, L., & Sickle, P. (2007). *Building moderate Muslim networks.* Santa Monica, CA: The Rand Corporation.

Rabasa, A., Pettyjohn, S., Ghez, J., & Boucek, C. (2010). *Deradicalizing Islamist extremists.* Santa Monica, CA: The Rand Corporation.

Salvatore, A. (2007). *The public sphere: Liberal modernity, Catholicism, Islam.* New York, NY: Palgrave Macmillan.

Salvatore, A., & LeVine, M. (Eds.). (2005). *Religion, social practice, and contested hegemonies: Reconstructing the public sphere in Muslim majority societies.* New York, NY: Palgrave Macmillan.

Schwedler, J. (2006). *Faith in Moderation: Islamist parties in Jordan and Yemen.* Cambridge, England: Cambridge University Press.

Schwedler, J. (2007). Democratization, inclusion and the moderation of Islamist parties. *Development, 50,* 56–61. doi:10.1057/palgrave.development.1100324.

Schwedler, J. (2011). Can Islamists become moderates? Rethinking the inclusion-moderation hypothesis. *World Politics, 63,* 347–376. doi:10.1017/s0043887111000050.

Schwedler, J. (2013). Islamists in power? Inclusion, moderation, and the Arab uprisings. *Middle East Development Journal, 5,* 1–18. doi:10.1142/s1793812013500065.

Skinner, Q. (1973). The empirical theorists of democracy and their critics: A plague on both their houses. *Political Theory, 1,* 287–306. doi:10.1177/009059177300100302.

Somer, M. (2007). Moderate Islam and secularist opposition in Turkey: Implications for the world, Muslims and secular democracy. *Third World Quarterly, 28,* 1271–1289. doi:10.1080/01436590701604888.

Somer, M. (2014). Moderation of religious and secular politics, a country's "centre" and democratization. *Democratization, 21,* 244–267. doi:10.1080/13510347.2012.732069.

Tepe, S. (2012). Moderation of religious parties: Electoral constraints, ideological commitments, and the democratic capacities of religious parties in Israel and Turkey. *Political Research Quarterly, 65,* 467–485. doi:10.1177/1065912911434473.

Tezcür, G.M. (2010). *Muslim reformers in Iran and Turkey: The paradox of moderation.* Austin, TX: University of Texas Press.

Tipps, D. (1973). Modernization theory and the comparative study of societies: A critical perspective. *Comparative Studies in Society and History, 15,* 199–226. doi:10.1017/s0010417500007039.

Turam, B. (2007). *Between Islam and the state: The politics of engagement.* Stanford, CA: Stanford University Press.

Warner, M. (2005). *Publics and counterpublics.* Cambridge, MA: Zone Books of MIT Press.

Wedeen, L. (2008). *Peripheral visions: Publics, power, and performance in Yemen.* Chicago, IL: University of Chicago Press.

White, J. (1999). Amplifying trust: Community and communication in Turkey. In D. Eickelman & J. Anderson (Eds.), *New media in the Muslim world: The emerging public sphere.* Bloomington, IN: Indiana University Press.

Wickham, C.R. (2004). The path to moderation: Strategy and learning in the formation of Egypt's Wasat party. *Comparative Politics, 36,* 205–228. doi:10.2307/4150143.

Young, I.M. (2001). Activist challenges to deliberative democracy. *Political Theory, 29,* 670–690. doi:10.1177/0090591701029005004.

CHAPTER 7

The Dilemma of Postcolonial and/or Orientalist Feminism in Iranian Diasporic Advocacy of Women's Rights in the Homeland

Mahmoud Arghavan

Introduction

Masih Alinejad, an Iranian U.S.-based journalist and women's rights activist launched a campaign on May 3, 2014 against compulsory hijab in Iran called My Stealthy Freedom. The campaign was initiated when she posted a photo of herself on her Facebook page. The photo was taken on a street in the U.K., where she used to live at the time, with wind blowing in her bushy hair. The Iranian women from inside Iran, who have been subjected to compulsory *hijab* for 38 years now, reacted to Alinejad's photo with various feelings of envy for her freedom, fury for the Islamic Republic's law, and enthusiasm to express their discontent with the current compulsory hijab in Iran. Thus, Alinejad, being aware of dual lives of the Iranian women who do not believe in the Islamic veil but are forced to submit to it in public, because otherwise they will be penalized, asked her followers on Facebook to use their stealthy freedom and send her their unveiled photos. She called it Stealthy Freedom because, according to the Islamic Republic's law, the Iranian women are not free to appear in public without hijab. However, they can and would remove the veil once they are somewhere beyond the borders of the realm of the Islamic law, such as in their private sphere or in the heart of nature. The campaign by now has won over one million followers.

Not only because of this campaign and her advocacy of the Iranian women's rights to wear or not to wear hijab, but also because of covering political issues, social problems, and cases of human rights violations in Iran, Alinejad was awarded the 2015 Women's Rights Award by the Geneva Summit for Human Rights and Democracy.

The Stealthy Freedom campaign received different reactions from various parties who concerned themselves with the issue of women's rights in the Middle East. Liberal feminists have praised Alinejad's campaign because from their perspective the Islamic veil represents the most tangible case of oppression of women in Muslim majority societies and women's liberation in these societies should and could begin with refusing the compulsory hijab. However, postcolonial feminists critiqued the campaign because it incites the old 'Orientalist cultural imaginary' in the West, which was built upon the tropes of the oppressed women in the Orient who must be liberated through adaptation of the Western values. In addition, Islamic feminists received this campaign as reinforcing the new wave of Islamophobia in Europe and the United States, which represents Islam as a misogynist religion.

In the speech that she gave for receiving the Women's Rights Award, Masih Alinejad countered her critics, who charged her campaign of provoking Islamophobic sentiments in the West, catering to the Western value system, and neglecting the gender complexities of the Muslim majority societies. She argued that in the West, because of the terrorist attacks, Islamophobia, Donald Trump's campaign in the United States, and other nationalist anti-immigrant movements, people rightfully defend Muslim people's rights as a minority in the West. But they totally ignore the Iranian women's struggle with compulsory hijab.[1] She calls into question the Western female politicians' integrity because they travel to Iran and wear the compulsory hijab without challenging the Islamic Republic for forcing them and Iranian women to veil their hair (Alinejad, 2015).[2] She called these politicians hypocrites because they spoke out against the Burkini Ban in France as a case of violation of religious freedom but fail to support the Iranian women in their campaign against the compulsory hijab.

She responds to four arguments that the Western female politicians have made for not challenging the compulsory hijab. According to Alinejad, Western female politicians have argued that "compulsory hijab is required by law in Iran and we have to respect the law." She responds that "Burkini Ban was a law in France, slavery used to be legal and so on. We have to protest against the bad law and alter it into a respectable law" (ibid.). The second argument has been that "hijab is a cultural issue and we want to respect the Iranian culture." Alinejad responded that "here we're talking about compulsion that is by no means any part of our culture. How could forcing a 7-year-old girl to wear hijab be a cultural issue?" (ibid.). The third argument is that "compulsory hijab is a domestic issue and an internal matter." Alinejad counters this argument by

1 https://www.youtube.com/watch?v=DCgysXS_zEo.
https://www.youtube.com/watch?v=OeYo3WCKbgA.
http://mystealthyfreedom.net/en/.

2 In the latest case, on Feb. 11, 2017, Sweden's Prime Minister, Stefan Löfven, led a Swedish delegation to Iran. He was criticized back home by Swedish feminists, because the female officials of the delegations including Ann Linde, Sweden's minister for European Union affairs and trade, conformed to the compulsory hijab rule in Iran and put on headscarves in Iran.

saying that "Islamic Republic forces all women who want to travel to Iran to wear hijab. Even Iranian women outside Iran have to wear hijab if they want to go to an Iranian embassy anywhere in the world. Moreover, burkini ban was a domestic matter in France. But we all protested against it" (ibid.). Finally, the European female politicians have argued that "the Middle East has got bigger problems than compulsory hijab." Alinejad contended that

> I know that by heart. I was expelled from Iran because I, as a journalist, was investigating bigger problems in Iran. I was the one who was wearing compulsory hijab in Iran because I wanted to address the bigger problems such as corruption in the political system. I was the one who exposed the voices of 57 individuals who were killed in the peaceful demonstrations in 2009 in Iran. Also, who said that compulsory hijab is not a big issue. Fighting against it is not a fight against a piece of cloth. We are fighting for human dignity. Our identity. Because from the age of 7 once we wanted to leave the house we had to be someone else.... While the Islamic Republic would deport you from the airport if you do not wear hijab, you will not be able to fix bigger problems in Iran because of this simple issue. (Ibid.)

Being conscious about her critical position, Alinejad concludes her talk by declaring that:

> I never called the western politicians to come and rescue Iranian women. Iranian women are strong enough to free themselves. I call the western female politicians hypocrite because they stood up with French Muslim women and condemned burkini ban but they travel to Iran, put on hijab, smile and call it a cultural issue. Compulsory hijab is the most visible symbol of oppression and we have to stand all together and bring this wall down.[3]

Alinejad claims authenticity by reminding her audience the fact that she grew up under the Islamic law in Iran, therefore, she has the authority to 'speak of' the voiceless women in her country of origin. Nevertheless, the controversy around the Stealthy Freedom Campaign has added up to the ongoing discourse around the orientalist representations of Muslim women, Islam, and the

---

3 According to Alinejad: "Last year, the Islamic Republic morality police warned 3.6 million Iranian women because of their inappropriate hijab and arrested 18 thousands of them. If this is a simple issue, why the Islamic republic spends some millions dollars a year to keep this wall. To me hijab is a wall and we need all to stand together and bring the wall down."

Middle East not only by the Western media, also by the writers and journalists such as Middle Eastern diaspora writers who come originally from the Middle East but reside in the West or particularly in the United States. The Orientalist representations of the Middle Eastern women in the West and the postcolonial critique of this imperialist politics, ever since 9/11, has been a major ground for postcolonialist critics to confront the neo-conservative supporters of U.S. imperialist 'War on Terror' in Afghanistan and Iraq.

In this chapter, we will study the theoretical confrontation that has occurred between Iranian postcolonial intellectuals in the American academy and Iranian American diaspora writers in relation to their representations of Iran, particularly their representations of Iranian women. This theoretical battle escalated as the U.S.–Israeli alliance began talking publicly about a strike on Iranian nuclear plants in order to prevent this country's controversial nuclear program from advancing any further. In this global context, Iran was represented as an evil regime in pursuit of a nuclear bomb and therefore as a direct threat to global peace and security. This discourse aimed at persuading American public opinion, as well as global public opinion, of the necessity of another military intervention in the Middle East. This, in turn, led Iranian academics in the United States and around the world to campaign against a war with Iran.

The postcolonial enlightened critiques that revealed the Bush administration's appropriation of Middle Eastern women's rights in its War on Terror for propaganda purposes have been discussed at length. This chapter is concerned with reemergence of another example of what Lowe (1991) has conceptualized as "Postcolonial Orientalism" through discursive challenges between the two discourses of Orientalism and the postcolonial critique of U.S. imperialist politics. It is worth stressing that our criticism of some postcolonial critics' arguments should not be read as a criticism of postcolonialism per se. The legitimacy of the postcolonial critic who strives to bring attention and disgrace to U.S. neocolonialist policies in the Middle East is unquestionable. Rather, some postcolonial critics' reproduction of a binary opposition between Orient and Occident in their battle against Western representations of Middle Eastern societies, and thus, their reproduction of the very logic underlying the discourses they seek to critique, is the matter in question. The notion of the Middle East or Islam as an Other to the West has taken shape within a conflict between Orientalist and postcolonialist discourses that challenge each other to represent it more accurately according to their discursive vantage points. Portraying the Orient not as a self-sufficient entity, but always as it corresponds to Western representations of it, exemplifies a situation that Lowe (1991) first called in *Critical Terrains: French and British Orientalisms* "Postcolonial Orientalism" while explaining French intellectuals' portrayals of Maoist China in the 1960s.

Postcolonial Orientalism

Edward Said's (1979) *Orientalism* explicates the idea that longstanding representations of the East by European travelers, writers, artists, missionaries, and academics have constructed a sense of superiority of the Occident over the Orient. This portrayal has aided the dominion of Europeans over the people of the East. Said conceptualizes this "Orientalism" as

> a style of thought based upon an ontological and epistemological distinction made between "the Orient" and (most of the time) "the Occident." … Orientalism can be discussed and analyzed as the corporate institution for dealing with the Orient—dealing with it by making statements about it, authorizing views of it, describing it, by teaching it, settling it, ruling over it: in short, Orientalism as a Western style for dominating, restructuring, and having authority over the Orient.
>
> SAID, 1979, pp. 2–3

Among other constructed contrasts between West and East, the Orientalist imagination of women in harems and the purported exoticism of the veiled women of the Islamic world have been consistently used to draw lines of separation between Occident and Orient. Middle Eastern women have been subjected to a long tradition of Orientalist representations. Thus Said's (1979) noble perspective has been highly influential in forming new debates centered on the issue of women in the Middle East. The publication of Said's *Orientalism* inspired a new postcolonialist approach within the discourses of feminism, women's studies, and gender studies related to Middle Eastern and third-world women. In this sense, the Middle Eastern woman's rights as a "multivalent signifier" (Lowe, 1991, p. 136) have been constructed within this intersection of plural discourses that are actively engaged with this topic, such as Orientalism, postcolonialism, and feminism. Postcolonial critics with a Middle Eastern background adopted a new position which aimed at revealing the gendered complexities of the real lives of Middle Eastern women. In responding to generalized portrayals of Middle Eastern women as 'passive, silent, and oppressed,' many of these scholars have attempted to explain how 'active, practical, powerful, and resourceful' Middle Eastern women actually are or to suggest that gender relations in the Middle East are simply much more complex than they are often portrayed (Lowe, 1991). Some scholars have strived to de-essentialize the rigid connection between Islamic law and patriarchy, in addition to demonstrating the local strategies and resources that lower-class Middle Eastern women use to empower themselves in work and marriage.

Abu-Lughod et al. (2001) summarize the four ways that Said's (1979) work has impacted Middle East women's studies:

> First, Orientalism opened up the possibility for others to go further than Said had in exploring the gender and sexuality of Orientalist discourse itself. Second, the book provided a strong rationale for the burgeoning historical and anthropological re-search that claimed to be going beyond stereotypes of the Muslim or Middle Eastern woman and gender relations in general. Third, the historical recovery of feminism in the Middle East, emerging from this new abundance of research has, in turn, stimulated a reexamination of that central issue in Orientalism: East/West politics. Finally, Said's stance, that one cannot divorce political engagement from scholarship, has presented Middle East gender studies and debates about feminism with some especially knotty problems, highlighting the peculiar ways that feminist critique is situated in a global context.
>
> ABU-LUGHOD ET AL., 2001, p. 101

In a similar vein, Deniz Kandiyoti (1996) argues in *Engendering Middle East Studies* that the field of Middle East gender studies has been negatively affected by the arguments of Orientalism in three ways: social analysis has been devalued in favor of analysis of representations; binary thinking about East and West has trained us to focus too much on the West and not enough on the internal heterogeneity of Middle Eastern societies; and, finally, it has also deflected attention away from "local institutions and cultural processes that are implicated in the production of gender hierarchies and in forms of subordination based on gender" (p. 18). Thus, she calls for "the necessity of internal critique of gendered power in Middle Eastern societies" (Kandiyoti, 1996, p. 18).

Observing this problematic situation, Lowe (1991) argues against "totalizing orientalism as a monolithic, developmental discourse that uniformly constructs the Orient as the Other of the Occident" (p. 4). Rather, Lowe suggests "a conception of orientalism as heterogeneous and contradictory" (p. 5). She continues: "[T]o this end I observe, on the one hand, that orientalism consists of an uneven matrix of orientalist situations across different cultural and historical sites, and on the other, that each of these orientalisms is internally complex and unstable" (p. 5). She also argues

> strongly for the heterogeneity of the orientalist object, whose contradictions and lack of fixity mark precisely the moments of instability in the discourse; although orientalism may represent its objects as fixed or stable, contradictions and non-correspondences in the discursive

> situation ultimately divulge the multivalence and indeterminability of those fictions.
>
> LOWE, 1991, p. x

As Lowe (1991) states: "The discourse of orientalism is never independent of the contiguous discourses that figure otherness" (p. 136). According to Lowe: "Orientalism must be understood as but one discourse in this complex intersection" (p. 137). Postcolonialism is one of the discourses that is 'bound' to Orientalism and operates actively in contradicting and criticizing its 'ruling figurations.'

According to Lowe (1991):

> the figuration of the Chinese Cultural Revolution and the People's Republic of China by French intellectuals during the early 1970s in Julia Kristeva's *Des chinoises* (1974), Roland Barthes's *Alors la Chine?* (1975), and the avant-garde theoretical journal *Tel quell* (1968–1974) (p. 13)

demonstrates a recent form of Orientalism. As Lowe affirms, "an assortment of discourses" created the "multivalent signifier of China" and circulated it in response to "urgent quests emerging from the social circumstances and discursive formations" of Paris in the 1960s and 1970s:

> In this sense the postcolonial discourse about China appropriated certain orientalist tropes in order to criticize the state apparatus of which the earlier colonialist orientalism was a product. Opposed to, yet in a dialogic relation with, traditional orientalism, this postcolonial form of orientalism departed from, yet was determined by, the discursive conditions of the previous orientalism. (p. 138)

Lowe's (1991) observations on the vision of French leftist intellectuals, such as Kristeva and Barthes, and their writings on the Maoist revolution in China and the subsequent cultural revolution indicate something of a preponderance among the French intellectuals of the 1960s and 1970s to search for, and construct, an Other in relation to Western democracies and modern societies. Lowe states that

> the embrace of Maoism by the theorists of the journal *Tel quell* in 1971, in which communist China is figured as the revolutionary Other of western society and western Marxist theory, occurs at the nexus of orientalism and the discourses of the French Left after 1968. (p. 137)

Lowe stresses the political disappointment of some French leftist intellectuals in the post-war era and during the 1970s as a reason for praising the cultural revolution in China as an alternative to Western liberal democracy. Although Kristeva's and Barthes' representations of China served their critiques of nationalist ideologies supported by earlier Orientalists, their figurations of the Orient utilized some of the very same terms, postures, and rhetoric employed in earlier texts.

What is absent from Lowe's (1991) observation of a postcolonial Orientalist construction of an Other to Western civilizations and societies by French intellectuals is Michel Foucault's analysis of the 1978 political crisis in Iran and the subsequent revolution in 1979. Although Said's (1979) *Orientalism* is indebted to Foucault's notion of the "power-knowledge" nexus, it seems Foucault's criticism of European modernist philosophy and "modern Western subjectivity" misguided himself to some extent in his interpretation of the events of 1978–1979 in Iran. Foucault's thoughts on the eruption of politico-religious opposition protests in Iran in 1978 appeared in an interview entitled *"L'Esprit d'un monde sans esprit,"* which was published in Claire Briere's and Pierre Blanchat's *Iran: La Revolution au nom de Dieu* in 1979. As Rosemarie Scullion (1995) in "Michel Foucault the Orientalist: On Revolutionary Iran and the 'Spirit of Islam'" reports:

> In this interview and numerous other writings on the subject, Foucault extolled the virtues of Iran's revolutionary "spirit," remaining, I shall argue, singularly uncritical in his appraisal of the emancipatory potential and of the new subjectivity it was to bestow upon the Iranian people. (p. 16)

In many of his writings and interviews on the topic of Iran, from the fall of 1978 to the spring of 1979, Foucault's Western intellectual perspective on Iran produced an Orientalist discourse wherein an Islamic spirit of the Revolution was to introduce a noble subjectivity to the people, who were unsatisfied with the modernization agenda of the Shah. In other words, Foucault's excitement about seeing his critique of Western modernity actualized in Iran, with a religious driving force behind it, left him blind to all the reactionary trajectories the revolutionary upheaval encompassed, particularly for women and ethno-religious minorities. Foucault's postmodern philosophy, which challenges the idea of Western-style industrialization as a universal imperative, led him to endorse anti-Shah demonstrations, regardless of the alternative to the Shah's modernist regime. According to Scullion (1995):

> In classic Orientalist form, in relating the high drama of Iran's revolutionary moment, Foucault fails to take into account crucial social and

> historical circumstances that contributed decisively to generating the mass revolt, performing, I would argue, a reading of the event that is more revealing of his own post-humanist political desires and anti-authoritarian reflexes than of the movement's complexities, contradictions, and, most importantly, of its potential eventualities. (p. 18)

Foucault's thesis, presented originally in the 1979 interview entitled "Iran: A Spirit of a World without Spirit," suggested that Iran's revolutionary movement was the expression of a transcendent, collective effort to re-inject "spirit" into "a world without spirit" (Foucault, 2005). Nonetheless, as Scullion (1995) states:

> In order to sustain the argument that the Ayatollah Khomeini was the 'mythic head of the revolt' which had a glorious vision of a wholly new form of politico-spiritual democratization and emancipation from Western values and domination, Foucault would have had to go through considerable analytical contortions to explain why the Islamic hierocracy had in fact supported the Shah and his illegitimate 1953 return to power on the wings of Anglo-American intervention, and participated in the destabilization of Mossadegh's government. (p. 28)

Thus, in Foucault's argument, Iran figured as an Other to the Western representation of the Middle East. The dichotomy of colonizer–colonized, or capitalist–communist, united many leftist political parties in their support of the Islamists during the 1979 revolution in Iran, which sought to overthrow the Shah, who was seen as the 'West's puppet' and installed in power by the CIA. Moreover, the anti-American feature of the Islamic Republic, or anti-Islamic Republic politics of the American Empire, employs a fabricated image of Iran as an Other in relation to American representations of the Middle East. Thus, the postmodern project of Foucault, Kristeva, and Barthes, in searching for an alternative to Western modernity, brought them to explore non-Western revolutionary societies such as China and Islamic Iran. Their construction of these 'Oriental' societies as Others in relation to Western civilization, refashioned the Orientalist approach, but from a postmodern leftist perspective, which Lowe (1991) calls "Postcolonial Orientalism."

If the anti-colonial liberation movements of the 1960s and 1970s in Africa, Asia, and South America generated a revolutionary excitement where some 'postcolonial Orientalists' endorsed the Cultural Revolution in China and the 1979 revolution in Iran, the post-9/11 era of the 'War on Terror' and the U.S. wars in Afghanistan and Iraq renewed the discursive challenge between neo-Orientalists and postcolonial critics of the U.S. empire.

The extensive discussion around Azar Nafisi's controversial 2003 memoir *Reading Lolita in Tehran* illuminates the contrast between these two discourses. It is worth noting the connection between the time of publication of *Reading Lolita in Tehran* in 2003 and the storm of criticism that targeted this book and other books by Iranian diaspora writers at the same time. Nafisi published her memoir in a hostile atmosphere that neoconservatives had generated against the Islamic Republic of Iran over its nuclear program. Neoconservatives supported Nafisi's book and other voices which purported to disclose the viciousness of the Islamic regime against its own people in order to legitimize a potential strike against Iran under the guise of preventing an outrageous Islamic regime from possessing nuclear weapons. It is no wonder that such discursive formations at the time of the 'War on Terror' required an appropriate response from postcolonial intellectuals such as Hamid Dabashi (2006a, 2006b, 2011) and Ali Behdad (2008). The issue of Iranian women's rights became a major point of controversy between neoconservatives' and postcolonial critics' discourses, who had constantly been striving to raise support for their respective arguments regarding U.S. attitudes toward the Middle East, particularly Iran. However, some critiques of the prominent Orientalist perspective that Nafisi conveyed in her book in effect legitimized the politics of the Islamic Republic.

It seems that these critics were unable to simultaneously criticize an imperial power and an Islamic regime, which both in one way or another oppressed women and violated their human rights. Dabashi's may be the only work which, in a Saidian manner, ties critiquing Nafisi's selective memory politics in recollecting the past of a nation to criticizing the Islamic Republic's oppressive gender politics. Other Iranian academics at American universities, such as Ali Behdad (2008), Roksana Bahramitash (2005, 2007), Mitra Rastegar (2006), and Parvin Paidar (1995), in their criticism of *Reading Lolita in Tehran*, however, barely point out the repressed conditions women face under the Islamic Republic.

Moreover, in negating Nafisi's (2003) claim that during the Shah's era Iranian women enjoyed the same rights that European women had at the time, some of these critics, such as Bahramitash, include statistics from international studies conducted in developing countries to show that Iranian women have made greater gains since the Islamic Revolution in 1979 in comparison to their position in the pre-revolutionary era. Using this type of comparison—which is not acceptable according to the research methods in social sciences—these critics have created a distorted picture of women's lives in Iran and their place within the Islamic Republic's politics; they thereby engaged in the logic of Orientalism, because they attempted to create an image of the Orient as an

Other in relation to the Occident. This Other had to contradict the West's image of Middle Eastern women. Because the picture they painted needed to be coherent, they may have felt the necessity to cover up shortcomings in the daily lives of Middle Eastern women. This picture of the Other is a picture of an 'Oriental' woman who has the agency to find local resolutions in order to realize her rights. Some Iranian critics of Nafisi's memoir charge her with portraying Iranian women and girls as incapable of leading independent and free lives due to wearing the veil and being limited by many other elements of Islamic law.

In contrast to this image, postcolonial critics introduced a picture of an Iranian woman who has strived to reach the higher ranks of professional life and lead a happy private life at the same time. Their argument appropriates the fact that young women constitute 60% of university students in Iran, in addition to Iranian women athletes who participate in many international competitions. They also point out that Iranian women can serve their country as government ministers or nominate themselves for parliament.

All of these theoretical endeavors, and their somewhat incomplete depiction by postcolonialists, are supposed to contradict the neoconservative representation of Middle Eastern women and convey that Iranian women do not need American marines to gain equal civil rights. Bearing in mind the legitimacy of this theoretical struggle, this line of argumentation betrays a thinking in binary oppositions, where negating one position necessarily entails endorsing the other. According to this logic, critiquing the politics of the Islamic Republic means confirming the neoconservatives' perspective, and critiquing the neoconservatives is tantamount to endorsing the Islamic Republic's politics.

Therefore, the theoretical strategies of anti-imperialist rhetoric, which asserts the value of self-determination for Middle Eastern women, result in reproducing the same Orient–Occident binary. The discourse of Islamic feminism or postcolonial feminism, in searching for an alternative to Western feminism, may find Iranian women as an 'object of desire' who refute the essential relationship between Islam and women's repression. Iranian women, these discourses point out, are Middle Eastern Muslims who can be elected to parliament, can compete in the Olympic games, and can perform various social roles due to their advancement in higher education. The big challenge for neo-Orientalists and their postcolonial critics centers on producing a 'regime of truth,' which should dominate the discourse on Iran. However, as Abu-Lughod et al. (2001) put it, "as long as we are writing for the West about 'the other,' we are implicated in projects that establish Western authority and cultural difference" (p. 105).

Authority and Authenticity

As Kandiyoti (1996) argues, a confrontation centering on the representation of the real world in the media could well become a prominent characteristic of the post-Orientalist era. Thus, the question of the authority and authenticity of the representing powers have turned into a determining factor. In contrast to the former monologue of the imperial powers in representing the Oriental colonies, in the postcolonial era the multiplicity of intersectional subversive voices of the anti-colonial forces have been engaged in forming their own discourse. Thus, native writers, scholars, and local media have claimed the authority to represent themselves, in contrast with depictions produced by mainstream media outlets. In this politicized climate, the positionality of the author or academic plays a significant role in generating approval or disapproval for their arguments. The literary works and scholarly books written in English by writers from the Middle East have emerged in response to this need for self-representation. In this sense, the Iranian-American writers and their academic critics from the community of the Iranian diaspora have positioned themselves in order to authentically represent their homeland. As Lowe (1991) is most concerned about China, or Said (1979) about Palestine, Behdad, Dabashi, and other Iranian scholars in the United States are obsessed with Iran. While observing Chinese intellectuals in the United States, Chow (2003) said that it is the "lures of diaspora" that create a feeling of responsibility to correct the image of their homeland in the West.

The Iranian American writers have either themselves claimed authenticity or have been accepted by their readers as authentic voices from inside an Islamic Iran. However, Behdad, Dabashi, and other critics of Iranian diaspora literature have negated the authenticity of Iranian-American writers' portrayal of Iran. Dwelling very far away from the reality of everyday life in Iran, Iranian diaspora intellectuals' academic analyses of the situation in Iran oppose the accounts of Anglophone Iranian writers and journalists residing in the United States. If these authors have to rely on their imaginations and memories, diaspora scholars can only invest in existing data and gather their information through media reports, images, and videos coming out of the country. Although the internet and social media have facilitated the spread of information, being in the field is still an invaluable source of accuracy. The ambivalence of dual belonging, to the homeland and to the host country, or the state of not belonging to either of the two, have, in the case of Iran and the United States, complicated the situation significantly.

In his article "Critical Historicism," Behdad (2008) proclaims that the aim of his project was to teach his students about the historical roots of post-9/11

Islamophobia and American hostility toward Middle Easterners; he presents an historical analysis of the formation of Orientalism since the late 18th century through European travelers' and artists' works about the Orient. Thus, he argues, 9/11 and its aftermath should be positioned "not as an exception, but rather as an occasion for exploring longstanding social and cultural tropes surrounding questions of nation, immigration, and belonging that have circulated in the collective imaginary of this country since the founding" (Behdad, 2008, p. 2). Behdad opens his article with an anecdote from his lived experience as a freshly arrived high school student in the United States. His arrival coincided with the Hostage Crisis of 1980 that made him, and other Iranian students, subject to tracking and investigation by the Immigration and Naturalization Service, which had required them to "report to ad hoc security centers to be interviewed, photographed, and fingerprinted" (Behdad, 2008, p. 1).

As a part of his project, Behdad (2008) calls on his colleagues to

> pay attention to forms of neo-Orientalism in the U.S. and Western Europe that have emerged since the Iranian revolution—forms which certainly are indebted to past representations, but which have distinctive features. Often deployed and perpetuated by Middle Eastern subjects who act as native informants—e.g., Azar Nafisi in *Reading Lolita in Tehran: A Memoir in Books* (2003) or Roya Hakakian in *Journey from the Land of No: A Girlhood Caught in Revolutionary Iran* (2004). (p. 8)

Behdad attempts to vilify Iranian American writers as neo-Orientalist. He states that they

> transform, for example, the trope of the veil and the figure of despot into discursive sites upon which to stake a-historical claims, readily appropriated by Western liberals and neo-conservatives alike, about the incommensurability of Islam with democracy, while cementing the connection in the popular imagination between Moslem identity, and the forces of fanaticism, oppression, and terror. (2008, p. 8).

Behdad (2008) refers to Dabashi's (2006b) description of Nafisi as a "native informant" who confirms "the Orientalist perception of the Middle East through a narrative that not only overlooks the rich literary tradition of Iran but also obscures the complex political and cultural history of the country" (p. 11). Dabashi argues that Nafisi acts as a comprador native intellectual whose task is "to feign authority, authenticity, and native knowledge by informing the American public of the atrocities taking place in the region of their birth, thereby justifying the imperial designs of the United States as a liberation" (2011, pp. 72–73).

Nevertheless, Behdad's (2008) reference to Dabashi is surprisingly selective. Because, unlike Behdad, who never criticizes the Islamic Republic's interior politics, Dabashi (2011) attempts to position himself as an irreconcilable critic of both American imperialist politics in the region and the Islamic Republic's interior gender policies that repress Iranian women. Although he also critiques memoirists of Islamic background, best represented by Nafisi's *Reading Lolita in Tehran* (2003), as authors recruited by U.S. institutions to cultivate world public opinion in favor of "the U.S. global warmongering" politics, he recognizes "concerns about the plight of Muslim women in the Islamic world" (Dabashi, 2011, p. 69) as a legitimate cause. From Dabashi's (2011) vantage point, *Reading Lolita in Tehran* "exemplifies the systematic abuse of legitimate causes (in this case the unconscionable oppression of women living under Muslim laws) for illegitimate purposes" (p. 70), such as a representation of the Orient designed to justify U.S. military hegemony.

Dabashi (2011) argues that Nafisi has transmuted from "a legitimate critic of the Islamic Republic into an ideologue for George W. Bush's empire-building" (p. 70). According to him, Nafisi's case "provides a crucial lesson in the way the new breed of comprador intellectuals and native informers is being recruited and put to use in the ideological build-up (and the cultural foregrounding) of an otherwise precarious claim to imperial hegemony" (Dabashi, 2011, p. 70). Dabashi clarifies his position with the following statements:

> Criticizing the calamity of the Islamic Republic—and recognizing the heroism of a nation that first invested its hope in it and now is fighting it to the bitter end—is a legitimate and even urgent project. But shamelessly joining the neoconservative takeover of the democratic institutions of the United States by helping to build a literary canon for a predatory empire is an entirely different matter. The former restores dignity and hope to a nation and its national resistance to imperial domination; the latter seeks to steal such dignity and hope. Generations of Iranian women—political activists, avant-garde writers, pioneering poets, creative artists, and celebrated filmmakers—have put up a heroic resistance to the brutalities of their domestic patriarchy and the obscenities of the colonial gaze. Nafisi is not among them; she has betrayed them. From Tahereh Qorrat al-Ayn in the nineteenth century to Mehrangiz Kar in the twenty-first, Iranian woman have demanded and exacted their democratic rights and shown noble aspirations to freedom. The function of *Reading Lolita*

> *in Tehran* is to obliterate that empowering memory and make it subservient to American empire. (2011, pp. 77–78)
>
> The Islamic Republic of Iran has an atrocious record of stifling, silencing, and murdering oppositional intellectuals. But the function of the comprador intellectual is less to expose such atrocities than to package them in a manner that best serves the empire they help to sustain. Under the guise of legitimate criticism they effectively perpetuate (indeed aggravate) the domestic terror they purport to expose. Plotting the enemy in a narrative of demonization and de-narrating a nation from its historical claim to authority both pave the way for the advance of the colonial combat battalion. (2011, p. 73)

Behdad (2008) accuses Hakakian (2004) of romanticizing pre-revolutionary Iran and misguiding the reader about life there. Accordingly, he says that Nafisi (2003) had distorted the historical facts by claiming that "When I was growing up, in the 1960s, there was little difference between my rights and the rights of women in Western democracies" (p. 261). As Behdad argues:

> None, however, entertains the idea that the quality of life has indeed become better in at least certain respects for many rural and working class Iranians after the revolution. In addition, the neo-Orientalists either repress or turn a blind eye to some of the important changes which have occurred since the revolution. (2008, p. 8)

He cites Bahramitash's 2005 article on "The War on Terror, Feminist Orientalism and Orientalist Feminism: Case Studies of Two North American Bestsellers," as proof of developments in post-revolutionary Iran. In said article, Bahramitash reported that according to data from the World Development Indicator:

> infant mortality dropped from 131.20 in 1975 to 25.50 in 1999; life expectancy at birth increased from 49 for men and women in 1960 to 70 for men and 72 for women by 1999; and the illiteracy rate for young women declined considerably, from over 55 percent in 1970 to 8.7 percent by 1999. (p. 233)

Regardless of how methodically wrong it is to conclude from these statistics that the Islamic Republic has achieved greater social development in Iran than the Pahlavi dynasty, this usage of statistics as detached from a historical and local context follows the logic of Orientalism. The Orientalist or neo-Orientalist representations of the Middle East and Iran have exaggerated some aspects of reality, such as misogyny, patriarchy, or extremism, while ignoring other aspects that may not fit in with their own agenda. Ignoring all the atrocities that the Islamic Republic has committed since the 1979 revolution—executing political dissidents, violating ethno-religious rights, systematic repression of women's rights—is a larger ethical flaw. Behdad may believe that his ethical mission is "to draw attention to the ways in which neo-Orientalists disavow certain historical facts in their narratives which purport to be authentic and objective representations of the Middle East" (Behdad & Williams, 2010, p. 291). However, his silence about one part of the truth in order to prove the other demonstrates the same illogicality in which neo-Orientalist authors have become mired. It is not an effective substitute for a full and unbiased approach to simply say, "Our intent here emphatically is not to offer a defense of or an apology for the policies of the Islamic government of Iran, but rather..." (Behdad & Williams, 2010, p. 291). Let us assume for a moment that Behdad's argument about all the positive developments in post-revolutionary Iran is true, then what, one might wonder, caused the mass migration of Iranians after the Revolution that eventually formed the Iranian diaspora and Iranian American literature? If Iran after the Revolution is a better place to live, why do 150,000 educated Iranians annually decide to go through all the trials of emigration? It seems it would undermine his argument significantly if Behdad admitted the fact that the Islamic Revolution generated a backlash against women's rights and potentially reduced human rights.

Behdad fails to entertain the idea that many of the recollected stories in this so-called neo-Orientalist literature, such as executions of political prisoners, cultural revolutions in the universities, and the political oppression of ethno-religious minorities in post-revolutionary Iran, recall some of the historically recorded brutalities committed by the Islamic Republic. No imperial power had explicitly sponsored or plotted the Revolution and its subsequent oppressive system.

However, acknowledging the fact that the Islamist revolutionaries established the Islamic Republic of Iran based upon the physical and political elimination of other numerous political parties that had collaborated to overthrow the Shah's system would weaken Behdad's campaign against the empire. One tangible example could be the 'cultural revolution' in Iran during the years 1980–1983, which shut down the universities for 3 years. Although it changed the lives of many Iranian academics and university students dramatically, Behdad (2008) does not include it in his thesis on 'critical historicism' apparently because a 'neo-Orientalist' figure such as Nafisi had criticized it. Thus, real historical events in the nation's past have been dismissed in a battle over media representations because they are represented in historical novels and memoirs that are discursively positioned as 'neo-Orientalist.'

Tahmineh Milani, an Iranian feminist filmmaker and writer, depicted the consequences of the 'cultural revolution' for Iranian university students in one of her films, *The Hidden Half* (Nimeh-ye Penhan; نیمه پنهان), in 2001. Milani had to spend 8 days in custody when her film was screened in Iran due to charges such as acting against national security and disturbing the public opinion through spreading lies. Despite recollecting similar stories to those Nafisi and Hakakian narrated in their memoirs, Milani's account of the 'cultural revolution' was never branded as 'neo-Orientalist,' thanks to her subject position as an Iranian feminist voice from inside Iran. Undoubtedly Nafisi's account draws on some Orientalist tropes in narrating her account of her homeland, probably to attract a wider audience. However, Behdad's advancing his argument at the expense of his silence about a dark period of the recent history of Iran is equally questionable.

In her attempt to portray Nafisi as a 'neo-Orientalist' whose experience fails to represent the experience of all Iranian women, and in order to respond to Nafisi's criticisms of the consequences of the 1979 revolution in Iran, Bahramitash (2005) distorts historical facts. She not only fails to mention the infamous 'cultural revolution in Iran' and the irreversible damage to the Iranian academy and subsequent loss of enormous numbers of students and professors accused of being 'liberal,' 'communist,' or 'anti-revolutionaries,' but her ideological commitment to defying the 'neo-Orientalists' leads her to transform the 'cultural revolution' into an opportunity for "many middle-class urban women, including many feminists to join programs that empowered women, such as the mass-based literacy program" (Bahramitash, 2005, p. 233). This misrepresentation of an historical event that influenced the lives of many Iranian men and women in one way or another and spread Iranian educated elites around the world may serve her discursive aim in constructing an 'Other' to the 'Orientalist' account of Iran. Nevertheless, it neither helps the Iranian women who still suffer from inequalities at a different level, nor is it morally acceptable to voice one part of reality and silence the other parts in order to advance a morally legitimate 'anti-imperialist' criticism. This constitutes 'postcolonial Orientalism,' which in its self-assigned mission to construct an 'Other' to the 'Orientalist account,' simply produces another 'Other' to the West, which is just as inaccurate.

Bahramitash's (2005, 2007) argument about the empowerment of Iranian women relies on recent statistics about women's enrollment in Iranian institutions of higher education and the presence of the winner of the Noble Peace Prize, Shirin Ebadi. She contradicts Nafisi's (2003) account of Iranian male-dominated universities by showing that, according to the official data, 60%

of Iranian university students are female. Undoubtedly, Iranian women have made significant progress against, and shown great resistance toward, the patriarchal system. However, using this data to prove that the Islamic Revolution and the Islamic Republic have been beneficial for women is unsound; rather, Iranian women have succeeded in making progress *despite* all the systematic obstacles that the Islamic system legalized after the 1979 revolution. In a similar fashion, mentioning Shirin Ebadi, the globally known Iranian women's rights and human rights lawyer and winner of the 2003 Nobel Peace Prize, as the most striking example of women's rights activism (Bahramitash, 2005) is self-contradictory and not in itself a sufficient argument.

It is critically important to remember that any progress Iranian women's rights have made after the backlash in 1979, and despite the Islamic Republic's misogynistic policies in Iran since the 1979 revolution, have been achieved as a precious result of numerous known and unknown feminist activists who devoted their lives to this cause. Ebadi is only one of many Iranian women whose resistance against gender discrimination in Iran has been recognized globally. How ironic would it be to name Ebadi's winning the Nobel Peace Prize in 2003, which she received thanks to her lifelong campaign for Iranian women's rights, as a sign of the successes of Iranian women under the rule of the Islamic Republic? A similarly absurd example would be to relate the success of the Iranian filmmaker Asghar Farhadi in winning the Academy Award in 2013 to the Islamic Republic's progressive cultural politics.

While Bahramitash's (2005, 2007) picture of Iran is more realistic, she still uses the same jargon as Behdad (2008) did, and she is led to a similar conclusion. In "Iranian Women During the Reform Era," Bahramitash (2007) affirms that many women lost their jobs and social positions after the Revolution. In some sense, she rightfully confirms what Nafisi (2003) reports in her memoir. However, Bahramitash criticizes the Orientalist feminist "depiction of 'Third World,' 'Muslim' women as a homogeneous category of powerless victims of a particular cultural and/or socioeconomic system" (2007, p. 87). She rightly believes that such claims overlook women's struggles in transforming their situation. However, this discursive polarization must not hide the socially obvious and historically proven fact that women's rights have been constantly violated since the Revolution. Fighting against the victimization of 'Third World Muslim Women' as a homogenous entity that needs to be liberated from Islam by means of a 'paternalistic guardianship' of Westerners, is a legitimate and morally right endeavor. Moreover, rejecting 'the essentialist view of Islam,' which 'ignores the fact that Islam is subject to change,' is a plausible argument. Nonetheless, it must not lead us to conclude that Iranians, and particularly Iranian women, have had a better life since the Revolution.

Bahramitash's main thesis in her article is to demonstrate that "during the reform era many women pressed for change through various interpretations of Islam" (2007, p. 88). This statement implies that the 1979 revolution deprived many women of their civil rights, as Bahramitash continues to report. Even claiming that only upper class and educated women suffered from Islamic law, while a religious majority of the society welcomed it, does not help her argument. Postcolonial critics critiqued Nafisi's (2003) account of Iranian women because Iranian 'subalterns' are absent from it. Yet the question is if the interests of all Iranian women, including educated Iranian women, are well represented in these postcolonialist accounts? If postcolonialism is about advocating minority rights, those secular women were in the minority at the time of the 1979 revolution in Iran. Also, using different interpretations of Islam in order to advance women's position in society during the reform era implies that an oppressive version of Islam had dominated the country after the Revolution up until the reform era, which spans almost 18 years. Therefore, Behdad's (2008) reference to Bahramitash's (2007) article in order to conclude that Iranians have been living better lives is morally inappropriate because Bahramitash had admitted to the oppressive gender politics present during the first decade of the post-revolutionary era. Also, both Bahramitash and Behdad misinterpret some statistical information about the mortality rate in order to show that the situation of women over the past three decades and after the Revolution has improved. They deviate this far from the actual reality in order to construct an Other out of the Middle East, for the benefit of the West. This Other was created mainly by diaspora intellectuals to contradict the Orientalist representation of their homeland. Defying the Orientalist image of Iranian women as victims in urgent need of liberation by Western military powers at the expense of waging a war against the nation is a valid position. However, offering a distorted image of the homeland and its people in order to contradict the neo-Orientalist imagination has resulted in postcolonial Orientalism, whose creation of an image of the homeland is mainly a reaction to the Orientalist representation.

Conclusion

Postcolonialism, either as a sociopolitical movement or as an intellectual project, challenges the traditional but still dominant order of societies around the globe. What one could consider as the prominent characteristic of postcolonial criticism is that it gives a voice to the subalterns through an intersectional critique of the global power structure and its dominant regime of truth. The inextricable intersectionality of the postcolonial critique would be more effectively demonstrated if we realized that the dominant regime of truth in the industrial societies of Europe has been produced predominantly by male, heterosexual, white Christian European colonizers, followed by their American counterparts. Thus each of these discursive subject positions needs to be criticized separately but also simultaneously. In his groundbreaking 1979 book, *Orientalism*, Said demonstrates the literary representation of the Orient by European writers as a part of the project of constructing an Other to Western civilization. Although Said initially concerned himself with the Orientalist tropes portraying the Islamic societies of the Middle East, Orientalism has now turned into a key concept in a variety of critical thinking. Postcolonial feminism, postcolonial gender studies, in addition to postcolonial literary criticism, are, among others, some of these discourses.

Said's (1979) *Orientalism* has been pronounced a turning point in criticizing the colonial strategies of domination; his work inspired the postcolonial critique of the binary of Orient-Occident. Nevertheless, postcolonial critics have shown a tendency to view the world in a dichotomy similar to that used by the colonialists. Moreover, Said's work demonstrates the historical fact that European representations of the Orient in literature and art have assisted Western powers in naturalizing their domination over colonized lands and their peoples. Besides all the enlightening perspectives that Said's work entailed, one consequence of his work could be described as a kind of displacement of the ground of West-East confrontation from the real world to the world of representation. In other words, in the postcolonial era a challenge between the rival local and global powers over media representation adds to the military and economic conflict between the former or current colonialist powers and the colonized world. The battleground's shifting from the reality to the representation of that reality in the contemporary postcolonial era has renewed the dichotomy of colonizer-colonized and Occident-Orient. As a result, the line between an Orientalist representation of non-Western societies as underdeveloped and a genuine critique of tyrannical local institutions in the decolonized world is very much blurred. Thus, any criticism of the local institutions which mainly portray themselves as anti-imperial could simply be understood with the same diachronic logic as the Orientalist degradation of the liberated people. In this sense, as Abu-Lughod et al. (2001) report, some critics have argued that "Said's Orientalism, and the broader approaches known variously as postcolonial and postmodern, have led us away from criticism of local institutions and political forces" (p. 111). Haideh Moghissi, an Iranian feminist scholar, in her 1999 *Feminism and Islamic Fundamentalism: The Limits of Postmodern Analysis*, questions the Middle East intellectual's anti-Orientalist adventure. Moghissi writes, "the uncritical fascination with western postmodernism can prove a costly intellectual experiment for Middle Eastern intellectuals, who inadvertently lend support to the most effectively cloaked repressive movement in the region: Islamic fundamentalism" (1999, p. 63).

Global context plays a determining role in creating and nurturing this dilemma. For instance, Abu-Lughod et al. (2001) demonstrate the doubts, fears, and probable accusations surrounding the publicity of reports on violence against women in the Middle East in

> a world already primed to think of the Middle East as a place of violence against women, especially because of the highly publicized issue of female circumcision [in Northern Africa]. And what accusations will be leveled against these feminists by government authorities and other defenders of Egypt's image? (p. 110)

Abu-Lughod et al. suggest that "the solution is to refuse the tradition/Western modernity divide, but how sophisticated do you have to be to manage this? One strategy seems to be to publish in regional languages" (p. 110).

The controversy, presented in this chapter, between Iranian diaspora intellectuals in general over the human rights situation in their homeland, particularly women's rights violations in Iran, exemplifies the struggles over the representation of Middle Eastern societies. However, what is missing in these representations, both in neo-Orientalist and in postcolonial Orientalist literature, are the individual struggles of Iranians, men and women, to lead a happy life despite all the economic, political, and cultural hardship that a system such as the Islamic Republic has burdened its people with. In this sense, what is largely 'the absent presence' in all of these literary texts and scholarly works produced in the Iranian diaspora is the local resistance that Iranian citizens have shown in their everyday lives, either their struggle against an Islamic repressive regime or against the imperialist policies of the United States that have put them through a harsh economic situation due to the international sanctions that have been in place for decades. Diaspora writers have endeavored to challenge the image of Iran propagated by the Islamic Republic through concentrating on stories of political oppression and human rights violations in Iran. On the other hand, Iranian postcolonialists are engaged in constructing an Iran that is an Other to Western civilization. In the latter case, Iran is represented as an example of an Islamic democracy in a Muslim-majority country in the Middle East, where women can actively lead their private and social lives. Yet one needs to go beyond this dichotomized world of Occident-Orient in order to appreciate the rich culture of the historically rooted people of Iran and at the same time criticize the patriarchal dimensions of the same culture. From the same subject position, one can value the ongoing endeavors of a nation to liberate itself from local oppressive regimes, before and after the 1979 revolution, and at the same time recognize the national struggle with the imperialist powers that have historically targeted the independence of the country.

References

Abu-Lughod, L., Yegenoglu, M., Arat, Z., Hoodfar, H., Tucker, J., Moghissi, H., ... Ward, R.V. (2001). "Orientalism" and Middle East feminist studies. *Feminist Studies, 27,* 101–113. doi:10.2307/3178451.

Alinejad, M. (2015, February 25). Speech at 2015 Women's Rights Awards. Available from https://www.youtube.com/watch?v=DCgysXS_zEo.

Bahramitash, R. (2005). The war on terror, feminist Orientalism and Orientalist feminism: Case studies of two North American bestsellers. *Critique: Critical Middle Eastern Studies, 14,* 221–235. doi:10.1080/10669920500135512.

Bahramitash, R. (2007). Iranian women during the Reform era (1994–2004): A focus on employment. *Journal of Middle East Women's Studies, 3,* 86–109. doi:10.2979/mew.2007.3.2.86.

Behdad, A. (2008). Critical historicism. *American Literary History, 20,* 286–299. doi:10.1093/alh/ajm040.

Behdad, A., & Williams, J. (2010). Neo-Orientalism. In B.T. Edwards & D.P. Gaonkar (Eds.), *Globalizing American studies* (pp. 283–299). Chicago, IL: University of Chicago Press.

Brière, C., Blanchet, P., & Foucault, M. (1979) *Iran: La Révolution Au Nom De Dieu.* Paris, France: Seuil.

Chow, R. (2003). Against the lures of diaspora: Minority discourse, Chinese women, and intellectual hegemony. In J.E. Braziel & A. Mannur (Eds.), *Theorizing diaspora: A reader* (pp. 163–183). Malden, MA: Blackwell.

Dabashi, H. (2006a, August 4). Lolita and beyond. *Hamid Dabashi's ZSpace Page.* Retrieved July 27, 2017 from https://zcomm.org/znetarticle/lolita-and-beyond-by-hamid-dabashi/.

Dabashi, H. (2006b, June 1–7). Native informers and the making of the American empire. *Al-Ahram Weekly,* Issue #797. Retrieved from http://www.campus-watch.org/article/id/2802.

Dabashi, H. (2011). *Brown skin, white masks.* London, England: Pluto.

Foucault, M. (2005). Iran: The spirit of a world without spirit. In J. Afary & K.B. Anderson (Eds.), *Foucault and the Iranian revolution: Gender and the seductions of Islamism.* Chicago, IL: University of Chicago Press.

Hakakian, R. (2004). *Journey from the land of no: A girlhood caught in revolutionary Iran.* New York, NY: Crown.

Kandiyoti, D. (Ed.). 1996. *Engendering Middle East studies*. Syracuse, NY: Syracuse University Press.

Lowe, L. (1991). *Critical terrains: French and British Orientalisms*. Ithaca, NY: Cornell University Press.

Mahmood, S. (2008). Feminism, democracy, and empire: Islam and the war of terror. In J.W. Scott (Ed.), *Women's studies on the edge* (pp. 81–113). Durham, NC: Duke University Press.

Milani, T. (2001). *The hidden half: A film by Tahmineh Milani*. Berkeley, CA: Iranian Film Society.

Moghissi, H. (1999). *Feminism and Islamic fundamentalism: The limits of postmodern analysis*. New York, NY: St. Martin's Press.

Nafisi, A. (2003). *Reading Lolita in Tehran: A memoir in books*. New York, NY: Random House.

Paidar, P. (1995). *Women and the political process in twentieth-century Iran*. Cambridge, England: Cambridge University Press.

Rastegar, M. (2006). Reading Nafisi in the West: Authenticity, Orientalism, and "liberating" Iranian women. *Women's Studies Quarterly, 34*(1/2), 108–128. Retrieved July 27, 2017 from http://www.jstor.org/stable/40004743.

Said, E.W. (1979). *Orientalism*. New York, NY: Vintage Books.

Scullion, R. (1995). Michel Foucault the Orientalist: On revolutionary Iran and the "spirit of Islam." *South Central Review, 12*(2), 16–40. doi:10.2307/3189968.

CHAPTER 8

Let the Oriental Perform: A Critical Approach to Neo-Orientalism at Work in Turkish Politics

Merve Kavakci

Statement of the Problem

The community of knowers who hold power in creating, shaping, and disseminating the information to do so in their own perspective, construing realities in particular ways to serve their own goal(s) divulging what is deemed important, undermining what is rendered trivial, unimportant, or worthy of dismissal. This, at the end, serves to create a reality different than that of the 'factual' or real. This chapter attempts to depict the ways through which Turkish political agency, at times, was represented by parameters accounted for the closest to the reality, if not by the 'reality' itself by the American academics, while at other times was misrepresented, hence rendered misinforming, based on its particularities, demarcated space, and time. The criterion that entailed a change within itself was a nebulous one, predicated upon the changes in day-to-day politics of all parties involved. This shift speaks to the vulnerability of the process of production of knowledge and the neo-Orientalist nature thereof.

Theoretical Perspective

Orientalism reads the world from the verge of Occidental and Oriental divide. The Orientalist, who is a member of the Occident (West), dwells into a research about the Orient (East) and its belongings. According to the Orientalist literature, the value attributed to the process of production of knowledge is intrinsic and pertinent to the Occidental community of knowers. That is to say, knowledge becomes of value if and when it is procured by agencies that represent a particular racial, ethnic, cultural, and sociopolitical stature. This process was engrained to be legitimized, starting with the European expedition that gave way to the colonial experience. With that, the dichotomized binaries of the two enterprises, namely Occidental and Oriental, entailed a hegemonic contextualization in oppositional standing with no room for scrutiny (Cox, 1992). The tumultuous pertinence between the West and the East or the North and the South was set off right then (Spivak, 1999). Here, the departure point in knowledge production processes was justified by racially white, culturally secular, ethnically European, predominantly male demography. As a result of a discursive process carried out by this group across the globe, the normative, invariably ascribed to the Occidental "self," was posited against the concocted reality of the "other" (Bhabha, 2004, p. 29). The former held ontological superiority over the latter, hence positioned itself equipped with certain systems of representation that divulged the hierarchy of power in every facet of life as opposed to the disadvantage of the latter (Said, 1978). This included a chasmic distinction between intellectual capacities as well, where the latter was subordinate to the former (Said, 1978). Biological incapacitation is no exception either, which in turn helps the process of de-humanization of the latter (Fanon, 2004). In this context, the Oriental 'other' carried generic particularities shared by all affiliated inhabitants of the assigned demographic demarcations (Said, 1978). The generalized 'one' transformed itself into uncontested man-made realities that serve as leverage for creating the quasi-facts of the former (Foucault, 1970). Parochial observations, rumination undertaken by the former, limited by personal attributions and ascribing processes, at the end of a repetitious continuum, are treated as unadulterated factuality deemed the absolute truth. The subjectivities defined by the Orientalist purport to concrete embodiments of the Orient not open to discussion.

Rooted in Marxist theory, postcolonialism argues that the Oriental, at a distance, becomes the subject matter under investigation only to be discerned, unpacked, deconstructed, and reconstructed anew in tandem, ready to perform for the disposal of the Orientalist. Here the former is made to speak (Spivak, 1998). The inequitable nature of the relationship between the two refers to the hierarchical structure of power that exudes in quotidian human activities shaping them time and again (Young, 2001). Among these is also the production of knowledge. The community of knowers in the Occident articulates the Oriental human agency and beyond thus the 'other' in the way he or she finds it fit. Needless to say, the monopoly over the production processes of knowledge renders the former the only viable source and disseminator of information entailing the close net relationship between knowledge and power (Said, 1978). Inextricable from all aspects of human experience, hegemonic stance over knowledge enterprise enables the Occidental community of knowers to shape the pertinent discourses ubiquitously from politics, culture, or economics to societal and theological sphere. Perceptions and perspectives that would serve the benefit of the Occident are prioritized through the hand of the Orientalist. Manipulating the vicissitudes on the Oriental ground, twisting the realities by divulging certain parts while concealing others, puts the circular motion of creating-recreating-reacting to-acting on 'realities.' The process required a particular language in order for its end product to be regarded as true (Foucault, 1981). The concepts of terror, war, violence, good, bad, rich, poor, even North, South, East, and West, were molded not by universalities but particularities of the 'other.' As a result, the Middle East was demarcated as the East of Europe while Africa was appropriated as North Africa that was annexed to the Middle East but separated from the rest of the continent. Along the same lines, what terror entailed in Europe or the United States was received differently than if it took place in Africa or Southeast Asia. The 9/11 attacks would change the history of humankind, as the United States leads the world to usher into a new era, for instance, while a similar tragedy, if it occurred in, say, India, would not. Terror attacks in France would justify rendering an immediate state of emergency and no one would pry into French politics to question the legitimacy of such a decision, but the same would not hold for Turkey. Turkey, a part of the Orient, in line with the Orientalist teaching, would not be left alone to govern itself on its own terms and wants. An African state inflicted with terrorism would not get the attention that a European country would receive under similar infliction. The value of life in the Orient would not be up to par with the value of a life in the Occident, hence could easily be undermined, ignored, or forfeited. In short, there is a systematic degradation of the Orient and its affiliations. It is almost considered a lost case, if you will (Salame, 2001).

It is important to note that as much as geography had played a fundamental role in the creation of dichotomous binaries of 'self' versus the 'other' at the outset, due to the imperial expeditions by European powers, currently it is not an absolute determinant in the Orientalist discourse. The Orientalist perspective can very well flourish within the Orient itself. In other words, one can find the Oriental Orientalist within the Orient imposing hierarchies of power against the Oriental in the Orient. One does not have to travel to Europe to observe the chain of thought of an Orientalist, but can see one in Burgiba's Tunisia, Shah Pahlavi's Iran, or Ataturk's Turkey as staunch admirers of European modernization. Moreover, Israel, albeit in the Orient, is rendered part of the Occident. A European, but more so American approach to the state of Israel grants it immunity and impunity in its relationship with the Palestinians. The Western world can easily pick on Muslim countries as part of the Orient vis a vis violations of human rights while it falls on deaf ears with respect to violations against Palestinians by Israeli perpetrators. Along the same lines, the West, which is known to be extremely meticulous about fighting anti-Semitism, not only does not fight Islamophobia but accommodates, if not promotes it. Here it is important to note that in the eyes of the Western academics in general, anti-Semitism and Islamophobia are not considered to be of the same kind. That is to say, hate towards a particular people can be less of an issue compared to hate towards another group of people of different origin based on race, ethnicity, culture, religion, or region.

Another example that refers to the double standardization of Orientalist discourse is embodied in the United States' obsession with democratization of the 'other.' Democracy, which is held as a shared reference by all Western powers, is to be imposed on the 'other' independent of its own take on the matter. With that, a satisfied population of nondemocratic governance would not be left to its own device to pursue. It 'must' be democratized. Furthermore, this must come in the form and format of European or American democracy to mimic the exact system of theirs. One-fits-all democracy speaks to the coercive nature of the Orientalist project. Nevertheless, the American administration wages a war against the dictatorial regime of Iraq but not against China. Or the United States, which bashes lack of democracy and human rights in Iran, does not notice similar abuses in Saudi Arabia. Borrowing from Mahmood Mamdani's (2002) "good Muslim and bad Muslim" (p. 766) juxtaposition, the Orientalist, albeit an outsider, constitutes what is acceptable hence permissible and what is not thus intolerable in the eyes of the Occidental.

Methodology

Qualitative research methodology was utilized. The data garnered for this chapter were derived from primary and secondary sources such as interviews, books, and academic journal articles. Data were analyzed through longitudinal historical analysis, historical events analysis, case study, and content analysis.

American Academics on Turkish Islamist Politics in the Post-9/11 Era

In order to have a clear apprehension of the American academics' stance on how they perceived Turkish political agency, one has to provide information on the 10-year span prior to the attacks. Such agency was represented by political actors including current President Tayyip Erdogan, former President Abdullah Gul, and former Prime Minister Necmeddin Erbakan. The 1990s was the marker of the reification of the failure of the homegrown 'Orientalist' regime of the country which, over time, is dubbed Kemalism. One can categorize the fervent defenders of Kemalism as committed Orientalists who believe in European superiority (Akural, 1984). They speak for the absent European Orientalist within to promote a coercive Westernization project for the Turkish society (Yavuz, 2000). Their efforts allowed Turkey to enjoy a kind of exceptionalism as far as its record on democratization was concerned. That is to say, the European and American intelligentsia looked away against the weaknesses in Turkey's political machinery that thwarted the process of reform for democratizing processes. At the center of Kemalist ideology was an unwavering commitment to French model of secularism. Turkey's secular fundamentalist façade helped to get away with scrutiny and accountability. The power hub within the country, namely the Orientalist Kemalists, turned to be the 'brat' in the house, so to speak. They enjoyed social and political perks provided as a result of the pacts they signed with the political machinery (Waterbury, 2001). In the larger, global picture, Kemalists were perceived as the guarantors of reproduction of the hierarchy of power between the Western Orientalist and the Turkish Oriental. In return for the Kemalist's loyalty, the Orientalist would reward him or her by not zooming in on Kemalist fallacies that are antithetical to democratization and or modernization.

Within this context, Turkish practicing Muslims came in office after the general elections in 1997; the expression of 'practicing Muslims' will be substituted by 'Muslims' for the rest of the chapter. Tayyip Erdogan was then the Mayor of Istanbul and Abdullah Gul was the Secretary of State in the newly formed cabinet under the leadership of Prime Minister Necmeddin Erbakan. The Western world had the jitters about this group of 'Muslims,' whom they referred to as 'Islamists.' In their eyes, they represented the 'other,' now in power in 'ally' Turkey, which was until then ruled by the friends of the West, under Kemalism committed to Orientalist value system. Eleven months into its rule, Kemalists represented by the military establishment and its extremities in bureaucracy and civil society joined hands to topple the government through a coup d'etat (Yavuz, 2003). The pretext was the rising Islamization in the country. Turkey, in the eyes of the Orientalist, was now inclined toward the East, namely the Muslim world, increasing economic and social ties with the peoples of Islamic heritage. Under Turkey's leadership, Iran, Pakistan, Nigeria, Bangladesh, Malaysia, Indonesia, and Egypt established Developing 8, in short, D8, to serve as an alternative outlet for cooperation amongst Muslim peoples (D-8 Organization for Economic Cooperation, 2014). American intelligentsia, including the academics, with a few exceptions, evaluated the coup process as an effort to protect the secular nature of the Turkish state, which was known for its commitment to Orientalist value system. Therefore, the patent breach of the democratic process has gone largely undermined as far as the American academics were concerned. The same was true for American policy makers. One, in a personal interview, submitted that they did not care for the Turkish democracy and that it was the 'Islamist' government's launch to increase economic ties with the Muslim world that actually led Washington to give a green light to the coup. Nonetheless, the increasing 'Islamization' was a fallacious argument. It was rather increasing democratization that the Muslim politicians in office were pushing for.

It is important to note that Turkey was not a democratic country until then. Under the auspices of Western allies, who made a conscious decision to look away from the problems such as the ailing human rights record, lack of transparency, and accountability, Turkey was easily getting away with its floundering democratization process. Now that the 'Islamist' government was striving to bring about change and challenge the status quo, the proponents of the status quo, namely no one other than the Kemalists, were to resist. This was expected.

On the other hand, the Western academics depended on the friends of the West for information flow. Kemalists committed to Orientalism were the Western academics' mere source. The way the former observed, discerned, articulated, analyzed, and finally communicated the information about the 'realities' on the ground to the latter was subjective to the particularities of the former. A Kemalist's approach to government's attempt to transform the country's secular fundamentalism, which is stifling in nature, into one that is more people friendly like that of the United States, in other words, a more Anglo-Saxon version would be perceived as more 'Islamization.' Yet, from a generalized American perspective, such an action would not be seen as more Islamization but rather as more 'religious freedom,' hence more 'democratization.' The example of Tayyip Erdogan's incarceration due to poetry is inexplicable in the eyes of an American intellectual. Yet it went mostly unnoticed since the 'source,' in other words, the Kemalists, had them believe that this was not simply an innocent action of poem-reading but rather an attempt to dismantle Turkey's secular regime. Furthermore, the rights of the Oriental would not be equally valuable as the rights of the Occidental. Hence while a case of abridgment of freedom of expression like that of Erdogan's poetry would normally heed much disparagement in the Western world, it was undermined, as the victim, in this case Erdogan, was a Turkish Muslim.

Along the same lines, the Western intellectuals invariably remained indifferent to the sufferings of Muslim women in the hands of the Kemalists. The way Muslim women dressed made them into a target for the Kemalists. Western academics mostly went along with the Kemalists, who argued that these women were donning the Islamic headcover not for personal religious expression but because they were ideologically intending to take the country backwards to the middle ages. They were "problems to be solved" (Said, 1978, p. 207).

This very process of shifting from the reality on the ground to first a subjective take, and secondly to a quasi-fact, depicts how the realities are marred on the way. This very shift leads to a circular motion of creating more 'facts' that, in fact, lack factuality. These are, rather, wanna-be-realities through "which truth claims are produced, circulated, consolidated, legitimated, and reproduced in the social formation" (Persaud, 2004, p. 68). The vicious circle emanating from this process serves to further exacerbate the situation within and without. The Orientalist who is to produce knowledge about the Orient theorizes based on the new data that comes in from the Orient, but a flawed one. As a result, the theory produced would lack veracity.

The byproduct of the postmodern coup of 1997 not only included ousting of the 'Islamists' from office, but also taking the necessary measures to preclude any possibility of the 'other' assuming office in the future. For that reason, all doors or possibility of doors had to be closed to the 'other.' With that in mind, the Kemalist establishment imprisoned Tayyip Erdogan for reading a poem at a public gathering, put Erbakan in house arrest, and closed their political party and banned its leading politicians. These violations received almost no criticism from American academics. The Kemalists who carried out the coup were the representatives of the Orientalist value system, hence their violation of the political rights of the 'other' could very well be tolerated. After all, they were considered one of 'us.' However, Kemalists did not stop there. They helped establish a new government from a coalition of parties who paid allegiance to the Orientalist values. Under the sway of Kemalist coup perpetrators, the new government crashed down the public school system that, in their eyes, raised the Islamists; banned symbols of religious expression such as the headscarf; and conducted a total crackdown on Muslim families in every facet of their lives including the private realm. A preponderance of Western academics chose not to see any of it; notable exceptions include Shively (2005), White (2002), and Yavuz (2003). As Orientalism would purport, from their perspective, the Muslim politicians and Muslims of Turkey whose human rights and civil liberties were violated did not deserve a reference, an investigation, or objective probing of their plight (Said, 1978). They were, in Mamdani's terminology, rendered 'bad' Muslims. They deserved no sympathy (Said, 1978). The same academics later would, on the other hand, be very much 'concerned' about the well-being of Fethullah Gulen, seemingly an imam who was then known for his religious leadership, a man who is now known to be the head of a terrorist organization, namely Fethullahci Teror Organization (FETO), in Turkey, and his disciples. In the eyes of the American academics they would be seen as 'good' Muslims. In the process of differentiating between the good and the bad, the Orientalist depends on the local representatives, in other words, the Turkish who believe in the Orientalist set of values, namely the Kemalists. Kemalists are the ones who think, act, and live their lives within the framework of Europeanized, modernized 'us' against the unmodernized, unWesternized, Muslim 'other.' Hence, they are trustworthy.

During the 1997 coup, Gulen, seemingly a devout Muslim, chose to stand with the Kemalists who victimized millions of Muslims and accused politicians like Erbakan and Erdogan "for creating tension with the Turkish nation" (Aktay, 2003, p. 146). Gulen, in accordance with his commitment to support Kemalism's Orientalist value system, as part of the crackdown at the aftermath of the postmodern coup d'etat, forced his female students and teachers working at his schools to take off their headscarves (Ozer, 2005). He did something more, though. He ordered his followers to percolate into the state apparatus, in particular, into security forces and the military, by concealing their religious identity behind a secular façade, until a time of sufficient power could be reached to overthrow the government. As it will be discussed below, that time arrived on July 15, 2016.

Unpacking the Implications of the 9/11 Attacks

Living close to the vicinity, when I literally heard a plane crash into the Pentagon on September 11, 2001, I was unaware that Turkey's ears would ring numerous times in the days to come. The political actors in the U.S. Congress as well as the pundits at the District's academic circles referred to Turkey as a model Muslim country that the rest of the Muslim states should follow (Kavakci, 2010). The reference invariably came as part of the new discourse at the aftermath of the attacks where American people were trying to figure out why and what did really happen (Tocci, 2011). The adumbration involved Turkey's role modelness. This discourse was not a new one. On the contrary, literature produced by the Orientalists for long pointed to the Turkish modernization, especially secularization with compliments allowing the Western intelligentsia to position Turkey differently in comparison to the rest of the Muslim world and the countries in the region. Here, the 'Orientalist' awarded such committed stance to modernization theory and the ensuing process of, in Homi Bhabha's wording, "mimicry" like that of Turkey (Ling, 2004, p. 116). Turkey was considered to be Muslim 'enough' but not 'too much,' right around the correct amount, so to speak, in other words, not to the extent that it would become a nuisance for the Western world. Furthermore, in the footsteps of France, which was the concocter of laic statehood in the world, Turkey was extremely committed to laic state building.

The downside of this, from the perspective of American Orientalists, was that the coalition government established at the aftermath of the coup d'etat led by the Kemalists, albeit committed to Orientalism, was in deep trouble due to the economic and political crisis. This was emblematic of failure of the secular regimes in the developing Middle East and North Africa (Burgat, 2003). In the November 2002 general elections, the nation, fed up with Kemalism's repercussions brought then the recently established Justice and Development Party to office. AKP won this election with a landslide. Now the Western world had no choice but to work with the Turkish politicians whom they had considered pernicious Islamists only a few years back. For the secular fundamentalist governance had failed like never before. The trepidation with respect to the Islamic identity of AKP, on the part of the Western powers, was still present though. After all, Turkey was going to be ruled by the same 'Islamists' one more time but now at a larger scale. Erbakan's Welfare Party assumed office, merely as part of a coalition, after gaining 21.4% of the votes in 1997. Justice and Development Party on the other hand, had won 34.3% of the votes. Nonetheless, the American administration needed Turkey to ameliorate the damaged relationship with the Muslim world at the aftermath of the invasion of Afghanistan. A project to win the hearts and minds of the people was launched by Bush Administration for that reason. Furthermore, the United States needed to be on good terms with Turkish authorities for geopolitical aspirations in order to be able to wage a war in Iraq. The United States had no choice but to start with a clean slate with the Islamists of Turkey. Erdogan, who was a nemesis before, now was an ally. The fluidity stemming from circumstantiality of the Orientalist's conceptualization of the 'good' and the 'bad' Muslim was evident. The inconsistency speaks to the hypocritical nature of the Orientalist. While the Orientalist decreed who the 'good' and the 'bad' would be, without utilizing a publicly voiced, universal set of criteria, he/she would hold the power to bail out on such classification to embark in a new 'good' and 'bad' grouping at any time. The Orientalist did not have to answer to any higher authority or explain him/herself. He was the only and the ultimate one with impunity. He could reformulate realities. What it was that rendered Tayyip Erdogan a 'bad' Muslim that he does not now do, to promote him to a 'good' Muslim, is not enunciated by the Orientalist (Moore-Gilbert, 1997).

The indiscriminatory rise of the anti-American sentiment across the globe as the United States waged its global war on terror was another incentive that strengthened the hands of the Muslim politicians of AKP. An old ally, not just of the United States but of the state of Israel as well, NATO member Turkey was needed for all proverbial reasons in the international community. In the meantime, at home, American academics were divided. Some stood by the hawkish politicians, the neocons arguing that Erdogan's Turkey, no matter what it does, poses a threat to Western democracies due to its political lineage (Rubin, 2016). In their view, the "once an Islamist, always an Islamist" argument held.

It is worth noting that the label of Islamist was one that was foisted on Turkey's Muslim politicians and activists by the West in the late 1980s and early 1990s. Once the term was winged among Orientalist community of knowers, it was used to define the 'other' involved in political action. When the postmodern coup of February 28, 1997 unraveled, neither the politicians such as Erdogan nor the representatives of Orientalism within, in other words, the Kemalists dubbed the 'other' Islamist. While the former's affiliation involved 'practicing,' 'religious,' or 'devout' Muslim, the latter's reference to the former comprised the 'reactionary.' It was rather the Orientalist, a European or an American intelligentsia who conspicuously referred to the Muslim politicians as 'Islamist.' That is to say, the 'Muslim' Oriental had no opportunity to define him/herself in the way he/she found it fit. He/she was either defined by the Orientalist (who called him/her Islamist) or the local representative of Orientalism (who labeled him/her reactionary).

Having been part of this political movement in the early 1990s in Turkey, I never defined myself as Islamist. I was merely a politician who was a Muslim. 'Islamist' reference, I argued, was a Western construct, thus foreign, to start with. Furthermore, what was intended off of the conceptualization of 'Islamist' was already intrinsic to what 'Muslim' entailed (Kavakci, 2013). During my years as a professor in the United States, however, I first resisted the labeling. After some time, I realized that it was almost impossible to fight it off within the academic and political circles of Washington D.C.; hence I caved in to the 'Islamist' identification. That was to say, the Oriental would not know himself the way an Orientalist would (Said, 1978); therefore, the process of naming was left to the latter. This was, actually, about the hegemonic exertion of power to flex the Orientalist's muscles to ensure that the Oriental did not undermine who held the power strings. Not to be able to define one's self and to be confined to a description from outside would also imply that the processes of de-humanization concomitant with de-emancipation were in place. Such processes, which strip the Oriental from his/her right to self-definition and self-determination, disempower the Oriental while channeling him/her to a defensive, hence apologetic stance.

There were also some academics in the United States who argued that Erdogan's AKP represented the end of Islamist politics (White, 2005). For some others, it was the new face of former Islamists (Esposito, 2010). AKP's own definition included the label of 'conservative democrats.' Party members referred to themselves as such within the local/national discourse. Moreover, in the international realm, they were also known as 'Muslim democrats.' This stuck to them among Western intellectuals who had some level of sympathy for Erdogan and his party. Within Turkey, 'conservative democrats' or simply 'conservatives' had preference in the eyes of AKP politicians. The nuance of 'Muslim' versus 'conservative' in domestic and foreign politics subsequently, had to do with the loaded meaning attributed to the former in domestic political vernacular. The Kemalist regime inculcated that all Turks were Muslims. Thus the distinction among varying degrees of importance ascribed to religion would only be possible through references such as conservative, secular, modern, reactionary, and the like. AKP, under Erdogan's leadership, adamantly wanted to divorce itself from Islamist identity (Edelman, Cornell, Lobel, & Makovsky, 2013). Therefore it grabbed the title 'conservative' in the naming process. This was not, though, due to an alteration in what people such as Erdogan and his colleagues in the leadership of the AKP stood for. It was simply for pragmatic reasons, such as to avoid the wrath of the Kemalist establishment who assumed decision-making positions, among which were the military, security forces, and the judiciary. Having come from a political tradition where affiliated parties were closed down one after another in sequence over the past 30 years, it was sagacious on part of the AKP members to be extra vigilant. Moreover, to combine that with 'democrat-ic' identity helped them to be received with more acceptance from differing facets of societal tapestry. On the other hand, 'Muslim democrats' became pervasive in the Western discourse, promoted both from within and without through an analogy of Europeans' 'Christian democrats.' Here, there are two ways of analyzing the process. According to one, the Orientalist, who only takes his/her own European or American experience as a departure point to understand the world, has to pull the Oriental into an Occidental discourse where the latter finds a spot to replicate the European/American political behavior. This also gives the Orientalist the ability, to some extent, to control the process of defining. Furthermore, it reasserts the Orientalist's position as the teacher, educator, trainer who holds the upper hand (Said, 1978). Or, the Oriental him/herself comes forth with finding an analogous definition that will help minimize the fear and consternation expected to occur in the Western mind. This stems from the inferior and defensive position that the Oriental is, invariably, put in. To speak the same language, per se, with the Western intelligentsia, might help the Oriental to dissipate prejudice toward the Oriental. Considering that there was a process of naming, AKP acted smartly to find an analogy that fit the party the best in order to appease the cloud around its 'Islamic' affiliation.

It is interesting to note that in the second half of AKP's reign in the post-2007 period, which also coincided with Abdullah Gul assuming office as the

President, AKP's Islamist affiliation was brought to the front as a caveat. To nobody's surprise, this was again the work of Orientalist academics in the West supported by the Kemalists within, who wanted to slow down the booming Turkish economy, flourishing political and social spheres. It is noteworthy to assert that it also had to do with AKP's effort to expand the public space for human rights and civil liberties. AKP put forth effort for rapprochement for all parties with frustrated aspirations to improve the plight of all religious minorities, particularly Alawites within the Islamic tradition, the Christians, the Jews, and others. It also pushed for the discussion of ethnic minorities, mainly the Kurds, to expand the realm of freedom of expression. In 2007, the Constitutional Court attempted to close down AKP for threatening secularism for aiming to lift the then-27-year-old ban on the headscarf for Muslim women. Apparently an attempt to open the way for such a basic matter of freedom of expression triggered the intolerance within the Kemalist structure. An electronic ultimatum from the Turkish military immediately ensued. The reaction in support of AKP from the American academia was flimsy. In the meantime, the corruption schemes within the military institution tapered the prestige of armed services, which was the stronghold of Kemalism, dramatically. Erdogan, a popular leader, could galvanize masses quickly to unite in the name of national solidarity.

Disturbed by Erdogan's fervency to introduce reforms for democratization that would render Turkey more independent of the sway of the Orientalist value system (Said, 1978), Kemalists turned to block the road to Erdogan's presidency. Utilizing his political savvy Erdogan, at the last minute, announced that he would not be a nominee and let his colleague Abdullah Gul run for the presidency. Not being able to block the road to presidency for Abdullah Gul, at the aftermath of election, the Orientalists turned to the good and bad Muslim game once more. This time, the good Muslim was embodied in Gul, while the bad Muslim was represented by Tayyip Erdogan (Cornell, 2013). Yet, President Gul and Prime Minister Erdogan worked in harmony for the duration of Gul's term. Futile attempts of disintegration were warded off. AKP's perseverance precluded plots of creating upheaval through the Gezi Park Incident as well. An environmentalist, Erdogan was declared a tree killer overnight (May, 2013). However, the ordinary citizens' utter trust in him, not just as a political figure but also as a human being, led the AKP and its constituents to overcome the stumbling blocks. Furthermore, the anti-green label did not fly as far as AKP's policies were concerned. "For the people, with the people" Erdogan submitted that since his government came into office the green area in the country increased by 1.5 billion hectare (Erdogan, 2017). Interestingly, the discourse of Gezi in no time evolved into one about laic-Muslim divide (Atay, 2013).

The attention of the Western world towards Gezi was enormous. The international media's coverage was intense, selective, and at times even fallacious. At one point, CNN International aired a large crowd claiming that people were protesting the government while in fact it was a gathering of support to Erdogan at Kazlicesme Meeting (Takvim, 2013). It apologized, arguing that there was a technical error (Hurriyet, 2013). Inundated with partiality of news, the American academics mostly turned against the ruling AKP. They questioned Erdogan's justified usage of power (Koplow & Cook, 2013). Nonetheless, the same media outlets later downplayed the coup attempt that would take a tragic turn resulting in the death of hundreds and wounding of thousands. The callousness put forth at this particular time period would later be substituted by extreme focus and probing when AKP went after the culprits.

Two other issues that played a role of turning point involved the 'One Minute' incident and Mavi Marmara Flotilla crisis. Both of these incidents, involving the State of Israel, served as a litmus test with respect to reiteration of Orientalist perspective in American academia. They played an indispensable role to mobilize neoconservatives of the United States against the AKP government. Behind all was the discomfort Turkey was causing as it was attempting to leave the safe, yet limiting 'zone' of the Orientalist's territorial hegemony (Falk, 2014). Furthermore, Turkey was a trailblazer among the Muslim countries to shed light to the atrocities, Israeli State carried out against civilians in the Palestinian Territories. Through the Mavi Marmara Flotilla crisis, Turkey was able to bring Israel, a state which is used to acting any which way it desires with impunity, to accountability before international community. As a result, Erdogan was relegated from a 'good' Muslim to a 'bad' Muslim once more. The Orientalist was capable of calling the shots in the relevant discourse referring to the "true colors" of Erdogan (Rubin, 2010, para. 6).

While the Orientalist can interfere with the works of the Oriental, the reverse is not true. From a distance, the Orientalist observes the Oriental opining on the changes it endures. Any development in economic, social, and political affairs is lauded to an extent with an undertone of oversight. Turkey's soaring economic and political independence caused discomfort in the American Orientalists. The chances were that Turkey would no longer be indebted to the West for "having transported" it "into modernity" (Said, 1978, p. 121). Furthermore, Erdogan ventured into a new code of behavior that the Orientalists were not expecting from the Oriental, that is, blatantly criticizing the Orientalist value system. For him to underline that lives do matter, no matter where they are lost, to stress that we, as humanity have a problem of lack of equity, to defy the United Nations' incapacitation and duplicity by his motto "the world is greater than five," Erdogan evoked the wrath of the Orientalist movers and shakers.

Coup Attempt of July 15, 2016

The most recent coup attempt of July 15, 2016 was a great indicator of how the Orientalist project plotters could remind one that in their eyes, the Oriental was always less than a human being (Said, 1978). The coup attempt that cost 249 civilian lives, resulting in some 2,000 civilians wounded, was an act of open violence before the eyes of the world. Yet the Turkish people were received with little or no sign of sympathy by the Western world. The world that arose after the Charlie Hebdo attacks in Paris would not show a similar gesture of sorrow and sympathy after the Turkish tragedy. On the very night of the coup attempt, I appeared on various television channels in the Western world. It was disappointing to see how the information was skewed and misrepresented as we were literally under attack by F16s, machine guns, rifles, and bombs across the board. While a sniper, ensconced on top of the Bosphorus Bridge, was killing civilians comprised of men, women, children, and elderly alike, I was asked by a BBC reporter if the authoritarianism of Erdogan would soar in case of the failure of the coup attempt failed. Another interviewee, an academic from the United States, commented on Skype that it very well could be the case. The focus of the Western intelligentsia was not the incentives, the perpetrators, and the victims of the coup, but rather, it was the alleged authoritarianism of the current government. The Orientalist was entitled to verify what was important and what could be dismissed. The fact that President Erdogan dogged an assassination attempt that very night with his family including his grandchildren, that the Prime Minister was caught under fire with his wife in the car that night, that the Turkish Parliament was bombed 8 times that night, that the special operations forces were bombed, killing 47 policemen right there, that the Presidency was bombed several times that night did not even raise eyebrows of the Orientalist. Throughout the country that night, under the command of the coup plotters, tanks took to the streets, smashing down pedestrians with no hesitation, driving over people in their cars, killing them all. Almost all went unnoticed by the American intellectuals. In the eyes of the Orientalist, Erdogan and his supporters who defied the coup attempt were "first an Oriental, second a human being, and last again an Oriental" (Said, 1978, p. 102). Hence, in Mamdani's terminology, a bad Muslim did not deserve attention and/or sympathy. Most political analysts and academics in the U.S. capital looked away as far as the density of the violence inflicted on the Turkish state and the civilians that night. A group of Turkish parliamentarians who met with American politicians and academics in the United States at the aftermath of the coup attempt to explicate the enormity of this tragedy faced rather accusative remarks concerning the domestic politics of Turkey. Moreover, some shifted their focus on

Erdogan's so-called "authoritarianism" rather than discussing the details of the coup attempt (Ravza Kavakci Kan, personal communication, March 28, 2017). Here the Orientalist is the one who sets the agenda for discourse, positioning him/herself at an upper point of departure with respect to the Oriental, channelling the discussion in a way to benefit his/her own stance. This allows the former to reassert him/herself as the power holder controlling "meaning and public discourse" (Peres, 2012, p. 78). This also speaks to what William Hutchison divulges, namely the fact that Americans see themselves at a higher place than they really are at (Crane, 2008).

The dismissal of facts on part of the Orientalist gives way to creation of new pseudo-realities about the Oriental. This is an offensive process for the Oriental. He/she would be deprived of the acknowledgement of the Orient's crucibles and the support to heal his/her wounds. Moreover, since the Oriental's own reality would be different than that of the Orientalist's 'concocted' reality of perceiving the 'other,' the Oriental would have to respond to the Orientalist's actions with respect to the new and updated plight of the Oriental. When the Orientalist blames Erdogan for Islamizing his country, while all Erdogan is actually doing is normalizing the public manifestation of religious expression that is intrinsic to the Occident, the Oriental has to don his/her guard to challenge the misconstrued perception thereof (Said, 1978). Furthermore, Erdogan's politics prodded both his allies and foes to meet on an equal footing with Turkey. To his contesters' chagrin, he leveled the playing field for the Oriental. This, further, agitated the Orientalist leading to more indifference towards the Oriental's reality.

The factual data provided by Turkish officials with respect to the identity of the perpetrators was largely ignored by the West. American officials did not want to see the conspicuous connection between the coup and their own political agencies such as the Central Intelligence Agency (CIA). The empirical evidence on the ground averred that the FETO terrorist organization under Fethullah Gulen's leadership was behind the coup attempt. Yet, experts concurred that Gulen could not have pulled this off alone. As soon as President Erdogan realized that there was a coup attempt, without respite, that night he flew to Istanbul to lead the nation on the streets. During his flight, FETO pilots in F16s tried to put his plane down. It was CIA-affiliated Stratfor that tweeted the coordinates of Erdogan's plane in the air (Milliyet, 2016). A few weeks into the post-coup period, the then-President-Elect Donald Trump tweeted that he had just been informed that "CIA officials helped Turkey coup attempt" (Veterans Today, 2016, August 24, para. 1).

Gulen, who is known for his cult, has resided in the United States under special status since 1999 (Abushanab, 2016b, July 19). Chief of the General Staff

General Hulisi Akar, who was taken hostage the night of the coup, explicates that it was FETO that carried out the coup. He saw it, he heard it, he experienced it. At some point, Akar was offered by his hijackers to speak with their leader. Brigadier Hakan Evrim told Akar, "Our leader Fethullah Gulen might persuade you to go along," Akar refused (Sabah, 2016, July 26, para. 15). The U.S. Chairman of the Joint Chiefs of Staff Joseph F. Dunford visited Akar in the weeks after the coup. Dunford stressed the importance of 'evidence' in order to pinpoint the perpetrators. A disconcerted Akar responded: "What else is for evidence? I am the evidence!" (Haberturk, 2016, August 2, para. 1). Again, the Oriental's input was dismissed. The Oriental's word against the Orientalist's would not hold. The latter overrides the former.

Former CIA agents Graham Fuller and Henry Barkey, who are known for their support of Gulen's cult, argue that Gulen only promotes a soft and moderate face of Islam, dismissing the evidence (namely, some 80 boxes of documents) about FETO's involvement in the coup (Fuller, 2016). Barkey was among some 10 CIA-affiliated people who met at Buyukada for a clandestine meeting the night of the July 15 coup attempt. Shortly after the coup attempt was halted, Barkey and others left the country quietly (Ozturk, 2016). The Orientalist stands close to the Oriental, yet at a distance to observe, understand, and intervene whenever it is necessary to shape the Orient and its people (Said, 1978).

From the perspective of the Orientalist, the decision of what moderate Islam entails is decided not by scholars from within the Islamic tradition but by the Orientalist academic of another faith. The Orientalist goes further to render the FETO leader a 'good' Muslim against millions of Muslims who are inflicted with the violence perpetrated under the so-called 'good' Muslim, 'bad' Muslim. Turkish officials' diligent probe and aggregation of hard evidence that divulges FETO's involvement in the coup plot is discredited with no explanation. The Orientalist does not believe anything the Oriental states, since the Oriental cannot know him/herself as the Orientalist would know. The Oriental is not heard. Furthermore, the Orientalist does not opine on *takiyya,* a particularity of the Gulen cult, a term used to describe one's disguising him/herself with the purpose of pursuing a greater goal. In his sermons, the FETO leader unremittingly promotes his disciples to resort to takiyya to infiltrate the state. Fuller (2016), who was eager to assume the position of a Muslim scholar earlier, this time refrains from opining on takiyya. Moreoever, he sees himself qualified to render FETO's Islam "most encouraging." I would ask "for whom?" For the Western powers who thrive on exploitation of the 'other'? Or for a Muslim country like Turkey, which harbors millions who are displaced, harmed, and shattered due to the insatiable wants of the countries of the West?

On another note, the sufferings of the Oriental are not real sufferings in the eyes of the Orientalist. For the Oriental is stripped of his/her humanness, thus does not deserve any attention or care. American intelligentsia, who had a tragic experience of terrorism in 9/11, ironically fail to acknowledge that terror is terror, independent of where it is inflicted. The tragedy of the July 15 coup attempt would not resonate with the Orientalist. Furthermore, the Orientalist can and does put him/herself in place of the Oriental to speak, decide, and perform on behalf of him/her. The latter, however, is not permitted to do the same. One, for instance, would wonder if the perpetrators of the 9/11 attacks were not treated as terrorists and say, even enjoyed protection in Turkey, what would be the reaction of the United States? The relationship between the Oriental and the Orientalist is not a reciprocal one; it is, rather, a one-directional interaction. The latter has the upper hand determining the ways through which the information about the former will be shaped. When Erdogan's AKP took action to bring the coup plotters to justice, he pushed for lustration (Abushanab, 2016a, December 14). Putting a twist to the Oriental's own reality, this was presented as a purge or crackdown over Orientalist-proclaimed 'innocent' people. Despite the fact that the process of lustration was not foreign to the Western academia (as in the example of Poland), the Orientalist did not utilize it in an effort to understand the July 15 coup plot. In the eyes of the Orientalist, lustration was an experience of the West within, therefore it was not up for the disposal of the Oriental 'other' to borrow or imitate. Albeit a similar experience, the Oriental's efforts were categorized as purging.

Conclusion

The neo-Orientalist approach in American intelligentsia affects the 'realities' of Turkish political discourse at two levels. First, the Orientalist value system is embodied in Turkish Kemalism. In the way that Orientalism creates a hierarchy of power between the Orientalist and the Oriental, Kemalism mimics Orientalism in the local context. Turkey is currently trying to move away from its engraved Orientalist value system to a less hierarchical, more egalitarian one based on universal values. The pains we attest today are mostly attributable to that internal process. Secondly, in an attempt to break away from the confines of the entrenched Orientalist value system, Turkey is challenging the impositions that come in the Orientalist package from outside. This involves taking on the Orientalist impositions and responding to them with Turkey's own unadulterated realities. Turkey's efforts to break the circular motion where Orientalism feeds off itself enables Turkey to present its realities based on its 'own' authentic experience but not of others. Here the caveat is that the process is twofold. Both prongs of the process have to be carried out contemporaneously. On one hand, Turkey tries to disseminate its own 'truth' as it sees it based on the genuine experiences from within. On the other hand, it fights off the concocted realities of the Orientalist to refute, demolish, and substitute them with its own. The coup attempt of July 15 forced Turkey to fight at both fronts against interrelated foes: Orientalism within, Orientalism without.

References

Abushanab, F. (2016a, December 14). Lustration in Turkey. *The Huffington Post*. Retrieved July 17, 2017 from http://www.huffingtonpost.com/entry/58518d8ce4b0320ed05a9a7c.

Abushanab, F. (2016b, July 19). A mafia-cult exposed in America. *Daily Sabah*. Retrieved from dailysabah.com.

Aktay, Y. (2003). Diaspora and stability: Constitutive elements in a body of knowledge. In M.H. Yavuz & J.L. Esposito (Eds.), *Turkish Islam and the secular state: The Gulen movement* (pp. 131–156). Syracuse, NY: Syracuse University Press.

Akural, S.A. (1984). Kemalist views on social change. In J.M. Landau (Ed.), *Ataturk and the modernization of Turkey* (pp. 125–152). Boulder, CO: Westview Press.

Atay, T. (2013). The clash of "nations" in Turkey: Reflections on the Gezi Park incident. *Insight Turkey, 15*(3), 39–44. Retrieved July 17, 2017 from http://file.insightturkey.com/Files/Pdf/insight_turkey_volume_15_no_3_2013_atay.pdf.

Bhabha, H. (2004). *The location of culture*. New York, NY: Routledge.

Burgat, F. (2003). *Face to face with political Islam*. London, England: I.B. Tauris.

Cornell, S.E. (2013). The diverging paths of Abdullah Gul and Tayyip Erdogan. *The Turkey Analyst, 6*(8). Retrieved July 17, 2017 from https://www.turkeyanalyst.org/publications/turkey-analyst-articles/item/42-the-diverging-paths-of-abdullah-g%C3%BCl-and-tayyip-erdogan.html.

Cox, R.W. (1992). Towards a post-hegemonic conceptualization of world order: Reflections on the relevancy of Ibn Khaldun. In J.N. Rosenau & E.-O. Czempiel (Eds.), *Governance without government: Order and change in world politics* (pp. 132–159). Cambridge, England: Cambridge University Press. doi:10.1017/cbo9780511521775.007.

Crane, R.D. (2008). Thank God for justice: Renewing the spirit in uncertain times. *Arches Quarterly, 2*(3), 27–30.

D-8 Organization for Economic Cooperation. (2014). President Erdogan: D-8 to be reinvigorated. *D-8 Journal, 3*(July 2014–June 2015), 4-4. Retrieved July 17, 2017 from http://www.developing8.org/image/Booklet/D8JOURNAL2015.pdf.

Edelman, E.S., Cornell, S.E., Lobel, A., & Makovsky, M. (2013). *The roots of Turkish conduct: Understanding the evolution of Turkish policy in the Middle East.* Bipartisan Policy Center, National Security Program, Foreign Policy Project. Retrieved July 17, 2017 from https://bipartisanpolicy.org/library/roots-turkish-conduct-understanding-evolution-turkish-policy-middle-east/.

Erdogan, R.T. (2017, March 21). Address at Insan icin Orman, Ekonomi icin Orman Bulusmasi, Dunya Ormancilik Gunu. *T.C. Orman Su Isleri Bakanligi.* Retrieved July 17, 2017 from https://m.youtube.com/watch?v=b5S46TdQ_Xc.

Esposito, J.L. (2010). Foreword. In M. Kavakci, *Headscarf politics in Turkey: A postcolonial reading* (pp. xiii–xxvi). New York, NY: Palgrave Macmillan.

Falk, R. (2014). Can the U.S. government accept an independent Turkish foreign policy in the Middle East? *Insight Turkey, 16*(1), 7–18. Retrieved July 17, 2017 from http://file.insightturkey.com/Files/Pdf/insight_turkey_16_1_2014_falk.pdf.

Fanon, F. (2004). *The wretched of the earth.* New York, NY: Grove Press.

Foucault, M. (1970). *The order of things: An archeology of the human sciences.* New York, NY: Pantheon Books.

Foucault, M. (1981). The order of discourse. In R.J.C. Young (Ed.), *Untying the text: A post-structuralist reader* (pp. 48–78). London, England: Routledge & Kegan Paul.

Fuller, G.E. (2016, July 22). The Gulen movement is not a cult: It's one of the most encouraging faces of Islam today. *Huffington Post.* Retrieved July 17, 2017 from http://www.huffingtonpost.com/graham-e-fuller/gulen-movement-not-cult_b_11116858.html.

Haberturk. (2016, August 2). Orgeneral Akar: Daha ne kaniti, kanit benim. *Haberturk.* Retrieved July 17, 2017 from http://www.haberturk.com/gundem/haber/1275360-orgeneral-akar-daha-ne-kaniti-kanit-benim.

Hurriyet. (2013, June 15). CNN International'dan Kazlicesme fotografi icin ozur. *Hurriyet.* Retrieved July 17, 2017 from http://www.hurriyet.com.tr/cnn-internationaldan-kazlicesme-fotografi-icin-ozur-23730158.

Kavakci, M. (2010). *Headscarf politics in Turkey: A postcolonial reading.* New York, NY: Palgrave Macmillan.

Kavakci, M.S. (2013). A theoretical critique: From secularism to politics of Islam. In M.S. Kavakci (Ed.), *International relations in the global village: Changing interdependencies* (pp.161–167). San Diego, CA: Cognella Academic.

Koplow, M., & Cook, S. (2013, June 3). How democratic is Turkey? Not as democratic as Washington thinks it is. *Foreign Policy Magazine.*

Ling, I.H.M. (2004). Cultural chauvinism and the liberal international order: "West versus Rest" in Asia's financial crisis. In G. Chowdhry & S. Nair (Eds.), *Power, postcolonialism and international relations: Reading race, gender and class* (pp. 115–141). London, England: Routledge.

Mamdani, M. (2002). Good Muslim, bad Muslim: A political perspective on culture and terrorism. *American Anthropologist, 104*, 766–775. doi:10.1525/aa.2002.104.3.766.

May, A. (2013). Twelve sycamore trees have set the limits on Turkish prime minister Erdogan's power. *American Foreign Policy Interests: The Journal of the National Committee on American Foreign Policy, 35*, 298–302. doi:10.1080/10803920.2013.836016.

Milliyet. (2016, July 28). ABD'li ozel istihbarat kurulusu Stratfor'dan darbe yonlendirmeleri. *Milliyet*. Retrieved July 17, 2017 from http://www.milliyet.com.tr/abd-li-ozel-istihbarat-kurulusu-gundem-2285537/.

Moore-Gilbert, B. (1997). *Postcolonial theory: Context, practices, politics.* London, England: Verso.

Ozer, G.D. (2005). *Psikolojik Bir Iskence Methodu Olarak Ikna Odalari.* Istanbul, Turkey: Beyan Yayinlari.

Ozturk, E. (2016, July 26). O gece bu otelde CIA mesaideymis! *Daily Sabah.* Retrieved from DailySabah.com.

Peres, R. (2012). *The day Turkey stood still.* Reading, England: Ithaca Press.

Persaud, R.B. (2004). Situating race in international relations: The dialectics of civilizational security in American immigration. In G. Chowdhry & S. Nair (Eds.), *Power, postcolonialism and international relations: Reading race, gender and class* (pp. 56–81). London, England: Routledge.

Rubin, M. (2010, June 2). Erdogan's Turkey is not a friend. *Forward.* Retrieved July 17, 2017 from http://forward.com/opinion/128501/erdogan-s-turkey-is-not-a-friend/.

Rubin, M. (2016, July 15). Erdogan has nobody to blame but himself for the coup. *Foreign Policy.* Retrieved July 17, 2017 from http://www.michaelrubin.org/19008/turkey-erdogan-coup.

Sabah. (2016, July 26). Orgeneral Hulisi Akar tum yasadiklarini anlatti. *Sabah.* Retrieved July 17, 2017 from http://www.sabah.com.tr/gundem/2016/07/26/orgeneral-hulusi-akar-tum-yasadiklarini-anlatti.

Said, E.W. (1978). *Orientalism.* New York, NY: Vintage Books.

Salame, G. (2001). Introduction: Where are the democrats? In G. Salame (Ed.), *Democracy without democrats? The renewal of politics in the Muslim world* (pp. 1–22). London, England: I.B. Tauris.

Shively, K. (2005). Religious bodies and the secular state: The Merve Kavakci affair. *Journal of Middle East Women's Studies, 1*, 47–72. doi:10.1215/15525864-2005-4003.

Spivak, G.C. (1998). Can the subaltern speak? In C. Nelson & L. Grossberg (Eds.), *Marxism and the interpretation of culture* (pp. 271–316). Chicago, IL: University of Illinois Press.

Spivak, G.C. (1999). *A critique of postcolonial reason: Towards the history of a vanishing present.* Cambridge, MA: Harvard University Press.

Takvim. (2013, June 18). CNN Yersen! *Takvim.* Retrieved from http://www.takvim.com.tr/guncel/2013/06/18/cnn-yersen.

Tocci, N. (2011). *Turkey's European future: Behind the scenes of America's influence on EU-Turkey relations.* New York, NY: New York University Press.

Veterans Today. (2016, August 24). Trump: CIA officers helped Turkey coup attempt; evidence available. *Veterans Today: Journal for the Clandestine Community.* Retrieved July 17, 2017 from http://www.veteranstoday.com/2016/08/24/trump-cia-officers-helped-turkey-coup-attempt-evidence-available/.

Waterbury, J. (2001). Democracy without Democrats?: The potential for political liberalization in the Middle East. In G. Salame (Ed.), *Democracy without democrats? The renewal of politics in the Muslim world* (pp. 23–47). London, England: I.B. Tauris.

White, J. (2005). The end of Islamism? Turkey's Muslimhood model. In R. Heffner (Ed.), *Modern Muslim politics* (pp. 87–111). Princeton, NJ: Princeton University Press.

White, J.B. (2002). *Islamist mobilization in Turkey: A study in vernacular politics.* Seattle, WA: University of Washington Press.

Yavuz, H. (2000). Cleansing Islam from the public sphere. *Journal of International Affairs, 54,* 21–42.

Yavuz, H. (2003). *Islamic political identity in Turkey.* New York, NY: Oxford University Press.

Young, R.J.C. (2001). *Postcolonialism: An historical introduction.* Malden, MA: Blackwell.

CHAPTER 9

(Neo)Orientalism: Alive and Well in American Academia: A Case Study of Contemporary Iranian Art

Staci Gem Scheiwiller

Introduction

Contemporary Iranian art, as well as contemporary Middle Eastern art and contemporary Islamic art, has been ushered into the North American and European academic discourses of postmodern and contemporary art or into the newest nomenclature of "global art."[1] Although scholarship on contemporary Iranian art has been taking shape since the 1960s, its presence in the discipline of art history and international art markets has grown dramatically since the events of September 11, 2001, and the later American colonial wars in Afghanistan (2001–present) and Iraq (2003–2011?), as interest in the cultures and lives of the Middle East has also grown exponentially (Hassan, 2010). This result may seem to bode well or to be a bittersweet outcome of these violent conflicts, but I suggest that the integration of contemporary Iranian art into the discourses of contemporary and global art has been awkward and not wholly successful because of the prevailing (neo)Orientalist views still well entrenched within the art market, the discipline of art history, and academia in North America and Europe. This unsettling marriage of contemporary Iranian art to the framework of contemporary art has produced weak scholarship, because many scholars who have never been to Iran or do not have the language skill set write about contemporary Iranian art—a condition that is atypical in other academic disciplines. What compounds the situation is that art markets continue to focus on a contemporary Iranian and Middle Eastern art that speaks heavily of an ethnic or cultural identity; hence, often when Iranian artists become internationally famous in a global art scene that already possesses defined tropes of 'contemporary Iranian art,' several of these artists have been accused of 'self-Orientalizing,' thus forcing them into particular

1 I would like to thank Hamid Severi, Amitis Motevalli, Elaine O'Brien, and Bavand Behpoor for their assistance and insightful comments. Reliable colleagues are a treasure, and I am grateful that they always have time to dialogue and to critique my work.

sidelines when 'white' artists from North America and Europe usually do not face similar dilemmas.

In this chapter, I also question this condition of 'neo-Orientalism' in relation to this subfield of 'contemporary Iranian art,' as Orientalism itself has never really left the field of art history. For instance, scholars writing on contemporary Iranian and Middle Eastern art continually invoke the terms 'East' and 'West' when describing artwork and artists, but 'East' and 'West' are really euphemisms for 'Orient' and 'Occident,' which still divide the world ideologically into ways similar to those constructed in Samuel Huntington's *The Clash of Civilizations and the Remaking of World Order* (1997) and that do not provide nuanced understandings of the artwork at hand. My definition of 'ideology' is based on the writings of Marx, Althusser (1971), and Freire (2005), referring to a set of beliefs and agendas of the ruling classes that are disseminated to the rest of society and normalized through discursive practices and institutions; thus, in participating through these apparatuses, ideology becomes invisible and difficult to extract and to criticize by the oppressed classes. Moreover, I seek to define neo-Orientalism as it exists in the discourses on contemporary Iranian art and to rethink approaching these artists and objects without attempting to replicate the limited attitudes and ways of thinking that postmodernism had sought to deconstruct in the first place.

(Neo)Orientalism: The Death that Never Came

I was only a year old when Edward Said (1935–2003) published his tour de force *Orientalism* in 1978 that would forever change all disciplines in radical ways, henceforth making him a great patriarch of postcolonial studies. Although the dialogue of problematizing Orientalism had already been in motion in American academia (Binder, 1976), I grew up in a world that was supposedly post-Orientalist, but it seems that the liberation of American and European academia from its perpetual racist stances toward the Middle East has continued to be an uphill battle. In that regard, if one considers the term "neo-Orientalism," there is the assumption that somehow Orientalism went away and has been revived (Abbas, 2011; MacDonald, 2003; Poole, 2002), especially after 9/11 (and on July 7, 2005, when the Tube in London was bombed) when it was presumed that Osama bin Laden (1957–2011?) and al-Qaeda (founded 1988) were the culprits in destroying the Twin Towers in New York City and murdering almost 3,000 people. Then the United States promptly began its colonial interventions into Afghanistan one month later. Former U.S. President George W. Bush (elected? 2000–2008) only exacerbated the situation soon thereafter when he called the quickly formulating "war on terrorism" a "crusade" (Ford, 2001, para. 4), thus emulating constructed medieval dichotomies between Christendom and the Caliphate and echoing Huntington's infamous work, which displaces the tensions in the Middle East caused by American imperialism into a power vacuum at the end of the Cold War (1947–1991) that would bring the Christian and Islamic 'worlds' into conflict.

It may be apt to define here what I mean by 'Orientalism' before probing deeper into the implications and consequences of neo-Orientalism in my particular field of study as an American scholar. Said (1979) defined Orientalism as a dialectal structure that European writers, scholars, artists, and politicians had constructed of an eastward (relative to them) geographical space that they called the 'Orient,' which they initially characterized by Islam. As European colonial expansion (and then American imperialism later) moved farther eastward, countries not usually identified with Islam, such as China and Japan, became included under this label of the 'Orient' (Said, 1979). This binary of the Occident and the Orient produced through various European (and later North American) institutional discourses emulated German philosopher G.W.F. Hegel's master/slave dialectic (1807), in which two opposing subjects are interrelated and dependent on each other for their identities. However, whoever held the master position would be deemed as positive and superior, thus displacing and relegating his negative traits onto the Other: "European culture gained in strength and identity by setting itself off against the Orient as a sort of surrogate and even underground self" (Said, 1979 pp. 2–3). By constructing representations of peoples and civilizations eastward of itself as barbaric, non-Christian, and incapable of ruling themselves, European powers could justify the institution of colonialism, thus dominating and manipulating these geographical spaces to bolster their own global images, to control natural resources, and to exploit strategic military positions. Moreover, what has been demonstrated as 'knowledge,' 'fact,' and 'truth' in North American and European academia until the 1970s was an epistemology of the Middle East and Islam seen mostly through European eyes.

In attempting to understand the phenomenon of neo-Orientalism, it might be useful to also address the term 'post-Orientalism.' After Said's publication, the impact was so great that studying the Middle East had to be reconsidered—supposedly, there was no going back to gazing at the Middle East through a seemingly positivist, colonial lens. In this aftermath, Frédéric Volpi (2010), an expert on political Islam, mentioned that scholars of the Middle East looked to postcolonial studies, specific case studies, and anthropological and economic factors that would fracture the monolithic modes of Orientalist thought. In *Post-Orientalism* (2009), Dabashi nuances and challenges Said's work in ways that allow scholars to think past Said's initial arguments. For example, Dabashi complicates the position of the Hungarian Orientalist Ignác (Ignaz) Goldziher (1850–1921), who was indeed imbued with certain ideological predilections, but who also possessed a profound sympathy with and desire to learn the Other, as much as was possible for him (see also Varisco, 2007). In this regard, although the overall project of Orientalism was flawed and consisted of knowledge wrought forth from colonial power relations and contestations, there may also be some examples of Orientalist scholarship worth salvaging, retaining, and disseminating, and the post-Orientalist moment is one that re-examines and reconsiders this scholarship. This case arises especially when scholars attempt to reconstruct historical moments of the Middle East and have to rely partly on the narratives of traveling Orientalists, for these recorded accounts are still valuable and cannot be completely dispensed with, although they should be viewed with skepticism due to their ideological contexts (Mahdavi, 2004; Rahimi, 2013).

In relation to the American academic context, the Iranian Revolution (1978–1979), the Iran Hostage Crisis (1979–1981), the Iran-Iraq War (1980–1988), the Lebanese Civil War (1975–1990), the bombing of Libya (1986), Gulf War I (1990–1991), and the First and Second Intifadas (1987–1993, 2000–2005) are only some of the conflicts within the Middle East, all of which involved the United States on serious levels and in different ways, looming in the back of American minds, even if peripherally or subliminally, and certainly on the radars of the American government when 9/11 occurred. To mark 9/11 as some sort of transition or milestone is ideological itself, or at least for Americans, because destructive conflicts have been pervasive in the Middle East, incurred by the U.S. government *ad nauseam*. With that said, what is happening in American and European academia is still Orientalism—it never died, it never went away, and it never subsisted. Perhaps one could argue that it only increased with the events of 9/11, but Orientalism was alive and well beforehand and continues to seep through every fabric of American life, such as through war and media, not just in academia, hence making the challenge to combat and to eradicate it an almost never-ending battle with no end in sight. Volpi (2010) also points out that those described as 'neo-Orientalists' never initially embraced the postmodern quest to eliminate 'Grand Narratives,' as the condition of postmodernity is characterized as a move away from a dominant center, as well as a dismantling of overall structures that could explain everything, hence postmodernity's other name, poststructuralism. In citing books such as Huntington's (1997) and Barber's *Jihad vs. McWorld* (1996), as well as the end of the Cold War leaving a lacuna for another political scapegoat for the United States, Volpi implies that Orientalists never disappeared from the academic scene after Said's publication.

What 9/11 did do, if to create a neo-Orientalist moment, was that it gave the U.S. government a carte blanche (in its own eyes) to wage colonial wars on Islamicate countries, such as Afghanistan, Iraq, and Libya, and threaten and harass others, such as Iran and Pakistan, in the name of protecting its own freedoms at the cost of others'. In Dabashi's *Brown Skin, White Masks* (2011), his main argument is that Middle Easterners have become the new Blacks and Muslims the new Jews in a post-9/11 American society. Moreover, it is not that Orientalism went away and was revived, but that the events of 9/11 and its aftermath only increased violence and prejudice toward the Other that was already there, enmeshed into American psyches. 9/11 became a catalyst for witch hunts against any American dissident, but particularly Middle Easterners and Muslims. On April 19. 2013, after the Boston Marathon bombings of April 15, 2013, Rep. Peter King (R-N.Y.), Chair of the House Subcommittee on Counterterrorism and Intelligence, declared that surveillance on Muslims should increase (Rayfield, 2013). On March 10, 2011, King had already conducted 'Muslim hearings' on Capitol Hill, analogous to 1950s McCarthyism of the Cold War. Among those who testified was the Muslim Rep. Keith Ellison (D-Minn.) who broke down into tears from the religious persecution endemic in such hearing proceedings. But most importantly, as argued by both Bayoumi (2010) and Dabashi (2011), the already living and breathing Orientalist discourses in American academia have reached new levels, because Orientalist agendas are now enforced and 'confirmed' by persons originally from Islamicate countries who condone and encourage American colonial interests, thus reassuring the American public that it is permissible to support these imperial interventions. Orientalism is no longer a European/North American project forced onto the world but has now co-opted seemingly 'authentic' voices that repeat and reinforce these older paradigms.

In relation to Islamic art history, one must note that the established discipline of art history is historically Eurocentric, as Johann Winckelmann's *Geschichte der Kunst des Alterums* (*History of Art of Antiquity*, 1764) is deemed the first official art historical text, privileging ancient Greek art, and the first professorships of art history were established at Göttingen, Germany, in 1813 (Minor, 1994). Like Orientalism, the field of art history until the 20th century has been constructed and viewed almost completely through European worldviews. As powerful empires, such as the British and French ones, colonized Africa, Asia, and the Pacific during the 19th century until World War II (1939–1945), scholars embarked on producing a discourse of 'Islamic art,' comprising partially the booty stolen from colonized entities (Vernoit, 2000). The ways in which Islamic art have been written about and categorized often affirmed ideological agendas of these colonial empires. For example, Sir Charles

Hercules Read (1857–1929) wrote in 1907 about the problems in collecting art from the Middle East in a catalogue of faience for the Burlington Fine Arts Club:

> One inherent and unsurmountable difficulty … makes these discoveries [of collectible materials] of far less value than they might be. This is the innate mendacity of the Oriental nomad who is mostly the purveyor of these relics. If a vase be really from excavations in Asia Minor he will surely declare that it comes from the neighbourhood of Teheran, perhaps in the belief that the buyer might … send an agent thither to buy direct.… [T]he story of the cosmopolitan oriental is untrustworthy.
>
> READ, 1907, p. xiv

What Read implied in this passage is that only Europeans are reliable in collecting and preserving 'Islamic art.' The 'Oriental' is too stupid to understand the pricing of objects and will dupe European collectors at any cost. The 'Oriental nomad' should not be the distributor of these precious objects or have such a strong hand in the art market, thus creating a 'white man's burden' for collectors who must protect both the Oriental and his culture from his own backward devices. When read within a broader context, if the Oriental cannot manage his artwork effectively, then how could he manage his own government and people, hence leaving no alternative but to be colonized by powers smarter and greater than he.

A perplexing problem that continues to haunt the scholarship and pedagogy of art history, but in other disciplines as well, is the continued monolithic labels of 'East,' 'West,' and 'non-Western' used to geographically place art, as well as to delineate what one studies in art history. The basic art historical surveys compose what is known as 'Western' art, although one initially discusses Iran, Egypt, and Mesopotamia, until the narrative switches permanently in favor of ancient Greece and Rome. An ideology of European hegemony is implicit in these surveys—the rise of European civilizations is clearly indebted to those of Africa and Asia, but they become Other, outmoded, 'non-Western,' and excluded once antiquity is fully entrenched as the backbone of European cultural production, despite Africa and Asia's own contributions and claims to a Greco-Roman inheritance (Bernal, 2006). The surveys could entail artists of color, such as the Mexican Muralists or several postmodern artists, but often their inclusions are framed to serve as tokens that reaffirm European-dominated narratives, such as when Andre Breton (1896–1966) proclaimed Frida Kahlo (1907–1954) as a great Surrealist when she herself did not initially label her work this way (Mahon, 2011).

My point here is that Said's *Orientalism* sought to show that the dialectic of the Occident versus the Orient was ideologically constructed to justify European and later American colonial interventions, but do not the substituted terms of 'East' versus 'West' actually imply similar baggage? Are they not just euphemisms for similar concepts? In fact, the language is possibly even more egregious, as what is deemed 'East' and 'West' is completely farcical. For example, the art of the United States is, for the most part, deemed 'Western' but not indigenous peoples' artwork, even though all the artwork is in the same hemisphere (Kleiner, 2010).

Furthermore, the political constructs of 'East' and 'West' appear strongly when one observes a Dymaxion (Fuller) map that depicts the land masses of Earth as connected in an icosahedron, and there becomes no discernible orientation. Naoki Sakai has assessed in "Modernity and Its Critique" (1989) that the geopolitical entities of 'East' and 'West' are not naturally but ideologically imbued:

> It goes without saying that the West is not simply and straightforwardly a geographic category. One need not refer to historical details to discover that the West has expanded and shifted arbitrarily for the last two centuries. It is a name for a subject which gathers itself in discourse but is also an object constituted discursively; it is, evidently, a name always associating itself with those regions, communities and peoples that appear politically or economically superior to other regions, communities, and peoples. (p. 94)

Sakai describes the 'West' as a semiotic sign with ideological coding that is actually not really associated with geography but with political agendas.

This East-West dichotomy has had its ramifications on the entire study of art history, including art from the Middle East, which occupies a schizophrenic existence in these narratives. For example, in both *Gardner's Art Through the Ages: The Western Perspective* (Kleiner, 2008) and *Gardner's Art Through the Ages: Non-Western Perspectives* (Kleiner, 2010), the same chapter on Islamic art appears twice, when no other chapter does; hence, I teach Islamic art in both the non-Western and ancient art surveys. The position becomes more bizarre when Islamic Spain is featured, occupying a space that is deemed both 'Western' and 'non-Western.' Islamic art was born out of the Greco-Roman tradition and its early buildings were either former churches or temples or subsequently built by Byzantine architects. As the third and final revelation of the Abrahamic religions, if Islam and Islamic art are going to be placed in a black-and-white paradigm, it would be 'Western,' not 'Eastern.' I do not promote these labels, but my purpose is to show how these world divisions and understandings of each other are completely fabricated to the point that they are contradictory.

A History of Contemporary Iranian Art

In the late 1960s and 1970s, the art scene in the United States seemed to be changing for the better. Thanks to the civil rights movement of the 1950s and 1960s (and earlier), the second-wave feminist movement (1960s–1970s), and the visibility of other oppressed peoples, such as the Chicano movement that began in the 1960s, more minorities began to appear on American art scenes, were shown in galleries and museums, and were written about by critics and scholars. Although the artwork of white American and British male artists still sells for the highest prices in the international art markets (Robertson, 2011), this increasing inclusion of artwork by people of color coincided with the rise of postmodernity and postcolonialism, both of which called for an end to white male domination and hegemony in politics and in art. The project of European modernism had been one of hypermasculinity, heteronormativity, and racism, comprised and constructed on the backs of women and people of color (Brennan, 2006; Connelly, 1994). The übermasculinity and appropriation of non-European art can be seen repeatedly within the narratives of modernism—Henri Matisse (1869–1954), Pablo Picasso (1881–1973), and Jackson Pollock (1912–1948) are just a few in the lineage of (artist) white father and son, engaged in an Oedipal avant-garde, incorporating non-European motifs as a snub toward academic art. Scholars have credited postmodernism as the inheritor of modernism's rebellion and the avant-garde's drive to push culture forward in critical, meaningful ways, thus holding promise for women and people of color to take the vanguard and to continue the revolution against hypercapitalist politics, institutional prejudices, and canonized art histories (Foster, 1996; Lyotard, 1992; Owens, 1980). Women artists and artists of color did revolutionize the art world for the better, but as the age of globalization and global art are among us (my take on post-postmodernism), the promises of postmodernism have eluded us, including in the subfield of contemporary Iranian art. (A different, but excellent, take on the cultural aftermath of postmodernism is Kirby's 2009 *Digimodernism.*)

A history of modern and contemporary art in and from Iran has weaved through several phases and labels since the 19th century. During the late 1800s and early 1900s, some called modern art in Iran *honar-e taraqi*, literally "progressive art," which indicated an avant-garde attitude that sought to push art forward (Khansari, 1990). Then efforts, such as those by Karim Emami (1930–2005),

Abby Weed Grey (1902–1980), Donna Stein, Akbar Tadjvidi (b. 1926), and Ehsan Yarshater (b. 1920), to name only a few, during the 1960s and 1970s usually discussed contemporary Iranian art as 'modern Persian art' as an historical connection to the rubric of 'Persian painting,' although sometimes these writers also used the national term 'Iranian' (Emami, 1971; Tadjvidi, 1962, 1967; Yarshater, 1979). Art was not always considered Islamic per se, or if there was a connection, for example, in relation to the art movement the *Saqqa-khaneh*, the movement itself was not Islamic. Then later after the Iranian Revolution, in 1984, the Pasadena Asia Museum showed *Contemporary Persian Art: Expression of Our Time*, still retaining "Persian" in its title, while in 1987, the Baltimore Convention Center exhibited *Contemporary Iranian Art: Four Women*, although it featured only one artist who was actually still working in Iran, Parvaneh Etemadi (b. 1948). Finally, in April–June 2001, the exhibition *Contemporary Iranian Art* at the Curve Gallery in London could be credited as a catalyst for what would be known officially in the art world as 'contemporary Iranian art.'

In 1989, the category 'contemporary Islamic art' also became more prominent in American academia through Wijdan Ali (1989, 1997), although exhibitions continued to use 'contemporary Iranian art' (as noted above) or 'contemporary Arab art' in their titles. Yet, it was in October 2001 when the auction house Sotheby's in London was selling "Arts of the Islamic World including 20th Cent. Middle Eastern Paintings" (Sotheby's, 2001). This combination continued until about 2012, although Sotheby's began separating 'modern and contemporary Arab and Iranian art' from Islamic art in 2007 and opened an office in Doha in 2008 (Sotheby's, 2007, 2012). The auction house Christie's also began marketing 'contemporary Iranian art' in 2006 with Bonham's following suit in 2008, both inaugural auctions coinciding with offices opening in Dubai. However, there continues to be international contemporary Islamic art exhibitions and conferences, thus still retaining the heading 'contemporary Islamic art.' Furthermore, this inconsistency of labels, changing labels, or multiple labels might imply that contemporary art from the Middle East in general has not been fully entrenched into one particular discourse or subfield, thus making it difficult to codify, which in turn becomes a problem when attempting to produce scholars and experts on the topic.

This continual identity crisis of the subfield 'contemporary Iranian art' is that there is no set course of study to become an expert on it. Currently, to study modern and contemporary Iranian or Middle Eastern art, one either studies Islamic art or modern and contemporary art, and rarely the twain shall meet unless the scholar makes a conscious effort to do so. If discussing contemporary Iranian photography, then one has a third subfield of photohistory to contend with that does not necessarily overlap the others. Therefore, Islamicists are not always conversant with the theories and approaches of modern and contemporary art historians, and likewise, modern and contemporary art historians do not have the experience, language skill set, or knowledge that Islamicists have. One has to make a very skilled, conscious effort to walk the line in multiple subfields to accomplish familiarity with the discourses, which is not easy, as these subfields are oriented so differently. Perhaps what I am suggesting is that 'modern and contemporary Middle Eastern art' has become a subfield all its own that cannot be sustained any longer within the current paradigms of art history, which, as mentioned earlier, were initially constructed by European epistemologies.

What this unstable position in the field of art history has done is create low-quality scholarship when writing on contemporary Iranian art, mostly on the part of contemporary art scholars, but Islamicists have also penned some poor scholarship too, imagining contemporary art to be a free-for-all that can be interpreted any way the viewer likes. Art historian and former Head of Research at the Tehran Museum of Contemporary Art Hamid Severi (2012) has suggested that the subfield of contemporary Iranian art suffers from a lack of rigorous academic research and writing, and this assertion seems to be proving quite true (Behpoor, 2012a; Keshmirshekan, 2011a). Even in premier peer-reviewed journals and publications, scholars not qualified as experts to speak on the subject are published, thus enmeshing themselves into the discourses that must be cited after the fact, even though a peer reviewer should have axed the manuscript dead on arrival. These types of articles contain no primary sources or sources in Persian (sometimes not in any language other than English). There is usually not a single reference to an interview with an artist, and if present, the interview was usually conducted in English. Artists' statements are generally missing too, unless a short statement in English is available. No article in English on Iranian history, linguistics, economics, and so forth could be taken seriously without primary or Persian sources, so why are these practices accepted only for articles on contemporary Iranian art? Is it that the academic bar for these articles is so low that the journals and publishers accept them written by scholars and graduate students who specialize on topics other than Iran and who can only use theory *ad nauseam* to speak about art in Iran, since there is no other substance or evidence utilized? Contemporary Iranian art as a subfield of both Iranian studies and art history and its discourses should be expected to have a similar academic caliber as any other. This type of opportunist capitalizing on contemporary Iranian and Middle Eastern art in general by those not qualified indexes a continuing colonial attitude alluding that this type of artwork is to be written or spoken about for the taking, and that a scholar does not need much training to speak or write of this artwork, while in fact, one does.

Self-Orientalizing

> Friends don't let friends self-Orientalize. We are all colonized, but to colonize yourself is just taking it a step too far.
>
> Artist JOSHUA H. BOLIN, February 28, 2013

In contemporary Iranian art discourses, a tension exists that involves the agency of speaking—who can speak for whom? Who is an Iranian artist? And most of all, what is contemporary Iranian art (Keshmirshekan, 2011b)? Is it art solely from Iran, or could it also include that from the Iranian diaspora? Is the only qualification that the artist is an Iranian, and if so, what is the implication of this identification? If one is discussing Iranian identity in his or her artwork but creating art outside Iran, then does that artwork also comprise the discourses? Several artists and art historians in Iran have made claims that only Iranian artists living and working in Iran can make 'contemporary Iranian art'—anyone working outside Iran is eliminated from that dialogue. As early as 1999, Ruin Pakbaz, an art historian in Iran, wrote in "Contemporary Art of Iran": "[I]n this article, no mention has been made of Iranian artists who live in other countries and have not directly affected the evolution of contemporary Iranian art" (p. 173). This particular view assumes nonporous borders, which allow a national art to flourish without any contact with the outside world—a notion that is probably impossible. But it is not only Pakbaz who holds this position, and it has gained popularity throughout the years, creating a striking blow to those Iranian artists working abroad (Allerstorfer, 2004; College Art Association Annual Conference, 2012; S. Entekhabi, personal communication, May 24, 2012).

Conversely, could Iranian artists (inside or outside Iran) make art that is not Iranian, i.e., not reflective of the state and/or of one's culture(s)? According to Althusser's (1971) ideas on ideology, the answer would be 'no,' as one is continually navigating through labyrinths of *a priori* sign systems since one's birth, but the more troubling issue is that what is deemed 'Iranian' and what is not have often been determined by the Orientalist fantasies still prevalent in the tastes of the art markets, collectors, collections, curators, and art historians who reside outside Iran. The dominance of American, European, and Arab art markets has played a large role in isolating contemporary Iranian art (Severi, 2012). The genre is a growing commodity on the art market, bringing in millions at auction houses (Christie's, 2017; Golshiri, 2011), oftentimes forcing Iranian artists to conform to styles and motifs that their foreign audiences and collectors would like to see as opposed to what they would like to express. Art historian Alireza Sahafzadeh (n.d.) has blamed the art market for diluting the quality of contemporary Iranian art, and artist Barbad Golshiri (b. 1982) has made artwork that critiques the art market's desire for artwork that suits their expectations of what contemporary Iranian art should be like. For example, in Golshiri's print *Quod* (2010), he creates a nauseating experiencing for those attempting to look at or to read the Persian calligraphy, as well as the notion of the print itself removes the artist's hand/brush (Shahandeh, 2011). His motivation in making the print was that "the art market is limiting Persian writing to 'formalist, harmless and exotic calligraphy made for those who cannot read it'" (Aaran Art Gallery Newsletter, April 18, 2013). This colonial identification and desire for Arabic and Persian calligraphy—specific markers that are in contrast to European and North American sign systems—become sought-after aesthetic commodities on their own without the collector bothering to know what the text says (Moussavi-Aghdam & Mahmoudian, 2011). Severi (2012) has stated that international exhibitions on contemporary Iranian art tend to focus on Iranian identity and culture at the expense of other artistic factors and interpretations. Severi writes:

> [G]lobal attention is not without disadvantages, mostly and particularly auctions and art fairs are looking for "Iranianness" ... With their hegemonic power of exposure and ability to pay high prices, they influence artists and become the trend-setters and taste-makers.... Unfortunately, it [the art market] encourages many artists to modify their styles to make artworks that sell well: this is seen in the use of calligraphy ... or Persian script in their artworks ... Persian patterns, or recognizable Iranian elements such as veils [known as Chador Art], Islamic motifs, etc. (n.p.)

Much like the 19th-century colonial archeological digs, raids, pilferings, and buying of objects abroad (often through black market venues) that resulted in fabulous collections of 'Islamic' art in European collections, the art markets spur a demand for contemporary Iranian art that speaks of 'Iranianness,' and in a postmodern context, one has to ask whether such a pure state actually exists. It is probably an impossible feat, and yet, the art markets hunger for more of what it has constructed and determined for itself as 'Iranian.'

The global art world also perpetuates its racism and insensitivity by showing Iranian artists together without contingence, just because they are Iranian in origin (Keshmirshekan, 2011c). This approach to contemporary Iranian art can lead to the indiscriminate lumping of artists, styles, and messages without discernment. Islamic art historian Sussan Babaie (2011) has commented that this model is strikingly similar to the ways 'Islamic art' has been shown in the past. For example, the exhibition *Iran Inside Out* (2009) at the Chelsea

Museum in New York showed artists who work inside Iran in relation to those who work outside, comparing and contrasting their motifs and trends in light of their geographic differences. Although the show was praised for its wide representation of women artists and its potential to elucidate stereotypes about Iran (Cotter, 2009), as its opening coincided incidentally with the Green Revolution (2009–2010), some critics thought that the show only compounded the monolithic thinking already prevalent in the United States. Melik Kalyan (2009), writer for *Forbes Magazine* and *The Wall Street Journal*, commented:

> What the show doesn't do is change our [American] perceptions, for this is exactly what we thought. Iranians on the whole, especially young Iranians—and most of the home-based artists are young—despise the regime. If that is a stereotyped perception, the show merely confirms it. (n.p.)

Kalyan's suspicions allude to American ideological desires that obsess over a disgruntled Iranian youth with the hope that they may overthrow the Islamic Republic and install a government more suited to placating American interests, and this show only replicated those desires. In the end, American audiences saw what they wanted to see or messages they already knew how to read.

A debate has arisen within the discourses of contemporary Iranian art called 'self-Orientalizing' or 'self-exoticizing' in relation to this racism of the international art markets and the competition between artists, both inside and outside Iran. These accusations include almost any Iranian artist using motifs or tropes within an Orientalist framework, such as veils, calligraphy, or violence, as visual strategies to attract buyers on the art markets. In comparison, film scholar Yoshiharu Tezuka (2012) has coined a term "legitimizing cosmopolitanism," a type of self-Orientalizing in relation to Japanese filmmakers after World War II who were consciously creating films for international markets and catering to these exotic tastes and perceptions of "traditional" Japan (p. 41). Modern narratives about everyday life were usually abandoned, as they did not sell well and were not titillating enough for foreign audiences. Furthermore, Tezuka bases his definitions of self-Orientalism on Sakai (1989), who argued that when Japanese identities were gazed at and absorbed by Europe and North America, they had to be differentiated as Other to retain their uniqueness. This recognition of the international gaze makes the Other consciously refashion oneself into an Orientalized object: "The only route left to a non-Western subject is to affirm one as having an 'otherness' that is worthy in the eyes of the West, thus resorting to self-Orientalism" (Tezuka, 2012, p. 40).

In a contemporary Iranian context, the production of artwork becomes problematic on several levels. My question to those who accuse artists of self-Orientalizing is "As opposed to what?" Behpoor (2012a) has also posed a similar question in relation to the statement that "Contemporary Iranian art is bad." In relation to what—Iranian art of the past, other art from the Middle East, or 'Western' art? The accusation supposes that there is an Orientalized identity and an 'authentic' one, when the assumed 'real' identity is just as fraught and performed as the one cultivated to foreign artistic demands. Yet attempting to disentangle this notion of 'self-Orientalizing' presumes freewill in constructing oneself—one can actively shape and fashion one's identity—but one can only act and react in a world of existing, floating signifiers. It takes more than just one person's effort to fashion one's identity into something desired, marketable, and Other, as those systems of signs convey meanings for larger international audiences that are already speaking in a colonial language and can only negotiate within that language. And according to art critic Behpoor (2012b), these accusations of self-Orientalism potentially silence others and do not help the situation for Iranian artists, because as one attempts to speak a global (colonial) language in international art markets, the language that one uses at 'home' will inevitably mutate into something else. Iranian artist Alireza Darvish (b. 1968), who lives and works in Germany, has also spoken of the need to change the symbols and language of his artwork to address a foreign audience who does not understand some of his deeper cultural references (Siegel & Gonzalez, 2013).

The artwork of transnational Iranian artist Amitis Motevalli (b. 1969) provides a liminal space to speak of both Orientalizing and self-Orientalizing, of criticizing both the colonizer and colonized, as she brings the viewer face-to-face with the codifications and oppressions brought about through hegemonic patriarchal powers dominant in the United States and abroad. Some of Motevalli's most powerful performance art comes through her alter ego, Sand Ninja, who is a warrior against colonialism. Sand Ninja is the ultimate Orientalized subject imagined and then materialized—hairy, sexual, money-driven, gold-obsessed, and exotic. Her harem-like den includes a hookah, pillows, carpets, and strap-on bombs. All the stereotypes combined that American and European viewers have dreamed of what a Middle Eastern woman must be like become manifest through this character. But the critique does not stop here. In an artist talk, Motevalli spoke in-depth about the multifaceted processes that brought Sand Ninja into life. Motevalli described an evening at a beach party where an Iranian-American actress was dancing around a bonfire (A. Motevalli, artist talk, February 28, 2013). According to Motevalli, the actress's movements were melodramatized and 'Orientalized' to the point of laughable exaggeration. Motevalli's reaction was repulsion and disbelief toward the actress's over-the-top performance, but she later reflected on the possible deep-seated identity crisis that the actress must have been going through as an exile who cannot return to Iran due to her family's former connections to the reign of Mohammad Reza Shah Pahlavi (r. 1941–1979). All this particular woman had were memories of her family's past and the Orientalized machinations present in her current country, and as Tezuka (2012) has pointed out, perhaps this self-Orientalizing was a way to differentiate herself from the white universalism imposed by mainstream American culture. In contrast, Motevalli is able to travel back to Iran, and it is possibly due to this ability to navigate between international spaces that she can see all sides and speak of the various layers that compose the accusations of self-Orientalizing. Sometimes the impetus to self-Orientalize is not just to become famous and to make money, but the core of who one is continually slips in-between the 'real' and the 'unreal,' as if that dialectic actually exists anyway.

Yet Motevalli tests the limits of actively Orientalizing in a performance of mimicry that demonstrates the absurdity of the Orientalist project. For instance, Motevalli makes on-site passports for persons for the empire of 'Ninjastan.' The passports are based on her own Iranian passport, but the geographic region of Ninjastan includes the entire 'Middle East.' In a passport photograph of artist Joshua H. Bolin (b. 1978), he is transformed into a citizen of Ninjastan with turban and full beard (Motevalli, 2013). To become part of this imaginary space (much like the 'Orient' itself), the person transforms into the appropriate 'Ninjastani.' The passport photograph is important, because it says much about citizenship and representation, making the body a system of signs that potentially signifies national identity. Inadvertently, through the passport, both its picture and the person holding it become representations of the state, country, and culture, whether the person carrying the passport wants to be or not. The material possession of the passport and its photograph, along with its signage, all work in tandem as one crosses international borders.

Through a transformation of the subject, the non-Middle Eastern American (although Motevalli makes passports for everyone, including Middle Easterners) becomes part of Ninjastan and 'Orientalized' when handed over the passport—the Iranian artist has flipped the power dynamic and made the non-Middle Easterner into an object—a representation—that can be manipulated by her willful desires, much like the co-opted American media props up images of the Middle East to accomplish political agendas. Motevalli's goals are not as devious though, because her agency in the global matrices of power is comparably mute, as well as she intends to demystify—not mystify—but her artwork in this case illustrates that anyone can be Other(ed) by having one's sense of self reconfigured by someone else's hand. Motevalli puts the non-Middle Easterner in the position of being Orientalized for just one photograph, for one single instance, whereas peoples from the Middle East in the United States and abroad fight a daily barrage of false representations imposed onto them from various sources.

In a 2013 conversation with Motevalli, we discussed what it means "to decolonize oneself" and discovered no answer. If one were to strip all the colonized components that create one's sense of identity, what would one find? If one kept renouncing all that had been forced and manipulated—about race, gender, class, religion, and so forth—would one find the true self? Or are our identities constructed in sync or in opposition to the constructions already imposed on us? Could one born and raised in the United States, studying and writing on the Middle East but not of Middle Eastern descent or Muslim, not be an Orientalist? Again, according to Althusser (1971), the answer would probably be 'no,' as anyone born and raised in the United States and Europe, regardless of one's race, religion, or ethnicity, will most likely be an Orientalist on some level, because (neo)Orientalism is still one of the dominant paradigms of knowledge in mainstream American and most European cultures. To break from those matrices completely or permanently is no easy task, if not impossible. Similar to the position of 'postcolonialism,' perhaps one cannot return to a time before Orientalism. Our world will always be in a state of flux between post-Orientalism and neo-Orientalism but never pre-Orientalism or completely rid of it. In my moment of reflection, it is a poignant state to be in, because the discourses of power have no beginning or end. I suppose all one can do is search for a ray of hope in a bleak, still colonized world: "Such darkness is only a simulacrum, only a vision through our own dark glasses. In reality, there is always a lot of light in the 'Heart of Darkness'" (Oguibe, 1993, p. 8).

References

Abbas, T. (2011). *Islamic radicalism and multicultural politics: The British experience.* London, England: Routledge.

Ali, W. (Ed.). (1989). *Contemporary art from the Islamic world.* London, England: Scorpion.

Ali, W. (1997). *Modern Islamic art: Development and continuity.* Gainesville, FL: University Press of Florida.

Allerstorfer, J. (2004). Im Spannungsfeld zwischen Tradition und Modernismus [In the field of tension between tradition and modernism]. *Kunst und Kirche, 4,* 251–252.

Althusser, L. (1971). *Lenin and philosophy and other essays* (B. Brewster, Trans.). London, England: NLB.

Babaie, S. (2011). Voices of authority: Locating the "Modern" in "Islamic" arts. *Getty Research Journal, 3*, 133–149. doi:10.1086/grj.3.23005392.

Barber, B. (1996). *Jihad vs. McWorld.* New York, NY: Ballantine Books.

Bayoumi, M. (2010). The God that failed: The neo-Orientalism of today's Muslim commentators. In A. Shryock (Ed.), *Islamophobia/Islamophilia: Beyond the politics of enemy and friend* (pp. 79–93). Bloomington, IN: Indiana University Press.

Behpoor, B. (2012a). Contemporary Iranian art is bad. *Herfeh: Honarmand, 44*. Retrieved July 23, 2017 from http://fa.behpoor.com/?p=1683.

Behpoor, B. (2012b). The aftermath of the image-production revolution in post-revolution Iran. *Nafas Art Magazine*, October 2012. Retrieved July 23, 2017 from http://u-in-u.com/en/nafas/articles/2012/the-aftermath/.

Bernal, M. (2006). *Black Athena: The Afroasiatic roots of classical civilization.* New Brunswick, NJ: Rutgers University Press.

Binder, L. (1976). Area studies: A critical reassessment. In L. Binder (Ed.), *The study of the Middle East: Research and scholarship in the humanities and the social sciences* (pp. 9–13). New York, NY: Wiley.

Bonham's. (2008). *Modern and contemporary Arab, Iranian, Indian and Pakistani art.* Dubai: Bonham's.

Brennan, M. (2006). *Modernism's masculine subjects: Matisse, the New York school, and post-painterly abstraction.* Cambridge, MA: MIT Press.

Christie's. (2006). *International modern and contemporary art: Including Arab, Indian, Iranian and Western art.* Dubai: Christie's.

Christie's. (2017). *Salerooms and offices: Dubai.* Retrieved July 18, 2017 from http://www.christies.com/locations/salerooms/dubai/.

College Art Association Annual Conference. (2012, February). *Question and answer discussion: The body as a site of political intervention in contemporary Middle Eastern art.* College Art Association Annual Conference, Los Angeles, CA, February 2012.

Connelly, F. (1994). *The sleep of reason: Primitivism in modern European art and aesthetics, 1725–1907.* Philadelphia, PA: Pennsylvania State University Press.

Cotter, H. (2009, July 23). Iran inside out. *New York Times, Art in Review.* Retrieved July 18, 2017 from http://www.nytimes.com/2009/07/24/arts/design/24galleries.html?pagewanted=all.

Dabashi, H. (2009). *Post-Orientalism: Knowledge and power in time of terror.* New Brunswick, NJ: Transaction.

Dabashi, H. (2011). *Brown skin, white masks.* London, England: Pluto Press.

Emami, K. (1971). Modern Persian artists. In E. Yarshater (Ed.), *Iran faces the seventies* (pp. 349–364). New York, NY: Praeger.

Ford, P. (2001, September 19). Europe cringes at Bush "crusade" against terrorists. *Christian Science Monitor.* Retrieved July 18, 2017 from http://www.csmonitor.com/2001/0919/p12s2-woeu.html.

Foster, H. (1996). *The return of the real: The avant-garde at the end of the century.* Cambridge, MA: MIT Press.

Freire, P. (2005). *Pedagogy of the oppressed.* New York, NY: Continuum.

Golshiri, B. (2011). For they know what they do. *Journal #3, 1* (3), 82–91.

Hassan, S.M. (2010). Contemporary "Islamic" art: Western curatorial politics of representation in post 9/11. In C. Dercon et al. (Eds.), *The future of tradition—The tradition of future, 100 years after the exhibition masterpieces of Muhammadan art in Munich* (pp. 34–42). Munich, Germany: Haus der Kunst.

Huntington, S.P. (1997). *The clash of civilizations and the remaking of world order.* New York, NY: Touchstone.

Kaylan, M. (2009, August 5). The view from here. *The Wall Street Journal, Life and Culture.* Retrieved July 18, 2017 from http://online.wsj.com/article/SB10001424052970203547904574280051845780902.html#articleTabs%3Darticle.

Keshmirshekan, H. (Ed.). (2011a). *Amidst shadow and light: Contemporary Iranian art and artists.* Hong Kong: Liaoning Creative Press.

Keshmirshekan, H. (2011b). A new wave of Iranian art. *Journal #3, 1*(3), 8–20.

Keshmirshekan, H. (2011c). Contemporary or specific: The dichotomous desires in the art of early twenty-first century Iran. *Middle East Journal of Culture and Communication, 4,* 44–71.

Khansari, A.S. (1990). *Kamal-e Honar: Ahval va asar-i Muḥammad Ghaffari Kamal al-Mulk* [Perfection of art: Life and works of Mohammad Ghaffari Kamal-ol-Molk]. Tehran, Iran: Elmi Publishing.

Kirby, A. (2009). *Digimodernism: How new technologies dismantle the postmodern and reconfigure our culture.* New York, NY: Continuum.

Kleiner, F.S. (2008). *Gardner's art through the ages: The Western perspective* (14th ed.). Boston, MA: Wadsworth.

Kleiner, F.S. (2010). *Gardner's art through the ages: Non-Western perspectives* (13th ed.). Boston, MA: Wadsworth.

Lyotard, J.-F. (1992). *The postmodern explained to children: Correspondence, 1982–1985.* Sydney, Australia: Power.

MacDonald, M. (2003). *Exploring media discourse.* London, England: Hodder Arnold.

Mahdavi, S. (2004). Reflections in the mirror—How each saw the other: Women in the nineteenth century. In L. Beck & G. Nashat (Eds.), *Women in Iran from 1800 to the Islamic Republic* (pp. 63–84). Urbana, IL: University of Illinois Press.

Mahon, A. (2011). The lost secret Frida Kahlo and the surrealist imaginary. *Journal of Surrealism and the Americas, 5*(1–2), 33–54. Retrieved July 18, 2017 from https://

repository.asu.edu/attachments/107983/content/JSA_VOL5_NO1_Pages33-54_Mahon.pdf.

Minor, V.H. (1994). *Art history's history*. Englewood Cliffs, NJ: Prentice Hall.

Motevalli, A. (2005). *That's Sand Ninja Not Sand*. Photograph by Ernesto Medina.

Motevalli, A. (2013). *Passport Photograph of Artist Joshua H. Bolin*.

Moussavi-Aghdam, C., & Mahmoudian, A. (2011). The artist-ethnographer in contemporary Iranian art. *Honar-e farda [Art Tomorrow], 6*, 114–121.

Oguibe, O. (1993). In the "Heart of Darkness." *Third Text* 23, 3–8.

Owens, C. (1980). The allegorical impulse: Toward a theory of postmodernism, Part 2. *October, 13*, 58–80.

Pakbaz, R. (1999). Contemporary art of Iran. *Tavoos Quarterly, 1*, 168–191.

Poole, E. (2002). *Reporting Islam: Media representations and British Muslims*. London, England: I.B. Tauris.

Rahimi, B. (2013). *Takkiyeh Dowlat*: The Qajar theater state. In S.G. Scheiwiller (Ed.), *Performing the Iranian state: Visual culture and representations of Iranian identity* (pp. 55–71). London, England: Anthem Press.

Rayfield, J. (2013, April 20). Peter King calls for "increased surveillance" of Muslims after Boston. *Salon*. Retrieved July 18, 2017 from http://www.salon.com/2013/04/20/peter_king_calls_for_increased_surveillance_of_muslims_after_boston/.

Read, C.H.R. (1907). *Exhibition of the faience of Persia and the Nearer East*. London, England: The Burlington Fine Arts Club.

Robertson, I. (2011). The art market in transition, the global economic crisis, and the rise of Asia. In J. Harris (Ed.), *Globalization and contemporary art* (pp. 449–463). Chichester, England: Wiley-Blackwell.

Sahafzadeh, A. (n.d.). *Varshastegi-e motlaq-e honar-e moaser-e Iran* [The complete bankruptcy of contemporary Iranian art]. Retrieved July 23, 2017 from http://www.scribd.com/mobile/doc/134515519.

Said, E. (1979). *Orientalism*. New York, NY: Vintage Books.

Sakai, N. (1989). Modernity and its critique: The problem of universalism and particularism. In M. Miyoshi & H.D. Hartoonian (Eds.), *Postmodernism and Japan* (pp. 93–122). Durham, NC: Duke University Press.

Severi, H. (2012, March). *Contemporary Iranian art: A golden age or time of crisis?* Contemporary Iranian Art—Searching for Identity? Conference, Bonn, Germany, March 2012.

Shahandeh, I, (2011). "And I regurgitate and I gulp it down": Barbad Golshiri, *Honar-e farda [Art Tomorrow], 4* (Spring 2011), 74, 150.

Siegel, M.Z., & Gonzalez, C.P. (2013). Painted and animated metaphors: An interview with artist Alireza Darvish. In S.G. Scheiwiller (Ed.), *Performing the Iranian state: Visual culture and representations of Iranian identity* (pp. 193–199). London, England: Anthem Press.

Sotheby's. (2001). *Arts of the Islamic world including 20th cent. Middle Eastern paintings.* London, England: Sotheby's.

Sotheby's. (2007). *Modern and contemporary Arab and Iranian art.* London, England: Sotheby's.

Sotheby's. (2012, April 24–25). *Turkish and Islamic week.* London, England: Sotheby's.

Tadjvidi, A. (1962). *Iranian contemporary paintings.* Tehran, Iran: Fine Arts Organization.

Tadjvidi, A. (1967). *L'art modern e Iran* [Modern art in Iran]. Tehran, Iran: Ministère Iranien de la Culture et des Arts.

Tezuka, Y. (2012). *Japanese cinema goes global: Filmworkers' journeys.* Aberdeen, Hong Kong: Hong Kong University Press.

Varisco, D.M. (2007). *Reading Orientalism: Said and the unsaid.* Seattle, WA: University of Washington Press.

Vernoit, S. (2000). Islamic art and architecture: An overview of scholarship and collecting, c. 1850–1950. In S. Vernoit (Ed.), *Discovering Islamic art: Scholars, collectors and collections, 1850–1950* (pp. 1–16). London, England: I.B. Tauris.

Volpi, F. (2010). *Political Islam observed: Disciplinary perspectives.* New York, NY: Columbia University Press.

Yarshater, E. (1979). Modern Persian painting. In R. Ettinghausen & E. Yarshater (Eds.), *Highlights of Persian art* (pp. 363–377). Boulder, CO: Westview Press.

CHAPTER 10

Neo-Orientalism, Neo-Conservatism, and Terror in Salman Rushdie's Post-9/11 Novel

Beyazit H. Akman

Introduction: From Cold-War *Mujahedeen* to Post-9/11 Jihadists

In 1985, U.S. President Ronald Reagan introduced all the leaders of the *mujahedeen* from Afghanistan to the domestic and international media, on the White House lawn with great fanfare: "These gentlemen," he said gravely and confidently, "are the moral equivalents of America's founding fathers" (cited in Mandani, 2004, p. 119). In the struggle against Soviet Russia, the United States chose to support and create extreme versions of political Islam, armed and ready to fight. The alliance of faith against the atheist communist regime was a Reagan trademark. Three years later, the industry of Reagan's previous occupation took center stage on the silver screen in depicting the American support to the 'freedom fighters' of Afghanistan; in the third installment, entitled *Rambo III* (Feitshans, Kassar, Munafo, & Vajna, Producers, & MacDonald, Director, 1988), Rambo helps the *mujahedeen* to fight against the Russians. With a young boy called Hamid, Rambo encourages the locals to organize against the Soviet troops. After all, the connection between Hollywood and the White House was more than only the particular case of Reagan. Yet, the alliance of the Cold War was not limited to these two. In the field of popular fiction, the top Tom Clancy bestsellers were also created, such as *The Hunt for Red October* (1984) and *Red Storm Rising* (1986).

This is a changing world. Three decades later, the discourse of the White House against the *mujahedeen*, literally the followers of *jihad* in Arabic, is shaped not around the "moral equivalents of American's founding fathers" (Mandani, 2004, p. 119), but around terrorism, suicide bombings, and killings of civilian targets. It seems that the *mujahedeen* were but the founding fathers of al-Qaeda, which emerged first and foremost in Afghanistan. The fight against atheism of several decades earlier is now a fight against extreme religious fanaticism. The position of the friendly Hamid was taken over easily by terrorist suicide bombers, Ahmeds and Hasans ready to kill the innocent, on the silver screen. The alliance was also at an international level this time, at least bilateral (although most times unilateral) with the support of the British for the

American cause in the Middle East, which also meant that the bestsellers of the New World would be supported by the 'literary' masterpieces as a result of the literary heritage of Europe.

Continuing the European Orientalist tradition in his 2005 novel, *Shalimar the Clown*, his first novel after 9/11, Salman Rushdie reinforces the rhetoric against Islam, which is the topic of this chapter. In this novel, rather than deconstructing the common *a*historical assumptions about the *Islamic* terrorist, one which is nowadays highly accepted in the Western collective conscious, Rushdie, the winner of the Booker of Bookers award, the most prestigious literary prize of England, represents Islam as an ideological hotbed for terrorism. In *Shalimar*, Rushdie applies almost all of the major characteristics of Orientalist discourse, defined by Said as the "distillation of ideas about the Orient—its sensuality, its tendency to despotism, its aberrant mentality, its habits of inaccuracy, its backwardness" (1978, p. 205). It is argued that Rushdie reinforces, empowers, and licenses the neo-Orientalist discourse of the axis of evil perpetuated by the Bush administration (and now continued by U.S. President Donald Trump through his anti-Islamic rhetoric) by applying the stereotypes and clichés about the East, without engaging in an attempt to understand the Other. Nor does he show any attempt to put this grave issue in a socially, politically, and historically relevant context. In the final part of this chapter, to be able to contextualize Rushdie's work with other similar post-9/11 novels and with an attempt at situating the post-9/11 novel in a more general critical framework, I briefly look at John Updike's (2006) *The Terrorist* (as an American example) and Ian McEwan's (2006) *Saturday* (as a British example).

Hollywood, American Hegemony, and the Neo-Orientalist Novel

Shalimar the Clown opens with a comparison of the sounds of the Arabic language to those sounds produced while clearing a throat (Rushdie, 2005). The very first page of the novel, despite associating a disgusting act with the speaking of Arabic, is albeit quick to include a reference to Scheherazade, to exhibit the phrase 'Arabian Nights,' quite an uncreative gesture at this point, especially for Rushdie. Yet, still, as this is the very first page to establish the tone and the discourse of the narrative, one should not forget the other proper names dropped here and there within the first paragraph: Sigourney Weaver, *Ghostbusters*, the science-fictional Klingon, "a galaxy far, far away" (Rushdie, 2005, pp. 3–4). The opening can be understood as a trailer of what is to come in the next three hundred or so pages, some sort of one-paragraph microcosm of images that indeed represents the nature and the context of the macrocosm of the novel. The Arabic culture, or, the Eastern one, on a much larger scale, as we will see, will not accept much of an appreciation rather than the now cliché allusions to *The Thousand and One Nights*, a fictional work of magic lambs and flying carpets, of enormous treasures of Ali Baba, of the amazing adventures of Sinbad the Sailor, and of adulterous, disloyal, and lecherous Arab women of the veil. The whole set of images of the East is trapped in that romantic and mystical place of everything extreme (Said, 1981): the best or the worst, nothing in between can take place in this fictional universe, where one is either as perfectly beautiful as Oronooko the slave or as ugly as the guy with a dagger trying to kill Indiana Jones in Cairo in the film *Raiders of the Lost Ark* (Kazanjian, Lucas, Marshall, & Watts, Producers, & Spielberg, Director, 1981).[1] The fusion of popular culture, especially an obsession with Hollywood, suggests that Rushdie allies himself with the producers of huge blockbusters, the forerunning media in perpetuating the discourse against the 'despotic' Orient. This network of media and popular culture references also confirms that Rushdie's novel "advances an elite vision of cosmopolitanism" (Siddiqi, 2007, p. 293). It could further be argued, as we will see below, that Rushdie forsakes the serious issue of terrorism for this kind of elite cosmopolitanism. This "pastiche of clichés," in the overall, "lacks any cultural and historical specificity" (Siddiqi, 2007, p. 307).

The protagonist of the novel, Max Olphus, takes his name from the famous movie director, a Jewish German who made movies in Germany, France, and of course in Hollywood. Although his life has nothing to do with the character in the novel, one should be quite conspicuous of these similarities in a Rushdie text, which might mean a lot in terms of understanding the theme and

1 As far back as 1981, Said points out, "Assiduous research has shown that there is hardly a prime-time television show without several episodes of patently racist and insulting caricatures of Muslims, all of whom tend to be represented in unqualified categorical and generic terms: one Muslim is therefore seen to be typical of all Muslims and of Islam in general" (1981, p. 69). References to popular culture and to works of literature are one of the defining characteristics of Rushdie's work, as there are innumerable references to icons of the popular culture, which suggests the alliance of the popular media with his literary text in the portrayal of the Muslim societies. Jay Leno, Marlon Brandon, Orson Welles, David Letterman, Clark Kent, Superman, and Keanu Reeves are only some of these instances, which are also the international, cultural commodities marketed to other countries, including the Middle East; that is to say that cultural imperialism is a driving engine for the Orientalist depictions, which leads the 'natives' of the third-world countries to self-loathing. This Hollywood discourse embodies the Western culture in the first quarter of the novel, which will then create a stark contrast with the next chapter on the Pachigam village, a topos of Orientalism, as will be analyzed later.

approach of the novel toward its subject matter, and it indeed does so. For one thing, the basic story line of the novel is as simple as a Hollywood movie premise. There is nothing wrong with being simple, yet, when simplicity is mixed with stolid and biased stereotypes, the problem arises: Max Olphus, the Jewish–American ambassador to India, is killed by a Muslim terrorist, a death machine of a unique kind, trained for the sole purpose of hunting Olphus (Pitkin, 2007).[2] In a 2007 interview about his novel, Rushdie says, "The novel should question everything," and goes on:

> When a new world opens up to you, you start questioning every piece of truth which you believed up until that time. ...A writer does not speak for an ideology; what he should do is just to say, "I see this in this way," and he does in an individual way. For we are not the puppets of a huge plan.
>
> *my translation*, RUSHDIE, 2007, pp. 12, 14

In another interview in the *Observer*, Rushdie says, "'Novel' itself is a word that means new, and the purpose of art has always been thought to make things new, so you don't see things through the same old, tired eyes" (cited in La'Porte, 1971, p. 89). One can only agree with these statements, which honor freedom of expression and the unique quality of artistic imagination, geared toward exploring new horizons, finding new solutions, and ultimately understanding people.

However, *Shalimar the Clown* never exhibits the kind of critical thought that the author expresses in his interviews about challenging the mainstream narrative. Rather, even the basic story line is an indication of the degree to which Rushdie submits to the neo-conservative discourse about the Middle East. His text does not question but confirms the already accepted images about the East and Islam. What could have been more interesting would be a reverse story line of what we have here. That kind of reversal would have led to true questionings of values and commonly held notions in the Western society against the so-called common enemy, Islam. Yet, without making further generalizations regarding the novel, we should at first see how Rushdie reduces the image of Islam to the belief of one horrendous terrorist and the Eastern culture to the most marginalized (fictional) sect of barbarisms.

---

2 Pitkin states, "When reduced to such equations, the plotlines are not very illuminating; some such plot points seem to be no more than cheap shots. Rushdie of course deserves better from his readers than mere reductionism, and there is tremendous richness of ideas, events and imagery in this book. And yet these problematic parallels do resonate in the book's pages. The doubleness of the story makes these parallels inescapable, and yet their superficiality works to undercut the power of the sequences concerning the fate of Kashmir" (2007, p. 261).

Misrepresentation of one's own culture (although we will also try to question to what extent Indian culture is Rushdie's 'own' in the next paragraph) starts with dissatisfaction with that culture, at least in the case of Rushdie's narrative. The position of another major character of the novel, the illegitimate daughter of Max Olphus, is clearly stated in the novel: "Her name was India. She did not like her name" (Rushdie, 2005, p. 5). According to her it should not be "okay to hang people's birthplaces round their necks like albatrosses" (Rushdie, 2005, p. 5). India has been raised in Britain and Switzerland, the 'cradle' of civilization (Schaebler, 2004),[3] and has chosen to live in California, United States (another allusion to Hollywood). If anything, she is not 'Indian' at all, not even mentioning her mother's Pachigam village in the deep Hades hole of India, where she was born. It is not unusual for the characters of Rushdie to feel a grudge against their own cultures. The most famous instance is Saladin Chamcha, one of the main characters in *The Satanic Verses* (Rushdie, 1988), considered by many scholars to be Rushdie's autobiographical character, who also "rejects his Indian roots and even when young [he] dreamt about London, England or Ellowen Deewen, Vilayet (as the novel terms it)" (La'Porte, 1971, p. 34).

But can India really be uttered as Rushdie's *own*? Is Rushdie an Indian writer or a British one, or, after all, does he have to belong to either of them? The answer to this question might require more elaboration than one might first think, as Rushdie's 'insider' position is most problematic. It is problematic not because he was raised in private British colleges and spent most of his life, including his earlier decades, in England, but because his Indian identity has been serving to the interests of postcolonial England. Sardar and Davies argue that in the perpetuation of the Westernization process, the colonizers needed the help of some 'sort' of native: "the deporting colonial powers had left an important not-so-departing legacy: the brown sahib" (cited in La'Porte, 1971, p. 82). This so-called brown sahib is essentially an intermediary between the ruler and the ruled, but in the most covert, and for that matter sinuous, way. This is described as one of the ways of colonizing the minds of the natives. These brown sahibs then have three common features: being wealthy enough to afford a Western education; having skills to be used in the manipulation of the minds of general folk; and above all, possessing a sense of 'hereditary right' in

3 Schaebler indicates, "Discourses on 'civilization,' even the term 'civilization' itself, a direct outcome of the French Enlightenment, are born in encounters with others" (2004, p. 3). In this article he also indicates how Eurocentric discourses since the 1950s have long credited colonization with the Westernization of the peoples of the Globe (p. 4). In the history of the encounter of Europe and its modernity with the rest of the world, the concepts of "civilization" and its dialectical antithesis, "savagery" serves as a means of self-authentication.

undertaking the mission of the ex-colonial administration. Special attention should be given to the final aspect; even the best British, in terms of having a sociocultural and educational background in India, cannot come close to his least qualified Indian counterpart, as the latter would have an unprecedented credibility.

Having an 'identity crisis' is also an essential feature, as these figures are supposed to have been made to feel alien both during their European education and among their national peers. Ultimately, Sardar and Davies (as cited in La'Porte, 1971) point out that all of these qualities are visible in Rushdie, who has studied at Cambridge and who comes from a wealthy background, and for whom the fluidity of identities is a major theme in most of his work, and for that matter a postmodern trademark. "The brown sahib, therefore, is a rapid defender of everything Western; and since he cannot banish his Oriental self within him, like Kipling, he turns on himself and his own kind" (Sardar & Davies, as cited in La'Porte, 1971, p. 82). In this regard, Rushdie can also be compared to V.S. Naipaul, who also has an 'insider' status, which thus makes both of them elicit more authority and respect: "His [Rushdie's] brown color ensures the eagerness of many Europeans to listen to his authentic voice and thus have their own prejudices confirmed" (Sardar & Davies, as cited in La'Porte, 1971, p. 83). This double-edged sword helps Rushdie to have intellectual authority on the domestic issues of India as well as providing him with plenty of credit (Fernandez-Kelly 2009)[4] to speak in the name of, according to, in defense of, or as he mostly does, *against* the Islamic culture in the international media. He is thus the sole literary authority on the Middle East, according to many.

Fanon (2005) points out the troubling nature of such intellectuals in their native cultures: "When the nationalist parties are mobilizing the people in the name of national independence," he argues, "the native intellectual ... feels like a stranger in his own land. It is always easier to proclaim rejection than actually to reject" (p. 206). According to Fanon, the intellectual, who by way of cultural orientation and education "has managed to become part of the body of Western civilization," (p. 206), or in other words, who has exchanged his own

4 Apart from Rushdie's 'insider' status because of his national and religious origin, there is also the sense among many Western intellectuals that he also has extra credibility because he was once the victim of religious fanatics. See, for example, Patricia Fernandez-Kelly's (2009) review where she notes that the novel is a "remarkable book" that gives "insights into the making of a terrorist mind." For her, "This is an achievement *doubly* impressive because Rushdie" is "a man who spent nearly a decade hiding from the murderous fatwa issued by Ayatolla Ruhollah Khomeni" (2009, p. 471). Again, it is important to note that these kinds of umbrella judgements about an author's work may be misleading.

for another, comes to understand that his identity cannot be so secure any more. "The cultural matrix which now he wishes to assume since he is anxious to appear original" can hardly supply any figureheads as comparable to *the* original (Fanon, 2005, p. 206). In another interview, Rushdie himself expresses his fluid identity as

> I have constantly been asked whether I am British, or Indian. The formulation "Indian-born British writer" has been invented to explain me. But my new book deals with Pakistan. So what now? British-resident-Indo-Pakistani writer? You see the folly of trying to contain writers inside passports.
>
> cited in AHLUWALIA, 2005, p. 501

It is clearly seen here that Rushdie does not want to solidify his cultural identity. We do not know whether he dislikes 'India' as the daughter of Max Olphus does or does not, yet we know that he is too Indian to call himself British or European, which suggests the anxiety Fanon briefly mentions.

This personal crisis and the desire for oneself to be oriented toward Europe becomes more problematic when, with the leadership of these 'brown sahibs,' who have held the most vital positions—political, administrative, social, educational, etc.—the country is transformed into a collective social schizophrenia. When the national–historical narratives are authored by those who are alien to their own culture as much as to those they aspire, generation by generation, the gap of true national identity is filled with the interests of the 'original' culture. Guha (2005) sees the reason of this phenomenon as the elitist historical narratives of the country: "The historiography of Indian nationalism has for a long time been dominated by elitism-colonialist elitism and bourgeois-nationalist elitism" (p. 403). Siddiqi (2007) approaches this issue by naming Rushdie's perspective as "elite cosmopolitanism" and draws attention to the risks and threats that it poses for real migrants with real problems: "Not only is this vision unmistakably an elite one despite the token acknowledgment of subaltern lives, the bird's eye view of culture that underwrites Rushdie's cosmopolitan vision flattens the geopolitics of migration" (p. 307). Building on Simon Gikandi's article, "Globalization and the Claims of Postcoloniality," Siddiqi further argues:

> Scholars of globalization have drawn on the vocabulary of postcolonial theory to foreground a view of global culture marked by "hybridity" and "difference." What the privileging of this vocabulary tends to do, according to Gikandi, is elide the other kinds of ways, ways often rooted in now

> discredited theories of modernization, in which subjects of the third world understand their own experience. This experience is determined by the discourses and practices of a neo-imperial world that shapes hopes but physically and economically constrains global migrants. Rushdie's cosmopolitanism is appealing because it infuses cosmopolitan values with the promise of an organic community modeled on the ideal of Kashmiriyat. (pp. 307–308)

This vision is, therefore, very problematic because "power in its various globalized and localized manifestations continues to smash into private lives but for the few exceptional scenarios where elite individuals may insulate themselves against such forces" (Siddiqi, 2007, p. 307). Siddiqi concludes, "Rushdie's own threatened physical existence exemplifies the limits of elite cosmopolitanism; and for the many subaltern migrants whose existences are economically and legally precarious, the ideal of vernacular cosmopolitanism is entirely utopian" (pp. 307–308). While discussing another novel by Rushdie, Morton (2008) also notes the risks of "romanticizing and mythologizing transnational migration" in a way "that elides the precarious lives of many immigrants" in the perception of the author's novels (p. 339).

The Civilized West vs. the Barbaric East

This elitist, colonialist historiography, which Guha (2005) rightly blames, also reinforces the clichés and grand abstractions about cultures. According to this framework, then, the Western world is innately civilized: scientific, rational, logical, and mathematical, whereas the East is the ultimate counterpart: illogical, exotic, irrational, and barbaric.[5] This contrasting set of characteristics regarding civilization is excellently executed in *Shalimar*.

Rushdie's East is epitomized in a small village in India, the ultimate representation of the Indian culture in the novel, where women are lecherous and sexual objects and men are vulgar and unmannered. Lechery has been always a part of Kashmir, according to the narrator. "In the matter of lovemaking Kashmiri women had never been shrinking violets" (Guha, 2005, p. 52); each one of them is ready to use the opportune moment to realize their (almost always sexually driven) desires; intuition rather than logic, sexuality rather than

5 The way the West knows the Orient has been a way of using authority on them, demonstrates Said (1978, p. 6). What follows this black and white differentiation is the need of the West to invade, dominate, and change the Orient toward civilization.

sensuality governs their minds. The very existence of India, the character, is possible due to the ambitious adventures of Boonyi, who achieved to break her bonds to her native village by the emergence of Max Olphus, the American ambassador to the region, whom one scholar defines as having "the shrewd negotiating skill of a Henry Kissinger and the charm and sexual energy of a Bill Clinton" (Stadtler, 2009, p. 197). Despite her long-term love affair with the acrobat Shalimar, she chooses to submit to the sexual wishes of the ambassador (fulfilling every bit of erotic fantasy with him), with India as a result.

The norm of romanticism in the Pachigam village is, moreover, about how far you can go in killing, the ultimate standard for love in this society. In a chronologically previous event, while Shalimar and Boonyi talk about their love, the former says, "Don't you leave me now, or I'll never forgive you, and I'll have my revenge, I'll kill you and, if you have any children by another men, I'll kill the children also" (Rushdie, 2005, p. 61). Boonyi answers, "What a romantic you are. You say the sweetest things." It is all the more ordinary in a village where magicians abound, use of incense is highest, and cutting off ears and little fingers for the love of women are everyday phenomena, which thus reminds us of Said's (1978) depiction that in texts such as this, "The Orient becomes a living tableau of queerness" (p. 103). In Rushdie's text, Kashmir or India or Pakistan is, thus, not a place but a topos,

> a set of references, a congeries of characteristics, that seems to have its origin in a quotation, or a fragment of a text, or a citation from someone's work on the Orient, or some bit of previous imagining, or an amalgam of all of these.
>
> SAID, 1978, p. 177

The parameters that Rushdie uses in the creation of this small village all seem to be aligned with the political discourse of Otherness, consisting of people who are dramatically different from the culture and norms of the Western reader who is holding this text.

The process of Otherization leads to further exclusion of Islam from modern life to the extent that it shows the religion as a complete antithesis to society's existence. Siddiqi argues in her 2007 article that Rushdie emphasizes the "external forces" (p. 297) as threatening the community's very existence. "The novel," she writes, "attributes the destruction of this organic community to the initially secular and then Islamic separatists in Pakistan and the militantly hypernationalist Indian state" (Siddiqi, 2007, p. 297). Therefore, "the clash of these external forces" leads to the "obliteration of Pachigam" (p. 297). It is exactly this kind of thinking, I believe, which sees Islam as an "external" force in the history and culture of the region and which creates tensions and conflicts in the first place. However, Siddiqi continues to say, "It is only under brutal threats ... Pachigam adopt the veil" (Siddiqi, 2007, p. 298). "In depicting the rise of communal violence in Kashmir," she concludes, "Rushdie emphasizes that communal identities in Kashmir are not 'natural' or 'given' but are produced when resources grow scarce and when outside forces intervene in local spaces" (p. 299). Both in the novel and in Siddiqi's analysis it is surprising to see Islam, or whatever is represented as such, as an 'outside product,' rather than 'natural' faiths of billions of people in the region. It is, of course, one thing to portray and criticize religious fanatics, and quite another to portray fanatics' beliefs as the ultimate form of Islam. This, of course, creates its own absurdity about a novel that already represents a somewhat Muslim village as a bizarre and queer topos.

On the other hand, one immediately realizes when the setting becomes Europe in the novel:

> In the city of Strasbourg, a place of charming old quarters and pleasant public gardens, near the charming parc des Contades, around the corner from the old synagogue on what is now the rue du Grand Rabbin Rene Hirschler, at the heart of a lovely and fashionable neighborhood peopled by delightful and charming folks.
>
> RUSHDIE, 2005, p. 138

If the people of the East are a cactus in the desert; those of Europe are a rose, a beautiful one, according to Rushdie's text. The folks of the West read newspapers; they are generous, 'highly-cultured,' and quite charming. Whereas Arabic is a language of clearing the throat, the languages of Latin and French are of elegance, used and italicized many times throughout the novel (and they always refer to a beautiful, clean street in a cultured city of Europe or some work of art of high quality). India, the character, can only belong to this "charming" culture; she feels most confident and at home when she utters lines from French poetry such as those by Baudelaire (Rushdie, 2005, p. 19) or sings in French: "*Alouette, gentille alouette / Alouette, je te plumerai*" (Rushdie, 2005, p. 41).

This self-identification with everything beautiful, elegant, sophisticated, and cultured, and the other-demonization with everything filthy and disgusting is one of the essential characteristics of the way the West has come to define itself. A monolithic perception of different cultures on semi-mythical fabrications helps Western nations define themselves in a much easier and superior way. Therefore, according to this Orientalist discourse, the West is both the cradle and the pinnacle of civilization, embracing all things rational, scientific, and mathematical, and the Orient is as all things negative, deprived of historical development and change. The East always lives in a world of oasis, deserts, camels, pyramids, and concubines ruled by barbarism. Stam and Shohat (2005) explain: "Eurocentric discourse is diffusionist; it assumes that democracy, science, progress, and prosperity all emanate outward from a western source" (p. 482). Therefore, "[This discourse] sanitizes western history while patronizing and even demonizing the nonwest; it thinks of itself in terms of its noblest achievements but of the nonwest in terms of its deficiencies, real or imagined" (Stam & Shohat, 2005, p. 482).

Rushdie's application of age-old stereotypes and clichés in the reinforcement of the dichotomies between the East and the West becomes most clear when the narrative revolves around Shalimar, the title character, the embodiment of a Muslim terrorist in the novel, which is thus the heart of the text (Rushdie, 2005). There are three basic Orientalist methods in the creation of this character, if he even is a true *character* as he is closer to being a *type*, borrowed from the Orientalist corpus (from a topos we mentioned earlier). These methods include (a) the fusion of pagan elements with Islam, a monotheistic religion, thus alienating Islam outside the modern age; (b) using historical details to enhance the reality of the work at hand, which thus has a claim to factual life or to reality *per se*; and (c) conflation of the ideology of a villain with the teachings of Islam, thus reducing the latter to its most marginal interpretations.

Rushdie's Pagan and "Jihadist" Islam

The second chapter of the book is opened in the Pachigam village, in opposition to the first chapter, which was set in California (Rushdie, 2005). The first pages of these chapters are about the Gods and the myths that the people in this area believe in, the ones they think they are entitled to. "There were nine grabbers in the cosmos, Surya the Sun, Soma the Moon, Budha the Mercury, Mangal the Mars, Shukra the Venus, Brihaspati the Jupiter, Shani the Saturn," goes on the narrative listing about a dozen "grabbers" (Rushdie, 2005, p. 46). The uttering of the names Budha and strange-looking exotic names already suggests that we are in a completely different world, a world where the norms of the first chapter, the metropolis of California, make no more sense. "They were also the dragon planets: two halves of a single bisected dragon. Rahu was the dragon's head and Ketu was the dragon's tail" (Rushdie, 2005, p. 46). Among these mystical words of shadow and beasts, we are introduced to Shalimar's father, named Abdullah, "the headman, the sarpanch, who held them all in the palm of his hand" (Rushdie, 2005, p. 46).

It is true that some of these names represent certain aspects of Hinduism, which may lead to the argument that the passage is more about this religion than it is about Islam. However, neither in the previous chapter nor in the rest of the book is there a hint on this piece of information, which is not easily accessible nor readily available for a typical Western reader, the target audience of this book. Rushdie first and foremost writes for Europe and the United States, parts of the world where people equate every religion in the Middle East and the rest of the world, which is considerably different from theirs, with Islam. Secondly, the very fact that Rushdie conflates these two religions plays on the typical method of Orientalist discourse that has a tendency to totalize all the belief systems in the East, despite the huge differences and important nuances. According to this set of thinking, everything that diverts from Christianity, from Eurocentric discourse, is something else, which is in most cases grouped under the umbrella religion of Islam, the host of everything non-Christian.

Yet, the biggest problem with the above passage, thus the most rational answer to the claim that the passage can be about Hinduism or other pagan beliefs around the region, comes from the name *Abdullah*, a most common typical Muslim name, which is Arabic and means simply and literally "the subject of Allah." It is not difficult to infer that the use of this name among such a belief system of dragons and shadow planets means that the narrative is supposedly about Islam, the kind of irrational, meaningless, and absurd religion which can thus easily create a terrorist, devoid of ration and logic but infused with hatred and darkness. After all, it is Abdullah's son, Shalimar, who is about to cut the throat of the Jewish American ambassador: "He [Shalimar] wanted to make his father proud of Shalimar the clown, his son" (Rushdie, 2005, p. 47).

The description of Shalimar's village and the people in it are also in the same vein of irrationality and illogicality; they are governed by instincts and emotions rather than by mind and thought. French is the language of poetry and singing, and Latin, of proverbs and enlightened ideas; but Kashmiri is used once in a while as the language of prophecy, one which uses, suggests, implies, or directly tells about death, blood, or simply poverty. Kashmiris are, furthermore, driven by "crummy motivations such as envy, malice and greed" (Rushdie, 2005, p. 63). Pitkin (2007) argues that

> Kashmiri story itself is not always done full justice, in the sense that Rushdie sometimes teeters on the edge of clichés in his evocation of the region, telling us of Kashmir's cool mountain streams, embroidered shawls, lacquered boxes, blue or green-eyed people and their cozy village life. (p. 260)

These are details that we can summarize as the romantic view of the Orient. "Kashmir itself deserves fuller characterization, central as it is to the novel" (Pitkin, 2007, p. 260). Especially, the prophecies of Nazarebaddoor, the fortune-teller of the village, shape a lot of what the villagers think they should do and how they should act in their life, suggesting a collective life imbued with magic and intuitions. Sorcery and witchcraft are also daily events for the inhabitants of Pachigam. It is needless to say that Islam openly forbids any act of witchcraft, fortune-telling, or any other resembling act. To argue against even the major misrepresentations of the religion in the novel within the boundaries of this chapter would be a futile task. It should suffice to show the one-sided nature of the narrative as an evidence of the huge misrepresentation in question.

A mosque in Shirmal is also mentioned in the novel, yet once again, a mosque which many Muslims would find quite unusual and, for that matter, quite alarming. "No provision had been made for ladies to attend prayers" (Rushdie, 2005, p. 119). In the majority of mosques around the world, half of the space is always allocated to women, although it is true that men and women should have separate spaces of their own (but it seems that Rushdie does not find this detail 'queer' enough). The roof of the mosque in the novel is wooden, the walls of white-washed earth. Of course, at this point one should not expect Rushdie to narrate the unique architecture of Islamic civilizations such as the Taj Mahal in India or the Blue Mosque in Istanbul or the Al Hambra in Spain; we need the kind of structure in which a terrorist will be trained. In the middle of the mosque stands a "frightening-looking scrap-metal pulpit ... complete with a bank of truck headlights (nonfunctional) bent fenders spearing upwards like horns, and a snarling radiator light" (Rushdie, 2005, p. 119).

The image of the mosque as a hotbed of fanaticism is also visible, Almond (2007) indicates, in several other important works of the writer, especially in *Midnight's Children* (Rushdie, 1981) and *The Moor's Last Sigh* (Rushdie, 1995). However, in these works, the approach is much more ambivalent and of a deconstructive nature, which leads Almond to conclude that "This game of good mosque/bad mosque played by Rushdie ... carries a certain semantic consequence for Islam itself; ultimately, it almost suggests that there is no central, identifiable signified called 'Islam' for all the references in Rushdie's books" (2007, p. 103). Yet, as is shown with enough evidence, there *is* a signified for Islam in *Shalimar the Clown*, and if not anything else, it not only exists in *difference* (to borrow Derrida's term) to Christian civilization but also poses a threat to its counterpart. Almond's argument would also make sense if in the text we are analyzing, there were 'good' Muslims or 'good' mosques, which would thus complicate things rather than applying almost caricature images of hatred. Yet, such a depiction, or anything close to it, does not exist in *Shalimar* (Rushdie, 2005).

"We Ambush Christians, We Bomb Christians, We Burn Christians"

This is also the very mosque where the 'iron mullah' declares some sort of jihad. Rushdie once again prefers to use the term as it is in the collective memory of the West, conceived as the ultimate goal of Islam and of Muslims to fight against and kill the Christians, the 'infidels,' another unquestioned instance that the writer borrows from the Orientalist repertoire. Rushdie, as an 'insider,' though, should have been familiar with the simple fact that *jihad* has a different meaning for many Muslims, a meaning stated clearly in the Qur'an: to fight against the self so that one becomes a much better person not only for himself but also for the society one lives in. This purification of the self against sins is tough, which is the reason why it is called the *greater jihad* in the teachings of Islam. The meaning that is also misinterpreted, but which dominated the related discourse, is only called as the *lesser jihad* to fight back for justice, which can only be executed at the state level, not by individuals. Mastnak, who emphasizes the fact that "the debate around radical political Islam is increasingly a debate on the meaning of jihad," explains:

> The Qur'an insists that a Muslim's first duty is to create a just and egalitarian society in which poor people are treated with respect. This demands a jihad (literally, effort or struggle) on all fronts: spiritual and social, personal and political. Scholars of Islam distinguish between two broad traditions of *jihad: al-jihad al-akbar* (the greater jihad) and *al-jihad al-asghar* (the lesser jihad). The greater jihad, it is said, is a struggle against the weaknesses of self; it is about how to live, and attain piety in a contaminated wolrd. Inwardly, it is about the effort of each Muslim to become a better human being. The lesser jihad, in contrast, is about self-preservation and self-defense; directed outwardly.
>
> cited in MANDANI, 2004, p. 50

As such, the Islamic *jihad* (the lesser one) can be thought to be comparable to the notion of what Christians call a 'just war,' not a 'holy war.' It is quite important to understand the true nature of *jihad* in Islamic philosophy; it was the idea of the Crusaders to fight a 'holy war' against the 'infidel,' especially against the Muslims in the Middle East. Modern Western representations have tended to portray *jihad* as an Islamic war against unbelievers by equating the history of Christianity to that of Islam and by projecting the terms and conceptions in the former over that of the 'enemy.' Mastnak thus insists that "Jihad cannot properly be defined as holy war: Jihad is the doctrine of spiritual effort of which military action is only one possible manifestation; the crusade and jihad are, strictly speaking, not comparable" (cited in Mandani, 2004, p. 50).

The figure who declares this *jihad*, on the other hand, brings us to another problematic aspect of the novel: the fusion of famous historical figures with the characters of the novel. When Shalimar swears to kill Max Olphus (not for religious reasons, actually, but for being duped by the coordination of his wife and the ambassador; Boonyi simply betrays her long-time fiancé), he is trained in a terrorist camp in the leadership of one Maulana Bulbul Fakh. It might not make any difference for the Western readers what *maulana* means, but the Muslim world would easily recognize the title, as it is first and foremost used for Jalal-uddin, the renowned Islamic Sufi and scholar who comes from the mainstream Islamic tradition and who is also known in the West by the name Rumi for his poetry, *Mesnevi*, which has initiated the Sufi tradition and the whirling dervishes. Rushdie applies the title used for a Muslim Sunni cleric into the leader of a terrorist camp. The fusion of the most profane with the most sinful and horrendous of acts indicates the attempt to conflate even the most purified Islamic areas (even in the minds of a Western reader) with the religion's most negative and marginalized sidelines. Rumi, maybe the kindest and the most mainstream voice of Islam, turns literally into 'iron' in Rushdie's narrative. The word *mulla* (as 'the iron mulla' is the title for Maulana Bulbul Fakh), in the meantime, means "scholar" in Arabic, but the writer of *Shalimar the Clown* is least interested in that meaning; for Rushdie (2005), the word is and should be associated with a 'bloodthirsty terrorist.' The language of Fox News is just what he needs; no one would be interested in Islamic *science*. We should also note that the year following the publication of the novel was declared as the Rumi celebratory year by UNESCO for the appreciation of this great Sufi. Can it be that Rushdie was troubled by this global interest in a Muslim cleric? The next name in the title, *Bulbul*, is the Turkish word for "nightingale," the recurrent motif used in the Sufi tradition for love, which again indicates the degree to which the writer wants to deconstruct everything positive in the Islamic tradition.

Therefore, it is very difficult to agree with Morton (2008) when he depicts Rushdie as offering "a non-partisan response to the political, military and technological forces of postcolonial modernity in the valley of Kashmir" (p. 345). It could only be a misreading to say, "Rushdie's metaphor of the iron mullah suggests that the 'firebrand Islam' Bulbul Fakh preaches is a historical product of an increasingly militarised and divided postcolonial Kashmir rather than an essential theological principle of Islam" (Morton, 2008, pp. 345–346). As we will see later on, he will leave no doubt that "this is about Islam." We will also see to what extent the excuse of 'allegory' might work for this text.

Moreover, when it comes to deconstructing the negative judgments about this religion or the cultures imbued with this religion, Rushdie remains most silent and passive. Rushdie loves playing with historical facts and prominent figures. La'Porte (1971) indicates that Rushdie's distortion of historical and significant names has a history of its own. In *Midnight's Children* (Rushdie, 1981) and *Shame* (Rushdie, 1983), "Rushdie's personal description of characters based on Indira Gandhi and Benazir Bhutto are hardly flattering. His portrayal of Indira Gandhi as 'the Widow' is fairly brutal" (La'Porte, 1971, p. 60). She further indicates that "Benazir Bhutto's counterpart depiction in *Shame* is also quite derogatory. In the novel, she is known as the Arjumand Harappa or 'virgin Ironpants'" (La'Porte, 1971, p. 60).

La'Porte (1971) also covers the distortion of important factual events in *The Satanic Verses* (Rushdie 1988) quite comprehensively. The *Jahilia* in this novel, historically the age of ignorance, according to the Muslim belief, before the arrival of Islam, is used as the time where Muslim Mecca is situated. Mahound, the corrupted version of the name of the prophet Mohammad (pbuh.) in the discourse of medieval Christian clerics, meaning devil or anti-Christ, is also the version preferred in the novel, where he is depicted, in line with the tradition of the established church of the Medieval Europe, as licentious, alcoholic, and "business-minded" (La'Porte, 1971, p. 62). As La'Porte further demonstrates, many companions of the prophet Mohammad also appear in the novel as characters, some of which are Salman the Persian, portrayed as "somewhat as a charlatan"; Bilal, the African, whom every Muslim reveres as the first person to recite the call to prayer, narrated as the "black monster"; and Khalid, another close companion, described as "the water carrier, some sort of bum" (La'Porte, 1971, pp. 66–67). Rushdie also distorts the personage of Ibrahim, who is called a "bastard" in the narrative (La'Porte, 1971, pp. 66-67).

Through the end, Rushdie's narrative becomes more and more straightforward and more audacious. In the last quarter of the novel, there is no question that the context is a Muslim society and the camp is an Islamic terrorist camp:

> The five daily prayers at the camp *maidan* [a Turkish word for the "field," the usage of which doesn't make any sense except for the sake of seeming exotic] were compulsory for all the fighters and the only book permitted at the site—training manuals excepted—was the Holy Qur'an.
>
> RUSHDIE, 2005, p. 265

It is also previously stated in the previous lines that "there were weekly seminars about, and real-time training exercises in, high-speed, guerilla-style strike-and-withdraw operations across the Line of Control. There was a bomb factory and a course in fifth-column infiltration technique, and above all there was prayer" (Rushdie, 2005, p. 265). This is the hotbed of "fidayeen," "suicide bombers," and many other types of "*insurgents*" (Rushdie, 2005, p. 312). One ambitious member, though not as much as Shalimar, expresses his ideology in the most conspicuous way: "We ambush Christians, we bomb Christians, we burn Christians, we kidnap Christian tourists for ransom, we execute Christian soldiers, and then we ambush them some more" (Rushdie, 2005, p. 320). These "Bearers of the Sword" do not need other words than "ambush," "bomb," "kidnap," "ransom," and "execute." This is the death squad of Islam against the 'infidel.'

After several years of arduous training in the Maulana's camp, Shalimar the *clown* turns into a killing machine of unique qualities. He is the Muslim 007, described in a set of superlatives no more realistic than those in a blockbuster Hollywood movie: "He was trained in many things. He could have caught the dogs by their jaws and ripped their head in half. He could have faced the security voice and shown it some tricks" (Rushdie, 2005, p. 321). He is also 'humble,' 'supplicant,' and 'mild.' This perfect *assassin* has five passports in five names, and he knows French and English in addition to Arabic and Kashmiri (Rushdie, 2005, p. 275). The time is ready; he becomes the private, elegant, and handsome driver of Max Olphus in the United States. More than a driver, he is a "valet, a body servant, the ambassador's shadow-self" (Rushdie, 2005 p. 330). When the right time comes, he "slaughters" the ambassador in California, "like a halal chicken dinner" (Rushdie, 2005, p. 4) (*halal* here means meat prepared according to Islamic law and dietary regulations). And "slaughtering" is on purpose, too, as he wanted to know

> what it would feel like when he placed the blade of his knife against the man's skin, when he pushed the sharp and glistening horizon of the knife against the frontier of the skin, violating the sovereignty of another human soul, moving in beyond taboo, toward the blood.
>
> RUSHDIE, 2005, p. 274

To understand the true nature of Rushdie's text, to see how he applies the Orientalist stereotypes so blatantly, it could be looked at as a brief overview of all the major figures, who are actually not *characters*, but already-existing types: the amazing Max Olphus, who is the typical successful politician but with the flaw of a weakness toward women; Shalimar, who is the typical deceived husband, ready to do everything to avenge his honor; Boonyi, who is the typical literary type who sells her body but whose soul money cannot buy; Western diplomats, who are adored by the bodies of the native women; and finally the Eastern men, who cannot take care of 'their' women. The character of Max Olphus is also suggestive of an alter-ego (of Rushdie himself): "an encyclopedia of Hollywood lore," "a Renaissance hero, the philosopher prince, the billionaire power-broker," "an expert at foreign affairs," "a bestseller writer," "an irresistible man," and the "maker of the world!" (Rushdie, 2005, p. 27). Siddiqi (2007) reads Max Olphus as "an allegorical figure for Western power brokership," "a mastermind of global finance," and a "veritable pastiche of movers and shakers in the New World Order" (p. 304). Yet, she is quick to add, "As a Jewish intellectual, he represents a minority cosmopolitanism" that is implicated in "an exploitative geopolitical relationship" (Siddiqi, 2007, p. 304).

Rushdie's *A*historical Fiction vs. the (Post)Colonial History of British Imperialism

Overall in the 2005 novel, Rushdie has the tendency to see the so-called 'Islamic' terror in isolation. According to him, Islamic culture is innately evil as in the Pachigam village, and Islamic scholars are the mullahs of terrorism, leaders of the jihad against the 'infidel.' In *Shalimar the Clown*, there is no awareness of the historical–political context that has led to the ontological and epistemological situation in the region. Neither Orientalism nor the postcolonial discourse emerged in isolation in the last couple of centuries. Rather, this discourse has a specific, detailed, and intricate history entangled in a web of power relations out of which the binary of the 'East' and the 'West' has been created.[6]

In his 2007 article, Pankaj Mishra articulates eloquently and with ample evidence the role of the Imperial Britain over the current situation of India, Pakistan, and Kashmir, the kind of information which is mostly missing in Rushdie's text despite the fact that Kashmir is one of the main topics of the work. "Many of the seeds of postcolonial disorder in South Asia were sown much earlier," indicates Mishra, in the previous two centuries of direct and indirect British rule, one which was (and has been after 'independence' of India and Pakistan) based on partition of the geography and cultures. In this article, he quotes Alex von Tunzelmann, who summarizes how the British administration in the area "damaged agriculture and retarded industrial

6 The process by which European powers colonized the rest of the world could briefly be mentioned here. The first stage, Schaebler (2004) describes, is the impetus of *Orbis Universalis Christianus* that ended with the victory over the Moors and the discovery of America. It is also important to note that the Christian mission was secularized into a civilizational one, which went along with colonialism in the next stage. From the end of the nineteenth century until WWII is the third stage, when the United States came to replace the world power. Since the Second World War, 'modernization,' 'development,' 'democracy,' and 'civilizing projects' have become the key words of the Cold War. Finally, 9/11 initiated a "simplistic discourse" on the forces of "civilization versus barbarity" (Schaebler, 2004, p. 6).

growth in India" as in another example, the destructive effect of the Belgians in the Congo, although the latter, Tunzelmann argues, has been on a much more rapacious scale (Mishra, 2007, para. 7).

The British rule in India also manipulated the shape of education by "limiting Indian access to higher education, industry and the civil service" (Mishra, 2007, para. 8), paving the way for the ignorant masses. It turned out that, Mishra (2007) continues, "while restricting an educated middle class, the British empowered a multitude of petty Oriental despots" (para. 8). In 1947, he cites, there were 565 of these feudations, often called *maharajas*, running states as large as Belgium and as small as Central Park (Mishra, 2007, para. 8). Moreover, the British administration's dislike of the culture of India is also comparable to the tone of *Shalimar the Clown*; Churchill openly expressed his hatred for the Indian culture: "I hate Indians," he once declared, "They are a beastly people with a beastly religion" (as cited in Mishra, 2007, para. 10).[7] He also viewed Gandhi as a "rascal" and "half-naked fakir," interestingly in the same vein as Rushdie does to *Maulana* and other historically prominent figures according to the Middle Eastern cultures.

In 1947 Britain's Indian Empire was divided into the nation-states of India and Pakistan in the leadership of Lord Louis Mountbatten, the last viceroy of India, in New Delhi. After the British realized that they had to leave India after WWII, they tried to find a way to both leave the subcontinent but at the same time continue their 'covert' rule. "Leaving India to God, or anarchy" was not a political option as it would leave an India "on its own" (Mishra, 2007, para. 2). Rather, Mishra (2007) explains, Mountbatten and his colleagues in Britain saw the solution in reinforcing the religious identities in the region, solidifying the binaries between Muslims and Hindus, thus dividing the empire into two, which has been one of the latest examples of the practice of 'divide and rule' in the history of imperial domination. The fight over Kashmir is a direct result of this practice (as opposed to the innately evil Muslims of Rushdie who butcher Hindus and Christians). Mishra gravely summarizes:

> The British Empire passed quickly and with less humiliation than its French and Dutch counterparts, but decades later the vicious politics of

7 The connection between imperialism and civilization also finds widespread expression, indicates Mandani, as the former sets out to "clear inferior races of the earth" (Mandani, 2004, p. 6). In 1848, Lord Salisbury, the then British Prime Minister, claims that "one can roughly divide the nations of the world into the living and the dying [...] imperialism is a biologically necessary process which, according to the laws of nature, leads to the inevitable destruction of lower races" (cited in Mandani, 2004, p. 6). Hitler was nine years old at this time.

> partition still seems to define India and Pakistan. The millions of Muslims who chose to stay in India never ceased to be hostages to Hindu extremists. In 2002, Hindu nationalists massacred more than two thousand Muslims in the state of Gujarat. The dispute over Kashmir, the biggest unfinished business of partition, committed countries with mostly poor and illiterate populations to a nuclear arms race and nourished extremists in both countries: Islamic fundamentalists in Pakistan, Hindu nationalists in India. It also damaged India's fragile democracy—Indian soldiers and policemen in Kashmir routinely execute and torture Pakistan-backed Muslim insurgents—and helped cement the military's extra-constitutional influence over Pakistan's inherently weaker state. Tens of thousands have died in Kashmir in the past decade and a half, and since 1947 sectarian conflicts in India and Pakistan have killed thousands more. (2007, para. 31)

Rushdie, however, never utters nor implies in *Shalimar the Clown* even a fraction of these historical realities that partly and mostly gave birth to the so-called Islamic terrorism. With this respect, his discourse is most similar to that of V.S. Naipaul, who clearly condemned the Muslim culture for lacking intellectual substance, therefore predicting its collapse soon (cited in Said, 1981). Oliver, on the other hand indicates:

> The problem with "Islamism [is that] we are not dealing with error, error that once detected and made manifest would bring down an entire system, but rather with a particular resurgence, a vertical revivalism virtually immune to error and human judgement in general." (2004, p. 208)

According to Oliver, "We cannot speak so soon of 'the failure of political Islam,' or for that matter, of any other form of twentieth-century fundamentalism, religious or other, quite possibly, we will never be able to do so" (2004, pp. 208–209). That is to say, any perspective that desires to see acts of extremism of fundamentalism as the results of a religion or any other doctrine will always be unsuccessful at shedding light on the true nature of events, by not taking into consideration the larger transnational political interests.

Mandani (2004) furthermore indicates that expressions such as 'Islamic terror' or 'Muslim jihad' are the essential cornerstones of what he defines as 'culture talk,' which has the disability to address issues from a factual perspective by its dominant tendency to label criminal activities to cultures or religions: "Culture talk assumes that every culture has a tangible essence that defines it, and it then explains politics as a consequence of that essence. Culture talk after 9/11, for example, qualified and explained the practice of 'terrorism' as 'Islamic'" (Mandani, 2004, p. 17). Mandani also reminds that President George W. Bush himself used this discourse most openly:

> After an unguarded reference to pursuing a "crusade," President Bush moved to distinguish between "good Muslims" and "bad Muslims." From this point of view, "bad Muslims" were clearly responsible for terrorism. At the same time, the president seemed to assure Americans that "good Muslims" were anxious to clear their names and consciences of this horrible crime and would undoubtedly support "us" in a war against "them." But this could not hide the central message of such a discourse: unless proved to be "good," every Muslim was presumed to be "bad." All Muslims were now under obligation to prove their credentials by joining in a war against "bad Muslims." (2004, p. 15)

Unlike Bush's remarks and Rushdie's ignorance of the fact that political Islam was not created in isolation, but in encounter with Western powers, it should also be emphasized that "political Islam was born in the colonial period" (Mandani, 2004, p. 14). As for the role of the United States, the Reagan doctrine called "rollback" should be mentioned here to be able to see the making of Islamic terror and oppressive regimes in the Middle East. According to this doctrine, Mandani explains, the newly emerging nation-states of the Middle East were to be put into good shape regarding their position toward capitalism and free market economy; it was mainly Russian ideas of communism which inspired many of these states: "The intellectual support for this comes from academics such as Lewis, Huntington and Kirkpatrick," indicates Mandani (2004, p. 96). These intellectuals made a distinction between two kinds of dictatorships, left-wing ('totalitarian') and right-wing ('authoritarian'). Totalitarian dictatorships are not able to reform from within and, therefore, they have to be overthrown by outside forces. On the other hand, authoritarian dictatorships are open to internal reform. This can be made through constructive engagement, which provided the rationale, explains Mandani, for why it is fine to make friends with right-wing dictators while doing everything to overthrow left-wing governments. Moreover, "The United States supported the Sarekat-I Islam in Indonesia [and] the Jamaat-i-Islami against Zulfiqar Ali Bhutto in Pakistan" (Mandani, 2004, p. 121), initiated by the rollback doctrine. Secular but violent regimes like that of Saddam Hussein in Iraq were also used as American allies (Mandani, 2004). "Both the contras in Nicaragua and later al-Qaeda (and the Taliban) in Afghanistan were [also] American allies during the Cold war" (Mandani, 2004, p. 13).

"Of Course, This Is About Islam"

Overall in *Shalimar the Clown,* Rushdie is historically not only blind but also synchronically selective in his depictions of concepts such as Islam, civilization, and barbarism. Almond (2007) claims that the impression of Islam in Rushdie's works "will not always be that of an alien, incomprehensible faith, but often that of a familiar background, a collection of lived conditions, rather than an exotic palette of colors" (p. 94). He is quite right, especially in his comparison of Rushdie to Borges in that the latter makes passing judgments about the Arabic world whereas the former comes from the midst of this culture (although we should also keep in mind the problematic nature of this insider status). Yet, it could also be argued that *Shalimar the Clown* not only centralizes the so-called Islamic lived set of conditions but also applies that very exotic palette of colors in the heart of the text. Yes, Rushdie's focal point is Islam, but it being so does not inhibit him approaching it from an Orientalist perspective; rather, it enhances the very misrepresentative quality of the work, as readers would now take it for granted that Rushdie has the sole authority to speak of Islam, with utmost credibility. Almond is also quick to note that the employment of intimacy with Islam does not mean that Rushdie will refrain from using "Orientalist sources, clichés and stereotypes" (p. 94) in an attempt to create some kind of meaningful distance between himself and Islam.

Yet, the problem with Almond (2007) is that he does not question the so-called plurality or multiplicity of different viewpoints in Rushdie's text. "The idea of the novel as a space where different vocabularies can freely interrogate one another," indicates Almond, "does go some way to explain the faintly kaleidoscopic sequence of different Islams in his work" (p. 106), pointing to the different representations of Islam. According to this viewpoint, Rushdie's different vocabulary and plurality "enable a kind of conference to take place, with each vocabulary presenting its own collection of metaphors, allowing the reader ultimately to decide upon the version of his choice" (Almond, 2007, p. 106). However, despite the fact that this might well be the case in Rushdie's previous works, the language *in Shalimar the Clown* is indeed one-sided and partisan, centered around the propagandist Islam, recurrent with lexicon such as 'terror,' 'jihad,' and 'bombing.' In a 2001 *New York Times* opinion entitled "Yes, This Is About Islam," Rushdie expresses his viewpoint quite clearly, almost with an attempt to eliminate all suspicion regarding his clear perspective:

> "This isn't about Islam." The world's leaders have been repeating this mantra for weeks, partly in the virtuous hope of deterring reprisal attacks on

> innocent Muslims living in the West, partly because if the United States is to maintain its coalition against terror it can't afford to suggest that Islam and terrorism are in any way related. The trouble with this necessary disclaimer is that it isn't true. (para. 1–2)

In the rest of the article, Rushdie tries to demonstrate why the problem is about Islam, why Muslims should modernize themselves, why the West is right about their assumptions about the Islamic culture, and why "of course, this is about Islam" (para. 4). Yet, a historical perspective that takes into account the postcolonial, imperial, and transnational interests in the area is nowhere to be found in this article. Rushdie has no doubt that the trouble is with Islam and its main theology.

In an interview, however, Rushdie indicates criticism on being too certain about issues: "Doubt, it seems to me," he starts, "is the central condition of a human being in the twentieth century. One of the things that has happened to us in the twentieth century as a human race is to learn how certainty crumbles in your hand" (cited in La'Porte, 1971, p. 45). His suspicion, it seems, is only limited to the teachings of Islam; Shalimar the clown, and his most recent perspective on the related issues, does not question at all the Western superiority—cultural and religious—over its Eastern counterpart.

Rushdie is of course not alone in his Orientalist discourse; Peter Heinegg (2006) argues that "[Rushdie] takes the grand abstractions of politics and gives them a terribly local habitation and an unforgotten name" (p. 24). Most probably, Heinegg has in mind the issue of terrorism and fanatical Islam while he is referring to the "grand abstractions of Islam" (p. 24). In "Stripping of Humanity in Salman Rushdie's *Shalimar the Clown*," Vijeta Gautam (2014) also indicates that the novel "delves deep into the roots of terrorism and explores the turmoil generated by different faiths and cultures attempting to coexist ... In this novel the globalization of terror has been shown brilliantly" (p. 310). However, Rushdie's story has the least bit of connections to this important notion; he cannot come close to analyzing the sociopolitical context behind terrorism. *Shalimar* is a story about the madness of a man deceived by his wife and what he can do, rather than of the roots and causes of terrorism, which requires a much more intricate and careful analysis of the historical-economic power relations in the region. Gautam also admits, "Max's murder, at first appears to be a political assassination of a Jewish American by a Muslim-Kashmiri fundamentalist turns out to be passionately personal" (p. 307). Moreover, unlike Heinegg's claims, Rushdie names not to make things concrete but to reduce complex issues to reductive and distorted images, to turn historically significant events and personages into charlatans and clowns.

"What then are we to learn from the novel's central depiction of a man who becomes a terrorist because his wife has left him for an American?" rightly asks Pitkin (2007, p. 262). Her answer is based on the common ground of irrationality of both acts.

> One wonders if there is not an attempt, via this storyline and the comparisons to cuckoldry and murder it evokes, to minimize the figure of the jihadist, to cut down to size the egomania of any person who believes that they have been given the religious, moral or political right to kill other human beings.
>
> PITKIN, 2007, p. 262

Yet, one can only "wonder" about this possibility, and although it must be the answer behind the Hollywood-simple story line of Rushdie, it does not dismiss (on the contrary, it actually reinforces) the fact that the writer sees terrorism as a simple act of evil; of irrationality, which thus eliminates the geopolitical realities in the region. As Mishra states, "The rival nationalisms and politicized religions the British Empire brought into being now clash in an enlarged geopolitical arena; and the human costs of imperial overreaching seem unlikely to attain a final tally for many more decades" (2007, para. 33). It is without question that terrorism is an act of evil, but one which has a historical background, which requires a much more comparative and transnational perspective rather than the comparison to cuckoldry.

Other Examples of Post-9/11 Neo-Orientalism

Before concluding, it should also be mentioned here that Rushdie's (2005) failure to portray the cultural-material realities of its subject matter, especially terror and conflicts in the region, are not exclusive to him. Other famous post-9/11 novels also bear similar risks. It is, of course, outside the parameters of this chapter to provide an all-inclusive summary of such novels, but it would be useful to look at some other samples. I will, therefore, briefly mention two sample works, one from a British and one from an American context: John Updike's (2006) *The Terrorist* (as an American example) and Ian McEwan's (2006) *Saturday* (as a British example). It is surprising to see similar judgments are made about the so-called 'Islamic terror' in these works.

Updike's 2006 novel revolves around an American Muslim teenager named Ahmad Ashmawy Mulloy, the son of a Catholic mother and an Egyptian father who left him several years ago. Ahmad can be described as a ticking bomb, not only because of his teenage cynicism but also because of his hatred for everything Western due to his Islamic beliefs:

> Devils, Ahmad thinks. These devils seek to take away my God. All day long, at Central High School, girls sway and sneer and expose their soft bodies and alluring hair. Their bare bellies, adorned with shining navel studs and low-down purple tattoos, ask, What else is there to say? ... The teachers, weak Christians and nonobservant Jews, make a show of teaching virtue and righteous self-restraint but their shifty eyes and hollow voices betray their lack of belief. ...They lack true faith; they are not on the Straight Path; they are unclean.
>
> UPDIKE, 2006, p. 3

Ahmad calls Christians and Jews around him "infidels," "drunks," and "Godless." He does not forget to remember the Qur'an while imagining the Hell's fire burning all these people. After all, he should be well versed in the holy book, as he is the disciple of one Sheikh Rashid, the imam at a local mosque, who assists him to be a suicide bomber. The good guy in this story turns out be none other than a nonobservant Jew, Jack Levy, who, as Ahmad's guidance counselor at school, tries very hard to change Ahmad's life for the better (Updike, 2006). Just like in Shalimar's story (Rushdie, 2005), Ahmad is educated by an Islamic cleric to be a terrorist and essentially contrasted with a charismatic Jew.

This threat to civilized man is also the theme of Ian McEwan's (2006) *Saturday*, which centers on the thoughts of the middle-aged, successful brain surgeon Henry Perowne on the day of Saturday, February 15, 2003 when there is a big demonstration in England against the invasion of Iraq. Henry Perowne is torn between these demonstrations and the brutalities of the Saddam regime:

> Everyone is thrilled to be together out on the streets—people are hugging themselves, it seems, as well as each other. If they think—and they could be right—that continued torture and summary executions, ethnic cleansing and occasional genocide are preferable to an invasion, they should be somber in their view.
>
> MCEWAN, 2006, p. 68

Perowne then remembers that "apostasy from Islam is an offense punishable by death" (McEwan, 2006, p. 71). The horrors of 9/11 are also looming in the background of the collective conscious of the people: "It is already almost eighteen months since half the planet watched, and watched again, the unseen captives driven through the sky to the slaughter" (p. 15). And once again, Islamic belief, and for that reason any kind of belief is to blame, according to the text, for this monstrosity because Perowne, just like Max Olphus of *Shalimar the Clown* (Rushdie, 2005) or Jack Levy of *The Terrorist* (Updike, 2006), is a nonbeliever.

In a 2005 article entitled "Civilization and Malcontents," Christopher Hitchens, who compares McEwan's 2006 work to Rushdie's *The Satanic Verses* (1988), concludes that McEwan's 2006 *Saturday* "shows us that civilization and culture and the life of the mind, fragile as they seemingly are, nonetheless have a resilience that can outlast barbarism" (para. 20). Put in this kind of grave abstraction such as 'civilization vs. barbarism,' 'secular vs. religious,' or 'nonbeliever vs. terrorist,' it does not take much to see that these novels cannot provide much to understand the true nature of politics and history of the world we live in.

Conclusion

Some scholars admit that such works are indeed incapable of telling us much about terrorism, if anything, at all. One such reader is Robert Eaglestone (2007), who argues, "these novels, despite their many merits, fail to address precisely the issues to which they lay claim" (p. 19). Talking particularly about Rushdie's *Shalimar the Clown*, Eaglestone says, "The very rhetoric of attempts, and the final collapse of Pachigam into an existence that is solely textual, marked only in a map and in a guidebook, reveals simply the inability of the text to enunciate the terror" (p. 20). It is impossible not to agree with Eaglestone, as I try to demonstrate in this chapter; however, what Eaglestone is actually arguing strikes a rather different tone than one might see at first sight. It is Eaglestone's argument that these novelists cannot truly grasp and thus cannot represent the issue of terrorism because it is such an 'Eastern,' such an 'Islamic' concept that 'Westerners' cannot understand this alien notion! "What is missing is precisely a sense of the world of the Islamist," argues Eaglestone (p. 21). Therefore Rushdie's novel "offers only a cipher of evil, lacking a real sense of motivation" (p. 21). Finally Eaglestone concludes:

> Despite their attempts, [these novels] show an inability to address the terror that is their proclaimed subject, and indeed perform their own failure and collapse of voice. And at the same time, on the other side of the coin, their refusal to come to terms with it leads to a simplistic refusal to engage with the otherness of the terrorists and their ideas.... There is little sense that there is, in the current crisis, a very different set of discourses that demand engagement, and that cannot simply be recapitulated within (retranslated into, as it were) a western intellectual framework.

> This movement itself is characteristic of western thinking, in its attempt to bring all "otherness" inside its own hegemonic discourse. (p. 21)

At this point, it is difficult to understand the true nature of Eaglestone's argument because it becomes confusing to differentiate between the text of the novel and that of the article; it is up to the reader to decide which one is more Orientalist and essentialist in content and tone. As an attempt at paraphrasing Eaglestone, Rushdie's novel is a failure to portray the true nature of 'Islamic terrorism,' but it is not Rushdie's fault; he is too civilized, Westernized, and even too intellectual to understand and portray Muslim terrorists.

There are also those who defend Rushdie's simplistic narrative as an allegory. As such, these scholars argue that behind the façade of these simplistic binaries, there lies the complexity of the subject matter. There are a couple of answers that need to be given to these arguments. First and foremost is that it is very easy to defend any simplistic narrative by using the 'allegory' genre as an excuse. In "The Literalization of Allegory in Salman Rushdie's *Shalimar the Clown*," Neil Murphy (2008) lists reasons why allegory or magical realism does not work in the novel, either. While trying to make sense of Shalimar's character, he observes:

> The intention, it would appear, is to reveal that people like Noman are motivated by personal grief and private grievances rather than by any meaningful ideology. This is of course, a grossly simplified explanation of the realities of contemporary violence, but the reason that Shalimar's violent acts are represented in such a basic manner has as much to do with the clumsiness of the transference of meaning from the literal to the allegorical—and with the implausible plot—as it does with any innate problem with the political vision, which ends up appearing extremely unsophisticated.
>
> MURPHY, 2008, p. 358

After explaining, "Central to magical realism is the delicately balanced relationship between the two elements, the absence of a hierarchy among the different levels of 'reality'" (p. 359), Murphy concludes that no such balance is struck up in *Shalimar the Clown*. As a consequence, "the literal textual material is so weakened that it fails to act effectively as allegorical co-relation, and much of the political intent is diminished because of loosely drawn narrative elements" (Murphy, 2008, p. 359).

In conclusion, La'Porte (1971) argues that "Rushdie cannot simply be termed an Orientalist. He is not a Western supremacist" (p. 113). However, in this chapter, it is argued that Rushdie is not only an Orientalist but also a Western supremacist, through a close reading of *Shalimar the Clown* and comparing the fictional text to factual realities of the region. Moreover, beyond a typical Orientalist, who is in most cases a Western writer, artist, historian, or politician, Rushdie's 'insider' status gives him unfair and undeserved credit that makes him all the more credible in the eyes of the Western reader, thus more influential over his readership, mostly the literary intelligentsia of the West. It is also possible to see that Rushdie's disturbing Orientalism is mirrored in other post-9/11 novels by Updike and McEwan.

When discussing Rushdie's portrait, Siddiqi (2007) is most right to note, "Not only is this vision unmistakably an elite one despite the token acknowledgment of subaltern lives, the bird's eye view of culture that underwrites his cosmopolitan vision flattens the geopolitics of migration" (p. 307). The excuse for the novel's simplistic, reductive, and abstractionist attitude toward its subject as an allegory or magical realism also fails; as Murphy (2008) demonstrates, the magical realism is "inexpertly constructed" in this novel. As such, unlike many intellectuals both in the United States and abroad, Rushdie positions himself among the right-wing neo-conservatives of the United States, and he establishes himself as an effective power to counter-balance the intellectual fight against the neo-colonial doctrines of the New World Order.

Acknowledgement

An earlier version of this article first appeared in *SEFAD: Selçuk University Journal of Faculty of Letters*, Vol. 36, Winter 2016: 19–40.

References

Ahluwalia, P. (2005). When does a settler become a native?: Citizenship and identity in a settler society. In G. Desai & S. Nair (Eds.), *Postcolonialisms: An anthology of cultural theory and criticism* (pp. 500–514). New Brunswick, NJ: Rutgers University Press.

Almond, I. (2007). *The new Orientalists: Postmodern representations of Islam from Foucault to Baudrillard.* New York, NY: I.B. Tauris.

Clancy, T. (1984). *The hunt for Red October.* Annapolis, MD: U.S. Naval Institute Press.

Clancy, T. (1986). *Red storm rising.* New York, NY: Putnam.

Dirlik, A. (2005). The postcolonial aura: Third World criticism in the age of global capitalism. In G. Desai & S. Nair (Eds.), *Postcolonialisms: An anthology of cultural theory and criticism* (pp. 561–589). New Brunswick, NJ: Rutgers University Press.

Eaglestone, R. (2007). The age of reason is over ... an age of fury was dawning: Contemporary Anglo-American fiction and terror. *Wasafiri, 22*(2), 19–22. doi:10.1080/02690050701336568.

Fanon, F. (2005). On national culture. In G. Desai & S. Nair (Eds.), *Postcolonialisms: An anthology of cultural theory and criticism* (pp. 198–220). New Brunswick, NJ: Rutgers University Press.

Feitshans, B., Kassar, M., Munafo, T., & Vajna, A.G. (Producers), & MacDonald, P. (Director). (1988). *Rambo III* [Motion picture]. United States: Carolco Pictures.

Fernandez-Kelly, P. (2009). On *Shalimar the Clown. Sociological Forum, 24*, 471–474. doi:10.1111/j.1573-7861.2009.01110_5.x.

Gautam, V. (2014). Stripping off humanity in Salman Rushdie's *Shalimar the Clown. International Journal of English and Education, 3*(1), 306–311. Retrieved July 27, 2017 from http://ijee.org/yahoo_site_admin/assets/docs/24.1154532.pdf.

Guha, R. (2005). On some aspects of the historiography of colonial India. In G. Desai & S. Nair (Eds.), *Postcolonialisms: An anthology of cultural theory and criticism* (pp. 403–410). New Brunswick, NJ: Rutgers University Press.

Heinegg, P. (2006, February 13). The political is personal: Review of *Shalimar the Clown*, by Salman Rushdie. *America: The National Catholic Review*. Retrieved July 27, 2017 from https://www.americamagazine.org/issue/culture/political-personal.

Hitchens, C. (2005). Civilization and its malcontents: Alongside a "peace" demonstration in London, a crisis of micro-terrorism. *The Atlantic, April*. Retrieved July 27, 2017 from https://www.theatlantic.com/magazine/archive/2005/04/civilization-and-its-malcontents/303841/.

Kazanjian, H.G., Lucas, G., Marshall, F., & Watts, R. (Producers), & Spielberg, S. (Director). (1981). *Raiders of the lost ark* [Motion picture]. United States: Paramount Pictures.

La'Porte, V. (1971). *An attempt to understand the Muslim reaction to* The Satanic Verses. Lewiston, NY: The Edwin Mellen Press.

Mandani, M. (2004). *Good Muslim, bad Muslim: America, the Cold War and the roots of terror*. New York, NY: Pantheon.

McEwan, I. (2006). *Saturday*. New York, NY: Anchor Books.

Mishra, P. (2007, August 13). Exit wounds. *New Yorker*. Retrieved July 27, 2017 from http://www.newyorker.com/magazine/2007/08/13/exit-wounds.

Morton, S. (2008). "There were collisions and explosions. The world was no longer calm." Terror and precarious life in Salman Rushdie's *Shalimar the Clown. Textual Practice, 22*, 337–355. doi:10.1080/09502360802045148.

Murphy, N. (2008). The literalization of allegory in Salman Rushdie's *Shalimar the Clown*. In N. Murphy & W.-C. Sim (Eds.), *British Asian fiction: Framing the contemporary* (pp. 351–364). New York, NY: Cambria.

Oliver, A.M. (2004). The scandal of literalism in Hamas, the Israeli-Palestinian conflict, and beyond. In B. Schaebler & L. Stenberg (Eds.), *Globalization and the Muslim world: Culture, religion, and modernity* (pp. 206–224). Syracuse, NY: Syracuse University Press.

Pitkin, A. (2007). Salman Rushdie loses his cheerfulness: Geopolitics, terrorism and adultery: Review of *Shalimar the Clown*, by Salman Rushdie. *Journal of International Affairs, 61*(1), 257–262. Retrieved July 27, 2017 from http://www.jstor.org/stable/24358092.

Rushdie, S. (1981). *Midnight's children.* New York, NY: Knopf.

Rushdie, S. (1983). *Shame.* New York, NY: Knopf.

Rushdie, S. (1988). *The Satanic verses.* New York, NY: Viking.

Rushdie, S. (1995). *The Moor's last sigh.* New York, NY: Pantheon.

Rushdie, S. (2001, November 2). Yes, this is about Islam. *New York Times*. Retrieved July 27, 2017 from http://www.nytimes.com/2001/11/02/opinion/yes-this-is-about-islam.html.

Rushdie, S. (2005). *Shalimar the clown.* New York, NY: Random House.

Rushdie, S. (2007, March 16–17). Interview. *Milliyet.*

Said, E. (1978). *Orientalism.* New York, NY: Vintage.

Said, E. (1981). *Covering Islam: How the media and the experts determine how we see the rest of the world.* New York, NY: Pantheon.

Schaebler, B. (2004). Civilizing others: Global modernity and the local boundaries (French/German, Ottoman, and Arab) of savagery. In B. Schaebler & L. Stenberg (Eds.), *Globalization and the Muslim world: Culture, religion, and modernity* (pp. 3–30). Syracuse, NY: Syracuse University Press.

Siddiqi, Y. (2007). "Power smashes into private lives": Violence, globalization and cosmopolitanism in Salman Rushdie's *Shalimar the Clown. South Asia Research, 27,* 293–309. doi:10.1177/026272800702700303.

Stadtler, F. (2009). Terror, globalization and the individual in Salman Rushdie's *Shalimar the Clown. Journal of Postcolonial Writing, 45,* 191–199. doi:10.1080/17449850902820035.

Stam, R., & Shohat, E. (2005). De-Eurocentricizing cultural studies: Some proposals. In A. Abbas & J.N. Erni (Eds.), *Internationalizing cultural studies: An anthology* (pp. 481–499). Oxford, England: Blackwell.

Updike, J. (2006). *The terrorist.* New York, NY: Knopf.

CHAPTER 11

The Jasmine in the Fist: International Democratization Strategies in the Arab Spring and Beyond

Emanuela C. Del Re

Foreign Actors in the Arab Spring

Who was behind the 2011 revolution in Egypt? This has been a deeply discussed issue during and since the so-called Arab Spring.

The controversial WikiLeaks (2015) itself, probably with the ambition of putting an end to all doubts, has published its 'truth,' diffusing a secret document sent by the U.S. Embassy in Cairo to Washington ("Egypt Protests," 2011), with the intention of unveiling the size and impact of the American support to the protesters in the Egyptian revolts. Was it a non-spontaneous revolution that took place in Egypt, then? A revolution piloted by the United States through groups trained and tested in the past in other theatres?

In the document revealed on Assange's website (WikiLeaks, 2015), which has winged its way around the world, there is also a reference to the story of a member of the Egyptian April 6 youth movement (hereafter referred to as April 6) pointing out that he took part in the Alliance of Youth Movements Summit in Capitol Hill in December 2008, meeting members of the U.S. government. Later he affirmed that on his way back home from the United States he was detained at the airport in Egypt by the then notorious State Security and Investigation Service (SSIS), today dissolved. He said that his notes were confiscated: in them he affirmed that there was a need to radically transform the Egyptian regime in a parliamentary democracy and also noted that various parties and opposition movements had developed an unwritten plan to enforce the democratic transition by 2011. In his notes, he affirmed, it was also written that April 6 wanted to overthrow the regime before the presidential elections. The U.S. Embassy in Cairo prudently affirmed then that this member of April 6 was making unrealistic affirmations and was not supported by the main opposition trends. What is certain is that the U.S. State Department itself in 2008 had announced in a press release the institution of the Alliance of Youth Movements Summit to promote freedom (U.S. Department of State, 2008).

It is clear that the events in Tunisia inspired the Egyptian protests, which came days after the Tunisian leader Zine Al Abidine Ben Ali was forced into exile by demonstrations in his home country. Nevertheless, in a more global dimension, the visit of the member of the Egyptian youth movement April 6 to Washington is significant and could demonstrate, as some maintain, that Washington was aware of plans to overthrow Mubarak's regime as early as 2008. Or maybe, as others maintain, the trip of the April 6 member to Washington was aimed at training youth leaders to organize demonstrations and a movement of opinion that could peacefully lead to the overthrow of Mubarak.

The discussion on the influence of foreign powers in revolutions all over the world is heated and often becomes ideological and instrumental. One interesting example is a video realized by Patrick H. Hafner and Alexandre Steinbach in June 2011, entitled *The Revolution Business*. In this short film, the authors tried to demonstrate that the Arab Spring was organized by foreign powers through the work of people trained for this specific aim, affirming in the video itself that "they mainly operate in countries in which the western world has a clear interest. Hardly a coincidence it seems" (Hafner & Steinbach, 2011, 00:31).

The idea that the revolution was 'made up' to the point that some events were fake, organized *ad hoc*, with the clear aim of making the tension escalate, is creating a movement of thought that paradoxically seems to have the same intensity of the nonviolent methodological pattern that it criticizes, because it is perceived as imposed by external actors. This movement of thought is in fact spreading successfully at a global level in many societies affected by undemocratic regimes or internal conflicts, with varying expectations, strategies, and results.

Yet, the global discussion on the actual results and consequences of the operations allegedly organized to overthrow regimes, such as the one in Egypt, is surprisingly limited. Hundreds of posts in blogs and Internet forums, which this author has analyzed in different languages and in different countries between January 2011 and June 2013, show that what really emerges is the fear of a global leadership that decides the destinies of all societies: a sort of 'applied conspiracy theory' by which (a) the concept of training is interpreted as 'manipulation'; (b) the concept of participation and influence of a foreign actor in a given local political situation is turned into 'interference'; and (c) the outcomes of a population's upsurge are seen as the driven 'plot' of the story, whose end had been already decided. The global political dimension of this movement of thought implies that all international crises can be analyzed according to this specific pattern.

Global Views

During the protests in January 2011, the streets of Cairo were dominated by the image of a clenched fist, the symbol of the movement April 6, which had adopted *tout court* the logo of the Serbian movement *Otpor* (see Figure 11.1). Born as a Facebook group, April 6 grew to count more than 100,000 members. The name of the group derives from the day in which in 2008 the workers of El-Mahalla El-Kubra—a big Egyptian agricultural and industrial center—went on strike. Among the organizers of the strike there was Ahmed Maher, who later became a leader in the January 2011 revolution.

In 2008, the activists of April 6 began to use Facebook to diffuse news regarding the strike. At the beginning the members of the FB group were only 300, but in just ten days they rose to 70,000. Despite the fact that the protest was later repressed and Maher arrested, April 6 continued its fight with remarkable results. In a 2010 interview with the Carnegie Endowment for International Peace, Maher affirmed: "Being the first youth movement in Egypt to use internet-based modes of communication like *Facebook* and *Twitter*, we aim to promote democracy by encouraging public involvement in the political process" (as cited in Jacob, 2011, para. 12). Further, Maher called the movement a youth coalition, saying that it was not a political party and that it would not contest elections. The Egyptian group adopted as a logo a clenched fist that was the symbol of Otpor (Resistance), the Serbian movement that greatly contributed to the end of Milošević.

Described as an heroic movement in *Bringing Down a Dictator*, a well-known film produced in 2002 by WETA and York Zimmerman Inc. and narrated by Martin Sheen, Otpor's strength is clearly identified in its strategy and pattern

FIGURE 11.1
Otpor logo
SOURCE: VECTOR, HTTP://4VECTOR.COM/FREE-VECTOR/OTPOR-32630.

(York, Ackerman, York, & Zimmerman, 2002). In the website that advertises the film, the endorsement reads:

> Their weapons were rock concerts and ridicule, the internet and email, spray-painted slogans and a willingness to be arrested. *Otpor* students became the shock troops in an army of human rights, pro-democracy, anti-war, women's groups, and opposition political parties. Their slogan: "He's Finished!"
>
> A force more powerful, n.d., para. 3

The ambition to universality of the movement's pattern is made explicit by this sentence in the discussion guide accompanying the film: "This documentary examines those ideas and how they might be used against the world's remaining non-democratic regimes" (A Force More Powerful, n.d., p. 2).

In his review of the film, Bacher (2002) underlined the process of training that Otpor underwent and the influence of peace movements in Serbia. He quoted the words of Miljenko Derata, the director of a Belgrade group named *Građanskih inicijativa* (Civic Initiative), who explains in the film that he received funding from the U.S. human rights organization Freedom House to print and distribute 5,000 copies of Gene Sharp's 1993 book *From Dictatorship to Democracy: A Conceptual Framework for Liberation.* Bacher then stressed the fact that Otpor translated Sharp's book into a notebook in Serbian language, which became the "Otpor User Manual."

The above-mentioned film *Bringing Down a Dictator* has a strong ambition of diffusing a specific message, as it is also accompanied by a study guide and lesson plan for use in schools (A Force More Powerful, n.d.). It clearly states that the movement that deposed Milošević was trained in nonviolent action and was partially financed by the United States and Western Europe.

What constitutes the link between April 6 and Otpor? It was difficult for April 6, after the experience of 2008, to be able to convince the tens of thousands members of its Facebook group to take to the streets once they logged out. In 2009 Maher and his fellows realized that they had to move a step forward and decided to involve those people who had more experience. In this spirit in the summer of 2009, Mohamed Adel, an April 6 blogger and activist in his twenties, made his way to Belgrade (Rosenberg, 2011).

Democracy Promotion Networks

Otpor has truly acquired a lot of experience. It has exported its nonviolent strategies to Ukraine and Georgia, and also to Zimbabwe, Maldives, and elsewhere, tracing out on the planisphere a rainbow of so-called 'color revolutions.' A wake of colors that has made and makes many worry, because they see in the actions of Otpor outside Serbia the signal of a U.S. strategy whose features are still not clear. In Italy, for instance, the left-wing newspaper *Il Manifesto* and the weekly journal *Il Diario* had noticed all of this already in 2009, publishing interviews with members of Otpor who declared themselves proud of receiving help from the intelligence service (CIA) of a great democratic country like the United States (Vigna, 2009). In this sense, the preoccupations of the Bulgarians would be confirmed: They, together with others, were already worried as early as 2000 about the interference of the U.S. intelligence in others' internal affairs (Doncheva, 2000).

Who is Otpor sustained by? No mystery, because the issue of the financial backers of Otpor is covered by hundreds of websites disseminating the list of organizations that pay out money, and in the end all seem to agree, more or less, both on the financing bodies and on the amount of funds.

Regarding the role of Otpor, everything seems to be well known. Those who were wondering who had really deposed Milošević (Cohen, 2000) find an answer in the words of Paul McCarthy, an official of the National Endowment for Democracy (NED). In a February 2011 interview (Proyect, 2011), McCarthy affirmed that in August 1999 money had begun to flow into Otpor pockets, and that out of the three million U.S. dollars spent by NED in Serbia, the major part has gone to Otpor. Besides, NED has a lot of experience in funding groups, because it was founded in the Reagan times, in the controversial period of the revolution in Nicaragua. NED's tradition continued in the Balkans with Milošević and then beyond.

Otpor underwent a very significant development in Ukraine during the Orange Revolution. At that time, the world journals started to fill in the lists of the American bodies financing the Serbian organization. According to *The Guardian* (Traynor, 2004), those directly involved were and are the Open Society Institute of George Soros, the NED, the International Republican Institute (IRI), the Freedom House and the National Democratic Institute (NDI), and the U.S. State Department and USAID. This list represents a very cross-party and wide-spectrum approach in the United States, as it sees all involved, from Republican to Democrats. Critiques towards this 'system' are equally cross-party and wide-spectrum, often eventuating in ideological interpretations.

In the *Foreign Policy Journal*, Bolton (2011) wrote: "NED and Soros work in tandem, targeting the same regimes and using the same methods.... At least ten of the twenty-two directors of NED are also members of the plutocratic think tank, the Council on Foreign Relations" (para. 8), mentioning the latter because it is the American equivalent of the Rothschild's Royal Institute of International Affairs in Britain, seen by some as instruments of plutocratic control hiding in plain sight.

'Plutocracy' is a key element that recurs transversally in the explanations of the involvement of foreign countries in North Africa. The following quotation is taken from an article by an unspecified author, which has been re-published in 2011 by innumerable blogs, mainly those that are extremely politicized and ideological:

> NED and Soros have been injecting millions of dollars into the training of North African, pro-democracy teachers, lawyers, journalists and youth activists. In 2009 they more than doubled their training efforts. Why, at this time, has the 30-year support of these dictators been undermined? The prize is the rapidly-rising economies of North Africa. It coincides with the efforts of Ben Ali to make Tunisia the financial centre of North Africa and to promote Islamic banking. The Rothschilds want North African Muslims to borrow from Rothschild banks and pay interest at rates the Rothschild central bank decides: they do not want them to be able to borrow from Islamic banks and not pay any interest. The Rothschilds want Muslims to trade their present political oppression at the hands of brutal dictators for future economic serfdom under the control of banker Lord Rothschild.
>
> professor 1, 2011, para. 80

The narrative used in this 2011 post has been particularly successful because it recurs to a simple terminology with clearly identifiable symbolic elements that can be understood cross-culturally by large audiences at global level. The repetition of the name of Lord Rothschild is used to transcend the contingency of events in order to reach a higher level of universal symbolism. The Rothschilds are seen as the emblem of plutocracy.

Another institution related to Otpor is the Albert Einstein Institute of Gene Sharp, an NGO founded by the man who is considered the ideologist of nonviolent resistance. It must be said that the inspiring principles derive from Sharp's book *From Dictatorship to Democracy*, published in 1993 in Thailand for the Burmese dissidents. Sharp is now considered the 'von Clausewitz of nonviolence,' using an oxymoron, noted also by *Scientific American* because of the 'vindication' of his nonviolent theories occurred specifically in Egypt's revolution (Horgan, 2011). More recently Sharp has been portrayed and his principles emphasized in relation with the Arab Spring in the film *"How to Start a Devolution"* by Ruaridh Arrow (2011). This confirms, to the eyes of the international community that is sensitive to peace activism, that the strategy behind the recent toppling of the Egyptian government was that of Sharp. In this era of free electronic communication, Sharp's ideas do not need to be smuggled into countries affected by dictatorships as it was in the past; it can be easily accessed and therefore can inspire generations of protesters.

Sharp's principles are echoed also in Otpor's manual, written by Srdja Popovic, Andrej Milivojević, and Slobodan Djinović, entitled *Nonviolent Struggle—50 Crucial Points: A Strategic Approach to Everyday Tactics* (2006). The manual has been opportunely diffused in any country where Otpor has carried out coaching and facilitating activities.

Through the creation of private foundations such as the Albert Einstein Institute, Washington filters the funds and provides strategic and political support to political groups and parties all over the world. Everything is public and transparent, so much so that in the recent case of the Middle East it is possible to consult the tables, elaborated by the Carnegie Endowment for International Peace (2006), which show all of the allocated funds. These funds represent money that has been well spent for democratization processes, some say. The projects favor contacts and train young people, above all through social networks and other current communication modes, with the great outcome of opening new windows to the world, although only to privileged sectors of the societies in which they operate. They work with groups that are already sensitive to social issues, activists, members of the élites, and members of educated middle classes.

Undoubtedly it is a noticeable effort that has allowed the creation of an efficient pattern of democracy promotion, which claims to be equally adaptable to very different contexts and scenarios. The positive outcome of this strategy is a network of democratic movements. Those who have become part of the network communicate globally, sharing and taking advantage and inspiration from lessons learned and past experiences, benefiting from one another, and in particular from Otpor, the emblem of success.

The negative outcome could instead lie in the fact that in the end, this system produces patterns of élites with identical characteristics, with young people from the middle class, educated, in some case activists labeled as extremists—the case of Venezuela will rise the issue later in this chapter—who base their strategy on the promotion of civil society, but cannot reach and involve the whole population with their message, which remains highly elitist.

Another relevant issue is that the pattern that these networks propose seems to be un-modifiable, with a top-down approach, always applied from above to a given situation, in this way restricting the contribution of the local people to a minimum. What the networks propose is an entire compact process, a 'democracy package,' not an approach to be developed according to the peculiarities of the single case.

The biases of such a system become apparent when one examines some issues spread on the Web that appear to be discrepant with the principles of the revolutions. This could be due to the fact that the principles of the revolution have not been completely absorbed or fully understood, given the fact that the pattern is brought to the population and enforced in a somehow a-critical way, or that the principles can be interpreted according to contingent circumstances, by leaders of the revolution who enjoy a certain degree of freedom of action. For example, Wael Ghonim, the marketing director of Google in Egypt, who had established himself as leader of the Egyptian movement and who appeared as first in the *Time Magazine*'s list of the most influential people in 2011, wrote on Facebook in February 2011 that after having met the leaders of the military, he ended up by trusting them (Levinson, Coker, & El-Ghobashy, 2011). This statement by Ghonim has been interpreted as a form of incoherence with the principles of the revolution and as a declaration aimed at pleasing the international spectators.

The Religious Dimension of Democracy

Another element to be discussed is the religious dimension of democracy. Is the pattern proposed by Sharp applicable to all religious contexts?

The issue of democracy and religion has been and is debated in the West as well as in Muslim countries. In the collective volume *Conflict, Identity, and Reform in the Muslim World* (Brumberg & Shehata, 2009), published by the United States Institute of Peace (USIP), the questions to which all contributors tried to give an answer are related to the analytical and policy challenges that escalating identity conflicts within Muslim majority states pose to both the Muslim world and the United States. In his chapter David Smock (2009) exhorted not to limit the issue to Islam. He stated that the United States must "devise a better strategy to effectively and respectfully engage" with a "religious realm" that includes representatives of all the major faiths of the Muslim world (p. 61). He affirmed that the United States has failed to recognize the positive role that Christian, Jewish, and Muslim leaders have played in mediating in many conflicts and must revise its attitude in such sense.

If there are weaknesses in Sharp's strategy, these can emerge in a situation like the Arab Spring, when it happens that while on one hand such strategy leads to revolt, training leaders to appeal to the civil society with a nonviolent attitude; on the other, the strategy is unable to face the fact that it is impossible to identify leaders who would be considered legitimate—in a Weberian sense—by all parts of the society and who could really be able to act as grantors for all parts of the society.

The wave of violence against Coptic Christians in Egypt after the Arab Spring could in this framework be interpreted as an indicator that the democracy pattern that had been promoted in the country, and the nonviolent strategy applied during the protests, did not take into account a long-term perspective, initiating deeply rooted changes. This has created a dilemma for American Christians because the Arab Spring has raised a double-edged issue: On one side there was a nonviolent movement aimed at establishing democracy in an authoritarian state; on the other hand there was a movement led by Arab Muslims.

Despite all of these biases and uncertainties, the capacity of absorbing foreign patterns by countries in transition is evident and strong. There are still crucial issues, though, such as whether there exists a concept of Islamic democracy that is different from the consolidated Western one, because it is based on Muslim principles. What are the differences? Do Westerners and Arabs aspire to the same kind of liberty? The mere fact that during the Arab Spring revolts the local population were applying nonviolent strategies defies the most common Western-Christian stereotypes about the Muslim world, even based on theological foundations sustaining that the Arabs are different because they are the 'sons of Ishmael.'

While the Arab Spring had seemed to make the aspirations of all populations of the world converge, as a consequence of the very high emotional tensions and empathy caused by the development of the events in Maghreb, more recent facts have again raised the issue of divergence, based in particular on religious differences.

For instance, democracies emerging from the Arab Spring, according to Dorrell and Lynch, do not contemplate the issue of religious minorities in a structured way, and this creates a renewed fracture in society, not to mention the casualties and the fear that this is diffusing (Dorell & Lynch, 2012). Sharp has made it clear that there is no direct connection between belief in nonviolent action and the use of nonviolent actions unless all this becomes an ideal: "People who believe in the ethical or religious approach to nonviolent means could assist, if they're not too arrogant, the development of pragmatic nonviolence to be used by the masses of people" (as cited in Pal, 2007, para. 19). Sharp has also stated that nonviolent movements have transcended religious boundaries:

> If people come from any particular religious group and are inspired to be nonviolent and to resist—not just to be nonviolent and passive—that's fine. But don't claim that they have to believe in a certain religion. Historically, for centuries and even millennia, that has not been true. Nonviolent

> struggle, as I understand it, is not based on what people believe. It's what they do.
>
> as cited in SCHNEIDER, 2011, para. 28

The issue of religion emerges also when reflecting upon the influence of foreign activists in a given situation. According to Ilić (2001), most Otpor activists are confessed believers. In fact, religion (Christian Orthodox) in Serbia has always been a fundamental element in the definition of the identity, especially when facing an enemy, for example the Muslim communities in Bosnia Herzegovina or in Kosovo. The members of Otpor were able to transcend their religious identity when involved in contexts that presented very different features from their own, because of their strong political realism and belief in opposition movements that allowed them "not to be bounded by purely structural and historical limitations of the domestic social structure and political culture" (Ilić, 2001, p. 51). Is the pattern of democracy exported by Otpor, which has interiorized it from the principles of democracy of the West, and its nonviolent strategy, based on Sharp's teachings, able to transcend the immanence of specific historical events?

A Question of Leadership

The picture of the veiled Egyptian woman who in 2011 wavered in front of the police a black banner bearing the white symbol of the clenched fist, has been published and seen all over the world, becoming 'viral.' That is probably the moment in which people started wondering about the meaning of that symbol. Those who knew the symbol wondered what Otpor was doing in Cairo. The link between Egypt and Serbia was consecrated by *Al Jazeera* (2011), that dedicated a chapter of its compelling video series *People and Power* to Egypt, entitling it "Egypt: Seeds of Change." The film starts from the protest on January 25, the national festivity in which the country celebrated the Police Corps, recalling the 25th of January in 1952, the day in which a murderous attack was perpetrated by British forces on a police station in the canal city of Ismailia, in which over 50 men were killed, sparking anti-British riots across the country. The Egyptian police in that occasion established itself as the heroic emblem of resistance against foreign occupation, remembered by a demonstration taking place every year since 1952.

In 2011 the demonstration acquired a different meaning and had a stronger echo, because it took place after the Tunisian events, characterizing it with a completely different value and new inspiration. *Al Jazeera* focused its video on the activists in the office of April 6, filming the debates, the meetings, the activities aimed at preparing of the demonstrations. It focused also on the leaders, and in particular on Ahmed Meher, during the most difficult days. The strong bond with Otpor is consecrated in the film by the interview with Srdja Popović, one of the funders and leaders of Otpor, who talks about the way he trained the Egyptians, about the videos and documents he gave them, about the way by which he promoted and taught nonviolent strategies and defense tactics in case of violent attack by the police. The video by *Al Jazeera* seems to demonstrate that the revolution in Egypt was not unexpected, as it had been prepared for at least 3 years, years in which the revolutionaries had been trained in the United States and elsewhere and had become professionals, certainly with the contribution of Otpor.

On the other hand, *Al Jazeera* wondered, how could a population that did not even know the meaning of the word *dissidence* because of the fierce repression, become emotionally and actively involved in an overpowering revolution without adequate preparation? It is Otpor that has managed to instill the fundamental principles that guarantee a positive outcome of the revolution: 'unity, discipline, planning,' also defined as the trifecta of civil resistance (Merriman, 2010). And then, it has taught tactics such as the fact that the leaders of the revolution must keep people always busy, even by just making banners and distributing leaflets, not to lessen the tension, not to disperse the forces.

With an unrelenting rhythm, in its film *Al Jazeera* shows the anxiety, the enthusiasm; the return from a demonstration that was put to an end by the truncheon blows of the police; the rough search carried out by the police in the office; three young people who scream in the streets while running to join a demonstration: "We have three PhDs in stubbornness, and three PhDs in ability to stay until he (Mubarak) goes!" (*Al Jazeera*, 2011).

A revolution prepared for years, as Kirkpatrick and Sanger (2011) affirmed. In fact, Maher had been a member of another group called *Kefaya* (Enough) around 2005; he later created a group called "Youth for Change," and then finally April 6. Many were the groups involved in the revolution: from *Kefaya* to the movement *We Are All Khalid Said*, all have played an important role.

Kefaya and April 6 are the groups to whom Egypt owes the ability to make people take the streets (Stratfor, 2011). A significant role was also played by the Academy of Change (2017), a group of expatriate Egyptians in their thirties who founded that organization in Qatar promoting the ideas of Gene Sharp. Hisham Morsy, one of the organizers of the association, was arrested during the protests in Cairo (Kirkpatrick & Sanger, 2011).

April 6, described as a group of educated and affluent young people, has grown to become a true leader in a revolution like the Egyptian one, which had instead been described by many as 'leaderless' (Editorial Board, 2011). Michael Hais and Morley Winograd (2011) affirmed that "the revolution was successful because it had no leaders, only coordinators of bottom up energy. Its use of social media was brilliantly conceived to meld online organizing with offline action, not supplant it" (para. 2). Is it a form of leadership simply difficult to understand for older generations, as Hais and Winograd say, or is it a form of leadership too fragile to set up long-lasting foundations for democracy?

Omar Ashour (2011), director of the Middle East Graduate Studies Program at the Institute of Arab and Islamic Studies of the University of Exeter, looked at the months following the overthrow of Mubarak. He commented that the wave of protests and the clashes in Tahrir Square that occurred in November 2011 reflect a particular issue:

> Unlike Egypt's revolts of 1882, 1919, and 1952, the revolution of 2011 is leaderless. That was a source of strength during the overthrow of Mubarak's dictatorship; now it is a source of weakness. The unity of opposition is usually a critical factor in successful democratic transitions, as in Poland, Chile, and South Africa, for example. In Egypt, the political unity was maintained—just barely—during the struggle against Mubarak, but began to splinter once the SCAF took over. Ideological polarization, leadership struggles, inflated egos, and inexperience in coalition management and negotiations caused serious rifts within the ranks of opposition politicians.
>
> ASHOUR, 2011, para. 3

A preoccupation expressed also by Wendell Steavenson (2011), who looked at Egypt's situation in November 2011, almost a year after the revolution.

> Meanwhile, liberal activist groups have remained fragmented and often divided by interpersonal rivalries. There are plenty of new parties, but no consolidated leadership has emerged, and at times the political fizz has seemed to amount to little more than Cairo gossip. For intellectuals, drawn from the politicized elites, and for the bloggers and Facebook activists who instigated the protests, the challenge is to translate their revolutionary spirit into a genuine political force. (para. 8)

In an interview carried out in November 2011 with Ahmed Maher, the founder of April 6, Elshami investigated deeply into the issue of the structure of the group and whether it was solid enough to resist present and future internal crises and external challenges. For instance, the group was challenged by a splinter group that was created by Tarek El-Khouly, putting in question the internal dynamics of April 6, affirming that in it there was a lack of democracy. Moreover, the situation had undergone radical changes in the country, and April 6 had to define its new identity and role. Maher said:

> Before the revolution any small demonstration had an impact. And day-by-day that does not work anymore, so we try to think about new things that can have an effect. After the revolution, million-people demonstrations on Fridays were very effective, but since numbers have decreased and they have lost their effectiveness. So we need to think of new tools to exert pressure.
>
> as cited in ELSHAMI, 2011, para. 72

Asked what new tools they were going to identify, Maher answered that they were still thinking about it.

There is also another important issue to analyze: Does an organization such as Otpor really possess the vocation to become an 'exporter' of democratic revolutionary patterns? Nenadic and Belcevic (2006) analyzed the Otpor involvement in the creation of organizations similar to theirs in other countries: "an issue that has not been demystified yet," they wrote (p. 17). In their view, Otpor never had the intention to be involved in processes of democratization outside of Serbia:

> Examples of Otpor members who took part in some seminars and trainings like participants, speakers or trainers were more likely to be individual engagement and the way of sharing their personal experiences and contributions to bringing down dictatorship. Objectively, *Otpor* as an example of successfully organized group was more used as an inspiration than it had concrete role in forming similar movements.
>
> NENADIC & BELCEVIC, 2006, p. 17

The events of 2011 seem to disprove this statement. Is the Otpor pattern able to keep up the pace of history, then?

The Structure of Nonviolent Resistance

Otpor has been defined as the 'Revolution Ltd.' (Lundin, 2011). Its true operational branch is the Centre for Applied Nonviolent Action and Strategies (CANVAS), the NGO founded by the members of Otpor that has worked in

50 countries. It has not always been successful because, despite the transversal pattern elaborated by Otpor, the context counts.

CANVAS, based in Belgrade, promotes its nonviolent principles: It has inspired the revolutionaries in Georgia, Ukraine, and Egypt. Its manual has been translated in Arabic and in 2009 also in Farsi, which is an indication of true and incisive global aspirations. Djinović and Popović decided to create CANVAS after a sojourn in South Africa to train young people from Zimbabwe.

Popović has often complimented the Egyptians for their way of leading the protest (Stojanovic, 2011), stressing that not only they have adopted the Otpor symbol, but they have also applied the rules of nonviolent resistance. Petar Milicević, one of the trainers of the Egyptians in a seminar that CANVAS organized in 2009, affirmed that the methods that had been presented on that occasion have been followed to the letter in the Egyptian revolution. He added that the success of the revolution was due to the fact that the leaders of the protest had fully understood the needs of their own society (*shadow*, 2011).

CANVAS has confronted many realities, from Burma to Zimbabwe, to Maldives to Georgia, and now Venezuela. Both Hugo Chávez and Aleksandr Lukashenko have condemned the organization, but it is a fact that many young people around the world perceive it as heroic and follow the principles and values it predicates.

The principle at the basis of the tactic it adopts is relatively simple: Identify a moment in the history of a population in which the dictators make the wrong move rousing the anger of the people, such as the murder of an opposition leader or exaggerating the rise in the prices of goods. The ability to identify that very moment and to channel the anger of the population in an organized force can make a dictatorship fall. Yet, preparation is needed.

In Georgia, the result has been positive because in that country there was an organization called *Kmara!* (Enough!), founded by a group of young activists, that made it possible for Djinović and other leaders of Otpor in 2002 to identify an adequate correspondent. They started to host in Serbia students who were members of Kmara!. In 2003 a movement led by Kmara! provoked the so-called 'Pink Revolution' with the subsequent fall of Eduard Shevardnadze. Then the 'Orange Revolution' in Ukraine followed, which saw former activists of Otpor involved, supporting the movement *PORA* (Now).

In Venezuela, CANVAS has faced and is facing a lot of difficulties. The group Otpor Juventud Activa Venezuela Unida (JAVU), El Organismo Táctico Para Orientar la Resistencia (OTPOR), which says it is proud of being affiliated to Otpor, gathered only a few dozen members on its Facebook group, although it launched appeals to mobilization and denounced violations of human rights. Do those appeals fall on deaf ears?

According to the Agencia Venezuelana de Noticias (2011), JAVU is supported by international organizations and, according to an article published on the website of the Centro de Alerta, the students who were on a three-week hunger strike in Venezuela (January 31st to February 23, 2011) to fight for freedom declaring to be 'political prisoners' had been manipulated by the United States, which trains young people in foreign countries for their own interests. The author of the article defined the strike as a 'reality show' whose intention has been uncovered, revealing a link between the young people and Washington, the real threat to the Venezuelan national sovereignty and to the future of the Bolivarian Revolution (Golinger, 2011). An old story—the interference of the United States—given that since 2003 there has been news circulating about activists from Venezuela who were trained in Colorado, according to various sources including Reuters (Logan, 2007). This training was carried out in collaboration with the Albert Einstein Institute.

What was the impact of those events? No *Golpe Suave* (soft coup) like those in the world of color revolutions? It is difficult, as stated by a commentator to the article of Tina Rosenberg on *Foreign Policy* (2011), to apply the Otpor/CANVAS pattern to a society that has re-elected its populist leader many times. According to the commentator, who echoes an old saying, the intention of CANVAS, USAID, and NED is only that of favoring the interests of the United States.

Yet Popović has repeatedly affirmed that CANVAS—of which he is the executive director—is 100 percent independent of any government. Many do not believe this, because, as it has been mentioned, the funds derive from U.S. institutions (Daragahi, 2008), and many say that there exists a global political élite, a solid network, that manipulates democracies (Barker, 2010). Some even define Otpor as "the CIA coup college" (Cartalucci, 2011a). In 2004, the well-known *Cafébabel* ironically stated: "Need to knock down a tyrant? Call Otpor!" (Dell'Arciprete, 2004, para. 1).

In 2014 the left-wing Italian newspaper *Il Manifesto* wrote about the role of Otpor and Javu in Venezuela after the clashes occurred on the 12th of February, recalling tactical ingerences already seen in former Jugoslavia, sustaining that in the case of Venezuela Javu (Otpor) is a very small group extreme right-wing oriented. "Look who's there" is the incipit of the article (Colotti, 2014).

End Games

An article by Toni Cartalucci (2011b), an analyst based in Bangkok, has bounced in thousands of activists' websites. In order to explain recent world events, in his article he theorized an end game that is a system of global governance that embraces all countries. It is a system controlled by Anglo-American bankers with their networks of global institutions, that make sure that the consolidated nations of the world conform to a single system that they can eternally exploit through the control of the populations, industries, and much more. The color revolutions would not be anything other than an instrument to fulfill this aim. To sustain this thesis, a document by the well-known Rand Corporation is often quoted. In 2007, Rand published a report by Rabasa, Benard, Schwartz, and Sickle entitled "Building Moderate Muslim Networks," in which a plan addressed to the networks of moderate Muslims is proposed, based on the lessons learned during the Cold War, with the aim of creating networks of civil society based on the Western model. One of the main problems is how to maintain the credibility of groups receiving outside support (Rand, 2007):

> The concern that US backing would discredit democratic organizations was substantial during the Cold War, as it is today. Policymakers in the late 1940s and early 1950s attempted to avoid this pitfall by keeping their support covert. The United States funded the organizations through foundations, both real and the United Initially, only a limited number of individuals knew about the covert backing of the new democratic organizations, and thus they avoided the negative repercussions of US support for a time. But, as is almost always the case, the covert US support was ultimately revealed. Once this occurred, the credibility of these organizations was compromised, and many never recovered. The credibility of the organizations was better maintained by providing a degree of real distance between the groups and the U.S. government, for example by supporting the efforts of private and non-governmental organizations with established relationships in the countries in which they operated. Another way of quietly influencing organizations while maintaining their credibility was through the appointment of reputable public figures as movement leaders. The reputations of these leaders lent the groups a degree of credibility that helped to mitigate any concerns about potential ties to the u.s. government. Finally, it is important to note that many individuals and organizations were happy to accept U.S. government funding. (pp. 31–32)

This statement, which could be accused of being an example of ethnocentric rhetoric, has caused the resentment of activists and is reported globally as a proof of the validity of the theory of the end game.

As regards the Arab Spring, the words of Bolton (2011) really seem to sum up the general state of mind of an active and reactive part of the political world, which is sensitive to the geopolitical superstructures that it perceives as uncontrollable:

> Given the keen interest NED has shown in Tunisia, it would seem naïve to think that the "Jasmine Revolution" is simply a "spontaneous manifestation of popular anger" and that it has not been planned well in advance, awaiting the right moment for a catalyst. (para. 17)

Perpetuation of Patterns

Is the pattern of transformation that Otpor exports able to last? Has April 6 work in Egypt made the population develop resilience skills? Has it made the embryo of democracy consolidate into a programmatic and pragmatic approach to future evolutions?

Mrvos (2010) analyzed the fact that while it seemed that Otpor was the most important factor in bringing democracy to Serbia, it had difficult times after the climax:

> After the overthrow of the dictator, all further results were disappointing. One question that comes up when we are looking for the reasons of *Otpor's* disappearance is the role of foreign aid. It has been concluded that the US with its Agencies gave significant financial support to *Otpor* to overthrow dictator Milošević. If the US really cared about the implementation of democracy, why did they stop any further financial or logistical assistance to *Otpor*? No one likes to come up with this question, but if the US is so concerned with spreading democracy, why do they appear to be only staying for elections? *Otpor* had so many pending tasks but it simply collapsed. (p. 20)

Analyzing the role of Ukraine's and Georgia's NGOs in the color revolutions, Laverty (2008) wrote that they were characterized by horizontal organizational structures, clever use of cultural politics and humor, nonviolence and discipline, collaboration with other sectors of civil society, political parties, and the media. He took as a striking example the above-mentioned Georgian Kmara! group, which was particularly effective, also because of its highly horizontal structure that made it more difficult for the state to suppress. He also stressed that Kmara! activists benefitted from the training and advice of civil society activists in other post-communist countries, such as members of the Otpor movement in Serbia. He concluded by affirming that civil society is necessary, but not sufficient for lasting transformation and especially consolidation, because in order to create lasting democratic change, civil society must be able to relate to sound institutions; he then enumerated a number of reasons why after the 'revolution' there is still a great degree of uncertainty in these countries. To be most effective, he maintained, civil society should be autonomous, but not alienated, from the state (Laverty, 2008).

After the regime changes in Georgia and Ukraine, civil society was either co-opted by the state (Georgia) or alienated from it (Ukraine), thus reversing some of the democratic progress of the revolutions. The wave of pessimism for the future of revolutions does not affect everybody. Rubin (2011) is trustful. Reflecting upon the lasting effects of the revolution in Egypt, Rubin first quoted the words of Ian Bremmer, the president of Eurasia Group, who said that we should not go looking at Egypt as if it is a successful revolution because it is "a managed transition" (para. 4) in which any new elected government will be weak and the military will remain the most powerful player. She then replied by saying that an important revolution has occurred in Egypt, and quoted the words of Hossam Bahgat, the young executive director of the Egyptian Initiative for Personal Rights, a human-rights advocacy group in Cairo: "For the first time, we are feeling that our problems must be solved by us, not by Americans, or by God" (para. 6). Rubin commented: "Anyone who has spent years focused on the Arab world will know that such a statement of personal responsibility for one's future is revolutionary indeed" (para. 7).

In fact, these revolutions have demonstrated that 'democracy' is not a privilege of the West—a notion still diffused—and that not only it can develop in countries traditionally considered as irredeemable, but it constitutes a true aspiration of all populations. Yet, this wiser awareness that is at the basis of the export of foreign patterns of democratization can be questioned by the issue of the dangers that this process implies. Beissinger (2006) listed a number of these dangers:

> First, democracy could come to be viewed as a tool of external statecraft rather than an indigenous development; second, human rights organizations could compromise their ability to act as independent monitoring organizations if they involve themselves with specific political movements or come to be identified as "revolutionary organizations"; third, efforts to promote democratic revolution could produce intensified ethnic conflict and even civil war; and finally, giving democratic revolution "a little extra shove" could lead to post-revolutionary situations in which democratic development is highly vulnerable to reversal. (n.p.)

Democracy Consolidation

It would be very unjust to consider the revolutions that took place from Ukraine to Egypt as completely organized by external actors. It is obvious that if there were not a fertile ground and germinating seeds of change, the influence of external 'advice' would fail or not take place at all.

Another important element is the "paradigm shift," as Adrian Karatnycky, senior scholar at Freedom House, and Peter Ackerman, chair of its board of trustees (2005) described the change in the pattern of democracy promotion: The pattern is now based on aid to those groups that make nonviolent civic resistance, encourage broad-based coalitions among opposition forces, transfer knowledge about civil resistance to opposition groups, invest in alternative media networks, and wield external sanctions to constrain the repression of democratic opponents.

> Yet Beissinger (2006) tries to abruptly bring us back to reality by saying that the outcomes of revolutionary upsurges are highly unpredictable and just as often lead to failure and prolonged civil war as to democratic success. Failed revolution can in fact be worse for democratic development than the protracted evolution of civil society—because widespread repression can lead to the decimation of democratic forces. (n.p.)

The problem is that if revolutions based on foreign patterns occur in contexts where the social and economic conditions cannot guarantee a healthy consolidation of the immediate outcomes of the revolt—is overthrowing a dictator enough?—then the development of the embryo of democracy is at risk.

A number of examples are brought to the attention of analysts, from Serbia itself to Georgia, Ukraine, Egypt, and other colored revolutionary countries. Not to mention the not-always-positive effects that such revolutions have had on other countries, such as China, for instance, where the Arab Spring has brought stricter security measures and more censorship on Internet and other means of communication (Del Re, 2012).

Egypt has been closely monitored month after month since the revolution, and many things have happened. Months after the revolution, the feelings of the population seemed to oscillate between a negative sense of frustration and a sense of reacquired dignity, which seems to be too little, though, to feel secure (Mashamoun, 2011).

Focusing on the achievements of democracy, it seems that the work done by the NGOs has had few long-lasting results. *IRIN Humanitarian News and Analysis* (2011) affirmed: "Egyptian NGOs hoping for greater freedoms and more space to operate after the fall of Hosni Mubarak's government say they have encountered just the opposite: an unprecedented clampdown by the post-revolution military rulers" (para. 1).

In a 2011 article by *IRIN Humanitarian News and Analysis* entitled "Egypt's NGOs Face Tough Post-Revolution Reality," there emerged a truly unpredictable issue in post-revolutionary Egypt. The issue regards Egypt's law 84/2002, which although it does not prevent NGOs from getting funding from abroad, requires NGOs to register with the government and for all funding to be approved by the ministry of social solidarity. In 2010, the government introduced a law that further restricted NGOs and gave state security the power to approve or deny international funding to the organizations. The government lamented that none of the registered NGOs had informed it about any funds they received. The minister of international co-operation, Faiza Abul-Naga, announced an investigation into foreign funding of unregistered NGOs, saying that such funding was considered "an intervention in our internal affairs" (*IRIN Humanitarian News and Analysis,* 2011, para. 10).

The Qualitative Aspects of Revolutions and Future Challenges

There are many theoretical and practical reasons not to believe that there could exist one single exportable pattern *à la* Otpor. In the above-mentioned video program by *Al Jazeera* (2011) entitled "Egypt: Seeds of Change," there is a moment in which it is shown that during the protest in Egypt, while the protesters were shouting slogans face to face with the anti-riot police, in a climate of highest tension, abruptly everything stops: The protesters bend on their knees to pray, and thus the policemen turn their backs in a sign of respect, as the narrator of the video explains. This is a qualitative element that cannot be underestimated. The variety of human sentiments is certainly a variable that cannot always be interpreted or identified and certainly cannot always be predicted in a democratization process. No manual can teach this.

There are other reasons, such as the awareness of having to accept a moral principle—that is becoming a global standard commandment—that implies 'do not impose patterns' or interpretations of facts, it could be added. For example, the expression *Jasmine revolution,* which has been used to describe the 2011 events in Tunisia by the international press, is in fact the least appropriate name, because there has already been a *Jasmine revolution,* for this is the name that the CIA gave to the 1987 coup d'état that had empowered Ben Ali. Elder Tunisians perceive that expression as it is used today with a sense of bitterness (Ben Sassi, 2011).

Where does this dissertation about the opportuneness of exporting patterns and its consequences, which started from Egypt, bring us? The challenge is Iran. According to the end-game interpretation (Cartalucci, 2011b), the revolutions in Maghreb would be the beginning of a route that tends to convince China and Russia that the United States is a shareholder, responsible for the events that determine the global scenario, which would in this way become unipolarly Anglo-American. Such a picture depicts a risk game that never ends, in which everyone shoots with his own little cannons.

In the meantime, on the Iranian blogs the freedom kit of CANVAS for Iran is being diffused. Otpor has been present in Iran for quite some time, and in 2009 there were denounces of secret seminars organized by Washington to train the anti-Ahmadinejad activists. Pictures with Iranian young people waving the Otpor symbol are disseminated on the Web. Oslobodjenje-Wordpress (2009) published a blog article by an anonymous writer, "Iranian Otpor activist," which was immediately bounced also by the *Pravda* and others; the article is entitled "Otpor Now in Iran, Courtesy of Uncle Sam," with a subheading that reads "Iranian coup d'état: Shade of green and the same clenched fist" (para. 1).

In January 2011, while so much was occurring in Maghreb, Ivan Marović, one of the leaders of Otpor, flew to Washington D.C., where he took part in the Iran Democratic Transition Conference, held in collaboration with the Confederation of Iranian Students (CIS). While talking with the Iranian students, he declared that he saw many parallels between the freedom fight in Serbia years before and the current fight in Iran (Cyrus, 2011).

There is still a binary view on the issue of exportation of democracy patterns developed by foreign powers and by the United States in particular. Popović, one of the founders of Otpor and later executive director of CANVAS, replies to critiques and preoccupations related to the role of organizations like Otpor and others on the online pages of *Foreign Policy* that has hosted his views in its Democracy Lab in 2016 (Popović, 2016). To the accusations moved to Otpor—and the initiatives derived from it—of being merely the product of foreign powers projects to create agencies that could be manipulated and monitored and would act on their behalf, Popović responds by saying that "even for clever people, it seems that conspiracies are weirdly comforting" and affirming that "despite the best efforts of authoritarian governments, democratic activists are not powerless against this false narrative" (Popović, 2016). Referring to what he thinks is a concretely potential new Cold War that could be started by the Kremlin, Popović warns that in order to prevent it "democratic governments need to apply some of the street-level lessons activists have learned to the arena of geo-strategy and public diplomacy" (Popović, 2016). In conclusion, he sustains that the formula is more than working today and mentions the need not only for Russia but also for Serbia, his homeland, to create alliances with the civil society to be able to flourish.

Meanwhile in fact, despite the past actions of Otpor and others alike, many serious unresolved social and political issues oppress the Balkans today, although great progress has been made, issues from which the world has distracted its attention because of the crises in Maghreb and in the Middle East.

But things develop, new scenarios emerge, social and political reference points change. For instance, some have started to worry when in 2011 the historical BBC World Service in the Balkan region closed down and was replaced by *Al Jazeera*. *Al Jazeera* can count on a network of 150 correspondents disseminated throughout all of the countries of South Eastern Europe, who report in the local languages. Considering that *Al Jazeera* has been the enthusiastic supporting voice of the revolutions in Tunisia and Egypt, Otpor or not Otpor, some leaders are probably wondering about the future, somewhere else in the world.

References

Academy of Change. (2017). *Home page*. Retrieved July 27, 2017 from http://aoc.fm/en/.

Al Jazeera. (2011, February 9). People and power. Egypt: Seeds of change [Video]. Retrieved July 27, 2017 from http://www.youtube.com/watch?v=QrNzodZgqN8&feature=player_embedded#at=26.

Arrow, R. (Director), & Shaw, R., Watt, C., & Otis, J. (Producers). (2011). *How to start a revolution* [Motion picture]. Los Angeles, CA: Seventh Art Releasing.

Ashour, O. (2011, November 27). Egypt's headless revolution: What was a source of strength in overthrowing Mubarak is now a source of weakness. *The Inquirer*, Philly.com. Retrieved July 27, 2017 from https://www.brookings.edu/opinions/egypts-headless-revolution/.

Bacher, J. (2002). Video review: *Bringing down a dictator*. *Peace Magazine*, July–September, 28. Retrieved from http://peacemagazine.org/archive/v18n3p28.htm.

Barker, M. (2010, April 19). Commentary: *Mother Jones* and the defence of liberal elites. *Swans*. Retrieved July 27, 2017 from http://www.swans.com/library/art16/barker47.html.

Beissinger, M.R. (2006, Winter). Promoting democracy: Is exporting revolution a constructive strategy? *Dissent*, Winter. Retrieved July 27, 2017 from http://www.dissentmagazine.org.

Ben Sassi, C. (2011, January 28). Enigme de l'expression "Jasmine Revolution" de 1987 à 2011. *Tunisie Numerique*. Retrieved July 27, 2017 from www.tunisienumerique.com.

Bolton, K.R. (2011, January 18). Tunisian revolt: Another Soros/NED jack-up? *Foreign Policy Journal*. Retrieved July 27, 2017 from http://www.foreignpolicyjournal.com/2011/01/18/tunisian-revolt-another-sorosned-jack-up/.

Brumberg, D., & Shehata, D. (Eds.). (2009). *Conflict, identity, and reform in the Muslim world: Challenges for U.S. engagement*. Washington, DC: United States Institute of Peace Press.

Carnegie Endowment for International Peace. (2006). Fact sheet: U.S. actors promoting democracy in the Middle East, 2006. Washington, DC: Author. Retrieved July 27, 2017 from http://carnegieendowment.org/2006/03/15/fact-sheet-u.s.-actors-promoting-democacy-in-middle-east/mfh.

Carnegie Endowment for International Peace. (2010, November 8). *Interview with Ahmed Maher, co-founder of the April 6 youth movement*. Washington, DC: Author.

Cartalucci, T. (2011a). The CIA coup college. *Land Destroyer*. Retrieved July 27, 2017 from http://landdestroyer.blogspot.com/2011/02/cia-coup-college.html.

Cartalucci, T. (2011b, February 18). The Middle East and then the world: Globalist blitzkrieg signals largest geopolitical reordering since WW2. *Activist Post*. Retrieved July 27, 2017 from http://www.activistpost.com/2011/02/middle-east-then-world.html.

Cohen, R. (2000, November 26). Who really brought down Milošević? *New York Times*. Retrieved July 27, 2017 from http://www.nytimes.com/2000/11/26/magazine/who-really-brought-down-Milošević.html.

Colotti, G. (2014, February 17). In Venezuela, Otpor e Javu. Ingerenze. Gli scontri del 12 febbraio richiamano tattiche già viste nella ex-Jugoslavia. 17 February. *Il Manifesto*. Retrieved July 27, 2017 from https://ilmanifesto.it/in-venezuela-otpor-e-javu/.

Cyrus, M. (2011, March 24). Serbian youth leader compares anti-Milošević campaign with Iran today. *Iran Channel*. Retrieved July 27, 2017 from http://iranchannel.org/archives/tag/otpor.

Daragahi, B. (2008, September 3). Georgian unrolls the "Velvet revolution." *Los Angeles Times*, 2A. Retrieved July 27, 2017 from http://articles.latimes.com/2008/sep/03/world/fg-velvet3.

Dell'Arciprete, N. (2004, December 6). ¿Queréis derrocar a un tirano? Llamad a la OTPOR. *Cafébabel*. Retrieved July 27, 2017 from http://www.cafebabel.es/article/12835/quereis-derrocar-a-un-tirano-llamad-a-la-otpor.html.

Del Re, E.C. (2012). From the Balkans to Caucasus: Paradoxes of the so called precedents. In D.A. Mahapatra (Ed.), *Conflict and peace in Eurasia* (pp. 36–53). London, England: Routledge Chapman and Hall.

Doncheva, B. (2000, August 9). Bulgarian paper says: "CIA is tutoring Serbian group, Otpor." *The Emperor's New Clothes*. Retrieved July 27, 2017 from http://emperors-clothes.com/news/cialectures.htm.

Dorell, O., & Lynch, S. (2012, January 31). Christians fear losing freedoms in Arab Spring movement. *USA Today*. Retrieved July 27, 2017 from https://usatoday30.usatoday.com/news/religion/story/2012-01-30/arab-spring-christians/52894182/1#mainstory.

Editorial Board. (2011, February 4). Egypt's true revolution: A leaderless movement fueled by universal values. *Christian Science Monitor.* Retrieved July 27, 2017 from http://www.csmonitor.com/Commentary/the-monitors-view/2011/0204/Egypt-s-true-revolution-A-leaderless-movement-fueled-by-universal-values.

Egypt protests: Secret US document discloses support for protesters. (2011, January 28). *The Telegraph.* Retrieved July 27, 2017 from http://www.telegraph.co.uk/news/worldnews/africaandindianocean/egypt/8289698/Egypt-protests-secret-US-document-discloses-support-for-protesters.html.

Elshami, N. (2011, December 7). Internal April 6 dynamics, Egyptian politics and outlooks for the future: An interview with Ahmed Maher. *Jadaliyya.* Retrieved July 27, 2017 from http://www.jadaliyya.com/pages/index/3429/internal-april-6-dynamics-egyptian-politics-and-ou.

A Force More Powerful. (n.d.). *Bringing down a dictator.* Retrieved July 27, 2017 from http://www.aforcemorepowerful.org/films/bdd/.

A Force More Powerful. (n.d.). *Bringing down a dictator: A discussion guide.* Retrieved July 27, 2017 from http://www.aforcemorepowerful.org/films/bdd/eo/bdad-discussion-guide.pdf.

Golinger, E. (2011, February 21). Huelguistas en Venezuela: Made in USA. *Centro de Alerta.* Retrieved July 27, 2017 from http://auto-hermes.ning.com/profiles/blogs/huelguistas-en-venezuela-made.

Hafner, P.H., & Steinbach, A. (Directors). (2011). *The revolution business* [Short motion picture]. United Kingdom: Journeyman Pictures. Retrieved July 27, 2017 from http://www.youtube.com/watch?v=lpXbA6yZY-8. Transcript retrieved July 27, 2017 from https://www.journeyman.tv/film_documents/5171/transcript/.

Hais, M., & Winograd, M. (2011, February 11). Victory for Egypt's leaderless revolution. *The Huffington Post.* Retrieved July 27, 2017 from http://www.huffingtonpost.com/michael-hais-and-morley-winograd/victory-for-egypts-leader_b_822228.html.

Horgan, J. (2011, February 11). Egypt's revolution vindicates Gene Sharp's theory of non-violent activism. *Scientific American.* Retrieved July 27, 2017 from https://blogs.scientificamerican.com/cross-check/egypts-revolution-vindicates-gene-sharps-theory-of-nonviolent-activism/.

Ilić, V. (2001). *The popular movement Otpor—Between Europe and re-traditionalization.* Budapest, Hungary: Central European University Files. Retrieved July 27, 2017 from pdc.ceu.hu/archive/00005016/01/Files05.doc.

Iranian Otpor activist. (2009, June 17). Otpor now in Iran, courtesy of Uncle Sam [Blog]. *Oslobodjenje.* Retrieved July 27, 2017 from http://oslobodjenje.wordpress.com/2009/06/page/2/.

IRIN Humanitarian News and Analysis. (2011, October 27). Egypt's NGOs face tough post-revolution reality. *The Guardian.* Retrieved July 27, 2017 from https://www.theguardian.com/global-development/2011/oct/27/egypt-ngos-clampdown-military-rulers.

Jacob, J. (2011, February 1). What is Egypt's April 6 movement? *International Business Times*. Retrieved July 27, 2017 from http://www.ibtimes.com/articles/107387/20110201/what-is-egypt-s-april-6-movement.htm.

"JAVU recibe apoyo de organizaciones internacionales." (2011, February 21). *Agencia Venezolana de Noticias*. Retrieved July 27, 2017 from http://www.avn.info.ve/node/44471.

Karatnycky, A., & Ackerman, P. (2005). *How freedom is won, from civic resistance to durable democracy*. New York, NY: Freedom House.

Kirkpatrick, D.D., & Sanger, D.E. (2011, February 13). A Tunisian-Egyptian link that shook Arab history. *New York Times*. Retrieved July 27, 2017 from http://www.nytimes.com/2011/02/14/world/middleeast/14egypt-tunisia-protests.html.

Laverty, N. (2008). The problem of lasting change: Civil society and the Colored Revolutions in Georgia and Ukraine. *Demokratizatsiya, The Journal of Post-Soviet Democratization, 16*(2), 143–162. doi:10.3200/demo.16.2.143-162.

Levinson, C., Coker, M., & El-Ghobashy, T. (2011, February 15). Strikes worry Egypt's military, youth. *Wall Street Journal*. Retrieved July 27, 2017 from http://online.wsj.com/article/SB10001424052748703584804576143824048718898.html.

Logan, T. (2007, April 30). Otpor and the US made coup attempts against Chavez in Venezuela. *Not My Tribe*. Retrieved July 27, 2017 from http://notmytribe.com/2007/otpor-and-the-us-made-coup-attempts-against-chavez-in-venezuela-81260.html.

Lundin, T. (2011, March 2). The revolution that came from Serbia. *Svenka Dagbladet*. Retrieved July 27, 2017 from http://www.voxeurop.eu/en/content/article/523241-revolution-came-serbia.

Mashamoun, G. (2011, September 14). Voices from Egypt: "What do you think of the revolution now?" *PBS News Hour*. Retrieved July 27, 2017 from http://www.pbs.org/newshour/rundown/2011/09/voices-from-egypt.html.

Merriman, H. (2010, November 19). The trifecta of civil resistance: Unity, planning, discipline. *Open Democracy*. Retrieved July 27, 2017 from https://www.opendemocracy.net/hardy-merriman/trifecta-of-civil-resistance-unity-planning-discipline.

Mrvos, D. (2010, April 23). *The rise and disappearance of Otpor: Nonviolent movement in the republic of Serbia*. Paper submitted to the 18th Annual Illinois State University Conference for Students of Political Science.

Nenadic, D., & Belcevic, N. (2006). *From social movement to political organisation: The case of Otpor*. Coventry, UK: Centre for Peace and Reconciliation Studies, Coventry University.

Pal, A. (2007). Gene Sharp interview. *The Progressive*. Retrieved July 27, 2017 from http://www.satyagrahafoundation.org/dictators-dont-like-us-the-progressive-interview-with-gene-sharp/.

Popovic, S. (2016). When dictators cry conspiracy. *Foreign Policy*. Retrieved July 27, 2017 from http://foreignpolicy.com/2016/02/03/when-dictators-cry-conspiracy/.

Popovic, S., Milivojevic, A., & Djinovic, S. (2006). *Nonviolent struggle: 50 crucial points: A strategic approach to everyday tactics.* Belgrade: Centre for Applied NonViolent Action and Strategies (CANVAS). Retrieved July 27, 2017 from https://www.usip.org/sites/default/files/nonviolent_eng.pdf.

professor1. (2011, April 13). Rothschilds and George Soros (the elites) stage revolutions in Tunisia and Egypt to kill Islamic banks in emerging North African markets [Blog]. *Itmakessenseblog,* Retrieved July 27, 2017 from http://itmakessenseblog.com/2011/04/13/rothschilds-and-george-soros-the-elites-stage-revolutions-in-tunisia-and-egypt-to-kill-islamic-banks-in-emerging-north-african-markets/.

Proyect, L. (2011, February 14). What is the connection between Otpor and the Egyptian youth movement? [Blog]. *Louis Proyect: The unrepentant Marxist.* Retrieved July 27, 2017 from https://louisproyect.org/?s=Otpor.

Rabasa, A., Benard, C., Schwartz, L.H., & Sickle, P. (2007). Building moderate Muslim networks. *RAND Center for Middle East Public Policy.* Retrieved July 27, 2017 from http://www.rand.org/pubs/monographs/MG574.html.

Rosenberg, T. (2011, February 16). Revolution U: What Egypt learned from the students who overthrew Milošević. *Foreign Policy.* Retrieved July 27, 2017 from http://foreignpolicy.com/2011/02/17/revolution-u-2/.

Rubin, T. (2011, April 21). Worldview: Egyptian revolution likely to have long-term ripple effect. Philly.com. Retrieved July 27, 2017 from http://www.philly.com/philly/columnists/trudy_rubin/20110421_Worldview__Egyptian_revolution_likely_to_have_long-term_ripple_effect.html.

Schneider, N. (2011). The science of people power: An interview with Gene Sharp [Blog]. *The Immanent Frame.* Retrieved July 27, 2017 from http://blogs.ssrc.org/tif/2011/02/17/the-science-of-people-power-an-interview-with-gene-sharp/.

Shadow. (2011, March 31). CANVAS, Otpor, Pora: Serbia's brand is non-violent revolution [Blog]. *Cafébabel.* Retrieved July 27, 2017 from http://www.cafebabel.co.uk/article/37103/egypt-revolution-serbia-otpor-pora-canvas-youth.html.

Sharp, G. (1993). *From dictatorship to democracy: A conceptual framework for liberation.* Boston, MA: The Albert Einstein Institution.

Smock, D. (2009). Religion in world affairs: Its role in conflict and peace. In D. Brumberg & D. Shehata (Eds.), *Conflict, identity, and reform in the Muslim world: Challenges for U.S. engagement* (pp. 60–69). Washington, DC: United States Institute of Peace Press.

Steavenson, W. (2011, August 1). Who owns the revolution? *The New Yorker.* Retrieved July 27, 2017 from http://www.newyorker.com/reporting/2011/08/01/110801fa_fact_steavenson.

Stojanovic, D. (2011, February 4). Serbian Otpor praises Egypt protesters. *The Times of India.* Retrieved July 27, 2017 from http://www.domovod.info/showthread.php?185-Otpor!-Serbia&highlight=Serbian+Otpor+praises+Egypt+protesters.

Stratfor. (2011, February 4). *A breakdown of Egyptian Opposition groups.* Retrieved July 27, 2017 from https://worldview.stratfor.com/analysis/breakdown-egyptian-opposition-groups.

Traynor, I. (2004, November 25). US campaign behind the turmoil in Kiev. *The Guardian.* Retrieved July 27, 2017 from http://www.guardian.co.uk/world/2004/nov/26/ukraine.usa.

U.S. Department of State. (2008, November 18). *Announcement on Alliance of Youth Movements Summit, December 3–5, 2008.* Retrieved July 27, 2017 from http://iipdigital.usembassy.gov/st/english/texttrans/2008/11/20081120122321eaifas0.3440363.html#axzz4bMtaaYIm.

Vigna, E. (2009, September 24). Le "ombre" di Otpor e della CIA in Iran. *Resistenze.* Retrieved July 27, 2017 from www.resistenze.org.

WikiLeaks. (2015). *What is WikiLeaks?* Retrieved July 27, 2017 from https://wikileaks.org/What-is-Wikileaks.html.

York, S. (Director), & Ackerman, P., York, S., & Zimmerman, M. (Producers). (2002). *Bringing down a dictator* [Motion picture]. Arlington, VA: WETA & York Zimmerman.

CHAPTER 12

Iranian Studies in the United States and the Politics of Knowledge Production on Post-Revolutionary Iran

Seyed Mohammd Marandi and Zeinab Ghasemi Tari

Knowledge Production on Post-Revolutionary Iran

Understanding and analyzing the politics of 'knowledge' and 'knowledge production' on post-revolutionary Iran in the United States academia is inseparable from the context of relations between the two countries. Iran was once a close ally and a strategic pillar for the United States. During the Cold War, Iran was considered as a bulwark against Soviet expansion and later, when it grew wealthier from oil income, it turned into a market for U.S. arms and investment. The close ties came to an end with the 1979 Iranian Islamic Revolution and when the Shah left Iran. Many Western countries regarded the 1979 Revolution as a beginning of an 'Islamic fundamentalism' in the region with political power. For the United States, "the political change had transformed Iran from a staunch ally into one of the most intractable opponents of the United States in the region and beyond" (Haass, as cited in Brzezinski, Gates, & Maloney, 2004, p. viii). Since then, "the revolution is a political prism through which the two countries view each other" (Litwak, 2000, p. 158). Currently, Iran is the only country in the region with no formal relations with the United States.

In the absence of diplomatic relations between the two countries, public and political understanding about post-revolutionary Iran in the United States was and is shaped by various sources such as think tanks, media, academia, and other popular and literary products such as memoirs and movies. The Iranian diaspora in the United States plays a major role in production of knowledge on post-revolutionary Iran. In general, diasporas play an important role in the United States. According to a study by the World Bank:

> By far the strongest effect of war on the risk of subsequent war works through diasporas. After five years of post-conflict peace, the risk of renewed conflict is around six times higher in societies with the largest diasporas in America than in those without American diasporas.
>
> COLLIER, HOEFFLER, & WORLD BANK, 2000, p. 5

Diasporas are able to influence world affairs in numerous ways; they can play passive or active, constructive or destructive roles toward their homeland (Shain & Barth, 2003). Moreover, diasporas are involved in complex and shifting power relations. Changes in the relations of power within diasporas and the "way these changes intersect with external configurations of power" (Smith & Stares, 2007, p. 5) are influential in the diasporas' knowledge production toward their homelands.

According to Bozorgmehr (1998), "After the Revolution many of the Iranian exiles turned to humanities and social sciences in order to explain what had happened in their homeland presenting themselves as viable alternative subjects" (p. 12). It is believed that the 1979 Iranian Islamic Revolution is the most significant factor that contributed to the growth of the Iranian diaspora. Karimi-Hakkak mentions the importance of the Iranian-American community in the expansion of Iranian studies programs in the United States:

> I mentioned to the university that the capacity for growth [Iranian/Persian Studies] was tremendous because Iranian–American community was highly educated professionals, etc. and so I insisted that if the university put in the resources at the beginning, the community will then contribute and we'll see phenomenal growth. That exactly has happened. (Podcast, 2008)

In the absence of a considerable degree of alternative voices and due to the unique status of exilic Iranians as "inside the people" (Shain & Barth, 2003, p. 451), their produced materials gain special authority and credibility. The knowledge produced by diaspora—either academic or popular—is often used by Iranian and non-Iranian academicians and politicians in the West as authentic sources of information on pre- and post-revolutionary Iran.

Iranians became increasingly influential in Middle Eastern and more particularly Iranian studies programs and Iranian academic journals in the United States. There was very little published about Iranians in the United States before the Iranian Revolution of 1979. According to the Middle East Studies Association (MESA) membership list, before the 1980s none of the 21 PhDs in sociology were Iranians, while during the 1980s 11 of the 19 who received their degrees were Iranians. Furthermore, a survey of publications of sociologist members of MESA in *Sociological Abstracts* for the 1985–1990 period showed that the three most frequently addressed areas were the Iranian Revolution, the historical sociology of Iran, and Iranian immigrants in the United States, in that order (Lorentz & Wertime, 1980).

Iranian Studies in the United States

The 1979 Iranian Revolution took Western academicians and Middle East experts by surprise. As Nikki Keddie, professor of Iran history at the University of California, Los Angeles (UCLA), puts it:

> U.S. scholars of modern Iran, who were doing research there in large numbers in the 1970s, did not predict anything like a revolution that occurred.... These scholars, who were inclined to be critical of the Shah's regime and not to echo official U.S. support for it, should, if anyone could, have provided predictions of serious trouble, but they did not. (1983, p. 592)

Even when signs of the revolution were quite visible in 1978, the Hoover Institution at Stanford University published a collected volume on Iran prepared by George Lenczowski, a political scientist and founder of the Center of Middle Eastern Studies at the University of California, Berkeley, praised[1] "Iran's modernizing monarchy and its stability" (1978, p. 475, as cited in Kramer, 2002, p. 15). He adds, "Thanks to Iran's reverence for monarchy, the country possessed an advantage over some newer nations, which could not point to the same remarkable legacy" (Lenczowski, 1978, p. 475).

Examination of the produced literature following the Iranian revolution reflects the deep shock among Iran's experts. According to Salem (1992), the Iranian Revolution proved to be more decisive to the field of Middle Eastern studies than the Arab–Israeli wars of 1967 and 1973. Yvonne Haddad, a MESA president, also believes that the Iranian Revolution changed the field drastically, stating that "since 1979 many members of MESA have had a meteoric rise in their careers," and "that if someone were tracking his achievements he should have a stamp engraved on his forehead reading 'Made by Khomeini'" (1992, pp. 1–2, as cited by Kramer, 2002, p. 55).

Iranian studies programs in the United States or Europe are neither internally homogeneous nor similar to each other. A close examination reflects some distinctive approaches in their political, institutional, and intellectual histories, and in their relationships with the disciplines. In general, Iranian studies programs in the United States can be categorized into two distinct types: (a) Iranian studies programs and (b) Persian studies programs. While the former is broader and often has an interdisciplinary approach and deals

1 The founder of the Center of Middle Eastern Studies at University of California, Berkeley.

with the study of history, literature, art and culture, contemporary politics, and sociology of Iran, Persian studies is more focused on the study of the modern Persian language (Farsi) and literature. Likewise, Middle Eastern centers, institutes, or programs also study Iran as a part of area studies programs. Many programs, centers, and institutions do not grant degrees but sponsor a number of courses as Iranian/Persian studies. They attract many undergraduate and graduate students from different disciplines such as the social sciences, humanities, and history. Such programs organize or support multi-disciplinary lectures, workshops, conferences, research, and projects as well as a wide variety of public activities.

The pattern of growth for Persian and Iranian studies in the United States can be classified into three eras, which might be reflective of the changing political relations between Iran and the United States: (a) an early approach, which was more concerned with the philology/archaeology of Iran; (b) as a part of Middle Eastern studies programs that attempted to study Iran from a more modern and international academic perspective (after WWII); and (c) an independent field of study that studies history/culture and politics as well as the Persian language.

The chapter will offer a brief overview of changes and evolution in Iranian studies. Iranian/Persian studies began in the early 20th century as part of the classical academic model of Orientalism in the United States. The program first began as a philological endeavor and had an archeological approach with more emphasis on ancient Iranian civilization and language. According to Hossein Ziai, director of Iranian Studies at the University of California at Los Angeles (UCLA), Persian was defined as "an ancient or dead culture ... Persian was never looked at from the perspective of a living language and culture, but seen only as Old Persian, as a classical but dead language, like Sumerian" (Cincotta, 2009, para.7).

The establishment of the American Institute for Persian Art and Archaeology in 1925 may be considered as the outset for Iranian studies as an independent field of learning in the United States as well as internal development within the field. The institute was founded by Arthur Pope and his wife, Phyllis Ackerman, both of whom were art historians. It later became the Asia Institute in New York and was regarded as a center that expanded Western understanding of Persian and Iranian civilization (Devos & Werner, 2014). Pope also developed a close friendship with the Pahlavi family, and along with his wife and served as advisor and dealer of Iranian art for many museums and private collections (Abdi, 2001).

After WWII, Iranian studies as a part of area studies programs began to expand. Ahmad Karimi-Hakkak, founding director of the Roshan Institute for Persian Studies at the University of Maryland, believes that Iranian studies in the United States started in earnest after the Second World War when the United States emerged as a world power (Cincotta, 2009). Ziai too maintains that in the late 1950s and early 1960s Iranian studies gained a distinctive significance, as "scholars began looking at modern Persian as distinct from its identity as an ancient language. It evolved into a separate discipline as a modern, living, international language and culture" (Cincotta, 2009, para. 13). Richard Nelson Frye, Professor Emeritus of Iranian Studies at Harvard University, is believed to have had a major role in expanding Iranian studies in the United States. He contributed to the founding of the Center for Middle Eastern Studies at Harvard University in 1954, which launched the first modern Iranian studies program in the United States. He served as director of the Asia Institute in Shiraz from 1970 to 1975 (Frye, 2005). A.V. Williams Jackson is another scholar who contributed to the development of Iranian studies by establishing a center for grammar of the Avestan language at Columbia University (Jackson, 1906). Other programs were founded at UCLA in 1963 with a focus on ancient and medieval Iran. In 1967 the Society for Iranian Studies (now the International Society for Iranian Studies [ISIS]) was founded by a group of Iranian graduate students and began producing the *Journal of Iranian Studies*.

A few institutions and centers for Iranian studies were founded during this era and they continue their work to present. The International Society for Iranian Studies (ISIS), was founded in 1967 in the United States as an academic society to support and promote Iranian studies at the international level. ISIS is also an affiliated member of the international Middle East Studies Association (MESA). Among the centers that were established during this era (1967) and that continues its activities to the present is the American Institute of Iranian Studies (AIIrS), which aims to promote an interdisciplinary study of Iranian civilization with Iranian studies scholars. AIIrS maintained a Center in Tehran from 1969 and with the 1979 Iranian Revolution its activities in Iran were suspended. In February 1988 relations were renewed by Iran's cultural ambassador to the United Nations. The declared aim is to create and maintain expertise on an important geographical region and maintain interest in bi-national cooperation. The program has been supported by the U.S. Department of State and the U.S. Department of Education (Hamilton, Congressional Record, 1998).

It is believed that during the 1970s the field expanded significantly, when a number of Americans who had served in the Peace Corps in Iran took up academic positions related to Iranian studies. Consequently, the close ties between Iran and the United States increased the number of academic programs as well as exchanges between Iranian and American scholars. Despite such efforts before the Revolution, there was very little published about Iranians in the United States (Bozorgmehr, 1998).

Bozorgmehr (1998) maintains that research and writings on Iranians in the United States can be divided into pre- and post-revolutionary phases. With the 1979 Iranian Islamic Revolution, Iranian studies gained more political significance than before, yet ironically this initially reversed the trend for expansion of the Iranian studies. The Iranian hostage crisis of 1980–1981 had further negative effects on research about Iran (Bozorgmehr, 1998).

According to Abbas Milani, the director for Iranian Studies at Stanford University:

> The interesting point about America and Iranian Studies is that after the revolution and particularly after the hostage crisis instead of the number for Iranian studies increasing they began to decrease. This is completely against the pattern that America has had about any other country. When America was worried about the Soviet Union, there was a massive amount of funding available for people to study Russian language, literature, economy. In the case of Iran, as Iran became more of a problem, the places that studies Iran were diminishing; till September 11. So as the need for knowledge was increasing the capacity for producing knowledge was decreasing. There was a true gap.
>
> A. MILANI, personal communication, November 16, 2014

A number of reasons may explain the reversed trend: With the Revolution the relationship between the two countries deteriorated and consequently the programs as well as exchanges between the two governments came to a halt; financial assets were seized by the United States as well. On the other hand, with the 'hostage crisis,' many Iranians did not want to disclose their nationality for fear of losing jobs, deportation, etc. (Bozorgmehr, 1998). Interestingly, instead of encouraging research, the 'Iranian hostage crisis' of 1980–1981 discouraged research on the topic, as Iranians were subjected to prejudice and discrimination and "given their vulnerable legal status they were concerned about making statements that would lead to their deportation" (Bozorgmehr, 1998, p. 15). It is claimed that researchers at that time were also concerned with allegations of collecting information on behalf of either U.S. government agencies or spying for the Iranian revolutionary government (Bozorgmehr, 1998). Moreover, it took a few years for the Iranian–American community to form and shape an approach toward post-revolutionary Iran. In addition, the educational and social formation of the Iranian community changed after 1979: Before the Revolution, most of the students were majoring in engineering (Askari et al., 1977), afterwards, "more Iranian students turned to humanities and social sciences to grapple with what had happened in their homeland." Hoshang Amirahmadi (1995) maintains that the post-revolutionary Iranian studies has taken two approaches toward the study of contemporary Iran. He believes that initially and in the early years after the Revolution, "scholars focused on the driving forces of the 1979 Revolution, Islam in particular. By the mid-1980s, attention shifted toward an understanding of the Islamic Republic in place, notably its theocratic nature and probable teleology" (Amirahmadi, 1995, para. 1).

Milani maintains that this pattern began to change by September 11, 2001: "By September 11 a number of rich and successful Iranians began to get involved in these programs" (personal communication, November 16, 2014). Milani refers to the Iranian studies programs at the Stanford University and UCLA as examples that were supported financially by Iranian Americans (personal communication, November 16, 2014). Karimi-Hakkak, too, believes that after September 11, 2001 many universities in the United States became aware of their critical shortage of Persian speakers along with Arabic and Urdu speakers (Podcast, University of Maryland, 2008). As a result, private individuals and institutional donors as well as the U.S. government increased support for Iranian studies programs financially.

The Iranian–American community played a significant role in the expansion of Iranian studies programs in the United States. Under the circumstances, "Iranian exiles and immigrants in the U.S. presented themselves as viable alternative subjects, especially since they were virtually unstudied at the time" (Bozorgmehr, 1998, p. 12). The contribution of the Iranian diaspora in Iranian studies programs comes in different forms, by providing financial support as well as being involved in teaching. For instance, the Roshan Cultural Heritage Institute provides the largest financial contribution, establishing centers and offering grants and fellowships to major American universities. Among the universities that receive grants from the Roshan Institute are University of California, Berkeley; Harvard University; University of California, Los Angeles; University of California, Irvine; University of Cambridge; University of Chicago; Columbia University; Georgetown University; University of Maryland; Massachusetts Institute of Technology; Northeastern University; San José State University; and Yale University (Roshan, Grants and Programs, n.d). Large numbers of Iranian Americans continue to support conferences and lecture series, fund undergraduate and graduate scholarships, and endow professorial chairs for Persian programs at universities across the country (Cincotta, 2009).

U.S. State Department's Programs on Iran

Since the 1980s, the United States government has provided funding for designated languages under Title VI, as Persian—similar to Arabic, Russian, Chinese,

Hindi, Urdu, and Korean—is regarded as a critical or strategic language for the United States. According to Kamran Talattof, "The resources provided by Title VI have been indispensable in the quality and quantity of Persian instruction" (as cited in Cincotta, 2009, para. 16).

According to statistics from a quadrennial survey last conducted in 2009 by the Modern Language Association (MLA), which looked at 2,802 U.S. colleges and universities, Persian continues to be the second most popular language in the United States after Arabic for student enrollment (Furman, Goldberg, & Lusin, 2007). From 2002 to 2006, Persian language enrollment jumped more than 90 percent in the United States, from roughly 1,200 to almost 2,300 students (Furman et al., 2007).

As a report by the U.S. State Department in 2009 explained, in recent years state universities have rapidly expanded their Persian/Iranian studies programs (Cincotta, 2009). Accordingly, the traditional centers for programs of Persian and Middle Eastern studies such as Columbia, Princeton, Harvard, and the University of Chicago, have grown less rapidly than newer programs at state universities. Ziai argues that the current growth in Persian and Iranian studies has been taking place almost exclusively at large state universities across the country (Cincotta, 2009).[2]

Several universities and institutions with Iranian or Persian studies programs receive funds from the U.S. government. Among them are the National Security Education Program Flagship Graduate Programs that offers a master degree at the University of Maryland for the Persian Flagship Program at the University of Maryland, College Park (National Foreign Language Center, 2014). The Undergraduate Internship Program Open Source Officer (CIA) is another program that offers internship to both undergraduate and graduate students. Farsi/Persian is one of the languages that are included in this program beside Kurdish, Arabic, Urdu, and Pashtu. The program requires relevant area knowledge beside language proficiency (Central Intelligence Agency, 2007). The National Security Agency Summer Language Program (NAS) is an intensive 12-week intern program with the purpose of improving language skills of high-potential college upperclassmen and graduate students. The program is currently hiring students who are studying Persian-Farsi (National Security Agency, 2014). It is also offered to students who are studying Arabic, Urdu,

2 Including Ohio State University and the universities of Maryland, Texas, Arizona, Utah, Washington, Berkeley, Los Angeles, Fullerton, and Irvine. Among the state universities that are supported by the U.S. government are Ohio State University and the Universities of Maryland, Texas, Arizona, Utah, and Washington. In California, Persian studies programs are offered at state university campuses in Berkeley, Los Angeles, Fullerton, and Irvine.

Russian, Chinese, Korean, and Pashto. National Security Education Program Scholarships of the U.S. Department of Defense is another program that is offered to both graduates and undergraduates for studying abroad in areas of the world that are considered critical to U.S. interests. It is funded by the National Security Education Program (NSEP). Iran is also among the countries that are listed as emphasized countries for the Boren Awards, which is a part of NSEP program (NSEP Annual Review, 2009).

Iranian Studies Journal: A Case Study

One of the main sources and expressions of academic knowledge production on post-revolutionary Iran may be found in academic journals and academic publications. To examine some of the properties of the mainstream academic discourse on post-revolutionary Iran, this chapter focuses on one of the leading journals in Iranian studies, the *Iranian Studies Journal*. The present chapter will examine passages from several articles that are currently available by the journal about post-revolutionary Iran. *Iranian Studies Journal* is a quarterly peer-reviewed academic journal covering Iranian and Persian history, literature, and contemporary society, published by Routledge for the International Society for Iranian Studies. It is published 6 times a year (with two special issues per year) and was established in 1967.

This chapter will discuss some of the articles that are published by female writers on post-revolutionary Iran from 1980, a few months after the Islamic Revolution, to August 2012. Book reviews are excluded and 27 original papers are analysed. The analysis attempts to address the following questions:

1. Access: Who can write and publish articles about Iran in the *Iranian Studies Journal*?
2. Framing or topic selection: What issues are raised and accentuated by the writers? It should be noted that topic setting and framing has social and political implications and is often done within the framework of dominant ideologies.

The method of analysis generally focuses on specific assumptions that exist about Iran and their implications, with occasional attention to greater details as well as arguments. Meanwhile some issues are discussed in slightly greater detail, although it will be impossible to provide a full critical account of the views expressed in the articles due to the many narratives and perspectives as well as the wide disparity of issues discussed with regard to post-revolutionary Iran.

Access and Framing

Gatekeeping and framing is related to mass media studies and focuses on the structure of newsrooms and events. This section will borrow the concepts to explain how scholarly productions of articles related to post-revolutionary Iran are framed, filtered, and disseminated in the *Iranian Studies Journal*. A frame is the central organizing idea for making sense of events and suggesting what is at issue. "Framing is often considered as a necessary tool for reducing the complexity of an issue, given the constraints of their respective media related to news holes and airtime" (Gans, 1979). Gatekeeping is defined as "the process of culling and crafting countless bits of information into the limited number of messages that reach people each day" (Shoemaker & Vos, 2009, p. 1). A gatekeeper is the one who decides about the dissemination of certain information, what may enter and get published in the scholarly production. Significantly, gatekeepers are able to control the public's knowledge about the actual events by letting some stories pass while blocking others. "The gatekeeper's choices are a complex web of influences, preferences, motives and common values" (Gupta, 2006, p. 34).

The decision about the publication of an article involves interaction between authors and the editorial board. Current methods of accepting and disseminating scholarly information by academic journals give the editorial boards an exclusive control and influence on the materials they accept and publish. Considering the volume of information product and paper submissions, filtering is inevitable and even crucial. While filtering and selecting is inevitable, it can also manipulate events or issues and provide a partial and sometimes distorted narrative by deciding what information to include and what to exclude based on preferences.

The pressure on academics to publish papers in order to get a job, tenure, grants, or other funds may result in the manipulation of the produced 'knowledge.' Therefore, the author has to arrange the manuscripts in a way that makes it appealing for the editors and reviewers. Accordingly, the content of the papers may change and in some cases become compromised in order to increase chances of publication. Strategies such as considering what topic is trendy and market worthy, exaggerating findings, or using those that fit well into the dominant discourse might be used to assure the publication of a paper. Though the papers are peer reviewed, a reviewer's personal perceptions and affiliations can interfere in his or her judgement. Reviewers and editors may prefer the trendy, common, and expected over the controversial and unexpected content. Moreover, the demographic formation of the editorial board is of significance.

It can be argued that the act of framing and filtering as well as the production and dissemination of 'knowledge' in the *Iranian Studies Journal*, like any other journal, is performed at two levels: the author who chooses to write about a specific topic and the journal that makes a decision about publishing a paper with certain content. Thus, both gatekeepers (author and journal) decide what information will be disseminated and what will not. Accordingly, the frame for a given article represents the effort of the writer and journal to convey a story in a particular yet meaningful way.

Significantly, a majority of the writers (almost 69%) who have published articles on different topics related to post-revolutionary Iran have Iranian origins, while 21% of the articles were published by non-Iranian writers (see Figure 12.1 below). The nationality of 11% of the writers was not clear.

Moreover, the majority of the writers (almost 86%) who have published articles in the *Iranian Studies Journal* are living/working in the United States or Europe, while only 4% (3 people) are living/working in Iran (see Figure 12.2 below).

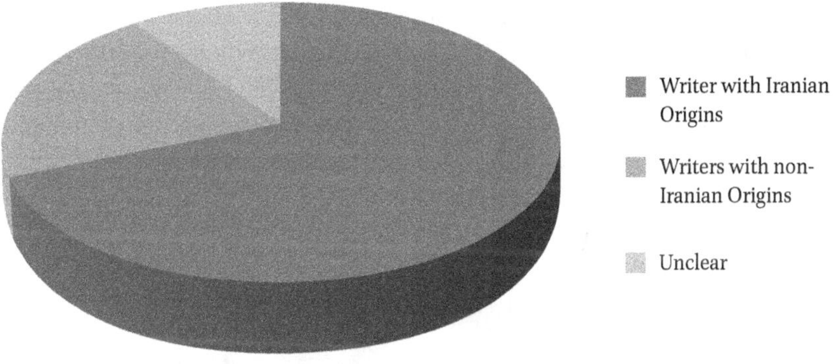

FIGURE 12.1 *Origin of* Iranian Studies Journal *writers*

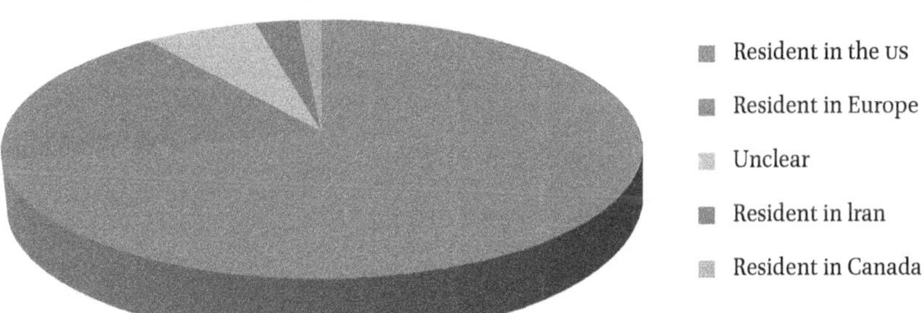

FIGURE 12.2 *Residence of* Iranian Studies Journal *writers*

More than half (57%) of the members of the editorial board of the journal have Iranian origins, while 45% are non-Iranians (see Figure 12.3 below). 52% of the editorial board of the *Iranian Studies Journal* are members of different universities in the United States, while less than 2% (only one person[3]) is from an Iranian university, which equals the number of members from Jordan, Japan, and Afghanistan. Almost 23% of the members come from universities in the United Kingdom.

One important aspect in framing an issue is paying attention to some problems (that are believed to be important or should be regarded as important) and ignoring or paying slight attention to others (Iyengar & Kinder, 1987). According to Entman, "Framing essentially involves selection and salience. To frame is to select some aspects of a perceived reality and make them more salient than a communicating text in such a way as to promote a particular problem definition" (1993, p. 52). It refers to "modes of presentations that journalists and other communicators use to present information in a way that resonates within existing underlying schemas among their audience" (Shoemaker & Reese, 1996, p. 12). While selection (choosing a topic or focusing on a specific issue) is inevitable and in many circumstances useful, it can ignore a substantial amount of information and lead to a partial understanding or factual distortion. The following discussion will consider how the articles published by the female writers in the *Iranian Studies Journal* often frame those issues that confirm the stereotypical image of post-revolutionary Iran and Iranian society (see Table 12.1 below).

FIGURE 12.3 *Origin of* Iranian Studies Journal *editorial board*

3 Mansoureh Ettehadieh—Tehran University.

Women and Sexuality under the Islamic Republic of Iran

Analysis of women and sexuality under the Islamic Republic in the *Iranian Studies Journal* can be perceived within the dominant Orientalist discourse toward Muslim women in general and Iranian women in particular. A brief overview of the development of the Orientalist discourse toward Muslim women may help in interpretation of the articles under study.

The images of Muslim women became a major component for the construction of the Orient and had a direct connection to Western imperialism, particularly that of France and Britain (Kabbani, 1986; Said, 1978; Sardar, 1999). In her book, *Western Representations of the Muslim Woman: From Termagant to Odalisque* (1999), Mohja Kahf historicizes nine centuries of European images of Muslim women, which runs from the medieval to Romantic periods. Despite the wide variety of literary models that Kahf uncovers—giantesses, princesses, harlots, and soldiers—she concludes that "all that Western culture retains today of its own ebullient parade of Muslim women is a supine odalisque, a shrinking-violet virgin, and a veiled victim woman" (1999, p. 179). Accordingly, despite some nuances in Orientalism, there is a constant and inseparable association between the Orient and sensuality. The obsession with the harem as a dominant signifier of the Orient in the Orientalist discourse of the 18th and 19th centuries was used constantly in popular literature, both literally and metaphorically. The harem had an erotic significance and was perceived as a site for forbidden sexual pleasures as well as a segregated space, which separated men from women. Moreover, the harem and eroticism associated with it has significance as it depicts the relationship between Oriental

TABLE 12.1 *A thematic presentation of articles written by female writers in the* Iranian Studies Journal

Dominant Themes in the Articles on Women	Number of the Articles	Percent
Education	4	15.0
Art (music, cinema, literature)	4	15.0
Sexuality (homosexuality, trans-sexuality, temporary marriage)	5	18.5
Female social status	6	22.5
Politics of post-revolutionary Iran	8	29.0

women, Oriental men, and their Western counterparts. Sardar pointed out that "symbolically, the violent and barbaric Muslim male and sensual, passive female, come together to represent the perfect Orient of the Western perception: they fuse together to produce a concrete image of sensuality and despotism and thus inferiority" (1999, p. 48).

The oppositional binary between the Western treatment toward women and their Oriental counterparts abound. By portraying the other as inferior, they legitimize their own conception of women. As Macfie puts it:

> Europe (the West, the "self") is ... essentially rational, developed, humane, superior, authentic, active, creative, and masculine, while the Orient (the East, the "other") (a sort of surrogate, underground version of the West or the "self") is ... irrational, aberrant, backward, crude, despotic, inferior, inauthentic, passive, feminine, and sexually corrupt. (2002, p. 8)

During the colonial era, Orientalist feminism served a purpose: The constructed image of suppressive and cruel Oriental males and submissive Oriental females justified the conquest of Eastern lands and even made it a moral imperative. This, according to Spivak, is the case of "white men saving brown women from brown man" (Spivak, 1999, p. 303). The contemporary example of this view toward the so-called Oriental women is the representation of Afghan and Iraqi women during and after the U.S. and NATO invasion to Afghanistan and Iraq, when the depiction of Muslim women in burqa or niqab (the face covering hijab) was prevalent in many Western and even some Eastern press and media.

Whereas the rhetoric of "saving Muslim women" is often used by feminist Orientalists, the debate around the "third world woman," the problematic history of the "feminist-as-imperialist," and the so-called "civilizing mission" of the colonialists (Gandhi, 1998, p. 83) raises serious doubts about the benign intentions of many Western feminists toward the issue of women's right in Islamic countries. According to Parvin Paidar (1995), feminist Orientalism basically makes three assumptions: first, the assumption of an oppositional binary between the West and the East in which Muslim women are oppressed while their Western counterparts enjoy full freedom in their societies. The second characteristic is the conception that the Oriental women are only victims of a male chauvinistic society and have no agency or resistant role in their social transformations. This approach tends to marginalize the so-called Oriental women and therefore, Muslim women need saviors, i.e., the Westerns, to emancipate them from Muslim men's tyranny. The third aspect is the construction of a monolithic entity of Muslims and therefore the belief that all Muslim women are living under the same condition and have no unique aspect or identity for themselves (Paidar, 1995). Therefore, non-Western women are represented as "ignorant, poor, uneducated, tradition-bound, domestic, family-oriented, victimized, etc." and Western women as "educated, modern ... having control over their own bodies and sexualities, and the freedom to make their own decisions" (Mohanty, 1984, p. 261) .

Gayari Spivak also suggests that the representation of the so-called "third world women" has housed her in an "identifiable margin" and by marginalizing her, the "superiority" of "first world" women is emphasized, "when a cultural identity is thrust upon one because the center wants an identifiable margin, claims for marginality assure validation from the center" (Spivak, 1993, p. 55). In this way, as Trinh Minh-ha argues, a hierarchy is established between the third world women and their Western counterparts in which the White woman plays the role of savior for the Oriental women: "The patronizing attitude towards unfortunate sister creates an insuperable division between I-who-have-made-it and You-who-can-not-make-it" (1989, p. 86). According to Leela Gandhi, the Western feminist approach toward non-Western and Oriental women is a type of neo-Orientalism (1998). This means that the constructed discourse surrounding the Orient is for the purpose of the imperial consumption and creates a self-congratulatory and self-consolidating project for the Western feminists.

In the late 20th century a series of female writers from Islamic countries began to write about their lives and experiences. Unlike their predecessors, these 'Oriental women' were not 'silent' but outspoken, Western-educated women, thus familiar to the Western audience. Compared with the instances of the 19th and early 20th centuries, these neo-Orientalist narratives are regarded as more authentic and reliable (Ahmed, 2009; Behdad & Williams, 2010; Marandi & Pirnajmuddin, 2009). Here the Oriental woman is not silent anymore but is allowed to speak within the stereotypical image of the traditional Orientalists that is familiar to the American audience.

A major question one may ask in a critical analysis is what topics in texts are accentuated and emphasized when discussing an issue/event or entity. In other words, how people write or speak (and 'problematize') about Iran/Iranian society in an academic debate is significant. While it can be argued that the articles published in the *Iranian Studies Journal* have more complicated perspectives about Iran/post-revolutionary Iran[4] compared with the memoirs or other popular productions on Iran in the West, the overall image often favors the stereotypical image of the Islamic Republic. When discussing Iran under

4 Like Pesaran, Hegland, Nashat, Javaheri.

the Islamic Republic, issues such as 'female suppression,' 'patriarchy,' 'insecurity,' and 'surveillance' are strongly highlighted in the articles. Moreover, it is argued that women's status under the Islamic Republic regressed and 'the return of Islam' is blamed. The following offers a few flaws from the articles published by the *Iranian Studies Journal.*

It is claimed that the Islamic Republic interferes and controls all aspects of Iranian life from education, and child-rearing to the sexual affairs of married couples. For instance, in her article *Enveloping Music in Gender, Nation, and Islam: Women's Music Festivals in Post-Revolutionary Iran* (2005), Wendy DeBano argues that the Islamic Republic's control is both symbolic and practical. She states that "as men and women bustle along the busy city streets of Tehran, they are watched by the stern gazes and ghostly stares of images of national leaders and martyrs, most of whom are male" (DeBano, 2005, p. 443). In a similar vein, Jane Afary, in her article, *The Sexual Economy of the Islamic Republic,* argues that the Islamic Republic is interfering in people's private and sexual affairs. In her analysis, she revives the old Orientalist discourse on the dichotomy of cruel sensual men as opposed to submissive Oriental women: Afary claims that men's sexual pleasure and their sexual interests and gratifications are prioritized by the Islamic Republic (2009). She alleges that the reason why the state attempts to keep the age of marriage low is to assure men's unrestricted access to sex, "and on the other denying women greater control in other areas of their lives. This was the secret of the Islamist state's sexual economy" (Afary, 2009, p. 16).

Schools and universities are claimed to be under total surveillance of the Islamic Republic to the extent that children are used against their own parents. For instance, Azadeh Kian-Thiébaut, in *From Motherhood to Equal Rights Advocates: The Weakening of Patriarchal Order,* purports that the Islamic Republic indoctrinates youth and in doing so it seeks weakening of the authorial parental relations, "though the post-Revolutionary power elite is, elderly and traditionalist, it did not openly oppose the youths' new value system.... On the contrary they actively participated in the weakening of parental authority that could have hindered the youths' ideologization" (2005, p. 62). Moreover, it is claimed that with the beginning of the Iran–Iraq war (1980–1988), the authorities weakened the parental relationships as they "needed volunteers and mobilized all the ideological state apparatus, media, Friday prayers, or mosques to encourage the youths to go to the war" (2005, p. 62). Elsewhere Kian-Thiébaut claims, without mentioning any references, about alleged intervention in family affairs by the Islamic Republic, which "attempts to control families through information it tried to obtain from school children on the mode of life" (2005, p. 63). As a result, "a lot of these innocent children caused trouble to their parents, some of whom lost their jobs, while others were even arrested" (Kian-Thiébaut, 2005, p. 63). However, Mary Hegland, another writer whose paper is published in this journal, argues that in post-revolutionary Iran, "Schools have a somewhat more open atmosphere than a quarter of a century ago, and offer more opportunities for initiative, performance and leadership" (2009, p. 54).

Moreover, pre-revolutionary Iran is usually represented as a modern and progressive society with a Shah who had hastened the process of modernization by unveiling women, as well as through promoting literacy and employment among Iranian women. This is juxtaposed with the alleged religious backwardness and repression of women under the 'clerical regime' of the Islamic Republic.

For instance, Guity Nashat, in her article, *Women in the Islamic Republic of Iran,* describes Reza Shah's ban of the veil "accompanied by official encouragement of women to enter into public life" in 1936 as helping women's progress, because "they [women] began to appear in a variety of capacities in the lower echelons of government" (1980, p. 176). She maintains that "this participation of women in public life [during the Reza shah] ran counter to centuries of social conditioning that was associated with the veil, religious piety, and propriety" (Nashat, 1980, p. 167). Nashat argues that besides the improvements in education during the reign of Reza Shah, female employment improved as well: "During the next two decades, as the economy began to expand at an ever-increasing rate, employment opportunities opened up for women, and as women's role in society changed, so did societal attitudes toward them" (Nashat, 1980, p. 168). Moreover, often the Family Protection Law of 1976 and the Family Protection Law and its amendments in pre-revolutionary Iran are referred to as a sign of advancement which was reversed with the 1979 Revolution (see, for instance, Kian-Thiébaut, 2005; Rahimieh, 2009).

Nashat blames "the return of Islam" for women's "oppression" under the Islamic Republic (1980, p. 174). Afary (2009) maintains that women's status under the Islamic Republic regressed and that the post-revolutionary state "revived pre-modern social conventions (repudiation, veiling, and flogging)" (p. 46). According to her, "Defunct and repressive Shi'i rituals of purity and penance were brought back, while polygamy and sex with underage girls were newly sanctioned" (2009, p. 6). Kian-Thiébaut argues that the application of the Shari'a laws in the aftermath of the Revolution deprived women of their civil rights and institutionalized gender inequality and the Islamic ideology denies women individuality, autonomy, and independence and "it perceives women as family members whose rights and obligations are defined in relation to their male relatives" (2005, p. 46). And that the function of women is reduced to "childbearing, childrearing and housework thus" (Kian-Thiébaut, 2009, p. 46).

Meanwhile Mary Elaine Hegland's *Educating Young Women: Culture, Conflict, and New Identities* (2009) compares women's status in an Iranian village, "Aliabad" in Shiraz, in pre- and post-revolutionary Iran. Hegland, maintains that the Islamic Republic has provided women with more opportunities, though she too claims that the Islamic Republic did not do it out of will but as an obligation. "Given the significance of women's participation in the Iranian Revolution of 1978/79 and also their support for the formation of the Islamic Republic of Iran, not surprisingly, the regime gave women attention and praise" (Hegland, 2009, p. 49). She maintains that "educational opportunities, services, and sources of information which the Reza Shah Pahlavi regime was working to make available for the upper and middle classes are now beginning to go to rural and lower urban class people as well" (Hegland, 2009, p. 51).

While some of the authors maintain that women's status under the Islamic Republic regressed (only with the exception of Hegland), others affirm the improvement in women's status but attempt to disassociate the progress with the Islamic Republic. In this way, the improvement in women's status is not a reflection of benign intentions of the Islamic Republic but despite it. This is to the extent that sometimes improvement in the statues of women is regarded as a sort of protest against the Islamic Republic. For instance, Jane Afary claims that women's status with regard to education and health has improved significantly (2009); she attributes these improvements with the "sexual economy of the Islamic Republic," which, she claims cannot be easily characterized as "puritanical" or "moralistic," unlike the popular perception (p. 6). However, she maintains that the policies had "unintended results" for the power elite (2005, p. 47). In her view, the Revolution and its policies toward women "triggered new forms of strategies within the female population, who increasingly reject traditionalist values and divine justifications for segregation policies" (2005, p. 46).

In reality, the age of marriage for Iranian women increased after the Revolution. By 2011 the average age for female marriage was 23.5 years (Iran Data Portal, 2011) and age at first marriage has sharply increased during the decades after the Revolution (Abbasi-Shavazi, McDonald, & Hosseini-Chavosi, 2009), not to mention the effective program for family planning after the Revolution, which has improved women's health and education. Comparing the statistics of pre- and post-revolutionary Iran with regard to basic infrastructure, human development, health care, and education can be revealing. In 1979, few cities in Iran had basic facilities such as electricity, gas, and clean water, and public access to education and health care was limited. The Islamic Republic's HDI value for 2012 was 0.742—in the high human development category. Between

1980 and 2012 (under the Islamic Republic), Iran's HDI value increased from 0.443 to 0.742, an increase of 67 percent or an average annual increase of about 1.6 percent. Between 1980 and 2012, Iran's life expectancy at birth increased by 22.1 years, mean years of schooling increased by 5.7 years, and expected years of schooling increased by 5.7 years. Iran's GNI per capita increased by about 48 percent between 1980 and 2012 (UN Human Development Report, 2013). The literacy rate of Iran was raised from 36.5% in 1980 to 82.3% in 2010 (UNHDP, 2013). Meanwhile the Islamic Republic has facilitated education and, to a significant degree, women's employment, through state education, which is contradictory with what Thiébaut claims.

The fact that many traditional and religious Iranian families were not willing to send their daughters to schools, universities, or work before the Revolution should be considered as an important explanation for the dramatic increase in the number of female students after the Revolution. Many families felt that the Islamic ambiance of post-revolutionary Iran was more suitable for their children. This is referred to in Hegland's paper, in which she states that with the Revolution, "conservative rural and lower class parents feel less trepidation at the thought of their daughters studying to higher levels" (2009, p. 53). In other words, what is perceived as 'restrictive' or prohibitory for a foreign observer may be considered as normal or even empowering for those living inside the country.

Credibility Problems with Unattributed Quotes

Use of unsourced or poorly sourced materials, secondary or tertiary sources, unattributed quotes, or inaccurate or controversial sources is a major problem in many of the articles that were analyzed. Significantly, Persian and original sources are very rarely used by the writers. Lack of translation of Farsi sources in English might be a possible reason, although the majority of those who published their papers were of Iranian origins and therefore most likely know the language. The main reason might be the bias toward the sources and references that write about Iran or the Islamic Republic in country itself. Statistical and political analysis of individuals and organizations that produce knowledge from inside the Islamic Republic is considered as less noteworthy or reliable. Moreover, the use of anecdotal evidence (stories one hears from unknown individuals and personal informants) and grand generalizations based on a few cases (according to the authors) are very common in the articles. Anecdotal evidence in many of the articles does not conform with the known facts or careful study as well as information passed along by word-of-mouth but not documented.[5] Such evidence runs the risk of partiality, as the writer may tend to collect and present those stories that illustrate a desired conclusion and thus make inaccurate generalizations about a large number of people.

Shahla Haeri's article *Power of Ambiguity: Cultural Imprecisions on the Theme of Temporary Marriage* (1986), which she later developed into a book, attempts to provide readers with information about the practice of sigheh (mu'ta)[6] in Iran. For this purpose, Haeri selects unreliable hadiths, then misreads and distorts them. In the article, Haeri provides a self-constructed typology of different forms of sigheh such as "Sigheh Associated with Pilgrimage" (p. 130), "sigheh Nazri" (p. 131), "group sigheh" (p. 146), and "penance sigheh" (p. 146), which are complete distortions of Islamic jurisprudence with regard to sigheh.[7] Haeri portrays the religious cities of Mashad and Qum as "sigheh cities" (1986, p. 131) and claims that women pilgrims make "Nazr" (vow) to have temporary marriages (1986, p. 131) in those cities. These are just a few examples of how she manufactures materials and how it fits well with the Orientalist discourse about Islam in general and religious Iranians in particular. The sources Haeri mentions for her claims are either "a mullah in Mashad" or her "informant in Mashad" (1986, p. 132), another mullah in Qum (1986, p. 146), or some of her personal friends and informants (1986, p. 139).

Shahla Haeri's other article, *Sacred Canopy: Love and Sex under the Veil* (2009), which was published by the *Iranian Studies Journal,* suffers from the inclusion of an extensive amount of what appears to be misinformation consorted with Orientalist stereotypes. Here she makes constant associations between Iran and sensuality. Haeri invites her readers to "take a moment to lift the veil of prohibition and secrecy in Iran and take a peek under the sacred canopy of patriarchy's laws and religion" (2009, p. 114). Haeri makes claims such as that Iranian culture is "preoccupied with sex segregation, walls and veils" (2009, p. 117) and that "one could easily be convinced of the presence of an active voyeur in every [male?] Iranian!" (2009, p. 121). Interestingly Haeri's attempt to persuade the readers that male (or female) Iranians are voyeurs is based on quotations she takes from a writer named Ibn Hazm (an Andalusian polymath born in Córdoba), who associates voyeurism to 'Arabs' of Córdoba; Haeri

---

5 See for example Shahla Haeri's *Sacred Canopy* (2009) and *Power of Ambiguity* (1986).

6 Ibid.

7 In reality, such typology does not exist and the woman engaged in temporary marriage has to wait for two months (Iddah) before which she cannot marry anyone else. Temporary marriage is discouraged when one has a permanent wife who is sexually available to him.

extends it to Iranian men. She does not explain the relationship between the Arabs of Córdoba and Iranian men in contemporary Iran. The paper, which is about the prevalence of "erotic desire in Persian poetry," contains mingled stories and misinformation about Islam that work within the Orientalist discourse of attributing Islam with oppression and sensuality. For instance, according to Haeri, "in present-day Iran and according to the mandate of the Islamic Republic, unrelated men and women are forbidden to touch one another (excepting apparently in some forms of domestic violence)" (2009, p. 114).

Another similar example is Faegheh Shirazi's article *The Sofreh: Comfort and Community among Women in Iran* (2005), where Sofreh-e-Nazri (a religious ritual) is distorted and reduced to mere superstition; for instance, see sofreh-e- "Bibi Seshanbeh" (2005, p. 304), or "ash-e amaj kumaj" (2005, p. 299). Some other obvious flaws show that the writer lacks a basic knowledge of Islamic history and culture; such as "Abu l'Fadl, among the martyrs of Karbala, is also known as Abu l'Fadl al-Abbas. His father was Imam Hasan" (Shirazi, 2005, p. 298), whereas his father was Imam Ali. Or that "Fatima, [was] grandmother of Abu l'Fadl" (2005, p. 299).

Significantly, a number of writers use the Iranian-American memoirs as sources or introduce them to the readers to gain more information about Iranian society, culture, and politics. Afary (2009) refers to Christopher de Bellaigue's controversial (2004) memoir to explain the reasons for Ahmadinejad's election. Hegland refers to Azadeh Moaveni's (2006) *Lipstick Jihad* so that readers can presumably learn about social life in Iranian cities and understand the discussion of "Iranian women's struggle against the current regime's repression through makeup, fashion, and body-modification in Tehran" (Hegland, 2009, pp. 75–77). Laudan Nooshin quotes Azar Nafisi's (2003) *Reading Lolita in Tehran* several times in her 2005 article *Underground, Overground: Rock Music and Youth Discourses in Iran*, as she believes that "she [Nafisi] so eloquently encapsulates the contradictions and complexities of cultural life in Post-revolutionary Iran" (2005, p. 464). Nooshin suggests Nafisi's book for "an interesting account of Iran during the 1980s and 90s" (2005, p. 463).[8]

8 It should be noted that *Reading Lolita in Tehran* by Azar Nafisi (2003) appears on course syllabi across North America in the disciplines of women's studies, international relations, English studies, and anthropology, with course titles such as "Understanding Totalitarianism," "Understanding Culture and Cultural Difference," and "Women and Islam." Also Satrapi's *Persepolis* is recommended for 7th graders and 11th graders by the Chicago Public Schools.

Conclusion

The present chapter provided a brief overview of the developments of the Iranian Studies programs in the United States. The pattern of growth for Persian and Iranian studies in the United States was briefly discussed and classified into three eras that reflect the changing political relations between Iran and the United States: an early approach, which was more concerned with the philology/archaeology of Iran; as a part of Middle Eastern Studies programs that attempted to study Iran from a more modern and international academic perspective (after WWII); and as an independent field of study that studies history/culture and politics as well as the Persian language.

The chapter then offered a brief analysis of the *Iranian Studies Journal*. It may be argued that articles published in the *Iranian Studies Journal* are a form of in-group production. The overwhelming majority of the writers (86%) are Iranians/non-Iranians who are educated and residing in the West (either in the United States or Europe). This is also true about the editorial board of the journal, with only one Iranian from inside Iran being a member of the editorial board. It could be concluded that Iranian writers writing from inside the country tend to be discriminated against; the discrimination might be partly due to the language barrier, as some Iranian academicians inside Iran may not be able to write and publish academic papers in English and many of them might not submit their papers to English language journals.

On the other hand, the process of text production and getting a paper accepted in a journal involves selecting or discarding certain elements of contents. This is often linked to subjective interpretations of writers as well as that of the editorial board. Though selection is inevitable and in some circumstances useful, it can ignore substantial amounts of information and lead to partial understanding or factual distortion. Consequently, not only is knowledge production often a politicized process, but also the very structure of such academic journals and their structures do not favor certain perspectives on Iran.

Accordingly, the issue of framing is of significance. The *Iranian Studies Journal* often frames different issues in a way that confirms the stereotypical image of post-revolutionary Iran and Iranian society. While the articles published in the *Iranian Studies Journal* have more complicated perspectives about Iran/ post-revolutionary Iran[9] compared with the memoirs, the overall image often favors the stereotypical image of the Islamic Republic.

In any case, because Iranian writings from inside Iran are virtually absent from the journal, this not only means that knowledge production in general is

9 Like Pesaran, Hegland, Nashat, Javaheri.

partial due to the one-sided perspective, but also that fundamental knowledge and issues related to Iranians and their experiences are usually lacking. On the other hand, issues that might be of significance for Iranians inside Iran are not comprehensively discussed and in some cases are completely ignored or distorted.

Interestingly, while academic articles often demand that authors provide accurate and academic references, many writers often use secondary and tertiary sources, some of which are strongly questionable or unreliable.

References

Abbasi-Shavazi, M.J., McDonald, P., & Hosseini-Chavoshi, M. (2009). *The fertility transition in Iran: Revolution and reproduction.* New York, NY: Springer. doi:10.1007/978-90-481-3198-3.

Abdi, K. (2001). Nationalism, politics, and the development of archaeology in Iran. *American Journal of Archaeology, 105,* 51–76. doi:10.2307/507326.

Afary, J. (2009). The sexual economy of the Islamic Republic. *Iranian Studies, 42,* 5–26. doi:10.1080/00210860802593833.

Ahmed, L. (2009). *Women and gender in Islam: Historical roots of a modern debate.* Philadelphia, PA: University of Pennsylvania.

Amirahmadi, H. (1995). The civil society approach to Iranian Studies, *Iranian.com.* Retrieved July 27, 2017 from http://iranian.com/Sep95/Amirah.html.

Askari, H., Cummings, J.T., & Izbudak, M. (1977). Iran's migration of skilled labor to the United States. *Iranian Studies, 10,* 3–39. doi: "https://doi.org/10.1080/00210867708701523" 10.1080/00210867708701523.

Behdad, A., & Williams, J. (2010). Neo-Orientalism. In B.T. Edwards & D.P. Gaonkar (Eds.), *Globalizing American studies* (pp. 283–299). Chicago, IL: University of Chicago Press. doi:10.7208/chicago/9780226185088.003.0011.

Bozorgmehr, M. (1998). From Iranian studies to studies of Iranians in the United States. *Iranian Studies, 31,* 4–30. doi:10.1080/00210869808701893.

Brzezinski, Z., Gates, R.M., & Maloney, S. (2004). *Iran: Time for a new approach.* New York, NY: Council on Foreign Relations.

Cincotta, H. (2009). *Persian studies in United States reflects dynamism and growth: Thriving academic program grew from 19th-century roots.* Washington, DC: Bureau of International Information Program, U.S. Department of State. Retrieved July 27, 2017 from http://www.payvand.com/news/09/jul/1266.html.

Collier, P., Hoeffler, A., & World Bank. (2000). *Greed and grievance in Civil War.* World Bank Policy Working Paper No. 2355. Washington, DC: World Bank, Development Research Group. Retrieved March 1, 2018 from https://ssrn.com/abstract=630727.

de Bellaigue, C. (2004). *In the rose garden of the martyrs: A memoir of Iran.* New York, NY: HarperCollins.

DeBano, W.S. (2005). Enveloping music in gender, nation, and Islam: Women's music festivals in post-revolutionary Iran. *Iranian Studies, 38,* 441–462. doi:10.1080/00210860500300812.

Devos, B., & Werner, C. (2014). *Culture and cultural politics under Reza Shah: The Pahlavi state, new bourgeoisie and the creation of a modern society in Iran.* Abingdon, England: Routledge.

Entman, R.M. (1993). Framing: Toward clarification of a fractured paradigm. *Journal of Communication, 43*(4), 51–58. doi:10.1111/j.1460-2466.1993.tb01304.x.

Furman, N., Goldberg, D., & Lusin, N. (2007). *Enrollments in languages other than English in United States institutions of higher education, Fall 2006.* New York, NY: Modern Language Association of America. Retrieved from https://files.eric.ed.gov/fulltext/ED498998.pdf.

Frye, R.N. (2005). *Greater Iran: A 20th-century odyssey.* Costa Mesa, CA: Mazda Publishers.

Gandhi, L. (1998). *Postcolonial theory: A critical introduction.* Crows Nest NSW, Australia: Allen & Unwin.

Gans, H.J. (1979). *Deciding what's news: A study of CBS Evening News, NBC Nightly News, Newsweek, and Time.* New York, NY: Pantheon Books.

Gupta, O. (2006). *Encyclopaedia of journalism and mass communication.* Delhi, India: Isha Books.

Haeri, S. (1986). Power of ambiguity: Cultural improvisations on the theme of temporary marriage. *Iranian Studies, 19,* 123–154. doi:10.1080/00210868608701672.

Haeri, S. (2009). Sacred canopy: Love and sex under the veil. *Iranian Studies, 42,* 113–126. doi:10.1080/00210860802593965.

Ḥakkākiyān, R. (2004). *Journey from the land of no: A girlhood caught in revolutionary Iran.* New York, NY: Crown.

Hegland, M.E. (2009). Educating young women: Culture, conflict, and new identities in an Iranian village. *Iranian Studies, 42*(1), 45–79. doi:10.1080/00210860802593866.

Iran Data Portal. (2018). *The Iran data portal.* Retrieved March 3, 2018 from http://irandataportal.syr.edu/.

Iyengar, S., & Kinder, D.R. (1987). *News that matters: Television and American opinion.* Chicago, IL: University of Chicago Press.

Jackson, A.V. Williams. (1906). *Persia past and present: A book of travel and research with more than 200 illustrations and a map.* London, England: Macmillan & Co.

Javaheri, F. (2010). A study of transsexuality in Iran. *Iranian Studies, 43,* 365–377. doi:10.1080/00210861003693893.

Kabbani, R. (1986). *Europe's myths of Orient: Devise and rule.* London, England: Macmillan.

Kahf, M. (1999). *Western representations of the Muslim woman: From termagant to odalisque.* Austin, TX: University of Texas Press.

Karimi-Hakkak, A. (2008). Podcast. College Park, MD: Roshan Institute for Persian Studies, University of Maryland.

Keddie, N.R. (1983). Iranian revolutions in comparative perspective. *The American Historical Review, 88,* 579–598. doi:10.2307/1864588.

Kian-Thiébaut, A. (2005). From motherhood to equal rights advocates: The weakening of patriarchal order. *Iranian Studies, 38,* 45–66. doi:10.1080/0021086042000336537.

Kramer, M. (2002). *Ivory towers on sand: The failure of Middle Eastern studies in America.* Washington, DC: The Washington Institute for Near East Policy.

Lenczowski, G. (1978). *Iran under the Pahlavis.* Stanford, CA: Hoover Institution Press.

Lorentz, J.H., & Wertime, J.T. (1980). Iranians. In S. Thernstrom (Ed.), *Harvard encyclopedia of American ethnic groups* (pp. 521–524). Cambridge, MA: Harvard University Press.

Marandi, S.M., & Pirnajmuddin, H. (2009). Constructing an axis of evil: Iranian memoirs in the "Land of the Free." *The American Journal of Islamic Social Sciences, 26*(2), 23–47.

Litwak, R.S. (2000). *Rogue states and U.S. foreign policy: Containment after the Cold War.* Washington, DC: Woodrow Wilson Center Press.

Moaveni, A. (2006). *Lipstick jihad: A memoir of growing up Iranian in America.* New York, NY: Public Affairs.

Mohanty, C.T. (1984). Under Western eyes: Feminist scholarship and colonial discourses. *boundary 2, 12*(3), 333–358. doi: https://doi.org/10.2307/302821.

Nafisi, A. (2003). *Reading Lolita in Tehran: A memoir in books.* New York, NY: Random House.

Nashat, G. (1980). Women in the Islamic Republic of Iran. *Iranian Studies, 13,* 165–194. doi:10.1080/00210868008701569.

Nooshin, L. (2005). Underground, overground: Rock music and youth discourses in Iran. *Iranian Studies, 38,* 463–494. doi:10.1080/00210860500300820.

Paidar, P. (1995). *Women and the political process in twentieth-century Iran.* Cambridge, England: Cambridge University Press.

Pesaran, E. (2008). Towards an anti-Western stance: The economic discourse of Iran's 1979 Revolution. *Iranian Studies, 41,* 693–718. doi:10.1080/00210860802518343.

Rahimieh, N. (2009). Divorce seen through women's cinematic lens. *Iranian Studies, 42,* 97–112. doi:10.1080/00210860802593957.

Sabagh, G., & Bozorgmehr, M. (1986). *Are the characteristics of exiles different from immigrants?: The case of Iranians in Los Angeles.* Los Angeles, CA: Institute for Social Science Research, University of California Los Angeles. Retrieved July 27, 2017 from http://escholarship.org/uc/item/54d5s0q5#page-11.

Said, E.W. (1978). *Orientalism.* New York, NY: Pantheon Books.

Sardar, Z. (1999). *Orientalism*. Open University Press.

Shain, Y., & Barth, A. (2003). Diasporas and international relations theory. *International Organization*, *57*(3), 449–479. doi:10.1017/s0020818303573015.

Shirazi, F. (2005). The *sofreh*: Comfort and community among women in Iran. *Iranian Studies*, *38*, 293–309. doi:10.1080/00210860500096345.

Shoemaker, P.J., & Reese, S.D. (1996). *Mediating the message: Theories of influences on mass media content* (2nd ed.). New York, NY: Longman.

Shoemaker, P.J., & Vos, T.P. (2009). *Gatekeeping theory*. New York, NY: Routledge.

Smith, H., & Stares, P. (Eds.). (2007). *Diasporas in conflict: Peace-makers or peace-wreckers?* New York, NY: United Nations University Press. Retrieved March 1, 2018 from http://archive.unu.edu/unupress/sample-chapters/1140-DiasporasInConflict.pdf.

Spivak, G. (1993). *Outside in the teaching machine*. London, England: Routledge.

Spivak, G. (1999). *A critique of postcolonial reason: Toward a history of the vanishing present*. Cambridge, MA: Harvard University Press.

Index

www.ingramcontent.com/pod-product-compliance
Lightning Source LLC
Chambersburg PA
CBHW070908030426
42336CB00014BA/2332

* 9 7 8 1 6 4 2 5 9 0 0 9 8 *